ASIAPACIFI *QUEER*

Rethinking Genders and Sexualities

Edited by

Fran Martin,

Peter A. Jackson,

Mark McLelland,

and

Audrey Yue

University of Illinois Press
Urbana and Chicago

Library of Congress Cataloging-in-Publication Data
AsiaPacifiQueer : rethinking genders and sexualities /
edited by Fran Martin . . . [et al.].
p. cm.
Includes bibliographical references and index.
ISBN-13 978-0-252-03307-0 (cloth : alk. paper)
ISBN-10 0-252-03307-8 (cloth : alk. paper)
ISBN-13 978-0-252-07507-0 (pbk. : alk. paper)
ISBN-10 0-252-07507-2 (pbk. : alk. paper)
1. Homosexuality—Asia.
2. Gays—Asia.
3. Gays in popular culture—Asia.
I. Martin, Fran
HQ76.3.A78A86   2008
306.76'6095—dc22   2007045200

CONTENTS

ASIAPACIFI*QUEER*

INTRODUCTION

Fran Martin, Peter A. Jackson,
Mark McLelland, and Audrey Yue

In July 2005, in the tropical atmosphere of Bangkok's wet season, the largest-ever gathering of queer studies scholars in Asia took place. Six hundred academics and activists from across the region, from Colombo to Seoul and from Tehran to Singapore, converged to deliver and listen to papers presented at "Sexualities, Genders, and Rights in Asia: The First International Conference of Asian Queer Studies." The three packed days of the conference, which consisted of seven parallel streams presented in multiple languages, demonstrated conclusively the emergence of a vibrant new academic field: queer studies of Asian contexts conducted by researchers working in Asia.[1] No longer the sole province of Western-trained "experts" drawing on imported theory to account for local sexual and gender cultures, Asian queer studies emerged decisively from this conference as an enterprise carried out by researchers working within Asia itself. Significantly, the self-confident field of Asian queer studies represented at this conference was not preoccupied with speaking "back" to the presumptive center of queer studies in the English-speaking West but rather sought to articulate direct intraregional conversations among diverse locations in Asia.

The Sexualities, Genders, and Rights Conference provided the most tangible marker to date of an intellectual movement that has been underway for a decade—the localization of lesbian, gay, and queer studies approaches within

Asia. One effect of experiencing this critical mass of Asian research that many conference participants commented upon was the manner in which the diverse perspectives on offer forced presenters to reconsider the meaning of many basic categories such as "gay," "lesbian," and "queer." The conference questioned many enduring Anglo-centric biases in the field of lesbian and gay studies and reflected what Foucault terms "discontinuous, particular and local critiques" based on the (re)emergence of "subjugated knowledges." As Foucault notes, "it is a reappearance of what people know at a local level, of these disqualified knowledges, that make[s] . . . critique possible" (Foucault 2003, 7). Prior to this conference, there had been no mechanism, no other large-scale international gathering, journal, or academic context in which local Asian GLBTQ histories could be discussed *alongside* each other without first referencing Western approaches and paradigms.

This movement—the (re)emergence of local Asian queer perspectives—is something that this volume both exemplifies and contributes to. While the papers gathered here were conceived prior to the conference, many of the authors in this volume attended and presented papers at the conference. The volume takes the first part of its title from the AsiaPacifiQueer project: a network of Australia-based scholars working on cultures of sexuality in Asia. The AsiaPacifiQueer (APQ) group co-organized the Bangkok conference in collaboration with the Office of Human Rights Studies and Social Development at Mahidol University, Bangkok, and the four editors of this volume are APQ members. The APQ Network developed out of our shared sense of disciplinary exclusion and professional alienation within the academy. Established Asian area studies departments are often unsympathetic if not hostile towards both critical theory and research on homosexuality and transgenderism, and it is not unusual to encounter senior members of these departments who remain entirely unaware that there are sexual minority communities in the regions in which they are supposedly experts.

Meanwhile, the still-emerging proto-discipline of lesbian, gay, and queer studies has tended to focus on the histories and cultures of Western societies, with the issues of linguistic, discursive, and theoretical translation that lie at the heart of the practice of Asian cultural studies and Asian queer studies tending to be overlooked. Since it was established in 2000, the aim of APQ has been to intervene strategically to confront these multiple exclusions, bringing together academics and research students in a collective attempt to inscribe queer studies within Asian studies and equally importantly to locate Asia, and the non-West, within queer studies.[2] APQ's activities have included convening a stream of six highly successful panels of two dozen papers at the

Third International Convention of Asian Scholars (ICAS 3) held in Singapore in August 2003. This queer stream within ICAS 3 brought together Asian and Western scholars working on a diverse range of Asian queer studies topics. An impromptu meeting of almost forty ICAS 3 participants recommended unanimously that the APQ initiatives be extended internationally and work towards convening an international Asian queer studies conference in Asia in the near future. That meeting provided the direct impetus for both the Bangkok conference in July 2005 and the production of this volume.

APQ's desire to facilitate intraregional linkages and to provide forums for Asia-based queer studies academics to publish their work for an international readership emerges from more than simply our discomfort with the marginalization of Asia-focused queer studies within the academy. It also relates to a series of persistent anxieties about the *placing* of queer studies in the current world order, geopolitically as well as academically. These anxieties relate most directly to the ongoing dominance of U.S.-based research and researchers within the field. Seen from outside the United States, the mainstream of North American queer studies appears solipsistic and dominated by an unquestioned assumption that the most interesting and most important sites for queer analysis are to be found within the borders of the U.S. nation-state. As those working outside of this presumed center (both in Asia and non-metropolitan Western countries like Australia) are all too aware, the effects of such U.S.-centrism are real and consequential. When the world's most richly funded research institutions, the most influential university presses, and the biggest market for English-language publications in the humanities and social sciences are all located within a single nation, a certain skewing of perspective is inevitable. This system is self-perpetuating and produces genuine difficulties for many researchers in finding publishers for work on Asian sexual cultures. North American publishers often assume that the market for such work is limited since the "most important" readership, that is, American readers, will be unfamiliar with the material.

The system also results in an uneven distribution of scholarly and cultural capital. While queer studies scholars from Delhi to Kuala Lumpur to Shanghai have no choice but to acquire an understanding of the intricate workings of contemporary sexual cultures in the cities of the USA, where the most widely disseminated theory is written, unfortunately, the reverse is seldom the case. Within American queer studies, North American sexual cultures—from subcultural scenes to media products, from gay and lesbian activism to everyday sexual and gendered practices—are presumed to be general and primary while non-American sexual cultures are framed as particular and secondary. APQ believes that the time is right to bring together the growing group of scholars working on sexuality studies in the Asian region to challenge this situation by consolidating a distinct intellectual movement: queer studies *in Asia*. We hope that this volume will contribute to a transnational dialogue that not only challenges the disciplinary isolation of Asian queer studies by the structures of the Western academy but, more importantly, strengthens emergent cross-linkages within queer studies within Asia.

Australia's Asia-Western Hybridity

The cultural location of APQ provides a timely intervention within the current world order, both geopolitically and academically. Central to the global post-9/11 milieu is the figure of the Asian as a marked object of increased racism, heightened ethnic stereotyping, and racial profiling.[3] At the same time, the Asian is also subject to dissonant representation as a marked object of exotic desire consumed in the seductions of shopping malls and on transnational multiplex screens. The former is the axiom of paranoid nationalisms and decentralized empiricisms; the latter is a consequence of reverse global flows and anxious genders. Common to both is a new border crisis characterized by the Asian as a signifier that is in but not of the West. To be in but not of is to be situated at the threshold. This liminal position, which is at once inside and outside, reflects the off-center or ex-centric location of APQ as an intellectual movement that first emerged from the networking of Australia-based scholars working on queer studies in Asia.[4] This location suggests how the spatial distinction of Australia, as a politically Western nation in the geographic space of Asia and the Pacific, can pragmatically and critically intervene in the current post-9/11 border paradigm. Crucial here is the singularity of the border as a cultural location and a theoretical site of decentering the West and reorienting Asia.[5]

Australia's anxiety about its border with Asia is constituted from its tumultuous history as a European settler society that has been both colonizer and colonized. From the moment Australia's first federal level government instituted the Immigration Act in 1901 (which began the notorious regime of White Australia that ended only in the early 1970s), the nation's crisis about its cultural and geographical location—whether it is of British heritage or of the Asia-Pacific region—has sparked controversial debates within the country and internationally. The Whitlam government's move to end the White Australia policy in 1973 and the subsequent formal embrace of a national policy of multiculturalism signaled the first moments in Australia's postcolonial turn.[6] Ross Gibson's critical reorientation of Australia as "South of the West" provides a useful spatial and theoretical distinction: "The South's status as a conundrum for the West . . . puzzles and provokes rather than welcomes and accommodates the West."[7] Gibson maps a cultural location for the nation at the edge of Asia, reflecting former prime minister Paul Keating's regional embrace of an Australia situated firmly in Asia. Audrey Yue and Gay Hawkins further suggest that Australia is not only south of the West, it is also south of Asia.[8] In this postcolonial turn, the West is decentered and Asia recentered. Ien Ang's more recent positioning of an Australia that is in between Asia and the West further adds to the theoretical possibility enabled by the country's spatial distinction. Her framework of hybridity as that which is "neither/nor, or both/and" provides a double consciousness about being both Western and Asian.[9]

This double consciousness has been consolidated in a second postcolonial moment in Australia in the last decade. Despite the rise of neoliberalism and the resurgence of anti-Asian and anti-Muslim sentiments in the wake of the post-9/11 bombings in Bali (2003) and the bombing of the Australian embassy in the Indonesian capital of Jakarta (2004), conservative former prime minister John Howard strategically renewed Australia's regional allegiance by publicly reiterating that Australia is a part of the Asia-Pacific.[10] Although these two postcolonial turns reflect the different policies of late-twentieth-century multiculturalism and early-twenty-first-century counterterrorism, they both produce an axis to critically locate Australia in relation to Asia— as south of both the West and Asia. At the micro-level of everyday lived cultures as well as the macro-level of political discourse, in the twenty-first century, Australia is both Western and Asian. This double consciousness of national hybridity, characterized by a de-forming of historical relations with the West and a reorientating towards Asia, and which can be understood in terms of what Teresa de Lauretis has theorized as an "eccentric" process of "displacement and self-displacement," has been self-consciously mobilized in the APQ project.[11]

At its inaugural workshop held during the Gay and Lesbian Mardi Gras in Sydney in February 2001, APQ introduced the theme of "Gender and Sexual Difference in the Asia/Pacific: Paradigms and Approaches." The aim of the workshop was to explore "queer perspectives on the circuits of understanding which imagine Australia and New Zealand both as sites from which to analyse gender/sex difference in the Asia/Pacific and as hybridised locations whose popular and intellectual cultures increasingly reflect the aspirations of diasporas from 'The Region.'"[12] The workings of hybridity characterize

APQ in two ways. First, as a site from which to contribute to queer studies in Asia, Australia's hybrid location offers an ex-centric perspective on critical research. Second, as a field of research, the study of queer Asia has also been torn between global versus nativist debates on hybridity.

"Global Queering" and Queer Hybridization

In recent years, the topic of "global queering"—the internationalization of gay, lesbian, and transgender identities and cultures—has become a focus of at-times heated debate in both popular and academic contexts.[13] One view, drawing on globalization studies paradigms, is that the emergence of ostensibly Western-style lesbian and gay identities beyond the boundaries of the Western world reflects the impact of "sexual Westernization" on a global scale. This view assumes the centrality of Western approaches and paradigms, positing globalization as a process through which "the Rest" variously imitates, appropriates, and resists the West. A second view, drawing primarily on ethnographic and historical sources, offers a contrary analysis that tends to reify "traditional" cultures, framing non-Western societies as repositories of presumptively authentic, local sexual identities. The entrenchment of this simplistic opposition between what may be termed "local essentialism" versus "global homogenization" analyses of global queering underscores the need for more critical theoretical work, as well as for more detailed empirical accounts of the development of local Asia-Pacific GLBTQ cultures and histories.

APQ challenges both of the above views to explore the complex processes of localization and interregional borrowing that shape sexual cultures in an increasingly networked world. This emergent third position—the queer hybridization model—moves beyond the reductiveness of earlier approaches that located the sexual cultures and practices of other societies along a continuum of sameness versus difference from those of the West. Instead, it underscores the way in which *both* Western and non-Western cultures of gender and sexuality have been, and continue to be, mutually transformed through their encounters with transnationally mobile forms of sexual knowledge. In seeking to challenge the simplistic opposition of local essentialist and global homogenization views of global queering, the queer hybridization model offers a productive framework for understanding transformations of sexual cultures and knowledges today.

Hybridity is not simply a third term that resolves the tension between the global and the local. Often, it has been used as a postmodern descriptive catch-all to refer to intermixing without regard for how different forms of modality and agency come to figure in the politics of its use. Ella Shohat, for example, notes that hybridity may variously come to stand for "forced assimilation, internalized self-rejection, political co-optation, social conformism, cultural mimicry, and creative transcendence."[14] As a strategy that shows how minority subjects challenge cultural hegemony, its ambivalence functions as an alternative third space of enunciation for the transformative potential of new subject positions and subversions. As nonreducible identity, hybridity attends to the complexities of disjunctive globalization and emphasizes how local particularities are produced through what Homi Bhabha calls "a contesting, antagonistic agency."[15] At its most basic, this agency refers to modes of survival using the resources that are most readily available and through codes that may sometimes seem discordantly incompatible. For example, how can we further theorize the popular appropriation of the image of the global gay in Asia as the desire for sameness without simply reducing it to a homogenizing effect of global queering? How can we make critical sense of Singapore's thriving gay cultures in an authoritarian nation-state that has yet to decriminalize homosexuality? And how can we articulate the detention of gay asylum seekers within the ostensibly inclusive logic of Australia's same-sex migration program? José Muñoz's concept of queer hybridity is a useful departure to reinvest and reinvigorate notions of hybridity. He suggests that queer, like hybridity, thrives on "sites where meaning does not properly 'line up'": "This moment where things do not line up is a moment of reflexivity that is informed by and through the process of queerness *and* hybridity. It is a moment where hybridity is not a fixed positionality but a survival strategy that is essential for queers and postcolonial subjects who are subject to the violence that institutional structures reproduce."[16]

As displacement and self-displacement, the critical reflexivity of queer hybridity is reflected in APQ's ex-centric cultural location. As cultural survival, it is also deployed theoretically by APQ to interrogate the differential politics of how hybridity has figured in queer studies in Asia as well as in the queer cultures in the Asia-Pacific.[17] The queer hybridization model is also accented by the queer diasporic positionality, as Gayatri Gopinath, writing on the Indian diaspora and the transnational reception of the film *Fire,* suggests:

> The concept of queer diaspora functions on multiple levels. First, it situates the formation of sexual subjectivity within transnational flows of culture, capital, bodies, desire and labor. Second, queer diaspora contests the logic that situates the terms "queer" and "diaspora" as dependent on the originality and authenticity of "heterosexuality" and "nation." Finally, it disorganizes the

dominant categories within the United States for sexual variance, namely, "gay and lesbian," and it marks a different economy of desire that escapes legibility within normative Indian contexts and homo normative white Euro-American contexts.[18]

The essays in this collection examine the ways in which queer hybridity functions as critical reflexivity and cultural survival. Studies of the Asian diaspora in Australia, where diasporic female masculinity contests normative ethnicities and sexualities; studies of dominant representations of queerness in the cinemas and popular fiction of the Philippines, Korea, Taiwan, and Japan; and studies of the regulation of Muslim transsexuals in Malaysia show how queer hybridity is mobilized creatively by new post-9/11 sexual and border subject positionings that resist both nativist essentialisms and global queer hegemony. This emphasis on border positionings is also reflected in the essays on how postwar Japanese homosexuality has been refigured through an ethic of self-fashioning; how a contemporary intellectual discourse on queer in Taiwan has emerged as an exclusionary edifice; how Hong Kong tomboys and Japanese lesbians challenge gender norms and normative speech acts through the inscriptions of their self-narratives; and how these self-narratives have emerged as a distinctive formation of *tom/dee* queer categories in Thailand.

Comparative Histories of Asian Queer Studies

While the essays in this volume, the July 2005 conference in Bangkok, and the activities of the APQ network all highlight the recent emergence of transverse, intraregional programs of Asian queer studies, the hegemonic dominance of Euro-America still remains the everyday reality of intellectual life in Asia. Until very recently, queer studies in Asia has been constituted in terms of each Asian country's distinctive relations to the Euro-American "centers" via diverse and locally contingent patterns of colonialism, semicolonialism, and postcolonialism.[19] The early history of Asian queer studies has reflected an overwhelmingly colonial intellectual pattern under which each nation-level community of queer studies researchers has been well-informed about Western queer histories, cultures, and theories but remained largely unaware of often parallel and contemporaneous projects of queer studies in neighboring Asian countries.

The July 2005 Bangkok conference marked a turning point in the pattern of (post)colonial Asian queer studies by privileging intellectual relations among Asian countries rather than between each country and one or other

Western metropole. However, it is nevertheless true that until recently Asian queer studies has been largely constituted as a series of parallel but mainly non-inter-communicating nation-level projects. While a broader transborder project of Asian queer studies is now being imagined by researchers in various countries, it remains the case that the history of Asian queer studies is a series of largely discrete national narratives. In this, the history of Asian queer studies is heavily marked by the unequal flows of cultural and intellectual capital between the West and all non-Western, non-metropolitan societies.

It is only possible to begin to understand the emergence of Asian queer studies as a regionwide intellectual project by first placing side-by-side the largely separate histories of queer studies in each Asian country. This somewhat discontinuous set of national narratives nevertheless reflects the genuine unevenness of intellectual flows across the region. It also demonstrates the continuing power of linguistic-cultural-discursive boundaries to limit the flow of ideas despite the intensified cross-border flows of capital, people, and images brought about by the current bout of globalization. Asian queer studies began as a series of nation-level projects that are only now beginning to become aware of each other.

Japan

In the case of Japan, it is only in the past decade that academic and activist communities have begun to seriously research the history of a range of *hentai,* that is, "queer" or "perverse," communities. Some of this work was influenced by trends in Anglophone scholarship and analyzed the prevalence of heterosexist structures in Japanese society. However, unlike much queer studies research in the United States, which takes place in English literature departments and is based on textual criticism, sexuality research in Japan, while hinting at queer theory, has tended to prefer sociological and historical research methods such as fieldwork, interviews, and investigation of archival sources. Two particular trends stand out among research being conducted by a new generation of academics: one focusing on the tension between the rigid categories of public sexual discourse and the lived experience of various sexual minority communities, and another that aims to describe and analyze the everyday practices of these communities through participant observation and discourse analysis.[20]

There are two reasons why queer studies in Japan tend to take place in the social sciences as opposed to Japanese literature departments. First, researchers such as Ueno Chizuko and Ehara Yumiko, who in the 1980s brought feminist analysis into the mainstream, are sociologists. Many young queer researchers supervised by these two senior scholars have been influenced by social-science methodology. The second reason is that in Japan, literature study has tended to be seen as an aspect of literary history, which is still largely concerned with the study of canonical texts (or "discovering" the literary merit of overlooked texts so that they can be admitted to the canon). As a result, there is little space within the mainstream for pioneering work offering alternative queer readings.

However, it would be a mistake to conclude that this recent upsurge of interest in a range of nonheterosexual identities and communities is a new development in Japan. While it is only in the last decade that the study of minority sexualities has been accorded a place in the academy, Japanese popular culture has shown consistent interest in the topic for over a century. For instance, as early as the 1920s there existed a range of publications that focused on the topic of *hentai seiyoku* or "perverse sexual desire." While this genre was censored and disappeared during the long war years, it rapidly reemerged during the occupation following Japan's defeat at the end of World War II. In the early 1950s, over five periodicals dedicated to the study of perverse desire were founded (two of which survived into the 1970s). An important feature of this genre was the space given over to submissions by readers, thus giving individuals who saw themselves as "perverse" the opportunity for discussion, both among themselves and with the many "experts" who also contributed opinion pieces and diagnostic tracts. So extensive is this literature that it would not be an exaggeration to say that during the 1950s, building upon the trajectory established in the 1920s, Japan had already developed a tradition of "queer studies." Recently, this body of material has begun to be archived and analyzed by both Japanese and foreign researchers.[21] Researchers associated with Chuo University's Postwar Japan Transgender Study Association have been particularly active in publishing reports based on this material as well as using it to track down surviving community members in an attempt to record their personal histories.[22] It is only in the past few years that both Japanese and foreign academics alike have become aware of the very extensive print records that exist in Japan relating to sexual minority history, and as these resources are archived and made more generally available, we can expect to see a boom in interest in Japanese queer studies.

Thailand

It is one of the paradoxes of Asian queer studies that while Thailand was host to the 2005 Asian queer studies conference and is home to some of the region's most visible and well-established LGBT communities, Euro-American queer theory has had a negligible intellectual impact in the country. Bangkok's transgender (*kathoey*), gay, and lesbian (*tom/dee*) cultures first attracted local media attention in the early 1960s, when they were typically stereotyped as "the homosexual problem" (*panha rak-ruam-phet*).[23] A local biomedically inflected discourse of homosexuality emerged soon afterwards in response to a perceived need by concerned Thai authorities to "control" the country's burgeoning queer cultures, and by the early 1970s Thai educators and health professionals were publishing studies on ways to "solve" the homosexual problem. While drawing on mid-twentieth-century American biomedical accounts of homosexuality, the Thai studies focussed on attempting (largely unsuccessfully) to conceptually differentiate the established local transgender category of *kathoey* from other identities that came to be labeled with English-derived terms such as *gay, tom* (from "tomboy"), and *dee* (from the second syllable of "la*dy*").[24] What emerged was a hybridized Thai academic discourse that drew on now-abandoned 1950s Western models to construct a formalized and ostensibly biomedical account of the local *kathoey* category. This discourse of the *kathoey* as a problem became hegemonic in Thai universities and the bureaucracy (especially the Ministry of Public Health) in the 1980s and remains entrenched to this day. The discourse is so powerful that popular understandings of other Thai identities, including gay men and lesbians, are refracted through the conceptual lens of the transgender *kathoey*. In Thai translations and appropriations of the biomedical literature, the Western discursive emphasis on (homo)sexuality is subverted, being reread as an "authoritative" and "scientific" basis for a formalized official Thai discourse in which transgenderism takes center stage and becomes the dominant trope by which all variations of same-sex desire are understood—and problematized. Local LGBT resistances to this state-sponsored discourse have emerged since the late 1990s. These Thai voices of "gay pride" and self-confident "women who love women" (*ying rak ying*) have had growing success in their local interventions. Under pressure from the Anjaree lesbian group, in 2003 the Thai Ministry of Public Health publicly announced that it no longer classified homosexuality as a mental illness, some thirty years after the American Psychiatric Association similarly declassified homosexuality.

While Thailand's LGBT cultures are integrally interconnected with Western and other Asian gay, lesbian, and transgender cultures, the Euro-American discourse of queer theory has had almost no impact locally. One reason for this appears to be the fact that Western queer theory focuses predominantly on sexuality while, as noted above, both dominant and oppositional discourses in Thailand are predominantly constituted upon understandings of (trans)gender.

Taiwan

Lesbian, gay, and queer studies emerged as a vibrant area of intellectual activity in Taiwan during the 1990s, paralleling the concurrent rise of a local gay/lesbian/queer (*tongzhi*) culture and political movement.[25] From early in the decade, a cohort of diasporic intellectuals began returning to Taiwan following graduate studies in feminism, lesbian and gay studies, queer theory and related humanities disciplines in the USA and Europe. Now teaching mostly in English departments at major universities including National Taiwan University and National Taiwan Central University, these scholars began offering courses that included material in lesbian and gay studies and queer theory, and were soon organizing regular conferences on sexuality studies. Due in large part to the strong links, forged by returning students, between English departments in Taiwan and concurrent developments in sexuality theory in the United States and England, Taiwan is one place where Euro-American queer theory has had a very strong impact and has for the past several years been in the process of creative adaptation and localization for research focusing on dissident sexual cultures within Taiwan. Partly as a result, at the time of writing, queer studies are far more institutionally embedded and are accorded a far greater degree of academic "respectability" in Taiwan than they are in the People's Republic of China, where such studies remain for the most part peripheral to the scholarly mainstream and exist only in embryonic form. In 1995, a group of scholars headed by Professor Josephine Chuen-juei Ho established the Center for the Study of Sexualities (*Xing/Bie Yanjiushi*) at National Taiwan Central University. The Center hosts regular conferences and visiting scholars in lesbian, gay, queer, and transgender studies and has a prolific publishing program that adds to the wealth of local publications on queer critical theory and cultural analysis in Chinese, analyzing local sites, cultures, and texts for a local and regional readership. In Taiwan, university campuses are a major focus of queer cultural life, with very active gay and lesbian student groups and Internet BBS groups based on university servers playing a key role in the formation of local sexual identities and communities.

Singapore

Although there is currently no formalized program in Singapore universities for gay and lesbian studies, queer studies in and of Singapore can be considered an emerging intellectual field as a result of three competing but intersecting forces. These are the globalization of queer studies, the impact of the local gay and lesbian social movement, and the rise of a gay consumer culture, which have all been central to coalescing the disparate voices of Asian queer capitalism, activism, and the academy in the island republic.

Academic writings on studies of sexuality in Singapore first appeared in the early 1990s on the relationship between sexuality and nationalism. Writing against the backdrop of the Singapore government's infamous population promotion policy on marriage and childbirth in the 1980s, local scholars such as Geraldine Heng and Janadas Devan focused on heterosexuality to foreground the relationship between postcolonial nationalism and reproduction.[26] More recently, Kenneth Tan followed this trajectory to further critique the state control of sex and romance.[27] These critiques on heterosexuality are accompanied by the concomitant emergence of writings that have come out of the publishing boom in global queer studies in the West and focus specifically on local gay and lesbian politics and identities. In *Journal of Homosexuality* and *Mobile Cultures: New Media in Queer Asia,* the writings of Russell Heng and Baden Offord use media communications and political economy to approach the regulation of homosexuality through the discourses of sexual citizenship and human rights.[28] These contestations are also recorded as activist history in the locally published collection *People Like Us: Sexual Minorities in Singapore.*[29] The growth of mediated GLBTIQ communities in Singapore is examined in Audrey Yue's work on class politics between English-speaking diasporic and local, Chinese-speaking working-class lesbians as well as in Ng King Kang's self-published *The Rainbow Connection: The Internet and the Singapore Gay Community.*[30] These publications map a nascent intellectual field by local cultural workers, diasporic and Western researchers mobilized around postcolonial sociology, social movement history, new media, and diasporic queer studies.

Local queer entrepreneurships and activisms have added dynamism and vibrancy to the movement, both intellectually and politically, to produce a unique feature about queer Singapore. Despite the criminalization of homosexuality and Internet censorship laws that prohibit content promoting homosexuality, Singapore has emerged as the queer Mecca of Asia in the last five years. Singapore's visible gay and lesbian and queer consumer cultures have exploded as a result of recent government initiatives that promote cultural arts, creative entrepreneurships, and material consumption. Since the early 1990s, state-subsidized gay and lesbian theaters, popular queer fiction, and local award-winning films have regularly portrayed themes of coming out, sexual identity, and transsexuality. More recently, enterprising gay businesses have revolutionized Singapore's nighttime economy with saunas, queer karaoke bars, annual Butch Hunt competitions, and the now iconic Nation parties. The co-sponsorship of the Sexualities, Genders, and Rights conference in Bangkok 2005 by Singapore-owned Fridae.com, the largest gay and lesbian queer Asia Internet portal, provides a new platform to further develop the connections between Asian queer capitalism, the grassroots, and the academy. The intricacies of these connections show a discordant sexual hybridity that usurps the straightforward logic of a statist, global, and even nativist hegemony and reflect how queer studies on and in Singapore have emerged by confronting the disjunctions of sexual rights, developmental materialism, postcolonial nationalism, and informational capitalism.

Intraregional Trends

In terms of emerging cross-border queer intellectual flows, two trends stand out. The Chinese language discourse of *tongzhi* ("comrade") is arguably the most extensive non-English language medium of queer imaginaries in Asia today. While limited to Chinese-speaking cultures, since its origins in the early 1990s *tongzhi* has provided a basis for a common—albeit hotly contested—queer discursive articulation across Hong Kong, Taiwan, the People's Republic of China, and overseas Chinese communities in Singapore, Malaysia, and elsewhere. While locally inflected by the history of modern China and Taiwan, *tongzhi* also functions as a new, politicized identity marker for homosexuality that is self-consciously related (and at times explicitly opposed) to Western discourses of sexuality and queer theory.

A second but less well articulated cross-border discourse links local understandings of transgenderism across Southeast Asia. Research on Thai *kathoey,* Filipino *bakla,* Malaysian *mak nyah,* and Indonesian *waria/banci* is increasingly conducted as part of a regional Southeast Asian dialogue on transgenderisms. In Chinese-speaking East and Southeast Asia, the discourse of *tongzhi* is arguably based more on local understandings of (homo)sexuality than on those of gender, and the frequent use of *tongzhi* to translate "queer" creates a discursive parallelism between English and Chinese discourses on this point. However, in non-Chinese-speaking communities in Southeast Asia, queer is overwhelmingly articulated through the lens of (trans)gender.[31]

Thailand, site of the 2005 conference, is located on the discursive fault line between the tectonic plates of Chinese *tongzhi* queer sexualities and Southeast Asian queer genders. Because of large-scale Chinese migration until the mid-twentieth century, 10 percent of Thailand's population today is of Chinese ancestry, and Chinese cultural and other influences remain significant. Thais of Chinese background are influential in business, politics, education, the media, and many other fields. One of the future tasks of Asian queer studies will be to trace how the rapidly intensifying intra-Asian queer cultural and intellectual flows are understood and negotiated in terms of intertwining but nonetheless distinctive imaginings of sexuality and gender. Indeed, it may only be possible to fully comprehend the form and nature of Asia's many hybrid queer identities once unresolved analytic tensions between sexuality and gender in queer theory have been more clearly articulated.

While both India and Japan have significant and rapidly emerging networks of queer studies scholars, research in these two important Asian societies has yet to have a significant impact in neighboring Asian countries. It also needs to be emphasized that while queer studies is growing rapidly in a number of Asian countries, the extreme unevenness of economic development and the diversity of political regimes across the region also mean that there is little if any research on LGBTQ topics in a significant number of poorer countries. For example, we know little if anything about LGBTQ cultures and communities in Myanmar, North Korea, or the former Soviet republics in Central Asia.

The Paradox of Theory in Asian Queer Studies

One of the greatest dangers among the many that inhere in traditional area-studies-style approaches to the study of Asia, which envisage the Western researcher applying his or her "expert knowledge" to mine the raw material of the "other" culture, is that such methods perpetuate the myth of (Western-derived) theoretical frameworks as general and universal and of local (non-Western) cultures as merely local and particular.[32] Dipesh Chakrabarty has discussed a related problem in his incisive critique of the universalizing tendencies of the discipline of history, in "The Time of History and the Times of Gods."[33] Chakrabarty is critical of history's underlying assumptions that, he proposes, render it unable to account for the radical and incommensurable plurality of contemporary cultures. History, the social sciences, and modern political philosophy, Chakrabarty argues, share "the idea of a godless, continuous, empty and homogeneous time . . . [that] belongs to [a] model of a higher, overarching language—a structure of generality, an aspiration toward the scientific—which is built into conversations that take the modern historical consciousness for granted."[34]

Elsewhere, Chakrabarty compares the higher, overarching language that social science claims to provide with the chemical notation H_2O used as a universal translator to mediate between the English term *water* and the Hindi term *pani*. The problem with this claim, for Chakrabarty, is that such a model of scientific translatability is unable to account for the radical singularity of cultures. If *water* and *pani* can only speak to each other through the inherently generalizing language of H_2O, then all of the complex cultural and linguistic associations and meanings of two local terms is sacrificed to the bland generality of the chemical sign.

Although the present volume is not concerned specifically with the discipline of history, nor primarily with social-science approaches to culture, Chakrabarty's meditations on the acts of translation entailed in making theoretical paradigms speak to specific situations of culture resonate interestingly here. Until now—indeed, arguably, such is still largely the case—the lingua franca or presumed universal scientific translator of LGBTQ studies has been provided by Anglo-American theory. If a scholar in Tokyo wishes to make a particular sexual culture there visible and comprehensible to someone working, say, in Jakarta, she would very likely translate that milieu into a familiar language involving concepts like "gender performativity," "butch/femme," "the invisible lesbian," "the lesbian continuum," and so forth. All of these, while undeniably handy, are concepts that developed out of a particular set of cultural and historical contexts: North American, English speaking, late twentieth century. These contexts are significantly distinct from—though not of course hermetically isolated from—those of either Tokyo or Jakarta. Yet paradoxically, for the researchers working in those places to have an intellectual conversation *precisely about what is local and particular* about the sexual culture each inhabits and studies, for better or worse they would more than likely be compelled to do so by means of the H_2O of Anglo-American lesbian theory.

But, to return to the article cited above, it is not the case that Chakrabarty has no faith at all in the possibility of cultural translation; his point is a different one. Later in the same article he specifies his intention to "appeal to models of cross-cultural and cross-categorical translations that do not, unlike sociological or social-scientist thinking, take a universal middle term for granted. The Hindi *pani* may be translated into the English *water* without having to go through the science of H_2O."[35] What is perhaps most exciting about the emergent intraregional conversations on sexual cultures seen in both the 2005 conference and this volume is the possibility that in the foreseeable future such conversations may be able to take place directly, as it were, skipping the universal middle term of Anglo-American queer theory. To continue with the example above, the primary question would then concern how cultures of same-sex love between women in Tokyo relate to cultures of same-sex love between women in Jakarta, with no *necessary* reference (though of course such reference would not be precluded, if useful) to lesbian cultures in the English-speaking world. At the time of writing, such transverse, relatively unmediated intraregional conversations are, for the most part, a future possibility rather than a present reality. Yet the energetic dialogues between geographically dispersed researchers made possible by projects like the Bangkok conference and, we hope, this volume indicate that the will and energy to pursue such intraregional critical conversations is building, and that the emergent field of Asian queer studies may eventually have as one of its hallmarks just such a critical recentering of the terms of discourse.

The Chapters in This Volume

Until very recently, there has been little written in either Japanese or English about homosexual identity formation in the context of postwar Japan. J. Darren Mackintosh's chapter on Japan's 1970s' *"homo"* magazines is an important contribution to our understanding of the specific dynamics at play in male homosexual identity formation at a crucial time in Japan's history—the 1970s—a period when the Japanese economy rose to rival that of established western powers and the Japanese nation state reemerged as a significant local and global player in world affairs. Rather than discovering, as was the case in the United States and other nations of the West, that homosexual identity was carved out in a countercultural space, opposed to mainstream or hegemonic values, Mackintosh discerns an attempt by some among Japan's male homosexuals to reposition their homosexual attraction and identity as a force supportive of, not contrary to, Japan's emerging role as an economic powerhouse. Mackintosh shows how men using the personals section in a range of *homo* magazines of the period sought to align themselves with the ideology of the "corporate warrior," especially through the notion of "moral seriousness." Mackintosh demonstrates that in the ads a range of terms relating to moral seriousness, hard work, and commitment "are found at the heart of a signifying economy that for some fused together a man's work, his bodily identity as a man, his desire for other men, and his sense of ethical being. At the most general level, seriousness acts as a context in which a man comes to be associated with characteristics like commitment, dedication, careerism, and singularity of purpose." It is precisely this identification with, rather than rejection of, codes of masculinity embedded in Japanese work practices that Mackintosh suggests resisted the acceptance of a U.S.-style countercultural approach to homosexual identity, an approach that still has minimal impact in contemporary Japan.

James Welker, too, in his chapter on the development of a range of queer female identities in Japan, focuses upon a particular period—the 1980s—and a specific genre of magazines, those dedicated to the love of "beautiful boys." While it might seem strange in an Anglophone context to look in texts dedicated to male homosexual love for signifiers of lesbian desire, Welker shows how this space was appropriated by women-loving women who negotiated a range of (trans)gendered identities, albeit "at the margins." Welker argues that the "beautiful boy" has long been a romantic trope of indeterminate gender in Japanese popular culture and that the postwar boom in representations of such figures, particularly in the world of manga, enabled Japanese women to question the "necessary" biologistic logic of mainstream, culturally endorsed gender performances. Welker notes how women writing to the personals columns of such "boy love" magazines as *Allan* and *June* played with a range of sexual identities and gender roles that were "inextricably linked to the figure of the 'beautiful boy' and the representation of 'boys' love.'" Therefore, these magazines "functioned as a crucial site of transgressive gender and sexual identity formation" while largely avoiding the rhetoric of Western feminist and lesbian discourse.

The particularity of Japanese queer culture is also picked up by Claire Maree in her chapter on the use of "hyperfeminine" language by lesbian-identified women in Japan in an attempt to oppose both "restrictive heteronormative femininity and stereotypes of the butch lesbian." Maree notes that the Japanese language is more clearly gendered than is English and that sociolinguistic norms often force individuals to align themselves with either a "male" or "female" speaking style. However, she argues that sophisticated language play is a hallmark of a range of communities within Japan's queer culture, particularly the use of *onē kotoba* (literally "big sister speech")—a camp, hyperfeminine mode of address usually associated with gay men.

Yik Koon Teh uses methods derived from sociology, sexual health, and political economy to examine how the postcolonial history of Malaysia has regulated transsexuality through the legacies of British colonization and assertions of Islamic cultural autonomy. She shows how Malay Muslim transsexuals face the double discrimination of inherited British civil law and Islamic *Syariah* law, and how these have criminalized homosexual and transsexual practices and shaped the mainstream negative perception of sexual minorities. She further displaces this history by indigenizing male-to-female transsexuality with the local term *mak* (mother) *nyah* (ladylike/feminine behavior) to allow for a proliferation of differentiated sexual identities: "the term was introduced to differentiate *mak nyah* from *pondan* or *bapok*, terms used to describe effeminate men or homosexuals . . . [it] includes both individuals who have undergone sex-change operations and those who have not." By revising the gendered discourses of Islam, Teh's account debunks the current post-9/11 stereotype of Muslim patriarchy and argues how Islam can be a critical site to reformulate the relationship between gender and sexuality.

Indigenous reformulations of gender and sexuality are also evident in Lucetta Kam's and Carmen Ka Man Tong's chapters on the Hong Kong tomboy and masculine woman. Like Teh's use of interviews and focus group studies, Kam and Tong frame their research through ethnography and sociology to inscribe the everyday experiences of masculine women and young lesbian schoolgirls. For them, the tomboy or TB (in its abbreviated form) is a localized identity that resists both Western theorizations of female masculinity and Confucian norms of gender and sexual identity. Kam's focus is on masculine women who recuperate the colloquial term "boy-head" (*nam chai tou*) as a renewed category to critically frame the TB. In her self-narratives, the cultural memory of the boy-head opens up the dissonance between the TB as a "a recognized masculine gender in girls' school culture" and as a gender identity that is "not restricted to lesbian women, but can be found on women with different sexual preferences." The boy-head potentializes a queer hybrid discourse that differentiates between the formation of gender and sexual identities in Hong Kong. Kam's observations of how local TBs resist through the interpellating effects of recognition and mis-recognition are also foregrounded in Tong's study of a group of working-class lesbian schoolgirls where everyday survival was "full of multiple and even conflicting ideologies; in which the identity was highly hybrid, being defined by and redefined by different discourses." Analyzing daily practices like *po-yan* (chain-smoking), letter writing, chatting, and sports to negotiate everyday life, Tong exposes the performativity of TB through a sexual hybridity that contests the tension between normative masculinity and conventional femininity.

Megan Sinnott's study of Thai masculine-identified *tom* (from "tomboy") and their feminine *dee* (from "lady") partners describes an Asian culture in which gender is the dominant field within which female same-sex desires and relationships are imagined. These Thai "women who love women" (*ying rak ying*) resist both local gender norms and Western accounts of the lesbian as a sexual being. For *tom* and *dee,* it is the remodulation of Thai norms of masculinity and femininity rather than female homoeroticism per se that is the most salient feature of both personal narratives and the broader culture of *ying rak ying.*

Heather Worth's essay on diasporic *faʾafafine* (self-feminizing Samoan biological men) in New Zealand continues the focus on alternative gendering as a constitutive feature of some non-normative sexual cultures in the Asia-Pacific region. Based on an a series of interviews with *faʾafafine* in South Auckland, Worth undertakes a deconstructive theoretical critique of sexual and gender norms, highlighting how for the *faʾafafine,* gender and sexuality are always already marked by the inextricable entanglement of identity (and processes of identification) with difference (and processes of differentiation). For Worth, the *faʾafafine* exemplify not so much a "third gender" or "third sex" as a fundamentally unstable and indeterminable position *between* sexes and genders that underscores the instabilities within those categories themselves.

J. Neil Garcia's nuanced study of three Filipino authors' representations of male homosexuality traces key historical shifts in the hybridization of local notions of the transgendered male (*bakla*) and American notions of the gay man. Highlighting the impact of multiple Spanish and American colonialisms over four centuries, he abandons any notion of the Philippines as an originary site of a "pure" non-Western culture of homosexuality. For Garcia, the recoverable histories of transgenderism and homosexuality in the Philippines can only be founded on an ever-more-complex hybridization of cultural patterns. His investigations of the past reveal only earlier moments of local/foreign intersection in which "local" signifiers such as *bakla* mark a history of constantly shifting negotiations between diverse cultural patterns of gender and eroticism. What is most stunning about Garcia's account of same-sex cultures in the Philippines is the extent to which the "inauthenticity" of an irredeemably and undeniably hybrid identity does not lead to an intellectual exercise in deconstruction but rather is a self-consciously celebrated feature of local queer cultures.

Queer Asian cinema has been a critical site for challenging normative "Eastern" and "Western" conceptions of homosexuality and rethinking the hybridity of Asia queer identities.[36] The three chapters by Ronald Baytan, Jin-Hyung Park, and Teri Silvio resituate this terrain by focusing on how different postcolonial forces have shaped the changing representations of queer sexuality in the cinemas of the Philippines, Korea, and Taiwan. Baytan examines "the homosexualization of *bakla*" in recent Filipino cinema. Using *Bala at*

Lipstick (Bullet and Lipstick, 1994), *Sa Paraiso ni Efren* (In Efren's Paradise, 1999) and *Duda* (Doubt, 2003), three iconic films produced between 1994 to 2003, Baytan traces how the *bakla* "has become a hybrid who is no longer the womanish man that he once was, nor is he simply the local version of the homosexual or gay of the West." By foregrounding how gay and film histories have led to the *bakla*'s postcolonial appropriation of the Western conception of gayness, Baytan argues that the queer hybridity of *bakla* subjectivities has emerged through a critical revisioning and self-fashioning of both globalizing and nativizing discourses of Filipino male homosexualities.

This critical reflexivity is also emphasized in Jin-Hyung Park's examination of how gay social movement discourses, queer theory, and art cinema have arrived in Korea in the mid-1990s to construct, discipline, and represent the homosexual in the cinema. Park examines the politics of reception surrounding *Road Movie*, a 2002 art house film acclaimed by local film critics and the mainstream audience as a "frontier gay movie [that] opens a new genre (of queer cinema) in Korean film culture." He shows how the film's genre as a road movie and melodrama have incorporated a marginal homosexuality into the heterosexual mainstream through a universalizing discourse on love. This incorporation, he argues, has de-eroticized the homosexual: "homosexuality is reregistered as the normalized other in mainstream discourses, while homoeroticism, a transgression that refuses to be recuperated by mainstream discourses, *cannot be represented*." Park's reading of *Road Movie* introduces and concomitantly problematizes the modernizing discourses of global Korean film and local gay cultures; in doing so, he offers a strategy for queer Asian film criticism that foregrounds how a politics of interpretation could become connected to ethics not only as a theoretical practice but also as "a way of life."

Teri Silvio attends to the ethics of interpretation in her rendering of the 1990 Taiwanese novel *The Silent Thrush* and its 1992 film adaptation. Like Park's *Road Movie, The Silent Thrush* also marks an iconic and defining moment in Taiwan's indigenous and queer histories. The novel was one of the first Taiwanese novels to deal with the theme of female homosexuality, and the film was seen both as a "Native Soil culture" (*bentu wenhua*) film and a "lesbian" (*nütongxinglian*) film. By situating the narrative within queer and regional politics of traditional Chinese opera and Hong Kong martial arts cinema, inscribing the novel within local reception of Native Soil discourse, and engaging the film genres of social realist melodrama, soft pornography, and art house nostalgia, Silvio's interdisciplinary mix opens up an ethics of interpretation to further consider the intersection between lesbian sexuality and indigenous (Holo) ethnicity and how "homosexuality is . . . fundamental to Taiwanese Holo identity." Silvio's perverse reinterpretation of Taiwanese mainstream cinema's representation of lesbian sexuality recuperates "the most abject aspects of Holo identity" to foreground how lesbian sexuality is integral not only to Taiwan's ethnonationalism but how this nationalism constructs a Taiwanese culture that is similar and at the same time different from Chinese culture.

Song Hwee Lim's paper, also focusing on Taiwan, shifts from Silvio's concerns with the intersections of lesbian representation and nativist identity through the Taiwanese opera film to the more rarefied urban middle-class realm of queer (*kuer*) intellectual discourse in 1990s Taipei. After providing a brief cultural history of the various terms that have been used to refer to homosexuality in modern Taiwan, Lim examines the complex transculturation and localization of queer theory and argues that in this context *queer* lost some of its critical edge. Despite young queer-identified intellectuals' rhetoric critiquing the normativity of old-style gay ideology and espousing the radical power of sexual and social perversity, Lim points out the exclusivity of the term in practice, confined as its currency often was to a relatively small group of middle-class, highly educated urban youth whose privileged social position exposed them to the latest trends in sexuality theory emanating from the United States. While underscoring the linguistic and cultural hybridity of *kuer* as a transformed localization of the English term "queer," Lim concludes by questioning the celebratory link that is often made between cultural hybridity and progressive politics, observing that *kuer*'s hybrid provenance has not guaranteed that the term has had radical—or even democratic—effects in practice.

Audrey Yue focuses on the Asian queer diaspora in Australia as a site of queer hybridity that destabilizes nativist homeland and settler hostland constructions of race, gender, and sexuality. She shows how the performances of Asian drag kings appropriate kung fu and Japanese salaryman masculinities to produce queer hybridity through postcolonial and diasporic female sexualities. She argues these sexualities are not only "characterized by the diasporic Asian Australian tomboy as a desirable form of hybrid sexual identity," they also inscribe "the gendered migration of the Asian Australian diaspora." Yue uses the displacement of "going south" to show how the physical migration from Asia to Australia is also a critical trajectory that differentiates the Asian queer diaspora in Australia from the global diasporas elsewhere. As migrants, lesbians, and multicultural performers, diasporic Asian drag kings in Australia share with an ex-centric Australia a doubly displaced cultural location in between Asia and the West. Yue shows how this cultural location is a useful critical platform to reorient queer Asian and diasporic queer studies.

Notes

1. An online archive of the conference is at http://bangkok2005.anu.edu.au.

2. Reports of APQ activities are listed at http://apq.anu.edu.au.

3. The term *Asian* here is mobilized as a discourse, a collective term for a heterogeneous group of people and a descriptive term for a disparate geographical region. In the West, it is a signifier of racial difference. For example, in Britain, it is a stereotype that refers to people of Indian descent, while in Australia, this stereotype refers to people of Southeast Asian descent. Since 9/11, the term has also been sensationalized in the media and state discourses to include Muslims and non-Muslims from Middle Eastern backgrounds, or anyone who "looks" like one. In the inter-Asia cultural politics of Japan, "Asia" has been historically constructed to refer not to race but to geographical demarcation. See, for example, Ang, *On Not Speaking Chinese;* and Sun Ge, "How Does 'Asia' Mean? (Part 1)."

4. See Hutcheon, "The Post-modern Ex-centric."

5. For a further elaboration of this cultural location, see Yue's chapter in this collection.

6. In the Cold War era, Australia experienced over two decades of unbroken rule by conservative federal governments. This conservative domination of Australian politics was broken in December 1972, when the charismatic Gough Whitlam led the Australian Labor Party to victory. The conservative Liberal-National Party Coalition reattained office in 1975, with the Labor Party—first under Bob Hawke and then led by Paul Keating—taking government from 1982 to 1996. From early 1996 until 2007, Australia once again had a conservative government, led by the staunchly pro-American John Howard.

7. Gibson, *South of the West,* ix–x.

8. Yue and Hawkins, "Going South."

9. Ang, *On Not Speaking Chinese,* vii.

10. See, for example, former prime minister John Howard's address to the Asialink-Australia National University National Forum, "Australia's Engagement with Asia: A New Paradigm," August 13, 2004, *Prime Minister of Australia News Room: Speeches,* http://www.pm.gov.au/news/speeches/speech1069.html (accessed August 18, 2005).

11. De Lauretis, "Eccentric Subjects," 139, 138.

12. "AsiaPacifiQueer 1: Conference Report," March 8, 2001, http://apq.anu.edu.au/conferencereporpt.html (accessed August 20, 2005).

13. See, for instance, the various responses posted to Dennis Altman's "On Global

Queering," *Australian Humanities Review* (July 1996), http//www.lib.latrobe.edu.au/AHR/archive/Issue-July-1996/altman.html (accessed June 4, 2003).

14. Shohat, "Notes on the Post-Colonial," 110. For a more recent criticism of the term, see Anthias, "New Hybridities, Old Concepts."

15. Bhabha, *The Location of Culture*, 309.

16. Muñoz, *Disidentifications*, 78, 84.

17. See, for example, Bhabha, *The Location of Culture*; Gillespie, *Television, Ethnicity, and Cultural Change*; Young, *Colonial Desire*; and Alderson, "Queer Cosmopolitanism."

18. Gopinath, "Local Sites/Global Contexts," 151–52.

19. *Semicolonial* is a term used in critical Thai and Chinese studies. Drawing originally from Maoist revisions of Marxism-Leninism, semicolonial societies—like Thailand, Japan, and the parts of China beyond the European colonial concession zones—remained politically independent of the West during the era of imperialism but nonetheless were economically and/or culturally subordinated to the West.

20. In addition to research conducted by a new generation of academics, queer studies is being advanced by activists who are not aligned with any particular academic institution or community organization but who address sexuality issues in their published works. The most prominent among these is the gay writer Fushimi Noriaki, whose books *Puraibēto gei raifu* (Private gay life, 1991) and *Kuia paradaisu* (Queer paradise, 1996) as well as the magazine *Queer Japan* (1999–2001), of which he was the chief editor, built bridges between researchers and members of minority communities.

21. So far Mark McLelland's *Queer Japan from the Pacific War to the Internet Age* is the only book-length investigation to be based on this material in either English or Japanese, although Fushimi Noriaki provides an overview of the usefulness, from a gay perspective, of the postwar perverse press in the history section of his collection *"Gei" to iu keiken* (The experience called "gay").

22. Unfortunately most of this remains untranslated and is published only in Chuo University's in-house journal. However, there is an attempt being made to make this research more accessible to English readers. See, for example, Ishida, McLelland, and Murakami, "The Origins of 'Queer Studies' in Postwar Japan"; and Ishida and Murakami, "The Process of Divergence."

23. Jackson, "An American Death in Bangkok" and "An Explosion of Thai Identities."

24. Jackson, "Thai Research on Male Homosexuality and Transgenderism."

25. For a more extended discussion of these parallel movements, see Martin, "Taiwan's Literature of Transgressive Sexuality."

26. Heng and Devan, "State Fatherhood."

27. Tan, "Sexing Up Singapore."

28. Heng, "Tiptoe Out of the Closet"; Offord, "Singapore Queering of the Internet."

29. Lo and Guoqin, *People Like Us.*

30. Yue, "Paging 'New Asia'"; Kang, *The Rainbow Connection.*

31. For an analysis on the need to imagine Thai queer history through the lens of gender rather than sexuality, see Jackson, "Performative Genders, Perverse Desires."

32. For a thoughtful critique of traditional area studies, see Morris-Suzuki, "Anti-area Studies." Peter Jackson has also written on the dual problems of traditional area studies and critical cultural studies in the study of non-Western societies; see "Space, Theory, and Hegemony" and "Mapping Poststructuralism's Borders."

33. Chakrabarty, "The Time of History and the Times of Gods."

34. Ibid., 39.

35. Ibid., 46.

36. Grossman, "Queer Asian Cinema."

References

Alderson, David. "Queer Cosmopolitanism: Place, Politics, Citizenship, and Queer as Folk." *New Formations* 55, no. 1 (2005): 73–88.

Ang, Ien. *On Not Speaking Chinese: Living between Asia and the West,* London: Routledge, 2001.

Anthias, Floya. "New Hybridities, Old Concepts: The Limits of 'Culture.'" *Ethnic and Racial Studies* 24, no. 4 (2001): 619–41.

Bhabha, Homi. *The Location of Culture.* London: Routledge, 2004.

Chakrabarty, Dipesh. "The Time of History and the Times of Gods." In Lisa Lowe and David Lloyd, eds., *The Politics of Culture in the Shadow of Capital.* Durham: Duke University Press, 1997. 35–60.

De Lauretis, Teresa. "Eccentric Subjects: Feminist Theory and Historical Consciousness." *Feminist Studies* 16, no. 1 (1990): 115–50.

Fushimi, Noriaki. *"Gei" to iu keiken* (The experience called "gay"). Tokyo: Pot, 2002.

Ge, Sun. "How Does 'Asia' Mean? (Part 1)." *Inter-Asia Cultural Studies* 1, no. 1 (2000): 13–47.

Gibson, Ross. *South of the West: Postcolonialism and the Narrative Construction of Australia.* Bloomington: Indiana University Press, 1992.

Gillespie, Marie. *Television, Ethnicity, and Cultural Change.* London: Routledge, 1995.

Gopinath, Gayatri. "Local Sites/Global Contexts: The Transnational Trajectories of Deepa Mehta's *Fire.*" In Arnaldo Cruz-Malav and Martin Manalansan, eds., *Queer Globalilzations: Citizenship and the Afterlife of Colonialism,* New York: New York University Press, 2002. 151–52.

Grossman, Andrew. "Queer Asian Cinema: Shadows in the State." Special issue, *Journal of Homosexuality* 39, no. 3/4 (2000).

Heng, Geraldine, and Janadas Devan. "State Fatherhood: The Politics of Nationalism, Sexuality, and Race in Singapore." In Andrew Parker, Mary Russo, Doris Sommer, and Patricia Yaeger, eds., *Nationalisms and Sexualities*, New York: Routledge, 1992. 343–64.

Heng, Russell Hiang Khng. "Tiptoe Out of the Closet: The Before and After of the Increasingly Visible Gay Community in Singapore." *Journal of Homosexuality* 40, no. 3–4 (2001): 81–97.

Hutcheon, Linda. "The Post-modern Ex-centric: The Center That Will Not Hold." In Linda Kauffman, ed., *Feminism and Institutions: Dialogues on Feminist Theory.* London: Blackwell, 1989. 141–65.

Ishida, Hitoshi, Mark McLelland, and Takanori Murakami. "The Origins of 'Queer Studies' in Postwar Japan." In Mark McLelland and Romit Dasgupta, eds., *Genders, Transgenders, and Sexualities in Japan.* London: Routledge, 2005.

Ishida, Hitoshi, and Takanori Murakami. "The Process of Divergence between 'Men who Love Men' and 'Feminised Men' in Postwar Japanese Media." Special Queer Japan issue, *Intersections* (January 2006). Available at http://wwwsshe.murdoch.edu.au/intersections/.

Jackson, Peter A. "An American Death in Bangkok: The Murder of Darrell Berrigan and the Hybrid Origins of Gay Identity in 1960s Thailand." *GLQ: A Journal of Lesbian and Gay Studies* 5, no. 3 (1999): 361–411.

———. "An Explosion of Thai Identities: Global Queering and Reimagining Queer Theory." *Culture, Health, and Sexuality* 2, no. 4 (2000): 405–24.

———. "Mapping Poststructuralism's Borders: The Case for Poststructuralist Area Studies," *Sojourn: Social Issues in Southeast Asia* 18, no. 1 (2003): 42–88.

———. "Performative Genders, Perverse Desires: A Bio-History of Thailand's Same-Sex and Transgender Cultures." *Intersections: Gender, History, and Culture in the Asian Context* 9 (2003). Available at http://wwwsshe.murdoch.edu.au/intersections/.

———. "Space, Theory, and Hegemony: The Dual Crises of Asian Area Studies and Cultural Studies." *Sojourn: Social Issues in Southeast Asia* 18, no. 1 (2003): 1–41.

———. "Thai Research on Male Homosexuality and Transgenderism and the Cultural Limits of Foucaultian Analysis." *Journal of the History of Sexuality* 8, no. 1 (1997): 52–85.

Kang, Ng King. *The Rainbow Connection.* Singapore: Kangcubine, 1999.

Lo, Joseph, and Huang Guoqin, eds. *People Like Us.* Singapore: Select Publishing, 2003.

Martin, Fran. "Taiwan's Literature of Transgressive Sexuality." In Fran Martin, trans., *Angelwings: Contemporary Queer Fiction from Taiwan,* Honolulu: University of Hawaii Press, 2003.

McLelland, Mark. *Queer Japan from the Pacific War to the Internet Age.* Lanham, Md.: Rowman and Littlefield, 2005.

Morris-Suzuki, Tessa. "Anti-area Studies." *Communal/Plural* 8, no. 1 (2000): 9–23.

Muñoz, José. *Disidentifications: Queers of Color and the Performance of Politics.* Minneapolis: University of Minnesota Press, 1999.

Offord, Baden. "Singapore Queering of the Internet: Toward a New Form of Cultural Transmission of Rights Discourse." In Chris Berry, Fran Martin, and Audrey Yue, eds., *Mobile Cultures: New Media in Queer Asia,* Durham: Duke University Press, 2003. 133–57.

Shohat, Ella. "Notes on the Post-Colonial." *Social Text,* no. 31–32 (1992): 99–113.

Tan, Kenneth. "Sexing Up Singapore." *International Journal of Cultural Studies* 6, no. 4 (2003): 403–23.

Young, Robert. *Colonial Desire: Hybridity in Theory, Culture and Race.* London: Routledge, 1995.

Yue, Audrey, and Gay Hawkins. "Going South." *New Formations* 40 (2000): 49–63.

ONE

EMBODIED MASCULINITIES OF MALE-MALE DESIRE

The *Homo* Magazines and White-Collar Manliness in Early 1970s Japan

J. Darren Mackintosh

The *Homo* Magazines of the Early 1970s: A "Failure"?

The first specialized, commercially marketed, professionally produced, and nationally distributed magazines catering exclusively to men who loved men—or *homo,* as these magazines' readers were called—appeared in the early 1970s in Japan. Starting with the publication of *Rose Tribes* (*Barazoku*) in 1971 and followed in quick succession by *The Adonis Boy* (1972), *Adon* (1974), and *Sabu* (1974), the *homo* magazines featured an eclectic mix of essays on male-male eroticism, lifestyle columns on Japan's popular and *homo* cultures, pornography, and regular readers' contributions sections, the most important of which were the personal columns where men sought contact with other men.

All of these items had been seen before. In the two decades following the Allied occupation of Japan (1945–52) to the early 1970s, publications catering to male-male sexuality generally took two forms. There were the "common interest journals" (*dōjinshi*) of a variety of unrelated private members' clubs organized by and for men who love men, which were made up of members' literary and/or artistic contributions. There also was a genre of "erotica magazine" (*fūzoku zasshi*) that treated male-male sexuality in feature sections as one of an array of male-female and male-male sexual desires. Because of the dispersed nature of this publication activity, the culture of male same-sex love was fleeting in its visibility for many. Moreover, its representation, created by a disparate range of authors and artists, was atomized and eclectic, reflecting the wide spectrum of male-male sexual performances, practices, understandings, and concepts that characterized the early- to mid-postwar era (1950s-1970s) ranging from the "transgendered" (*gei*) to the hypermasculine.[1]

Barazoku challenged this situation when it first hit the bookstands in 1971. Marketed in mainstream bookshops, it broke the barrier separating mainstream society from its underground to bring the largely hidden world of *homo* into the public gaze. Moreover, the visibility was to be sustained since the magazine would appear regularly (published every other month after its launch and monthly from 1974). *Homo* desire could now be explored in a venue that was accessible to anybody across the nation. As a result, the atomization characterizing previous decades was potentially eclipsed, if momentarily. *Barazoku* and the magazine genre it generated were a success, expanding and enduring to help define the culture of male-male sexuality in Japan in the last quarter of the twentieth century.[2]

Despite their relative success and longevity, the significance of the *homo* magazines to the postwar history of male-male sexuality has been judged by some as doubtful. Ethnographer Wim Lunsing, for example, suggests that the influence magazines like *Barazoku* had on fostering lasting gay networks and stimulating gay political activity was limited at best.[3] Writer Nōkami Teruki is more ambivalent on the ability of the magazines to raise sociopolitical awareness, arguing that they were undermined by their close association with the commodified sexual world of bars, sex clubs, and cruising areas that had emerged in postwar Japan's major cities. Gay activist Minami Teishirō is the most critical, asserting that the *homo* media activity of the early 1970s and especially *Barazoku* (the vanguard publication) all failed to incite the *homo* voice politically.[4] These are important arguments that serve to highlight what seems to be an unavoidable conclusion concerning the *homo* magazine genre. Despite the optimism of its founders to effect positive change for the lot of *homo*—*Barazoku* editor Fujita Ryū predicted a "new dawn" —very little resulted. Certainly, a gay movement such as is witnessed in the Anglo-American West has not been mirrored in Japan in terms of numbers or sociopolitical influence.[5] Most crucially, antihomosexual prejudice continues to affect the lives of many.

Despite their varied perspectives, Lunsing, Nōkami, and Minami share a common approach. They all extol a model of sociopolitical change informed by a theory of global convergence according to which the Japanese case is measured against the historical experience of gay liberation and the gay movement as it evolved and is evaluated in societies like the United States or Britain. They critique the *homo* magazines according to two criteria: the degree to which they stimulated gay political consciousness and community and the degree to which they enabled gay men to legally and socially resist the norms of (male) heterosexual society in a bid for equal rights. In short, they are concerned with the problem of whether or not the magazines helped effect a new and powerful (Western-style) liberationist discourse of male homosexuality. According to them, the *homo* magazines of the early 1970s appear to have failed.

As incisive as these critiques are, they raise a crucial question regarding the postwar history and culture of male-male sexuality in Japan. Is the interpretive lens of gay liberation as contextualized by sociopolitical global convergence a relevant way of understanding the aspirations that characterized the *homo* magazines? To be sure, the gay movement was known in Japan, and there were attempts by activists like Minami—himself influenced by the Japanese student and civic protest movements of 1950s and 1960s—to import gay liberation to Japan. Although Minami's personal experiences help to explain his criticism of *Barazoku,* this is nevertheless a problematic perspective. Importantly, it overlooks the possibility that the magazines *did* help to create the conditions for a form of "liberation" that, while diverging markedly from the goals of Western gay liberation, reflected current and local circumstances to help "liberate" certain expressions of male-male sexuality in profound ways.

This chapter explores how the *homo* magazines of the early 1970s may have constituted a form of "movement," one aimed less at issues of sociopolitical equality since what was at stake for some of the magazines' readers was the search for a sense of subjectivity. Drawing on research I conducted on the personal columns in the *homo* magazines, this chapter details one specific idiom of how men may have understood themselves as (men who love) men, namely, the place of white-collar employment in the highly embodied project of self-perception/construction and self-representation.

It should be noted that white-collar work was only one of many ways that masculinity was configured. Other ways included manual/blue-collar labor; leisure activities; aesthetics, for instance, of the city and nature; popular and counterculture; different types of male-male relationships, some romantic and others not; and sex in all its varied forms. I have chosen to focus on what can be understood as "white-collar masculinity" since it throws into sharp and problematic relief the relationship of the men who love men with patriarchy and narratives of the nation. It importantly interrogates the taken-for-granted conflation of male male sexuality with "subaltern" positions to suggest that many white-collar men imagined themselves, their personal narratives, and love of men as integral to dominant and official conceptions of work, Japan, and its history.

In the first section of this chapter, the results of a quantitative analysis of a sampling of the personal advertisements reveals that white-collar work was possibly privileged in the depiction of men's employment. Through a discursive cultural analysis of the ads, the second section suggests that the work that men valorized implied specific kinds of manliness as manifested in both their physical and affective (emotional, cognitive, personality, and spiritual characteristics) bodies. Overall, this chapter will argue that the binary of resistance to and complicity with mainstream society—a pivotal strategy of the early Anglo-American gay movement—does not easily fit the case of early 1970s Japan, a place where the white-collar worker was officially held as the epitome of masculine achievement and identity. Instead, *homo* "liberation" was pursued through highly individualistic, creative, fluid, and, above all, potent engagements with the discursive field of masculinities to promote what Foucault defines as a "practice of the self."[6]

Regarding the sample, 1,098 advertisers of around 3,875 (28 percent) were randomly selected from the personal columns of the four magazines. Two sets of complete personal columns were analyzed from each magazine in the first year of their publication. It must be noted that the personal ads are not here taken as representative—though they may be indicative—of the magazines' readerships at large or of men who loved men in early 1970s Japan. The ads' authors comprised a specific group of men who possessed a combination of qualities that were not common to the majority of men, namely, the desire, means, and circumstances that enabled them to present themselves as lovers of men in a public venue. Furthermore, while the ads often contain information that detail their authors' backgrounds, the development of a market profile is statistically unfeasible due to the lack of consistency of information. As for the readership overall, information necessary to complete a market survey is unavailable. This analysis of the ads is therefore impressionistic. It is designed to map the imaginative field of meanings, emotions, images, and ideals concerning male-male sex and masculinities that a reader would have encountered. How he interpreted this field and how it relates to the overall readership is a question this chapter does not seek to answer.[7]

Work: The White-Collar Ideal in Quantitative Perspective

Masculinities studies scholar Stephen Whitehead conjectures that "paid employment provides an important arena through which the discursive subject can achieve a sense of identity—the accomplishment of being (an individual). In this respect, paid work is more than merely a provider of some material or social comfort or an opportunity to exercise power; it is a primary vehicle for the otherwise contingent and unstable subject to achieve a sense of self, to become grounded and located in the social world."[8] Whitehead's observation is particularly relevant to this Japanese case where nearly one-third of men in the personal ads (32 percent) indicated their occupations. It is tempting to conclude that work was a fundamental influence in the configuration of masculine identity for a large minority of men in this sample. Yet the picture is more complicated, since it does appear that some occupations were worth mentioning more than others. Indeed, when that contingent of men who made reference to their working lives is broken down according to occupation, a distinct bias favoring the white-collar sector is detectable.

Firstly, white-collar work is conspicuously overrepresented in the ads. The number of men who may be listed as white collar (62 percent) significantly outnumbered those found in all other categories of work put together (38 percent). When these figures are considered within the context of the distribution of occupations among the gainfully employed male population as listed in the *Japan Statistical Yearbook* for 1973–74, this trend is even more conspicuous.[9] Consider those men who listed unspecified nonprofessional white-collar occupations: "salaryman" (*sarariiman*), "office worker" (*kaishain*), and "public sector employee" (*kōmuin*).[10] Taking these terms as roughly corresponding with "administrative," "managerial," and/or "clerical" work (to use the nomenclature of the Bureau of Statistics), the following is observed. Whereas around 17 percent of the total employed male population of Japan in 1970 worked in the nonprofessional white-collar sector, nearly 60 percent of the men in the personal ads can be estimated to have done so.[11]

The comparison between the national case and the magazines is not unproblematic. Critically, the terms employed by men to describe their occupations are ambiguous. *Kaishain* is a case in point. Translated literally, it simply means "company employee," which, depending on the kind of business concerned, might include blue-collar laborers as well as white-collar paper-pushers. Because it does imply membership in the company, however, *kaishain* status tends to be more permanent with the result that remuneration may be based less on wages in favor of salaries. As such, it has an aura of legitimacy not far from that which attends the white-collar office worker.

With this in mind, two questions emerge to qualify the observations made above. Can all the men who listed themselves as *kaishain* be legitimately classified as white-collar workers? Probably not. In any event, this does not wholly belie the bias that favors white-collar men, for even if all self-designated *kaishain* are subtracted, the overall white-collar category still remains the largest of any single group. More significantly, if those who listed themselves as *kaishain* are not white-collar workers, what are they? To categorize them as blue collar is to replicate the problem encountered above regarding the classification of ambiguous terms like *kaishain*. In the end, many men listing unspecified nonprofessional white-collar occupations cannot be classified with certainty.

For some of these men, perhaps, this may have been precisely the point. Assuming that there is a bias towards white-collar status or at least a desire to share in some of the legitimacy it lends, it might be possible that labeling oneself *kaishain* was a performance of calculated obfuscation through creative self-enhancement. In the same way that a man of thirty-nine might attempt to suggest a more youthful persona by using the ambiguous phrase "in my thirties," *kaishain* might be used to either deflect attention away from work that is perceived as less than prestigious or inflate an average job into something more attractive, thereby enhancing in the eyes of a prospective partner the desirability of its holder. Of course, none of this can be proven since there is no way of testing the veracity of the information in the ads. Yet there is corroborating if circumstantial evidence to suggest why it may have been desirable to beef up one's work image.

Shifting attention to non-white-collar occupations, the bias favoring white-collar status appears to be buttressed by the minority of those who were willing and/or able to identify themselves with non-white-collar status, roughly one-third (38 percent) of that part of the sample that indicated employment. Not only is this far less than the 77 percent of all men across the nation working in the same or comparable kinds of work, but the distribution of occupations that are specified is curious.[12] Whereas jobs that might generally be classified as blue collar and/or manual labor (in the Bureau of Statistics typology, laborers, craftsmen, and production-process workers, workers in transport and communication, miners and quarrymen, farmers, lumbermen, and fishermen) account for around 60 percent of the employed male population nationwide, these make up a mere 6 percent of men in the sample of personal advertisements who listed their work. Non-white-collar occupations and, in particular, those that can be identified as coming from the blue-collar sector, are distinctly underrepresented in the personal columns of the early 1970s.

This survey is admittedly impressionistic. Fundamental discrepancies between the sets of terms employed make a precise comparison between the magazine sample and the national case extremely difficult. Moreover, as stated above, it cannot be claimed that employment figures derived from the magazines are representative of the advertisers let alone the readership. My purpose here in bringing attention to the advertisers' occupations as compared with the national case, however, is to suggest that white-collar employment may have disproportionately influenced the overall imaginary field of masculinities in the personal ads as configured by employment. It may have indeed been the case that the ads were representative with white-collar men being more likely to buy the magazines and/or advertise in them. It may have been equally true that class prejudices were in operation. The mid-postwar period was a time when the figure and ideal of the white-collar worker—the "corporate warrior" (*kigyō senshi*) spearheading Japanese economic growth—was in its ascendance. As a result, men may have been more apt to indicate their occupation if they worked in the white-collar sector and less inclined to do so if they were employed in many forms of non-white-collar work. Either way, as far as the imaginative field of masculinities is concerned, the white-collar model appears to be of significance for many *homo* appearing in the personal advertisements of the early 1970s. It was also fundamentally implicated in the way men perceived and represented their physical and affective bodily selves and male-male sexuality.

Seriousness: The Bodily Idiom[13] of White-Collar Masculinity

"I'm 25 years old: a serious, able, and committed company man," states "Anchan" with the formalism of a business letter.[14] In as terse a style, Y.Y. writes, "20 y.o., 168cm, 52 kg, *kaishain*. Partner I am seeking is a 38–60 year-old 'reliable, honest' [*kenjitsu na*] *sarariiman*, a dominant person who will lead me."[15] Finally, S: "'Normal and serious' [*Heibon de majime*], 45 y.o. *sarariiman*."[16]

These three ads exemplify how white-collar ethics helped some men shape a sense of manly self. Direct, confident, and unemotionally factual, each replicates the tone of a standard "self-introduction" (*jiko shōkai*) that a man had to learn to recite as a first step to mastering the protocol of corporate life in Japan in the 1970s.[17] Even if these statements are followed by an incongruous description of the "bulging pouches of Japanese-style loincloths," as was the case with one "serious and committed" (*shinmenmoku*) *sararii-man*, for example, the crucial first impression is nonetheless of a man who is both "sincere" and "reliable" (that is, *shinmenmoku, kenjitsu*) and "serious" (*majime*).[18]

In the personal columns, the importance of work as expressed through the idiom of seriousness to one's self-understanding cannot be overestimated. In terms of percentages, seriousness was one of the most commonly cited of all adjectives describing one's individual character and the ideal traits of a prospective partner: one in eight ads made references to seriousness with regards to oneself while one in seven held seriousness as desirable in an ideal partner.

The importance of seriousness is not belied from a qualitative perspective, either. Adjectives like *kenjitsu, shinmenmoku,* and *majime* are found at the heart of a signifying economy that for some fused together a man's work, his bodily identity as a man, his desire for other men, and his sense of ethical being. At the most general level, seriousness acts as a context in which a man comes to be associated with characteristics like commitment, dedication, careerism, and singularity of purpose.[19] The forty-year-old "Student of *Shinmenmoku*," for example, seeks "a person who works to the utmost of his ability, earnestly and sincerely."[20] Pitched at a register of politeness characteristic of a formal business setting, the ad conveys the importance its author attaches to seriousness for himself and a desired partner.

Seriousness was not concerned only with a man's public role. The kind and quality of a man's work fundamentally informed the (self-) perception/ construction and (self-) representation of his entire masculine identity. One forty-eight-year-old *kaishain* seeks a person who has a "respectable occupation" (*majime na shokugyō*). Numaguchi speaks of a "steady, regular job" (*teishoku*). His ad is worth citing at length since it demonstrates how pivotal seriousness can be:

> *Numaguchi Fumio* 24 years old, . . . 160cm tall, 54 kg, *kaishain*. Hobbies = cinema, music, travel. Not interested in "sado-masochism," possible active or passive role in anything except anal sex. Normal looks, small and slim build, but passionate. Ideal if you are a foreign male who understands Japanese. Seeking chiselled face and gentle heart. Bonus if you are intelligent as well. Looking for somebody who is 20–60 y.o. if foreign and 30–60 y.o. if Japanese "of solid and manly character" [*shikkari shita jinbutsu*] with steady, regular job, and financially stable.[21]

A "steady, regular job" is a highly embodied description that links the physical and affective body in ways that confirm a manly—and Japanese—

character. For Numaguchi, it brings together the desired affective qualities in a prospective partner of solidness and manliness, which are imagined physically: the sharply defined, perhaps square-jawed face of a possibly older Caucasian, as Japanese often imagine the "foreigner" to be.[22] Importantly, ethnicity serves here to emphasize the instrumental role of work in the construction of manliness and sexual desirability in this ad. Reflecting cultural stereotypes that imagine *gaijin* as less serious, Numaguchi's ideal foreigner is depicted in terms of non-work-related traits—his face, gentleness, and intelligence. As for a prospective Japanese partner, his masculinity is premised upon white-collar achievement—a steady, regular job and financial stability—and seriousness—a solid, manly character.

As for Numaguchi himself, his seriousness is possibly signified by his *kaishain* suit, white shirt, tie, and company lapel pin: seriousness clothes his body. Finally, seriousness takes corporeal and erotic form in a rather average stature that practices serious sex only, that is, no sado-masochism and arse play, which, for many in the personal ads, are depicted as an extreme form of sexual play.

Ikigai: The Ethic of White-Collar Masculinity— Mainstream Complicity?

Finally, seriousness as defined by a "steady, regular job" is an ethical statement. It defines not simply how one should go about one's job. Rather it signifies a standard that idealizes how one should live one's life. The advertisement of "Older Brother" (*Aniki*), for example, desires the kind of younger brother whose "reason for being" (*ikigai*) is "to be able to work with all one's might" (*harikitte hatarakeru*).[23]

As the quintessential expression of seriousness, the appearance of the concept of *ikigai* is unsurprising. In his research on men's employment in the 1990s, Gordon Mathews finds that men who were in their working prime, that is, their thirties or older in the 1960s, often characterized their work as "that which most makes life worth living."[24] The words of some of the company executives he cites are worth revisiting. "For the past thirty years, my *ikigai* has been the companies I've worked for; they've been more important to me than my family," admits a corporate executive with pride.[25] Another company executive frets about his younger colleagues: "There are fewer and fewer company men like me these days . . . I've never said no to any of my job assignments—I was always there when they needed me. I like men who do that: manly men (*otoko rashii otoko*)."[26] Conveying the paramount importance that work and seriousness might have to masculine identity in the white-collar context, a fuller idea is provided in both of these statements by Mathews's informants of why some men may have wished and even felt compelled to make their occupations a central feature of their advertisements.

As the most clearly illustrative of the white-collar model, the appearance of *ikigai* also puts some of the serious men in the personal ads in an apparently paradoxical position. By identifying themselves with the white-collar model, these men appear to have been complicit with what Roberson and Suzuki define as the "salaryman doxa," the "taken-for-granted [norm of] 'hegemonic masculinity.'"[27] Far from simply being a dominant "(self-) image, model and representation of men and masculinity in Japan," the figure of the white-collar worker *is* the index of discourses in postwar Japan on gender, sexuality, class, and the nation.[28] It is a public-sphere institutional role that was and is advanced as an ideology of patriarchal heteronormativity as premised on the following: productivity (the economically powerful male), a Japanese work ethic of absolute loyalty to company and nation (the uniquely Japanese male), the primacy of marriage (the heterosexual male), and fatherhood (the virile male who ensures the survival of his family name).

It seems, then, that some men in the personal advertisements subscribed to the very system that rendered their desire for other men illegitimate. It is a contradiction that scholars and activists have emphasized to explain the failure of the *homo* magazines of the early 1970s to spark a sustained form of gay consciousness and movement for gay liberation. According to Lunsing, for example, male-male eroticism was and is a form of "play" (*asobi*) that in Japanese society is opposed to either the serious—hence real—world of heterosexuality or the sociopolitical—thus genuine—gay communities that have evolved in the West.[29] Minami, for his part, is highly critical of postwar patriarchal heteronormativity. He explains that it is inimical to the emergence of gay consciousness, voice, movement, and liberation: "male-female sex is deemed legitimate because it is necessary to the maintenance of the race and the protection of the system of private property; . . . any other kind of sex is discarded."[30] As one of Japan's first gay activists whose "coming out" was attended by large personal sacrifices, he is critical of gays in the early 1970s. Fearful of the scorn and hatred that would emerge from heterosexual society if its ideology were challenged and thinking of only their bodily safety, gay men, he asserts, did not take any significant steps that might see their presumed aspirations for equality and will to freedom realized. What's more, the activity that did seem to emerge in the form of Japan's first gay magazine *Barazoku* was little more than a false start, since the "gay voice" was in actual-ity that of heterosexual publisher Itō Bungaku. Admittedly sympathetic to the plight of gays, Itō "managed" the "gay voice" to unwittingly obstruct it. In short, the gay movement that *homo* magazine activity ostensibly promised was, according to Minami, bound to fail because of gay men's complicity with "hegemonic masculinity," the structures and ideology of their own oppression.[31]

Work, Seriousness, and *Ikigai:* "Practices of the Self"

There is another way to interpret work, seriousness, and *ikigai.* The mention of one's occupation in the personal columns is not simply a statement of what a man does; it is a signifier of men's lives, ones that are characterized by a daily regimen of work: the commute, the mastering of complicated sutra-like codes of formal language and behavior, long arduous hours at the expense of one's personal life, and endless sacrifices all for the sake of the "harmony and strength" of the company and nation.[32] In retrospect, this regimen of work, compounded by the struggle to survive materially and morally, especially through the extreme hardship following the defeat of Japan in World War II, reads very much like what Foucault refers to in the *History of Sexuality* as a "practice of the self," a "relentless combat" akin to moral and ethical "training": "the task of testing oneself, examining oneself, monitoring oneself in a series of clearly defined exercises, [which] makes the question of truth—the truth concerning what one is, what one does, and what one is capable of doing—central to the formation of the ethical subject."[33]

The physical and moral mastering of one's body through the training of work is not simply a tale of hardship and success. Rather, a man's life and history are in effect the elaboration of "ethical work (*travail éthique*)" that Foucault defines as the acts one "performs on oneself, not only in order to bring one's conduct into compliance with a given rule"—in this case the white-collar model, company, and nation—but to become the subject of his behavior, that is, personal triumph over tribulation.[34]

From the perspective of the "practices of the self," complicity with a form of masculinity that is grounded in "the subordination of homosexuality"[35] can equally be understood as "the practice of freedom" in the sense of making a choice "to construct oneself as an ethical subject, in relation to the self and to others."[36] This "practice of freedom" may be interpreted as a displacement of male-male sexual desire from the center of their gendered personhood. But this "practice" may equally be understood as the integration of historical narratives of national reconstruction (Japan emerging in the 1950s like a phoenix from the ashes of total defeat) and the "economic miracle" (Japan rising to become the world's third largest economy in 1970) into one's bodily sense of self. Here, men's bodies enduring hardship through serious regimes of work signifies the ethical—and for the men who love men, eroticized body—regimes through which the historical narratives of postwar Japanese national power are understood and validated. The white-collar model, far from being inimical to the desire that finds beauty in male-male love, is integral to its expression for some men. It is an important means through which many individuals in the personal ads explored and articulated a sense of subjectivity and desire, a necessary condition of freedom. By freedom, I don't refer to social and legal equality as defined in the context of gay liberation. Far from it: in the personal advertisements, individuals were asserting their control over the right to perceive/construct and represent themselves, in other words, a freedom to decide who they were and who they should become as both man and citizen. Accordingly, the white-collar model, seriousness, and *ikigai* must be understood as vital components of an embodied project of self-liberation, one that is largely not premised on considerations of complicity with or resistance to "hegemonic masculinity," and one that, in turn, is not relevant to the moral imperatives of gay liberation at a time when this movement was rapidly expanding overseas.

Conclusion: A "Movement" of the Men Who Love Men

The case of work is indicative of a wide variety of expression in the personal columns and, by extension, the *homo* magazines in the early 1970s. To be certain, each of the personal advertisements varied greatly. Some men highlighted their hobbies and interests while others created detailed self-portraits, bringing into play an array of idioms to portray their bodily selves: sincerity, romance, muscularity, chubbiness. Many ads were autobiographical, a number of them recounting in highly evocative ways their author's dreams and aspirations, tragedies and regrets. In some cases running up to as much as a page in length, personal advertisements, especially in the very first personal columns, were often less statements of self-promotion to find a prospective partner than a tableau of one's own life. Secrets were confessed, emotions were expressed, and the physical body was depicted: men wrote themselves into being less in a will to know an objective truth concerning homosexuality but a subjective will to feel and celebrate their love for other men. This is precisely what one witnesses time and again in the very first personal columns of the early 1970s, an outburst of emotion: joy, hope, desperation, and, above all, an awakening. "When I came across *Barazoku*," wrote one man in the personal advertisements, "my eyes were opened."[37]

Something quite special seems to have occurred in the early 1970s that was located in the personal columns of Japan's first *homo* magazines. Many men who had hitherto been isolated geographically or through ignorance not only came to realize that they were not alone, but the magazines, designed first and foremost as a venue to help men locate each other in the forum of the personal advertisements, at once gave thousands of men across the nation an opportunity to affirm the fact of their existence and desire. Yet, when men declared "I'm here" in that unique historical moment that was the novelty of their first encounter with the personal columns, there did not emerge a new discourse of homosexuality, politically inspired and socially powerful. Rather, there were multiple projects of the self according to which men creatively engaged with discourses of gender and sexuality, normative and otherwise.

Insofar as the *homo* magazines in the early 1970s acted as a venue of self-expression, they can be understood collectively as a form of "movement" of, by, and for the men who love men. Its spirit and trajectory differed markedly from the movement for gay liberation and for good reason. The personal columns and the writings of the readership emerged largely out of the post-war Japanese circumstance with little reference to the overseas rallies and demonstrations then being reported in the Japanese news media. Some like Minami did try to take up the banner to introduce Japan to Anglo-American gay politics. But for many, issues of identity and solidarity were not to be found in the globalization of the gay movement with its polarization of society into mainstream and "subaltern"; there was little to be gained through the alienation of oneself from society in order to be part of a reclaimed subculture. Rather, as the case of the white-collar model and the personal columns of Japan's first *homo* magazines demonstrate, "liberation" was located in highly particular ethical projects of the bodily self.

Notes

1. On the early- to mid-postwar history of male-male sexuality, see McLelland, *Queer Japan from the Pacific War to the Internet Age,* and Fushimi, "The Gay 'Experience.'"

2. According to *Barazoku* founder Itō Bungaku, the first number sold 70 percent of its print run of 10,000 copies, a figure which grew to 30,000 copies a few years later (Itō interview with author). Although *Barazoku* could nowhere near compare with million-selling first-rate magazines (Kinsella, *Adult Manga,* 43), it nevertheless

singled out *homo* sexual identity from the vast array of male-male and male-female sexual performances, practices, proclivities, and understandings to carve out a market that was viable in terms of future growth, competition, and endurance. *Barazoku* was discontinued in 2004, although it has subsequently been re-started (Barazoku Web site [2007]). *The Adonis Boy* was reformatted and released in 1974 as *Adon* and lasted until 1996. *Sabu* was discontinued in 2002.

3. Lunsing, "*Kono sekai* (The Japanese Gay Scene)," 303, 309.

4. Minami, "The Gay Movement in Postwar Japan," 128–29. Although Minami founded *The Adonis Boy* and *Adon* to help spur a movement for *homo* civil rights, he acknowledges that his magazines had limited impact. As far as he is concerned, the gay movement belatedly arrived in Japan in 1984 when the president of the International Lesbian and Gay Association visited with the express purpose of establishing a branch of the organization (131).

5. Lunsing, "*Kono sekai* (The Japanese Gay Scene)," 315–16; Delfosse interview with author.

6. Foucault, *The Care of the Self* and *The Use of Pleasure*.

7. Regarding the citation of personal advertisements, the following system has been adopted for endnotes: magazine title and volume number, date, ad number. For example, *Barazoku* 1, 07/71, #5 refers to *Barazoku* no. 1, July 1971, ad number 5.

8. Whitehead, *Men and Masculinities*, 124.

9. Prime Minister's Office, *Japan Statistical Yearbook*.

10. Professional occupations include education-related and intellectual professions, engineering, medicine, and journalism. With 5 percent listing those occupations in the personal ads, the proportion of men who can be identified in terms of professional white-collar occupations closely matched the national percentage of men (6 percent) who fall into this category.

11. Prime Minister's Office, *Japan Statistical Yearbook*, 50–51.

12. Prime Minister's Office, *Japan Statistical Yearbook*, 50–51.

13. "Bodily idioms" refer to basic clusters of meanings concerning the perception/construction and representation of men's selves as derived from a word-by-word analysis of the personal advertisements. For example, the bodily idiom of "husky, muscular, and brawny" is drawn from all adjectives and phrases appearing throughout the sample that conjure this physical—and affective—bodily image, for example, "muscular" (*kinnikushitsu*), "solid" (*gatchiri*), and a "strong physical body" and/or a "solid character" (*takumashii*).

14. *Adon* 2, 07/74, #38.

15. *Adonis Boy* 1, 12/72, #3.

16. *Barazoku* 1, 01/72, #175.

17. Involving the formulaic exchange of information including one's name, company, and position, the *jiko shōkai* is highly structured and ritualized. Proficiency requires mastery of business etiquette that translates verbally into the manipulation of honorific styles of address and that is expressed physically by one's deportment, level of bowing, and the giving and receiving of name cards.

18. *Adon* 2, 07/74, #84.

19. Whitehead, *Men and Masculinities,* 128.

20. *Barazoku* 3, 01/72, #127.

21. *Adonis Boy* 2, 01/73, #10.

22. Creighton, "*Soto* Others and *Uchi* Others," 212.

23. *Adon* 2, 07/74, #67.

24. Mathews, "Can 'a Real Man' Live for His Family?"

25. Ibid., 110.

26. Ibid., 111.

27. Roberson and Suzuki, *Men and Masculinities in Contemporary Japan,* 1, 3.

28. Ibid., 1–2, 4–5, 8.

29. Lunsing, "*Kono sekai* (The Japanese Gay Scene)."

30. *Adon* 1, 05/74, #27.

31. Minami, "The Gay Movement in Postwar Japan," 129.

32. Rohlen, *For Harmony and Strength.* In his 1974 ethnography of a Japanese bank, Thomas Rohlen details the pseudo-religious and quasi-military practices that constitute a regime according to which male employees are trained to "work like seasoned soldiers" in a spirit of purity and sincerity for the sake of (as the company motto declares) "harmony and strength." The successful mastery of this regime helps to forge a sense of manly self, one that, as Rohlen argues, was contextualized by the conflation of the company and the Japanese nation-state. For a contemporary exploration of the white-collar regime and its role in the production of masculine identity, see Dasgupta, "Creating Corporate Warriors."

33. Foucault, *The Care of the Self,* 68.

34. Foucault, *The Use of Pleasure,* 27.

35. Connell, *Masculinities,* 78.

36. Danaher, Schirato, and Webb, *Understanding Foucault,* 148.

37. *Barazoku* 7, 09/72, #22.

References

Primary Sources: Magazines and Newspapers

Adon, 1974 (nos. 1–7).
The Adonis Boy, 1972, 1973, 1974 (nos. 1–14).
Barazoku, 1971, 1972 (nos. 1–7).
Prime Minister's Office. *Japan Statistical Yearbook,* no. 24. Tokyo: Mainichi Shin-bunsha, 1974.
Sabu, 1974–1975 (no. 1–6).

Interviews

Delfosse, Alain. Interview with author, September 28, 2002, Zurich, Switzerland.
Itō Bungaku, owner of Dai ni shobo and founder of *Barazoku.* Interview with author, March 21, 2002, Tokyo, Japan, tape recording.

Secondary Sources

"Barazoku Monthly's Chief Editor Itō Bungaku's Discussion Room—Festival" (Gekkan Barazoku henshūchō Itō Bungaku no sōdanshitsu—Matsuri). Available at http://www.barazoku.co.jp; accessed Ocotber 2, 1997.

Connell, R. W. *Masculinities*. Cambridge: Polity Press, 1995.

Creighton, Millie. "*Soto* Others and *Uchi* Others: Imaging Racial Diversity, Imagining Homogenous Japan." In Michael Weiner, ed., *Japan's Minorities: The Illusion of Homogeneity*. London: Routledge, 1997. 211–38.

Danaher, Geoff, Tony Schirato, and Jen Webb. *Understanding Foucault*. London: Sage, 2000.

Dasgupta, Romit. "Creating Corporate Warriors: The 'Salaryman' and Masculinity in Japan." In K. Louie and M. Low, eds., *Asian Masculinities: The Meaning and Practice of Manhood in China and Japan*. London: Routledge Curzon, 2003, 118–34.

Foucault, Michel. *The History of Sexuality*, vol. 3: *The Care of the Self*, trans. Robert Hurley. New York: Vintage Books, 1988.

———. *The History of Sexuality*, vol. 2: *The Use of Pleasure*, trans. Robert Hurley. New York: Vintage Books, 1990.

Fushimi, Noriaki. *The Gay "Experience" (Gei to iu "keiken")*. Tokyo: Pot, 2002.

Kinsella, Sharon. *Adult Manga: Culture and Power in Contemporary Japanese Society*. Richmond, Surrey: Curzon Press, 2000.

Laner, Mary Riege, and G. W. Levi Kamel. "Media Mating I: Newspaper 'Personals' Ads of Homosexual Men." *Journal of Homosexuality* 3, no. 2 (1997): 149–62.

Lunsing, Wim. "Japan: Finding its Way?" In Barry D. Adam, Jan Willem Duyvendak, and Andre Krouwel, eds., *The Global Emergence of Gay and Lesbian Politics: National Imprints of a Worldwide Movement*. Philadelphia: Temple University Press, 1999. 293–325.

———. "*Kono sekai* (The Japanese Gay Scene): Communities or Just Playing Around?" In Joy Hendry and Massimo Raveri, eds., *Japan at Play: The Ludic and the Logic of Power*. London: Routledge, 2002. 57–71.

Mathews, Gordon. "Can 'a Real Man' Live for His Family? *Ikigai* and Masculinity in Today's Japan." In James E. Roberson and Nobue Suzuki, eds., *Men and Masculinities in Contemporary Japan: Dislocating the Salaryman Doxa*. London: Routledge Curzon, 2003. 109–25.

McLelland, Mark J. *Queer Japan from the Pacific War to the Internet Age*. Lanham, Md.: Rowman and Littlefield, 2005.

Minami, Teishirō. "The Gay Movement in Postwar Japan" (Sengo nihon no gei mūbumento). *Impakushon* 71, "Special Collection: Gay Liberation" (Tokushū: Gei Riberēshon). Tokyo: Impakuto Shuppankai, 1991. 124 32.

Roberson, James E., and Nobue Suzuki. Introduction to James E. Roberson and Nobue Suzuki, eds., *Men and Masculinities in Contemporary Japan: Dislocating the Salaryman Doxa*, London: Routledge Curzon, 2003. 1–19.

Rohlen, Thomas P. *For Harmony and Strength: Japanese White-Collar Organization in Anthropological Perspective,* Berkeley: University of California Press, 1974.

Ueno, Chizuko. Introduction to section 5, "Corporate Warriors" (Kigyō senshitachi). In Inoue Teruko, Ueno Chizuko, and Ebara Yumiko, eds., "Feminism in Japan, Special Issue—Men's Studies" (Nihon no Feminizumu, Betsu—Danseigaku). To-kyo: Iwanami shoten, 1995.

Whitehead, Stephen M. 2002. *Men and Masculinities: Key Themes and New Directions.* Cambridge: Polity Press, 2002.

TWO

LILIES OF THE MARGIN

Beautiful Boys and Queer Female
Identities in Japan

James Welker

Interest in and research on genders and sexualities that trans-
gress heteronormativity in Japan has been increasing steadily since the early
1990s, both domestically and abroad. Over the same period, the representation of transgressive gender and sexual practices in Japan's *shōjo* manga
(girls' comics) has attracted far greater academic attention. Some research has
examined intersections between these two spheres, exploring the correlation,
or lack thereof, between the realities of men who have sex with men and these
representations of male-male romance and sexuality in a genre originally
called *shōnen ai* (boys' love) that has come to be referred to as BL or *bōizu
rabu* (boys' love) and *yaoi*.[1] In the 1970s, the "beautiful boy" (*bishōnen*) of
"boys' love" manga was a lithe, androgynous, and sexually ambiguous figure
with twinkling eyes whose femininity allowed readers to identify with him
and escape to his distant world, most often a romanticized and historic Europe. Researchers and critics alike have long argued that "boys' love" appeals
to its readers because it is situated outside local heteronormative discourse
and, as a consequence, liberates readers to vicariously experiment with gender
and sexuality. Ironically, such analysis has tended to assume heteronormative
female readers.[2] This chapter, in contrast, explores intersections between the
sphere of "boys' love" and the gender and sexual identities and practices of
women who resist heteronormativity.

Such linkages are, in fact, not difficult to find. Lesbian activist, "boys' love" fan, and academic Mizoguchi Akiko, for instance, has declared that she "'became' a lesbian via reception, in [her] adolescence, of the 'beautiful boy' comics of the 1970s."[3] Personal histories of those who might be included in the Japanese "lesbian" (rezubian) community similarly reflect the influence of "boys' love" manga on the development of transgressive gender and sexual identities.[4] While the lesbian community, including bars, organizations, and (noncommercial) publications, was well-established by the early 1970s in Tokyo and Osaka, awareness of and access to the community was limited, particularly in the 1970s and 1980s when "boys' love" manga was in its hey-day.[5] Doubtless these conditions contributed to the use of magazines focused on the "beautiful boy" and "boys' love" as critical sites of experimentation and play with transgressive gender and sexual identities for girls and young women who found themselves at odds with prescribed gender and sexual norms. The most significant of these magazines were June (1978–79, 1981–96) and Allan (Aran; 1980–1984). As can be observed in their pages, during the late 1970s and early 1980s, young Japanese women-loving and transgender women carved out a space for themselves literally and figuratively on the margins of a community of female fans of beautiful young men.[6]

The dialogue among these readers demonstrates the emergence of identities and practices that draw heavily on "boys' love" and the "beautiful boy," and that unsettle categories of gender, sex, and sexuality, creating such a diversity as to leave one at a loss for words to discuss it. Even "female" and "male" are rendered suspect categories. Faced here with the task of describing this "multiplicity of masculinities,"[7] femininities and sexualities, to the extent possible, I let individuals speak for and name themselves. I also employ the term "queer," not in reference to individual identities but as it is used in Euro-American queer theory, to tentatively encompass the unencompassable diversity and the fluidity that can be found in genders and sexualities that exist outside local heteronormative paradigms.[8] And, while Judith Halberstam judiciously cautions that the "use of the term 'lesbian' erases the specificity of tribadism, hermaphroditism, and transvestism,"[9] I cautiously make use of the term because—reflecting interaction with lesbian communities abroad—it is a key word in local discourse among and about women who are not heterosexually inclined; unless specifically indicated, however, my use here indicates female-female desire rather than the identities of those who experience it.

Confronted with their own personal lexical conundrums, some readers of and contributors to Allan and June chose to reframe their discussion of gender and sexuality in and on their own terms, often borrowing from or playing off *shōjo* manga images of male-male desire. It is the construction of the gender and sexual identities of these reader-contributors, as well as the terms with which they are discussed, that is the focus of this chapter. I begin with a brief history of the "boys' love" sphere, followed by an examination of the contents of *Allan* and *June*. I then turn to *Allan*'s personal ads column to focus on the terminology used by, and the gender and sexual identities expressed by its reader-contributors. In the concluding section, I examine several alternative sites of expression of female genders and sexualities that incorporate "beautiful boy" and "boys' love" imagery.

Gay Boom or Bust

While transgressive on multiple levels, the gender-bending and ambiguous sexuality represented in "boys' love" manga and related magazines are part of a larger tradition of performing gender in Japan that stretches back at least to Edo era (1603–1868) *kabuki* performances in which specifically trained male actors performed female roles (*onnagata*), but it is more intimately connected with the twentieth-century all-female Takarazuka Review, which, while capitalist and patriarchal in intent, has inspired some fans and critics to read homoerotic subtexts into the performances if not the lives of the performers.[10] Takarazuka inspired cross-dressing female manga characters who evolved into "beautiful boys" whose graphic appearance was a composite of nineteenth and early twentieth century aesthetes, members of the Vienna Boys Choir, and the androgynous British and American rock musicians and local counterparts popular in Japan in the 1970s and 1980s.[11]

Interest among Japanese women specifically in male-male romance can be traced back at least as far as several novellas written in the early 1960s by Mori Mari[12] and seems to have peaked during the 1990s "gay boom" (*gei būmu*), that is, the decade's surge of representations in the mass media of (predominantly male) homosexuality. Unsurprisingly, the boom itself began in women's magazines.[13] While perhaps not as widespread now as it was a decade ago, this interest in evolving representations of male-male sexuality and related cultural productions continue to thrive, particularly in the amateur and commercial manga scene.

Critics and artists alike have maintained that the "homosexuality" (*dōseiai*) in classic "boys' love" is simply a trope, as seminal artist Takemiya Keiko explains, "to mentally liberate girls from the sexual restrictions imposed on us [as women]."[14] This widespread denial that the narratives portray homosexuality may be motivated by the fear that, if readers see girls in and identify with the "beautiful boy" characters, they might read the "beautiful boys" and the "boys' love" narratives as lesbian.[15] The genre's openness to such readings, however, may explain why "boys' love" manga were so influential to many women in their own queer identity formation. Moreover, in spite of critics' and artists' insistence to the contrary, many readers have indeed been making the connection between "boys' love" and the lives of real homosexuals, as their contributions in *June* and *Allan* make clear. Editorial content sometimes explicitly suggested such linkages: for example, *Allan*'s special feature on Tokyo's well-known gay district of Shinjuku ni-chōme, which the feature notes is crowded with "beautiful boys like those in the world of *shōjo* manga."[16]

According to *June*'s editor, Sagawa Toshihiko, the magazine was created to capitalize on the growing fixation on "beautiful boys" among creators of "amateur manga magazines" (*dōjinshi*).[17] This obsession was most visible at Tokyo's annual celebration of amateur manga, the "Comic Market" (*Komiketto* or *Komike*), an event long dominated by women and highly influential in the development of "boys' love" and *yaoi*.[18] Yet, in spite of *June*'s "beautiful boy" focus, every issue in its first year of publication had at least one reader writing in with calls for more lesbian representation or bemoaning the paradoxical misunderstanding of lesbians among fans of "boys' love."[19] Ostensibly created for the same purpose, the less widely known *Allan* differed from *June* in the greater frequency and prominence of the depiction queer female genders and sexualities. While *June* was more graphic and *Allan* more textual, both ran articles, stories, anecdotes, confessions, photos, drawings, and manga, often contributed by readers, rendering these publications overtly collaborative productions of readers, writers, and editors. It is worth noting, however, that while most of the contributors to both magazines were women, like the vast majority of Japanese periodicals, they were edited by men.

In addition to "beautiful boys," gender-bending men were occasionally featured, which in *Allan* included lengthy interviews with well-known male-to-female cross-dressing and transgender entertainers Peter (August 1982), Matsubara Rumiko (October 1982), and Miwa Akihiro (February 1984).[20] While sympathetic in tone, these articles nonetheless positioned the transgendered, like the "beautiful boy," as objects of the female gaze. In spite of the popularity of the "male-role players" (*otokoyaku*) in the all-female Takarazuka Review, however, from the editorial end, female-to-male cross-dressing performers were not given such prominence. Unlike other *shōjo* magazines at the time, such as the manga magazine "Girls' Friend" (*Shōjo furendo*), however, while females were also occasionally presented as erotic objects,

Allan and early issues of *June* contained no advertisements for products pushing images of women as mothers, wives, or sex objects.[21] Instead, most advertisements were for amateur manga magazines, which further attests to the magazines' collaborative nature and illustrates the separation between the world presented within their pages and the world looming outside.

Allan's focus on erotic male beauty and homosexuality, and the literary roots thereof, is indicated by the tag line on the cover of most issues: "an aestheticist magazine for girls."[22] "Aesthetics" (*tanbi*) as used in this community refers broadly to male beauty and homoeroticism, as well as more specifically to such European aesthetes and decadents as Oscar Wilde, Paul Verlaine, and André Gide. Similar to the name *June* intimating famously homosexual French decadent Jean Genet—in Japanese *June* and Genet are spelled and pronounced the same—*Allan*'s name, as it is spelled on the cover, suggested the dark, sexually ambiguous figure of Edgar Allan Poe.[23] Long popular in Japan, Poe's writing appealed greatly to early-twentieth-century sexually radical feminist Hiratsuka Raichō and, decades later, inspired Hagio Moto's popular *shōjo* manga "The Poe Clan."[24] The continuing queer appeal of this imagery can be seen in one young woman's declaration that Hagio's "Poe" "opened [her] eyes" to female-female desire.[25]

Literary allusion was also the site of the magazine's mention of lesbian desire in its inaugural issue. An article introducing (male) homosexuality in history—one that mentions "lesbians" (*rezubian*) only in passing—ends with a cryptic reference to Baudelaire's infamous assessment of *"les lesbiennes"* as *"femmes damnées"* (damned women),[26] casting an alternative light on the article for readers who caught the allusion. Tomoko Aoyama argues that such intertextuality is "in fact central to *shōjo*-hood" and that "parody, allusion, quotation, adaptation, and travesty play significant roles in *shōjo shōsetsu* [girls' fiction] as well as in *shōjo manga,* and in the new genre called *yaoi.*"[27] As will be discussed below, this intertextuality is also a significant component of the gender and sexual identities expressed in the personal ads in *Allan*.

Aside from a few editorial references, during *Allan*'s first two years of publication, most expression of female-female desire and female masculinities could be found in letters from readers and personal ads, the latter of which first appeared literally on the margins of pages toward the rear of the magazine. These were eventually placed in a regular personal ads column aimed at female readers seeking romantic and/or sexual relationships with each other. Accompanying the inclusion of this column, and marking an editorial shift from the twelfth issue (October 1982), was a sudden increase in overt lesbian representation, including articles, some running several pages, about topics such as American and European actresses who look good in male drag, lesbian activism abroad, and book reviews, often of imported books in Japanese translation. Under the subheading "The Lavender Kimono," for example, an article about lesbian representation in magazines in the United Kingdom and the United States offers a history of Japanese lesbian activism and (noncommercial) magazines.[28] That issue also contains an interview with Itō Bungaku, editor of *homo* magazine *Barazoku* ("Rose tribe").[29] Rather than focusing on *homo* culture and *homo* men, which would seem logical given *Allan*'s ostensible raison d'être, half of this interview was devoted to a discussion of the need for a commercial lesbian magazine. Such editorial content supported the readers' efforts to turn *Allan* into a discursive space for girls and young women whose gender and/or sexuality situated them, like the "beautiful boy," outside heteronormative discourse. The significance of this space was acknowledged by Japan's first and then largest lesbian organization, Wakakusa no kai (Fresh Green Club), with its insertion in the June 1983 issue of an advertisement recruiting new members and promoting its (noncommercial) publications.[30]

By Any Other Name

Printed on the margin of a page toward the back of the third issue of *Allan*, in April 1981, is a message from a twenty-seven-year-old reader who described herself as a "Lesbienne" and wrote that she had bought a foreign "Homo" porn magazine that she was willing to send to a "Sodomite" or a "Lesbienne" for free.[31] She added that she was looking for friends. While most such marginalia in the first year of *Allan* was from readers looking for new (female) friends to join their clubs, help make manga magazines—again reaffirming the connection between *Allan* and the amateur manga scene—or trade photos and magazines, a few female readers wrote in looking for (male) "*homo*" friends or "big brothers" (*oniisama*), and, like the "Lesbienne," women-loving women and variously gendered individuals quickly began using the space to reach out to others like themselves and/or whom they desired. In December 1981, for instance, a "masculine" (*otokoppoi*) seventeen-year-old from Fukuoka Prefecture wrote that she was looking for an "older sister" (*onēsama*) or a cute "kitten" (*koneko*)[32] (139)—defying not merely the gender performance expected of her but also the expectation that she would be interested in *either* an older partner *or* a younger one. While her ad merely begins to suggest the diversity of queerness represented among *Allan*'s readers, the vocabulary she chose to describe herself and her desire would be echoed and redefined by hundreds of other young women in the soon to emerge "Yuri tsūshin" (Lily Communication)[33] personal ads section.

A common point of entry among studies dealing with gender and/or sexuality in personal ads is to first classify advertisers and/or those being sought and then perform statistical analyses.[34] In one study, Gayle Kaufman and Voon Chin Phua treat as synonymous "men seeking men and 'gay,' and men seeking women and 'straight,'" a problematic approach even when identity categories are perceived to be stable and dichotomous.[35] That is, "men" seek *either* a "male" *or* a "female" partner. Such categories seem all the more stable when reduced, as they often are, to a series of codes such as SWF, GAM, and BHF (namely, single/straight white female, gay Asian male, and black Hispanic female) to spell out a person's "essential" characteristics. In contrast, the gender and sexual diversity inscribed by readers on the pages of *Allan* defies classification and emphasizes the performative rather than essential nature of readers' genders and sexualities. The types of relationship being sought were likewise obscured by the shifting meanings of the terms used to describe them.

In spite of its eventual popularity, "Yuri tsūshin" got off to a slow start. Aside from a tiny "pen pal" section in the fourth issue, in which two of the three advertisers express dissatisfaction with their female gender, all such personal ads were found on the margins until the August 1982 issue, which included a formal personal ad section. This section contained eighteen ads, largely signed with female names, which expressed a mix of requests varying little from the marginalia of the intervening five issues. In stark contrast, the personals section in the next issue was given a Franco-English headline, spelled out in capital letters "For Lesbiens Only [*sic*]" boldly announcing the nature of these fifty-seven ads. The title "Yuri tsūshin" was finally settled on in the April 1983 issue, which contained 226 "*yuri*" (lily) ads. The term *yuri* was borrowed from the *homo* magazine *Barazoku*,[36] in which *bara* (rose) was used to indicate male-male sexuality and, subsequently, *yuri* to indicate female-female desire, beginning with the November 1976 introduction of a column for female readers called "Lily Tribe's Room" (*Yurizoku no heya*),[37] if not earlier. In effect returning the favor, the June 1983 issue of *Allan* included the first "Bara tsūshin" (Rose Communication) column for its male readers, although it held a mere eight *bara* ads alongside nearly 300 *yuri* ads. In October an "other" section was added for those unable to classify their ad as "pure *yuri* or pure *bara*."[38] All three sections, however, were crowned with the francophone "Lesbiennes." "Other" included *yuri* and ostensibly heterosexual women seeking *bara* friends, transgendered people, and individuals like "Franz"[39] who wished to dispense with the labels *yuri* and *bara* altogether and love "people" (*ningen*) as people.[40]

While loan words such as "lez" (*rezu*) and, less frequently, "lesbian" were used in these magazines to describe female homosexuality, "*yuri*" (lily) was the most preferred term to indicate female-female desire. Several women who wrote in to *June* and *Allan,* however, expressed resistance to if not outright rejection of the terms "lesbian" and "lez" in reference to themselves.[41] In the pages of *Allan* at least, while "homo," "homosexual," "gay" (all generally transliterated into Japanese), and "*bara*" were used to name male homosexuality, the latter term was prevalent. "Bisexual" and "bi" (both transliterated) were also occasionally used with their common English meaning, but the labeling of interviews with cross-dressing and transgender celebrities as "bisexual interviews" demonstrates the instability of the terms.[42]

Indicating that *yuri* was not synonymous with *rezubian,* however, contributions to *Barazoku*'s column came from women with queer gender and/or sexual identities, as well as women who were fans of "boys' love." Likewise, in the pages of *Allan* it is clear that *yuri* did not mean the same thing to all who used it. Many advertisers sought *yuri* "relations," including those with and without *yuri* "experience." Some of those seeking a *yuri* relationship specified that they were looking for a "platonic" relationship, while others noted they were willing to go up to "first base." One woman from Ibaraki Prefecture wanted someone with whom she could "play lily,"[43] and another woman from Saitama Prefecture explained that, while she was willing to have a "physical relationship," she would not do anything "scary."[44] Women like sixteen-year-old "Raccoon" from Osaka, on the other hand, made it quite clear they were seeking replies only from those with whom they could get physical.[45] In addition to the terms' popularity in the pages of these magazines, rose and lily imagery has been used to indicate male-male and female-female sexuality in *shōjo* manga from the early 1970s, attesting to Itō's claim that *Barazoku* had a large female readership or at least a large influence on the "boys' love" community of readers and writers.[46] Today, *yuri* continues to indicate manga and anime (animation) works that depict female-female romance and sexuality.

Other key terms in the personal ads were as unstable as *yuri.* The employment by advertisers of Japanese words such as "older sister" (*onēsama*) and "younger sister" (*imōto*) demonstrated an unsettling of both the meanings of the terms and the roles they represent. "Older sister," for example, at once ostensibly indicates the gender, age, and role such a person is expected to take in a relationship. Advertisers seeking an "older sister" sometimes explicitly requested one willing to "spoil" them, to "hold" them, or—particularly among advertisers who described themselves as a "cat" (*neko*) or "kitten"—to "rear" them. Those seeking "older sisters" consistently and, in the earlier issues overwhelmingly, outnumbered those seeking "younger sisters," possibly explained by the fact that a majority of advertisers indicated that they had little or no actual romantic or sexual experience with other women and wanted someone willing to "take the lead." While in earlier issues, only a handful of advertisers announced that they would be happy with either an older or younger sister, after an editorial comment about the high demand for and dearth of older partners,[47] advertisers became increasingly flexible. Even the age of an "older sister" was rendered unstable, as some advertisers noted that they were open to having an "older sister" who was the same age or younger. Requests for partners with whom the advertiser might have such a vertical homosocial or homosexual relationship, including a willingness to bend the rules regarding age and role, have also been observed in advertisements in *Barazoku* in the 1990s, indicating that the desire to either spoil or be spoiled is by no means unique to *Allan*'s readers.[48] Finally, while *onēsama* is written with the Chinese character for "older sister" and the honorific title *sama*, "Yuri tsūshin" advertisers disrupted the gender of their desired partner by seeking "masculine" (*otokoppoi*) or "boyish" (*shōnenppoi*/*boisshu*) "older sisters," or those who were "dandy beauties" (*dansō no reijin*).[49] Or they sought not "older sisters" but "older brothers," while indicating either parenthetically or by implication (by virtue of advertising in a *yuri* personals column) that the "older brothers" they desired were biologically female.

Norman Fairclough suggests that the struggle over ideology is also a struggle over language, explaining that texts impose "common sense" on readers and that ideology is, in turn, disseminated by placing responsibility on readers to make sense of a text by understanding its implicit assumptions.[50] While use of a common vocabulary among reader-contributors of *Allan* established a sense of community, the choice by some to redefine those terms made explicit their assertion of a right to self-definition that extended to the very words they employed to do so, unsettling the ideologies inherent in both communal and societal "common sense" in the process. Although language may indeed "keep . . . heteronormative stances in the foreground of daily life," as William Leap suggests, *yuri* advertisers were still able to "construct their own sense of sexual/gendered possibilities and apply their own meanings to those constructions."[51]

Sexuality in a Gender Blender

While the term *yuri* was used to encompass a "multiplicity of masculinities," femininities, and sexualities, some advertisers in "Yuri tsūshin" chose to go further and unsettle the very category of female/woman. In June 1981, one reader using the unisex name Kaoru and employing male vocabulary wrote, "I (*ore*) am a female who wishes I had been born male."[52] In linguistically claiming a male subject position (*ore*), Kaoru explicitly exposes the dissonance between her "natural" physical self and her declared identity, challenging Judith Butler's assertion that "the substantive 'I' only appears as such through a signifying practice that seeks to conceal its own workings and to naturalize its effects."[53]

As Claire Maree shows, for many women (and men), the choice of self-referent in Japanese is a complex process that involves negotiating one's own shifting and multiple identities and social status.[54] Among the most common self-referents ("I") at Japanese speakers' disposal in the "standard" Tokyo dialect of Japanese are *watashi* (female neutral or formal; male formal), *atashi* (female informal, feminine), *boku* (male informal), and *ore* (male informal, masculine). The structure of Japanese grammar, however, means that very often self-referents to mark the subject position in a sentence are naturally omitted; and while to use self-referents in the abbreviated language of the personal ads discussed in this chapter was not unnatural, it was certainly not necessary, adding a certain significance to the choice to use one, even a normative one. Of the three pen-pal seekers in June 1981, one uses no self-referent, one *watashi* and one *ore*. While some fluctuation can be seen in use of self-referents from April 1982 to June 1984, no trend is apparent. Over the two years, in each issue roughly half of advertisers used no self-referent, between 30 and 40 percent used *watashi,* roughly 10 percent used *boku,* a handful used *ore,* and fewer still used *atashi.* Maree argues that in their choice of words, rather than making a choice between female words and male words, speakers are choosing between heterosexual female words and heterosexual male words, which for at least some is done consciously.[55] This suggests some speakers are choosing self-referents not merely to speak as either one or the other, but rather to speak *against* one or the other or both, that is, to speak in transgression against the choice society compels them to make when referring to themselves.

References to "beautiful boy" manga characters, sometimes used in pen names and other times in self-descriptions, are also used in the ads to illustrate degrees of masculinity and femininity. These references further demonstrate both the powerful influence of *shōjo* manga on readers' identity formation and varying degrees of "boy" or "beautiful boy" identity, as well as attesting to the intertextual nature of identity itself. For instance, several advertisers modeled themselves or those they were seeking after the androgynous and masochistic nymphomaniac Gilbert Cocteau, Gilbert's lover Serge, or his sexually abusive father Auguste, characters in the highly influential manga, "The song of the wind and the trees" (*Kaze to ki no uta* by Takemiya and originally published between 1976 and 1984). Identification with or as a "beautiful boy" was, however, more commonly indicated by advertisers who simply described themselves as being and/or seeking someone who *was* or *was like* a "boy." Among them, some advertisers indicated biological sex parenthetically—either with the character *onna* (female/woman) or the symbol ♀—while others perhaps saw no need given the context. It should also be noted that masculine identification by no means indicated a desire to take the lead in a relationship, as can be seen from the male-identified advertisers who sought either an older sister or brother to show them the way. A connection between *yuri* manga characters and boys was drawn by a twenty-year-old woman who named herself after the *yuri* character Schnak in the manga "Applause, Applause" (*Apurōzu—kassai;* Ariyoshi 1981–82/1982) and sought a "boyish person."[56] The unisex name Kaoru, used by multiple advertisers, also has powerful lesbian intertextual implications.[57] Other reader-contributors described themselves or those they were seeing as "androgynous," sometimes explicitly expressing dissatisfaction at being placed in the sex/gender category of woman. However readers labeled themselves and others, it is clear both that many readers resisted to varying degrees culturally prescribed femininity and expressed through various means culturally prescribed masculinity. It is also clear that the figure of the "beautiful boy" as represented in "boys' love" narratives played a significant role in this process.

The layering of transgressive desire on top of equally radical gender constructions exponentially complicated the sexuality of these reader-contributors. "Roman," advertising in the *yuri* rather than *bara* section (the "other" section had not yet been created), described himself as a "bi" male looking for "a lez, a boyish girl, or a girlish boy," specifically "a passive younger sister (brother)."[58] "Mari" was a "bi" sixteen-year-old girl willing to go to first base with a "bi" female or "*bara* beautiful boy."[59] Several individuals advertised for a female partner with whom they could "play *homo,*" including "Evil Angel," a woman who considered herself "straight" (*nonke*), "masochistic," and "passive" and was seeking a *yuri* "big brother," yet who herself used a masculine self-referent (*boku*).[60] A fifteen-year-old from Chiba Prefecture who was "neither *yuri* nor straight (*sutorēto*)" wrote in to the "other" section seeking a girl who "wants to become a male" so they could be "boys" together.[61] Another gender and sexual transgressor, "Kanda Gypsy" writes, "I (*ore*) . . . want to become a pure-blood man. My current girlfriend is a male and a *homo*. I (*ore*) am a woman."[62] A few individuals offered to adapt their gender performances to suit a potential partner's taste. Someone who wrote into the "other" section looking for partners with whom to have sex "via writing" explained that, "being able to become male or female, perhaps I (*boku*) am biologically amphibious."[63] A seventeen-year-old wrote to "Yuri tsūshin" that "she" would "become male (♂) or female (♀) as you like."[64]

Though clearly identifying as a male, "Roman" chose not to express his taste for androgynous individuals of either sex in "Bara tsūshin"; neither did he make clear whether, in fact, he was looking for a younger sister *or* a younger brother, or for a younger brother willing to perform a younger sister role. He also seemed to assume there might be a lez interested in him. "Evil Angel" and "Kanda Gypsy" on the other hand, like many advertisers, expressed multiple, seemingly contradictory gender and sexual identities with the hope or expectation that someone would read and understand their ads and respond. These and other advertisers demonstrate "a distance," in the words of Judith Butler, from gender and sexual norms—"an ability to suspend or defer the need for them, even as there is a desire," or at least the sense of a need, "for norms that might let one live."[65] For many, the gender and sexual experimentation and play inspired in part by "boys' love" was a passing phase on the way to, or even alongside, heterosexual relationships and eventual marriage and children—either by choice or by necessity.[66] Some members of this readership community, however, appear to have surpassed mere play or experimentation with norms, choosing instead to "live in ways that maintain a critical and transformative relation to them" and establish identities and lives not contained within the heteronormative paradigm.[67]

Beyond the "Beautiful Boy"

Gender and sexually transgressive women have been reaching out and writing to magazines in Japan for much of the postwar era. While terms such as "Lesbos love" (*resubosu ai*) were used as early as the 1950s in letters to popular sexology magazines, comparisons were also drawn to and terminology borrowed from contemporary male homosexual culture. Such letters and panel discussions increased throughout the 1960s, surpassing those by and about male *homo*s, although the editorial interest also became more prurient and pornographic as the 1960s progressed.[68] While the "Lily Tribe's Room" column in *Barazoku*, noted above, did not function as a personals column, it offered female readers the opportunity to reach out to others who might be playing or struggling with gender and sexuality. From the early 1980s, Lily Tribe's Corner (Yurizoku kōnā) began to regularly appear as a tiny section of the magazine's Rose Communication (Bara tsūshin) personal ad column, upon which point the number of other types of contributions from female readers began to decrease greatly. Also in the 1970s, lesbian organization Wakakusa no kai's newsletter ran personal ads from women vetted by the group's founder, Suzuki Michiko.[69] Its self-financed magazine "Eve & Eve" (*Ivu & Ivu*) had a personals section called "Eve communication" (*Ivu tsūshin*).[70] Another magazine, "The Gay" (*Za gei*), ran women-seeking-women ads in a lesbian section of the magazine under the headline "Lesbian Communication" (*Rezubian tsūshin*).[71] "Luna" (*Gekkō*), *Allan*'s successor,[72] included "Luna Communication" (*Gekkō tsūshin*), a column in which classification of gender and thus sexuality was further complicated by the multiple meanings of gendered and sexual terms used by a jumble of biologically female and male advertisers. In the mid-1990s, while "Luna Communication" was slowly losing its function as a significant site of *yuri* ads, the commercial lesbian magazines "Phryné" (*Furiine;* 1995) and "Anise" (*Aniisu;* 1996–97, 2001–3), which both contained personal ads sections, were published.

Although advertisers in these other personal ads columns show a similar diversity of genders and sexualities to those represented in "Yuri tsūshin," references to the "beautiful boy" and "boys' love" are much more limited but significant nonetheless. In a 1982 issue of *The Gay*, for instance, among the twenty-two advertisers is twenty-one-year-old "Marahi," who sought an "older big sister" who understood "boys' love."[73] A decade later in "Labrys Information" (*Jōhō Labrys*), a personal ads publication associated with the noncommercial magazine *Labrys,* "Tsugumi" requested letters from people who liked *June* and *yaoi*, and "Kaoru" wrote that she enjoyed watching "English-language gay male porn." "Luna Sea," whose pen name refers to a popular androgynous all-male band, commented that she loved talking about *gays* and was a big fan of the TV drama "Reunion" (*Dōsōkai* 1993), which portrayed male homosexual relationships.[74] Another woman wrote into "Phryné Club" from Fukuoka Prefecture under the pen name "Torch Song Trilogy," a reference to the 1988 gay-themed American film.[75] While such references were relatively infrequent in these contexts, an interest in "beautiful boys" and "boys' love" among queer women can clearly be seen outside the pages of *June* and *Allan*, illustrating both its broad influence in the Japanese lesbian community and a link between images of male homosexuality and lesbian desire.

As we have seen, in the 1970s and 1980s, expression of same-sex desire and transgressive gender identities among women was in many ways a marginal practice, manifested in print in magazines focused on "beautiful boys" and "boys' love" as well as in magazines for lesbians and for homosexual men. Some women found in this imagery the freedom to express their own transgressive gender and sexuality, in the process radically unsettling gender, sex, and sexuality and the terms used to name them. Reader-contributors to *Allan* displayed varying degrees of discomfort and conflict in expressing gendered and sexual identities. Some readers of *Allan*, for instance, rejected all labels, perhaps in the hope that their "identity speak itself out of a willed namelessness."[76] Yet for many others, the choice to redefine labels in and on their own terms prevented the establishment of any sort of hegemonic ideology among *Allan* readers.

It would be impossible to estimate how many readers were, in their "*yuri* communications," just temporarily experimenting with gender and sexuality, how many succumbed to heteropatriarchal pressure and married in spite of their queer desire and/or identity, and how many went on to construct queer lives. It is, however, unquestionable that, for some Japanese women, *Allan* and "Yuri tsūshin," inseparable from the image of the "beautiful boy" and the representation of "boys' love," functioned as a crucial site of transgressive gender and sexual identity formation.

Notes

1. For a discussion of the lack of correlation, see McLelland, *Male Homosexuality in Modern Japan,* and Satō, "Shōjo manga to homofobia" (*Shōjo* manga and homophobia). *Yaoi* stands for *yama nashi, ochi nashi, imi nashi* (no climax, no point, no meaning) and initially referred to amateur manga more focused on sexual acts than narrative development. In her history of the genre, Mizoguchi asserts that *yaoi* is an appropriate transhistoric label for both graphic and textual male-male romance narratives "by and for women" ("Male-Male Romance by and for Women in Japan"). To foreground the pivotal role of the "boy" (*shōnen*)/"beautiful boy" in the identity formation discussed here, however, I will employ "boys' love."

2. Fujimoto, *Watashi no ibasho wa doko ni aru no?* (Where do I belong?); Aoyama, "Male Homosexuality as Treated by Japanese Women Writers."

3. Mizoguchi, "Male-Male Romance," 49.

4. The boundaries of the Japanese lesbian community have long been unfixed. It has included women who feel romantic and/or sexual desire toward other women as well as, to varying degrees, transgender and transsexual people, both female-to-male

and male-to-female. For a lengthier discussion of the composition of the Japanese community, see Welker, "Telling Her Story," 120–22; see "Komyuniti no rekishi"; Yajima, *Josei dōseiaisha no raifu hisutorii* (Life histories of female homosexuals); and Sei ishiki chōsa gurūpu, *Sanbyakujū nin no sei ishiki* (The sexual consciousness of 310 people).

5. The existence of a formal lesbian community in Japan has been dated back to the early 1970s, and, in terms of bar culture, began a decade or more earlier. This scene was centered around Tokyo and, to a lesser extent, Osaka. While some community publications were produced from at least the early 1970s, they were not commercially distributed and were thus out of reach for all but those who happened to learn of their existence and subscribe. This situation remained largely unchanged until the 1990s, which saw an increase in mass media representation of "gays" and "lesbians," the advent of commercial lesbian magazines, and, finally, a Japanese "lesbian" presence on the Internet. See Welker, "Telling Her Story."

6. Not all readers were female, however. *Allan* editor Nanbara Shirō estimates that its readership was approximately 10 percent male (personal correspondence, July 15, 2004). Their limited contributions make clear that at least some of these male readers identified with the "beautiful boy" characters and/or as *homo*.

7. Halberstam, *Female Masculinity*, 47.

8. While "queer" (*kuia*) has some currency within academic discourse, it is not widely used in the *lesbian* or *gay* communities in Japan.

9. Halberstam, *Female Masculinity*, 51.

10. Robertson, *Takarazuka*.

11. Fujimoto, *Watashi no ibasho wa doko ni aru no?* (Where do I belong?). Articles and reader contributions to issues of the magazines *June* and *Allan* attest to the interest in this diverse mix of artists and performers. See also Matsui, "Little Girls Were Little Boys: Displaced Femininity in the Representation of Homosexuality in Japanese Girls Comics," and McLelland, *Male Homosexuality in Modern Japan*.

12. Aoyama, "Male Homosexuality as Treated by Japanese Women Writers," 191–94.

13. For a discussion of the gay boom, see Izumo and Maree, *Love Upon the Chopping Board*, 120–21, and McLelland, *Male Homosexuality in Modern Japan*, 32–33.

14. Cited in Satō, "Shōjo manga to homofobia" (*Shōjo* manga and homophobia), 162. This quote is taken from an interview that originally appeared in the women's magazine *CREA*, in March 1991.

15. For a discussion on the openness of boys' love manga to lesbian readings, see Welker, "Beautiful, Borrowed, and Bent."

16. Ruporutāju: Shinjuku ni-chōme (Reportage: Shinjuku ni-chōme), 15.

17. Cited in Schodt, *Dreamland Japan*, 120.

18. Kinsella, *Adult Manga*.

19. E.g., see the letters from "Machita Mayumi" and "Bekku fujin" in "Readers' Writers' and Editors' Bedroom."

20. For a background on the emergence and popularity of male-to-female cross-dressing celebrities in Japan, see McLelland, *Queer Japan from the Pacific War to the Internet Age.*

21. The June 1981 issue of "*Shōjo* Friend Special Edition" (*Bessatsu shōjo furendo*), for example, contains full-page ads for a basket-making kit (162), a correspondence school offering courses in everything from mothering to cooking to doll-making (262), and three advertisements for slimming products (212, 362, 441).

22. "Shōjo no tame no tanbiha zasshi" in the original Japanese.

23. As pronounced in Japanese, *June* has two syllables, *ju* and *ne*, and is not pronounced like the English month June. *Allan* editor Nanbara Shirō explains that the spelling of the title was a design choice and that the magazine's creators had Alain Delon in mind in naming the magazine (personal correspondence, July 15, 2004). Regardless, it is Poe's name that adorns the cover.

24. Hagio, *Pō no ichizoku.* No fewer than twelve of Hiratsuka's translations of Poe appeared in the feminist literary and political journal *Seitō* from September 1911 to December 1912.

25. *Allan,* June 1984, 169, ad 46. Poe also inspired the pen name of the mid-twentieth-century male author Edogawa Ranpo, a name that mimics the Japanized version of Poe's name, "Edogā Aran Pō." Edogawa is well-known for his attraction to beautiful young men and was an occasional contributor to popular sexology magazines. See McLelland, *Queer Japan.*

26. Harada, "Shōjo no tame no dōseiai nyūmon" (An introduction to homosexuality, for girls), 98, 100. This reference comes from his *Les fleurs du mal* (1861), which was initially published under the title of *Les fleurs du mal—les lesbiennes.*

27. Aoyama, "Transgendering *Shōjo Shōsetsu*," 56–57.

28. Yurino, "London Lesbian Report."

29. While *gei* (gay) is likely the most frequently used term at present to refer to male homosexual identity and culture, at least within the community, in the 1970s and 1980s, *homo* was the term with the most currency both inside and outside the community. See McLelland, *Queer Japan.* On *Barazoku,* see Itō, "Itō Bungaku."

30. Wakakusa no kai was founded in 1971 and disbanded fifteen years later due to financial problems. This translation of the group's name comes from Ishino and Wakabayashi, "Japan," 95. The ad is on p. 179 of *Allan,* June 1983.

31. *Allan,* Apr. 1981, 190. Though this reader wrote in Japanese, she wrote all terms for homosexuality in French or English; I have reproduced her use of capitalization.

32. *Neko* (cat) has long been used in the Japanese lesbian and gay communities to indicate the sexually and/or socially passive partner.

33. Although this section went through a number of name changes, I use "Yuri tsūshin" to indicate the column in general, both because it was the name for the longest stretch of time and because the multiple meanings assigned to *yuri* come the closest to expressing the broad range of genders and sexualities of advertisers.

34. See Kaufman and Phua, "Is Ageism Alive in Date Selection among Men";

Bartholome, Tewksbury, and Bruzzone, "I Want a Man"; and Child, Graff Low, Mc-Donnell, McCormick, and Cocciarella, "Personal Advertisements of Male-to-Female Transsexuals, Homosexual Men, and Heterosexuals."

35. Kaufman and Phua, "Is Ageism Alive in Date Selection among Men," 228.

36. Nanbara Shirō, personal correspondence, July 15, 2004.

37. The editor's note at the end of this section indicates that the increasing number of women writing in for various reasons led to its inception ("Yurizoku no heya" [Lily tribe's room], *Barazoku*, Nov. 1976, 70). The earliest female voice in *Barazoku* was an article-length letter from a woman who "cannot love the opposite sex" in the September 1972 issue (see Shimizu, "Watashi wa isei wo aisenai onna" [I am a woman who cannot love the opposite sex]). Within a year, letters began to appear sporadically from female readers whose gender identities and sexual desires were not always clear. Editor-in-chief Itō explains, however, that the mostly homosexual male editorial staff resisted his decision to provide a space for women's voices (Itō Bungaku, unpublished interview with the author, June 2005).

38. *Allan*, Oct. 1983, 176.

39. For ease of reading, throughout this chapter, I have translated or transliterated the pen names of "Yuri tsūshin" advertisers. For words and names originally in English, I have preserved the writer's choice of capitalization.

40. *Allan*, Oct. 1982, 182, ad 8. Personal ads from the October 1982 issue onward were assigned numbers, which I indicate in the respective citations.

41. E.g., see the letter from "Eiko Robinson," "Readers' Writers' and Editors' Bedroom," 167.

42. See Peter (*Allan*, Aug. 1982) and Matsubara (*Allan*, Oct. 1982). Among other significant loan words, readers were taught the meaning of "come out" (*kamu auto*) in the April 1981 issue (189); however, its use did not catch on in Japan until the 1990s "gay boom," perhaps due to its use in the popular TV drama *Dōsōkai* ("Reunion," 1993).

43. *Allan*, June 1984, 168, ad 16.

44. *Allan*, Apr. 1983, 171, ad 31.

45. *Allan*, Apr. 1984, 164, ad 138.

46. Itō, "Itō Bungaku," 99. Hagio's *Tōma no shinzō* ("The heart of Thomas," 1974/1995) and Takemiya's *Kaze to ki no uta* ("The song of the wind and the trees," 1976–84/1995) employ the rose as an obvious reference to male homosexuality. The use of lilies has been more ambiguous, particularly in the 1970s. Both roses and lilies are used as overt markers for homosexuality in general and lesbian desire specifically, however, in Tsukumo Mutsumi's lesbian manga narrative "Moonlight Flowers" (1991).

47. *Allan*, Dec. 1982, 133.

48. McLelland, *Male Homosexuality in Modern Japan*, 145–49.

49. This term has been used to describe the *otokoyaku* (trouser roles) of the all-female Takarazuka musical review and female bartenders in male drag, particularly in the 1960s and 1970s.

50. Fairclough, *Language and Power*, 69.

51. William Leap, "Language, Socialization, and Silence in Gay Adolescence," 263.

52. *Allan*, June 1981, 151.

53. Butler, *Gender Trouble*, 144.

54. Maree, *Hatsuwa no gengo sutoratejii toshite no negoshiēshon kōi no kenkyū* (Research into negotiation as linguistic discourse strategies).

55. Ibid., 157–59.

56. *Allan*, Apr. 1983, 175, ad 159.

57. Kaoru, for example, has been used to mark the more masculine of female-female pairings in several significant manga works. See Ikeda, *Futari pocchi* (Just the two of them); Ikeda, *Oniisama e* (To my big brother); Tsukumo, "Moonlight Flowers."

58. *Allan*, June 1983, 183, ad 292.

59. *Allan*, June 1983, 181, ad 206.

60. *Allan*, Aug. 1983, 177, ad 164. Two common words used in queer communities in Japan for "straight," as in "heterosexual," are the transliteration from English, *sutorēto*, and *nonke*, a term combining the English "non" with "*ke*," here roughly indicating "preference."

61. *Allan*, June 1984, 173, ad 31.

62. *Allan*, Dec. 1983, 63, ad 44.

63. *Allan*, June 1984, 176, ad 101.

64. *Allan*, Apr. 1984, 160–61, ad 31.

65. Butler, *Undoing Gender*, 3.

66. Yokomori, *Ren'ai wa shōjo manga de osowatta* (I was taught about love by *shōjo* manga), 102.

67. Butler, *Undoing Gender*, 3.

68. McLelland, *Queer Japan*. While, as McLelland acknowledges, many of the letters about "Lesbos love" appear to have actually been written by men, many others genuinely seem to be from women, often conflicted over societal pressure to conform with norms that proscribe their own gender and/or sexual identity.

69. Fukunaga, *Rezubian: Mō hitotsu no ai no katachi* (Lesbian: Another shape of love), 88.

70. Only two issues of this magazine were published. See "*Komyuniti no rekishi*," 29.

71. See "The Gay," Nov. 1982.

72. First published by *Allan* editor Nanbara Shirō in late 1984, *Luna* was initially similar in format and content to *Allan*.

73. "*Rezubian tsūshin*," *Za gei* (The gay), Nov. 1982, 166, no. O.

74. *Jōhō Labrys*, Mar. 1994. See p. 1, ad 6; p. 2, ad 15; p. 5, ad 48.

75. "*Furiine kurabu*," 81, ad 323.

76. Robert Kroetsch, "No Name Is My Name" cited in Cook, "Exploring Transnational Identities in Ondaatje's *Anil's Ghost*."

References

Allan (*Aran*) Complete publication run, aa iuuuvu. (Oct. 1906, Jan. 1901, then bi-monthly Apr. 1981–June 1984).

Aoyama, T. "Male Homosexuality as Treated by Japanese Women Writers." In G. McCormack and Y. Sugimoto, eds., *The Japanese Trajectory: Modernization and Beyond*, Cambridge: Cambridge University Press, 1988. 186–204.

———. "Transgendering *Shōjo Shōsetsu*: Girls' Inter-text/sex-uality." In M. McLelland and R. Dasgupta, eds., *Genders, Transgenders, and Sexualities in Japan*. London: Routledge, 2005. 49–64.

Ariyoshi, K. *Apurōzu—kassai* (Applause, applause). 3 vols. Tokyo: Shūeisha, 1981–82.

Bartholome, A., R. Tewksbury, and A. Bruzzone. "'I Want a Man': Patterns of Personal Attraction in All-Male Personal Ads." *Journal of Men's Studies* 8, no. 3 (Spring 2000): 309–20.

Bessatsu shōjo furendo (Shōjo friend special edition) 17, no. 6 (June 1981).

Butler, J. *Gender Trouble: Feminism and the Subversion of Identity*. New York: Routledge, 1990.

———. *Undoing Gender*. New York: Routledge, 2004.

Child, M., K. Graff Low, C. McDonnell McCormick, and A. Cocciarella. "Personal Advertisements of Male-to-Female Transsexuals, Homosexual Men, and Heterosexuals." *Sex Roles* 34, no. 5/6 (1996): 447–55.

Cook, V. "Exploring Transnational Identities in Ondaatje's *Anil's Ghost*." *Comparative Literature and Culture* 6, no. 3 (Sept. 2004). Retrieved from http://clcwebjournal.lib.purdue.edu/clcweb04-3/cook04.html on July 18, 2004.

Fairclough, N. *Language and Power*. New York: Longman, 2001.

Fujimoto, Y. *Watashi no ibasho wa doko ni aru no?: Shōjo manga ga utsusu kokoro no katachi* (Where do I belong? The shape of the heart reflected in *shōjo* manga). Tokyo: Gakuyō Shobō, 1998.

Fukunaga, T. Rezubian: *Mō hitotsu no ai no katachi* (Lesbian: Another shape of love) Tokyo: Tairiju Shobō, 1982.

"Phryné Club." *Furiine* (Phryné), Nov. 1995, 69–82.

Hagio M. *Pō no ichizoku* (The Poe clan). Tokyo: Shōgakukan Bunko, 1998 [1972–76].

———. *Tōma no shinzō* (The heart of Thomas). Tokyo: Shōgakukan, 1995 [1974].

Halberstam, J. *Female Masculinity*. Durham, N.C.: Duke University Press, 1998.

Harada, N. "Shōjo no tame no dōseiai nyūmon" (An introduction to homosexuality, for girls). *Allan* 1 (Oct. 1980): 96–100.

Honda, M. "'S'—Ta'ainaku, shikamo kongenteki na ai no katachi" (S: The Shape of Essential Yet Frivolous Love). *Imago* 2, no. 8 (Aug. 1991): 68–73.

Ikeda, R. *Futari pocchi* (Just the two of them). Tokyo: Shūeisha Manga Bunko, 1976 [1971].

———. *Oniisama e* (To my big brother). 2 vols. Tokyo: Chūokōron Shinsha (Chūkōbunko), 2002 [1974].

Ishino, S., and N. Wakabayashi. "Japan." In R. Rosenbloom, ed., *Unspoken Rules: Sexual Orientation and Women's Human Rights.* London: Cassell, 1996. 95–101.

Itō B. "Itō Bungaku." Interview. *Allan* 12 (Oct. 1982): 98–99.

"Ibu tsūshin" (Eve communication). *Ivu & Ivu* (Eve & Eve) 1 (Aug. 1982): 191–97.

Izumo, M., and C. Maree. *Love upon the Chopping Board.* North Melbourne, Australia: Spinifex, 2000.

Jōhō Labrys (Labrys information). 5 (March 1994).

Kaufman, G., and V. C. Phua. "Is Ageism Alive in Date Selection among Men: Age Requests among Gay and Straight Men in Personal Ads." *Journal of Men's Studies* 11, no. 2 (Winter 2003): 225–35.

Kinsella, S. *Adult Manga: Culture and Power in Contemporary Japanese Society.* Honolulu: University of Hawai'i Press, 2000.

"Komyuniti no rekishi 1971–2001: Nenpyō to intabyū de furikaeru" (Community history 1971–2001: Reflecting back with timelines and interviews). *Aniisu* (Anise) (Summer 2001): 28–78.

Leap, W. "Language, Socialization, and Silence in Gay Adolescence." In M. Bucholtz, A. C. Liang, and L. Sutton, eds., *Reinventing Identities: The Gendered Self in Discourse.* New York: Oxford University Press, 1999. 259–72.

Maree, C. *Hatsuwa no gengo sutoratejii toshite no negoshiēshon kōi no kenkyū* (Research into negotiation as linguistic discourse strategies) Tokyo: Hitsuji Shobō, 2007.

Matsubara, R. "Burikko mankai: nyū hāfu Matsubara Rumiko-chan no maki" (A cutie in full bloom: The story of new half Matsubara Rumiko). Interview. *Allan* 12 (Oct. 1982): 42–44.

Matsui, M. "Little Girls Were Little Boys: Displaced Femininity in the Representation of Homosexuality in Japanese Girls Comics." In S. Gunew and A. Yeatman, eds., *Feminism and the Politics of Difference.* Boulder, Colo.: Westview, 1993. 177–96.

McLelland, M. *Male Homosexuality in Modern Japan: Cultural Myths and Social Realities.* Richmond, UK: Curzon, 2000.

———. *Queer Japan from the Pacific War to the Internet Age.* Lanham, Md.: Rowman & Littlefield, 2005.

Miwa, A. "Intabyū: Shikon no heya nite" (Interview: In a purple and gold chamber). *Allan* 5 (Feb. 1983): 9–16.

Mizoguchi, A. "Male-Male Romance by and for Women in Japan: A History and the Subgenres of *Yaoi* Fictions." *U.S.-Japan Women's Journal* 25 (2003): 49–75.

Peter. "Piitā: onēsan" (Miss Peter). Interview. *Allan* 11 (Aug. 1982): 75–79.

"Readers' Writers' and Editors' Bedroom." *Komikku Jun* (Comic Jun) 1 (Oct. 1978): 160–61.

———. *June* 7 (Aug. 1979): 164–67.

"Rezubian tsūshin" (Lesbian communication). *Za gei* (The gay). 7 (Nov. 1982): 165–67.

Robertson, J. *Takarazuka: Sexual Politics and Popular Culture in Modern Japan.* Berkeley: University of California Press, 1998.

"Ruporutāju: Shinjuku ni-chōme" (Reportage: Shinjuku ni-chōme). Special feature. *Allan* 2 (Aug. 1983): 9–36.

Satō, M. 1996. "Shōjo manga to homofobia" (*Shōjo* manga and homophobia). In Kuia sutadiizu henshū iinkai (eds.), *Kuia sutadiizu '96* (Queer studies '96). Tokyo: Nanatsumori Shokan, 1996. 161–69.

Schodt, F. L. *Dreamland Japan: Writings on Modern Manga.* Berkeley, Calif.: Stone Bridge Press, 1996.

Sei ishiki chōsa gurūpu. *Sanbyakujū nin no sei ishiki: Iseiaisha dewa nai onnatachi no ankeeto chōsa* (The sexual consciousness of 310 people: A survey of women who are not heterosexual). Tokyo: Nanatsumori Shokan, 1998.

Shimizu, J. "Watashi wa isei wo aisenai onna" (I am a woman who cannot love the opposite sex). *Barazoku* 7 (Sept. 1972): 28–31.

Takemiya, K. *Kaze to ki no uta* (The song of the wind and the trees). 10 vols. Tokyo: Hakusensha Bunko, 1995 [1976–84].

Tsukumo, M. 1991. "Moonlight Flowers." In Tsukumo M., *Moonlight Flowers.* Tokyo: Shūeisha, 1991. 3–142.

Welker, J. "Telling Her Story: Narrating a Japanese Lesbian Community." In A. Germer and A. Moerke, eds., *Grenzgänge. (De-)Konstruktion kollektiver Identitäten in Japan. (Japanstudien. Jahrbuch des Deutschen Instituts für Japanstudien* 16). Munich: Iudicium, 2004. 119–44.

———. "Beautiful, Borrowed, and Bent: Boys' Love as Girls' Love in *Shōjo* Manga." *Signs: Journal of Women in Culture and Society* 31, no. 3 (2006): 841–70.

Yajima, M., ed. *Josei dōseiaisha no raifu hisutorii* (Life histories of female homosexuals). Tokyo: Gakubunsha, 1999.

Yokomori, Rika. *Ren'ai wa shōjo manga de osowatta—ai ni ikite koso, onna!?* (I was taught about love by *shōjo* manga; woman, living in love!?). Tokyo: Kuresutosha, 1996.

Yurino, R. "London Lesbian Report: Global Lesbianism." *Allan* 12 (Oct. 1982): 129–32.

"Yurizoku no heya" (Lily tribe's room). *Barazoku* (Rose tribe) (Nov. 1976): 66–70.

THREE

GRRRL-QUEENS

Onē-kotoba and the Negotiation of
Heterosexist Gender Language Norms and
Lesbo(homo)phobic Stereotypes in Japanese

Claire Maree

In contemporary Japan, elements of the Japanese language such as personal pronouns, sentence-final particles, and verb inflections are said to constitute gendered language use, and the notion of "women's language" (*joseigo/onna-kotoba*) and "men's language" (*danseigo/otoko-kotoba*) continues to mold contemporary notions of gender-appropriate speech. Due to this notion, the queer is imagined as much by the use of flamboyant gendered speech as by flamboyant drag. Stereotypes of lesbian women and gay men inevitably invoke notions of hypermasculine women and hyperfeminine men. Furthermore, the camp speech style known as *onē-kotoba* (queen's language [literally, older sister's language/speech]), a parody of stereotypical women's language that is generally used by *gay* (*gei*)[1] men in a performance of (hyper)femininity, is recognizable within both queer communities and the mainstream. In *gei* community magazines, short articles on *onē-kotoba* position it as an integral part of "gay bar" (*gei bā*) and *gay* culture, while on mainstream television *onē* and/or *okama* (faggot/poofter/queen)[2] personalities—who use *onē-kotoba* and sharp-tongued comments in their public performances[3]—regularly appear on popular "variety" (*baraitei*) programs.[4]

This chapter examines *onē-kotoba* from the starting point of a roundtable discussion on "sexuality and language" coordinated as part of a study on Japanese language, gender, and sexuality in 1998.[5] The initial discussion between the seven volunteer participants at the roundtable indicated that the topic "sexuality and language" invoked the notion of "men's language" used by women, and onē-kotoba used by "gay men" (gei otoko). Furthermore, one interesting point that emerged from the discussion was the use of onē-kotoba by two "lesbian" (rezubian) identified participants who were in their twenties and partners at the time. In the following, I discuss the negotiative strategies of these two participants, Sayuri and Oka.[6]

Throughout the roundtable discussion, Sayuri and Oka spoke extensively of their own use of onē-kotoba, which led them to be referred to as "girl/female queens" (onna-onē) by their peers. The other "lesbian" (rezubian) or woman-loving-women participants, and the only "gay" (gei) male participant were all familiar with this speech style, which is widely associated with gay male culture. However, none of them professed to use it in everyday interactions. In this way, Oka and Sayuri were unique because they articulated an aversion to using "women's language" yet spoke of consciously choosing to employ onē-kotoba, itself generally considered to be a hyperfeminine speech style. I focus on their metalinguistic explanations, that is, their talk about talk, because these explanations offer an insight into the way that individual speakers negotiate stereotypes of language and existing speech styles according to their present-time sense of self and "personal histories of discourse."[7] In particular, Oka and Sayuri's metadiscursive explanations of their self-reference choices illustrate the complex relationship between the speaker's image of self, the gendered norms of the Japanese language system, and contemporary cultural expectations. Similarly, their explanation of onē-kotoba leads the discussion to the functions of onē-kotoba in contemporary queer communities based on current field work being carried out in Tokyo.

As will become clear from the following discussion, for Oka and Sayuri, onē-kotoba functions to resist both restrictive heteronormative femininity and stereotypes of the butch lesbian. By focusing on their creative use of language to negotiate these restrictive stereotypes, I hope to underline the ways in which creative language is fundamental to queer communities in Japan. Similarly, I hope this discussion will contribute to dialogue with other languages regarding strategies enacted by queer speakers and queer critiques of existing language and gender literature.

Recognizing and Resisting Stereotypes

Research on gender and the Japanese language has long been a focus for Japanese language specialists. As Yukawa and Saito note in their overview of the area, "scholars in *kokugogaku* 'national-language studies' have described and cataloged features of normative women's speech style (personal pronouns, sentence-final particles, honorifics, and so on) since the beginning of the twentieth century."[8] In fact, Jugaku Akiko's 1979 work noted the careful manipulation of various features of "Japanese to create the appearance of 'natural' femininity."[9] Despite this, much work in Japanese language and gender studies that has been influenced by English language sociolinguistics and informed by commonsense notions of "women's language" (*joseigo/onna-kotoba*) and "men's language" (*danseigo/otoko-kotoba*), has essentialized notions of gendered language used by homogeneous groups of women and men.[10] Studies employing traditional frameworks of "women's language" and "men's language" generally prescribe different pronoun usage (for example, the first-person pronouns *watashi* or *atashi* for females and *boku* or *ore* for males), different sentence-final particles (for example, uprising *wa* for females and *ze* or *zo* for males), and different levels of politeness (higher politeness for females than males) for *female* and *male* speakers.

Influenced both by the turn in language and gender studies towards the construction of identity in language and by the reevaluation of early Japanese language work, since the 1990s researchers have come to question the correlation of linguistic forms to the sex of the speaker.[11] The notion of a monolithic women's language, and consequently the notion of a monolithic men's language, has also been contested.[12] Emerging from this research is work focusing on gender, sexuality, and language that seeks to shed light on the linguistic work done by gendered and sexualized bodies. The most recent work does so from a perspective that acknowledges the intertwining of gender and sexuality but also problematizes the mapping of heterosexuality onto statically gendered fe/male bodies.[13]

Examining the intersections of gender, language, and sexuality (or sexual identities) first requires acknowledgment of dominant discourses of gendered speech. In other words, it is necessary to work within a framework that can access contemporary ideas relating to the way(s) women and men (should and can) speak. In terms of the Japanese language, this means acknowledging commonsense notions of gender-appropriate speech that operate in women's language and men's language and subsequently inform notions of *onē-kotoba*, while leaving those stereotypes open to contestation. Furthermore, it is imperative to avoid (re)establishing new regulatory or restrictive discourse of so-called gay or lesbian speech.

It is with these points in mind that I approach Oka and Sayuri's use of *onē-kotoba* as one example of speakers' negotiations of heterosexist gender norms. I do so with the understanding that language users repeatedly and reflexively negotiate complex contexts wherein positioning and performing the complexity of their multiple identities.[14] Taking a Bahktinian approach, I acknowledge the ceaselessly shifting power relations between words. For, as Bahktin has shown, language is synchronically informed by contemporary language and diachronically informed by historical rules and anticipated rules.[15] Finally, I understand gender as not something we are but something we do.[16]

As outlined above, this chapter focuses on the negotiative strategies of Sayuri and Oka, two speakers who identify as women and as lesbians and who employ onē-kotoba to varying degrees. By focusing on Oka and Sayuri's "personal histories of discourse"[17] and their metalinguistic accounts of their own language use, we are offered an insight into the negotiative practices language users employ in their short-term and long-term language use. In particular, we get an insight into the ways individual speakers negotiate restrictive stereotypes while simultaneous engaging other stereotypes, stressing the need to rethink gender and sexuality norms as enacted in language.

Contextualization One: Turns at Talk on "Language and Sexuality"

To contextualize Oka and Sayuri's talk on their use of onē-kotoba, let us first consider the original site of production. Oka and Sayuri's metalinguistic discussion of their personal language use was made during a roundtable discussion on language and sexuality, as outlined above. At the roundtable, seven volunteer participants, some partners, some friends, and some first-time acquaintances were asked to speak freely about the research topic.

At the opening of the session, when asked to share what thoughts the topic "language and sexuality" had provoked, Oka explained that the first thing that popped into her mind was onē-kotoba and a style of language used by women. Oka introduces this style with the example "Yo, hi, I'm Kenji" (ussu, dōmo. Kenji desu).[18] This example is greeted by laughter by the other participants. It is interesting to note here that while onē-kotoba has a name and needs no introductory example, the latter style used by women to which Oka refers is without name but seemingly recognizable to the group. Furthermore, none of the participants claimed to use this style; however, both Sayuri and Oka spoke extensively of their use of onē-kotoba.

Oka and Sayuri explain that their use of onē-kotoba leads to them being referred to as onna-onē ("girl/woman queens") by their peers. Oka states that *lesbian* friends respond with exclamations of "sickening" (*kimochi warui*). She says, however, that this reaction does not worry her too much. Sayuri maintains that Oka uses *onē-kotoba* even at work. In one section of the roundtable, Oka mimics her own use of *onē-kotoba* at work giving the example, "Eh? Whaat do you meean?" (*ee? dō iu kotoo?*).[19] Feigning surprise at some state of affairs, she speaks exaggeratedly, her intonation rising sharply in an excessive arc and her last syllable lengthened. Oka describes this as being "over the top" (*ōgesa*). Immediately following this description, Marina, another participant, likens it to that of a "drag-queen type of queen" (*doraggu-kuiin kei no onēsan*) to which Oka agrees. Sayuri adds further to this segment of the conversation by lowering her voice, slowing her speech, and lengthening each vowel of the phrase "that's nooo problem" (*ii wa yooo?*), which she offers as an example of Oka's reaction when asked to do something at work. The combination of sentence-final particles, uprising *wa* and *yo*, used in this example is traditionally classified as "women's language." Coupled with the slow speech style, the effect is to produce the slow, drawling qualities instantly recognizable as *onē-kotoba*.

Oka and Sayuri explain that the major difference between *onē-kotoba*, and stereotypical women's language lies in the exaggerated intonation and extended vowels. Sayuri maintains that even if used by women, this style is undoubtedly *onē-kotoba*. This is because, she says, this style parodies stereotypical women's language by "overdoing by about 50 percent the way women speak" (*onna no hito ga, hanashite iru koto wo, 50 pāsento gurai kajō ni shite*). Sayuri says this produces an accent that is different to "women's language." Furthermore, as *onē-kotoba* is based on men's parodying of stereotypical women's language, women who use the style do so in a voice that is lowered—that is, the voice is effectively reproduction of a lower pitched base voice mimicking a higher pitched "feminine" voice.

In the latter part of the roundtable, *onē-kotoba* is also compared to *ojōsan-kotoba*[20] (lady's language: a semisophisticated style used by young ladies from supposedly respectable homes). In this comparison, participants refer to *onē-kotoba* as being more stylish and trendy. Here too, emphasis is also placed on intonation and voice qualities. Sayuri uses the example of *yoku te yoo* ("faabulous" [lit. "no problem"]), which could be interpreted as stereotypical women's language. As Sayuri explains, when spoken in *onē-kotoba* style, the voice is lowered and the particle *yo* is extended, something she attributes to a difference in "vocalization" (*hassei*). Sayuri notes that if written down, *onē-kotoba* would appear almost identical to stereotypical women's language. It is only when spoken that the drawling qualities can be fully appreciated. Oka and Sayuri also describe *onē-kotoba* as having the potential to be very "aggressive" (*kōgeki-teki*) and "hard" (*kitsui*) at the same time as being a straightforward way of speaking that incorporates a pleasurable level of performance.

The importance of intonation and pitch to *onē-kotoba* is underlined by Oka when talking about one of her close friends. In one section, Marina recounts how she met Oka at the local gym one day and was introduced to someone Oka originally called her "little sister" (*imōtō*), but who actually turned out to be a *gay male* friend. Oka takes up this story by introducing Nobue (real name Nobuyuki) into the conversation by quoting his speech in hers. Note here that Nobuyuki has made a feminine version of his own name by dropping the character "*yuki*," a common component of Japanese boy/men's names and replacing it with "*e*," a common component of girl/women's names. The English language equivalent might be something like a Christopher becoming Christine. Oka's reenactment of Nobue's self-introduction "Ii'm Nobue" (*Nobue desuu*) shows an upward shift in pitch, a reduced speed, and exaggerated force. In particular the gerund *desu* is stressed and lengthened (see the excerpt below).

(1) Oka recounts introducing Nobue to Marina at the gym

1	*Marina:*	<laughing, exhale> dakara saisho wa ne (umarete) hajimete sono ko tachi ni au no ni,
2		<exhale> jimu ni itte "aa mō sugu imōtō ga kuru kara" tte, "un un."
3		⌈to ka itte, zenzen imōtō ja <exhale> nai ja nai mitai na kanji <laughing>
4	*Oka:*	⌊sō, shōkai suru ne? "Nobue **desuu**" to ka itte nan ka Nobuyuki kun no koto nan da
5		ke do. "Nobue **desuu**" to ka tte, chanto ne?
6	*Marina:*	sō ne ⌈go aisatsu wo,
7	*Oka:*	⌊aisatsu to ka shite,
1'	*Marina:*	but at first right <laughing> I'm going to meet those guys for the first time,
2'		<laughing, exhale> I was at the gym, and she goes "my little sister will be here soon,"
3'		(I say) like "yeah yeah." ⌈but it's like not <exhale> (your) little sister at all,
4'	*Oka:*	⌊yeah, "(I'll) introduce (you) okay?" "**Ii'm** Nobue"

5'   (he) says like right this is Nobuyuki but you know. "**I i'm** Nobue"
         (he) says like, real well mannered wasn't (it/he)?
6' *Marina:* right sure, ⌐greeting,
7' *Oka:*   └(he) does a greeting,

The above extract is a cacophony of voices. Oka playfully and theatrically brings Nobue's voice to the current interaction by directly quoting him,
mimicking both speech style and intonation. Here, the playful qualities of
onē-kotoba are skillfully underlined. This almost theatrical device underlines
onē-kotoba's parodying of "women's language" and reinforces the instability of positioning "women's language" as the only true or factive version of
women's speech.[21]

Let us look briefly at the discourse that follows this interaction. Here Sayuri
and Oka talk of another "gay boy" (*gei no otoko no ko*) friend who refers to
himself as "Kazuko" in their playful interactions. Kazuko, like Nobue, has
feminized his name by replacing the final character of his given name with
ko (literally "child"), a character that is traditionally and very commonly used
in women's names. In the extract below, Sayuri stresses that even though
Kazuko uses *onē-kotoba* he is not "woman-like" (*josei ppoi*).

(2) Sayuri describes Kazuko

9   *Sayuri:* demo, sono gei no otoko no ko wa, betsu ni josei ppoi to iu koto
              wa naku jimu ni
10   itte, karada wo kitae te [Oka: sō] kami no ke wo mijikaku shite,
              uwagami o fu tto tate
11   te, hontō ni ano gei, yoku iru gei no otoko no ko na
12 *Oka:*   betsu ni onna ppoi kara Kazuko desu to iu wake ja nai mo ne,

9' *Sayuri:* but, that gay guy, it's not like (he's) particularly feminine, (he)
              goes to the gym, works
10'   out (Oka: yeah), (he) has (his) hair short, and the front is spiked
              up, (he's) really um
11'   gay, like your usual type of gay guy,
12' *Oka:*   it's not as if (he) says "I'm Kazuko" because (he's) feminine or
              anything really is it,

In this conversation, the fact that gender presentation and the use of a
recognized speech style do not have a one-to-one relationship is emphasized.
To support her description of Kazuko as a "usual gay guy/boy" (*yoku iru gei
no otoko no ko*), she notes that he frequents the gym and that his hair is short
and spiked up. Oka joins in, noting that overt femininity is not what causes

him to introduce himself as Kazuko. Note here she uses the terms *onna ppoi*, literally "womanish." Oka and Sayuri articulate that interlocutors use more than just spoken language in their multifarious gender performances. This point underlines the fact that interlocutors recognize and employ the ambiguities and contradictions of so-called fixed gender stereotypes.

Contextualization Two: Parody and "False Evil"

As is clear from the description of *onē-kotoba* jointly carried out by the participants in the 1998 roundtable, *onē-kotoba* is not simply an attempt to mimic stereotypical women's language, it is much more a parody of what "women" say, and how they say it. This description of *onē-kotoba* as parody is not unique to the roundtable discussion. Well-known *gei* ("gay") writer, artist, and bar owner Takashi Ōtsuka refers to *onē-kotoba* in his notes on drag in the following way: "Just as *onē-kotoba* is not women's language, so too is drag not mimicry of what women do. For gays, it is the act of throwing bad eggs at a society that forces a gender image on us. It is also an expression through which we can laugh off our daily feelings of oppression by borrowing the structure that 'the most unmanly of men are not men = women.'"[22]

Ōtsuka's alignment of *onē-kotoba* and drag gives us an idea of the complex multiplicity of the style itself. Ōtsuka posits drag, and by extension *onē-kotoba*, as a challenge to compulsory gender stereotypes that is simultaneously a subversive playful technique of social survival. In this way, it is possible to understand *onē-kotoba* as one method of negotiating the social confusion and conflation of gender and sexuality.

As Ōtsuka comments, drag, and by implication *onē-kotoba*, borrows the construct of "not man = woman," an act that underscores general institutionalized homophobia and misogyny. At the same time, Ōtsuka's reference to *onē-kotoba* underlines the fact that drag queens and gay men do not employ it in an effort to studiously reproduce women's language. An interpretation of *onē-kotoba* as an attempt to faithfully reproduce women's language and the elusive femininity indexed therein is no more than an application of the compulsory gender image the style self-consciously parodies.

In his short essay in answer to the hypothetical question "do all gay people speak *onē-kotoba*?" another popular gay writer, Noriaki Fushimi, stresses that while *onē* (queen[liness]) is an extension of *jo-sei* (institutionalized femininity) it is far more theatrical/performative (*enshutsuteki*).[23] He writes that *onē* conversations may indeed be a product of "gay bar" (*gei bā*) culture and that these conversations are a performance of an "irresponsible and falsely evil female/woman" (*musekinin de giakuteki na onna*). Fushimi refers to well-known television personalities film critic Osugi, fashion critic Piiko, and *enka* singer Mikawa Kenichi, all famous *onē* personalities who, Fushimi maintains, are popular because they are able to make vitriolic comments that other personalities do not dare to utter on television.

The vitriolic aspects of *onē-kotoba* were also discussed in the roundtable. As Sayuri and Oka noted, *onē-kotoba* allows them to be frank and open, and one of its intrinsic characteristics is that is can be used in a scathing way. This feature is also emerging from ethnographic interviews I am currently conducting with drag queens and gay men in Tokyo. In an interview conducted in March 2005, the interviewee identified "maliciousness" (*dokke*) as a characteristic of *onē-kotoba*.

Unfortunately, mainstream discourse posits *onē-kotoba* as no more than mimicry of so-called women's speech by gay men, therein failing to recognize its power as either a flamboyant parody of so-called women's language or a performance of "false evil." In fact, until the late 1990s, reference to *onē-kotoba* in linguistic literature was virtually nonexistent.[24] In one of the very few references to the language used by *okama* (faggots/poofters/queens) to be found in pre-1990s linguistics literature, Nakanishi writes, "By using women's language, *okama* are able to more fully express femininity" (*okama wa onna kotoba o tsukau koto de, yori kukkiri onna rashisa o hyōgen dekiru*).[25] While this comment underlines, albeit in passing, aspects of gender performativity that are central our discussion here, it is inherently defective because it is supported by the dichotomy of (hetero)gendered language. Furthermore, Nakanishi does not pause to consider the elements of parody or maliciousness that are vital to understanding *okama*'s use of "women's language" and *onē-kotoba* as it is employed in real life. I suggest that *onē-kotoba* can be read as a negotiative practice that resists and desists the coercive heteronormative language styles that are "women's language" and "men's language."

Onna-onē: Negotiation of Heterosexist Gender Norms

In the same way that Ōtsuka assures that gay men do not use *onē-kotoba* to reproduce so-called women's language, Oka and Sayuri's usage is not a simple reproduction of normative feminine speech. For Oka and Sayuri, the decision to use *onē-kotoba* is anchored in their shifting relationship with complex social norms and stereotypes.

As seen in the extracts above, both Oka and Sayuri emphasize the difference between *onē-kotoba* and so-called women's language. For, as Sayuri says, "if so-called women's language was really forced onto me I would hate it" (*hontō ni iwayuru onna kotoba tte oshitsukerare tara atashi iya na n da na*). Oka agrees with this, and explains that speaking *onē-kotoba* is fun, and a way of establishing rapport as *women* with gay men. She expresses this rapport as "a sense of solidarity between women" (*onna dōshi no rentaikan*).

During the roundtable, Oka frequently describes herself as "frank" using expressions such as *sappari shite iru* and *saba-saba shite iru*. Furthermore, as the talk in the roundtable discussion drifts to talk about self-referencing strategies of the participants, Oka makes it clear there was a time when she used the first person pronoun *watashi*—the pronoun most frequently labeled as a polite semiformal pronoun used by men in more formal situations and women in both formal and more casual situations. However, Oka explains that she has recently switched to using the less formal and more feminine *atashi*, which is generally referred to as used only by women in casual situations. In regards to this conscious shift in language use, Sayuri refers to Oka's "unfeminine inner self" saying "internally you don't have so-called womanly/ feminine characteristics, do you" (*naimen-teki ni wa . . . josei-teki to iwareru yō na yōso wa nai n da yo ne*). Oka agrees with this comment, echoing that she does not possess "many so-called feminine characteristics" (*josei-teki to iwareru yō na yōso wa sukunai*).[26] Immediately following this, she explains that she "doesn't lean towards femininity" (see lines 13–14 below) and maintains that she uses *atashi* rather than *watashi* because of this. Subsequently we can see that Oka's shift from *watashi* to *atashi* expresses her conscious decision to appeal to her being a "woman." Note here that this is not an appeal to femininity, for, as we have seen already, Oka continuously refers to her lack of "internal femininity." Rather, Oka stresses that her choice of pronoun is a way of letting everyone know that she is a "*woman*" (*onna*).

(3) Oka's self-reference

13 *Oka:* de tsuka- a dakara motomoto wa watashi datta n dakedo, watashi ja chotto kō, watashi

14 tte hanashiteiru to amari, jibun jishin ga josei: ni katayo- katamuit-einai na to omotte,

15 naimen- naimen ga sugoi josei teki ja nai kara, kō atashi tte tsukat- u to nan ka a a kō,

16 atashi tsukau to yatto mina san ni, atashi wa onna da to iu koto wo kō wakatte

17 moraeru no ka na to ka omou,

13' *Oka:* and us- ah because originally it was *watashi* but, but with *watashi* it's a little so, if (I)

14' speak using *watashi* then (it's not) very, I myself don't lea- lean toward girl(ishness) I

15' don't think, because inner- (my) inner isn't very woman-like, so if (I) u- se *atashi* or

16' something ah ah so, when I use *atashi* at last to everyone, I think or something that I

17' can have it understood that so I'm a woman or something

Directly following this exchange, Oka further explains, "I'm not very feminine inside, so I really hate being thought of as masculine" (*naimenteki ga amari josei teki ja nai kara, dansei teki ni omowareru no ga sugoi iya na no ne*). What is important to remember is that even though Oka maintains she does not want to be thought of as manly (or masculine), as Sayuri points out, she won't have femininity forced on her either. For example, when Sayuri checks whether "because if you were told to wear a skirt you'd hate that too"—*sukāto mo haite to iwaretara, sore mo iya dakara*—Oka agrees with her, but once again adds that she doesn't want to be seen as a man either.

In the segment below, Sayuri explains the reasons behind Oka's negotiative choices. Sayuri begins by saying that "rather than wanting to speak (women's language) (4) it's that (she) doesn't want to use men's language or something," ([*onna kotoba*] *o hanashitai to iu koto yori mo,* [4] *otoko kotoba ni naru no wa iya to ka*). She goes on to comment that perhaps if Oka was heterosexual (*heterosekushuaru*) she wouldn't be as concerned about using so-called men's language. In her account, Sayuri uses examples that focus on sentence-final particles "*yo ne,*" the combination of which is traditionally classified as "women's language." Sentence-final particles are also referred to as interactive particles and are an integral part of spoken Japanese.

(4) The stereotype of the boyish lesbian

18 *Sayuri:* demo sore wa sugoku jibun no naka de rezubian da to kajō ni ishiki shite te: tabun, ano:

19 Oka wa (1) otoko kotoba o tabun, moshi heterosekushuaru to dattara, otoko kotoba o,

20 kaiwa no naka ni ima ko gyaru no yō ni tsukatemo, anmari, ishiki shinakatta n darō

21 keredomo, (ima wa) jibun ga, otoko otoba o tsukau koto de, (2) "anata wa rezubian

22 dakara bōisshu na n de shō?" to omowareru koto o, kajō ni osorete iru no de, gyaku

23	ni "nan to ka yo ne" to ka "(nan to ka) da yo ne" to ka kajō ni tsukatte iru (ka mo
24	shirenai.)
18' *Sayuri:*	but that's (because) really inside her (she's) too aware of being lesbian, maybe, well
19'	Oka is (1) maybe men's language, if it was with a heterosexual, men's language,
20'	even if (she) used it in the middle of conversation like *kogyaru* do, not too much,
21'	(she) wouldn't be conscious of it but, (now) she is, by using men's language, (2)
22'	being thought that "you're boyish because you're lesbian," (she) is excessively
23'	worried so, in reverse "blah blah, right (*yo ne*)" or something (like that), (she)
24'	excessively uses "(blah blah), isn't it (*da yo ne*)" or something, perhaps.

Sayuri hypothesizes that Oka avoids using so-called men's language because of the general stereotype that lesbians are mannish. It is interesting to note that Sayuri introduces this stereotype in the form of a direct quote ("you're boyish because you're lesbian"; see lines 21–22). In doing so she effectively reports the stereotype to the other participants as something spoken and already out there, while at the same time representing it as an idea that generates from another person's speech, and therefore not her own personal view.

Sayuri offers the interpretation that Oka (and by extension she herself) fear being told that "you act boyishly because you're a lesbian." This stereotype, the stereotype that mannish (masculine) women are lesbian (or women who use men's language are lesbian), is a product of the conflation of gender and sexuality. Needless to say, not all women who use men's language are lesbians, and neither are all lesbians masculine. This stereotype attributes a false consistency or sameness to woman-to-woman desire.

As Sayuri astutely points out, if Oka identified as "heterosexual," she might not fear this stereotype in quite the same way, and she might be able to use men's language in much the same way that "gals" (*gyaru*)[27] in Japan do. However, as a self-identified lesbian, it is considerably more difficult for Oka to escape the construct of boyish = lesbian, no matter how inadequate (or inaccurate) she feels it to be.

Sayuri's comment indicates the way in which an individual's interpretation of heterosexist gender norms influences their negotiation of language.

It is only by looking at an individual's personal history of discourse that the linguistic choices that individuals make become clear. These choices are anchored in the restrictions of specific languages and language styles and are informed by normative practices and an individual's personal sense of self. This reinforces the importance of studying language use in context and of accounting for analysis of individual uses of language.

As Sayuri herself relates, her use of self-reference terms has changed with her changing image of self. Sayuri currently professes to use the self-reference term *watashi*. However, like Oka, her use of *watashi* is a conscious choice highly influenced by personal experience. In the roundtable discussion, Sayuri relates how she used her first name as a reference term in her pre-teen years and shifted to the so-called boyish pronoun *boku* when she formed her first relationship with a girl in high school. For Sayuri, her romantic relations with women have heavily influenced her choice of pronouns. As she notes in the roundtable discussion, when she was doing her best to act boyish, she did try to avoid using pronouns, which are heavily marked for gender in spoken Japanese, as much as possible. However, she now chooses to use *watashi* or *atashi*. In fact, Sayuri says she is careful to avoid so-called men's language as much as possible. She avoids coarse language, particularly verbal endings and final particles that are widely considered to be used by men. Sayuri maintains she uses so-called feminine particles (she uses phrases such as *sō yo ne* and *na no yo ne* to elaborate on this). Sayuri explains that her speech often draws comments and that "even now, lesbians called femmes tell me that it's like talking to a queen (when they speak to me)" (*ima de mo rezubian no neko to iwareru onna no ko ni okama to shabeteiru mitai* [laughing] *to iwaretari*).

Ongoing Negotiation of Gendered Linguistic Norms

Japanese discourses of gender traditionally prescribe differences in language use for women and men. On paper, these stereotypes appear to be faithfully reproduced in interactions. However, as the above transcripts indicate, speakers' negotiations of language prescription and gender/sexuality norms intersect with their sense of multiple selfhood and with contextual/situational pressures to result in creative uses of language that may exploit available sociolinguistic and cultural rules. Oka and Sayuri's metadiscursive explanations of their use of *onē-kotoba* and self-reference choices illustrate the complex relationship between the speaker's image of self, the gendered norms of the Japanese self-reference system, the multiple or compound meanings of the Japanese final particle system, and contemporary cultural expectations.

For Sayuri and Oka, their personal friendships with gay men have undoubtedly influenced their linguistic choices. *Onē-kotoba,* though seriously underresearched, is generally envisioned by the mainstream to be an *okama* speech style hinging on reproduction of femininity. The *onē* or *okama* character continues to reappear on commercial television, and the use of so-called women's language by male personalities is said to index homosexuality. However, from the interactions studied here alone it is clear that this representation does not tap into the creative well of language use that *onē-kotoba* provides.

As Fushimi and Ōtsuka maintain, *onē-kotoba* is much more than an attempt by *gay* men to reenact stereotypical women's speech. *Onē-kotoba* is an integral part of Japanese queer culture and community formation; it can invoke feelings of belonging despite, or perhaps, because of its potential maliciousness. Furthermore, as Sayuri and Oka's metadiscourse shows, *onē-kotoba* is not the property of *gay* men alone, a fact that Fushimi himself comments on. Fushimi not only refutes the fact that all gay men use *onē-kotoba* but also acknowledges the possibility of *onna-onē.*[28] My recent field work on *onē-kotoba* further underlines the need for comprehensive research on this speech style.

Within a language that has clear hegemonic discourses of gendered speech, language users creatively negotiate complex boundaries therein. The stereotype of the mannish lesbian and their close relationships with *gay* male friends motivate Oka and Sayuri's conscious adoption of traditionally highly feminine pronouns that are also employed in *onē-kotoba.* In this way, both negotiate diachronic and synchronic rules of gendered language speech (cf. Bakhtin). Needless to say, these strategies are not employed by all of the participants in the 1998 roundtable discussion.[29]

Our discussion of *onē-kotoba* as used by self-identified lesbian speakers underlines the necessity to attend to coercive heteropatriarchal femininity posited by Japanese socioculture when conducting research into gender and language issues in the Japanese language context. It is imperative to incorporate notions of negotiation and speakers' relationships with gender and sexuality norms in research on gender and language.

Notes

1. For a discussion of terms used for homosexuality in Japanese, see Long, "Miscellany"; McLelland, *Male Homosexuality in Modern Japan* and "Gay Men, Masculinity, and the Media in Japan"; Valentine, "Pots and Pans."

2. The term *okama* connotes a gender-bending male homosexual and is used as a self-defining term by two or three popular television personalities to market their media personas. In contemporary Japan, the term is used positively by many queer

men, but like many colloquial terms for homosexuality, it also contains highly derogative connotations for others. For those who do not identify with the linking of male homosexuality to effeminacy implicated within, it continues to be a highly contentious term when used as a generic label.

3. In a recent ethnographic interview, the interviewee commented that he did not feel that more recent *onē* personalities use *onē-kotoba* in what he considered to be its pure form.

4. For discussions of gay men and the media, see McLelland, "Gay Men, Masculinity, and the Media." For a brief account of the resurgence in popularity of *okama* (queen/faggot/poofter) personalities Osugi and Piiko, see Fushimi, *Gei to iu "keiken"* ("The 'experience' of being gay").

5. Data used in this chapter comes from the following: (a) roundtable discussion on "sexuality and language" of approximately 120 minutes held in June 1998 between seven speakers, including myself, six women, and one man; (b) conversation of approximately 120 minutes in duration between the roundtable participants joined by one more woman recorded at an informal dinner directly after the roundtable discussion; (c) follow-up interviews with the seven participants in the roundtable conducted between July 1988 and March 2000. For further discussion of this data, see Maree, Nihongo to jendā oyobi sekushuariti—negoshieshon—jibun ga Jibun (atashi, boku, ore) de iru tame ni (Negotiation of Japanese language, sexuality, gender—maintaining "[my]self"); Lunsing and Maree, "Shifting Speakers."

6. As is standard for ethnographic and/or conversation analysis, pseudonyms are used for all of the participants. Oka, a shortening of the common surname Okamoto, reflects that participant's use of a shortened version of her surname. Sayuri reflects that participant's use of her given name, a well-known Japanese girl/women's name.

7. Silverstein and Urban, *Natural Histories of Discourse.*

8. Yukawa and Saito, "Cultural Ideologies in Japanese Language and Gender Studies," 24.

9. Jugaku, "Nyōbō kotoba," 22, as quoted in Yukawa and Saito, "Cultural Ideologies," 27. For a translation of Jugaku's related work, see Jugaku, "Nyōbō kotoba."

10. Abe, The Speech of Urban Professional Japanese Women, Maree, "Sei(sa) no gengotai"; Yukawa and Saito, "Cultural Ideologies."

11. For overviews, see Abe, "From Stereotypes to Context"; Yukawa and Saito, "Cultural Ideologies."

12. For recent developments in this area, see the collection of work in Okamoto and Shibamoto Smith, *Japanese Language, Gender, and Ideology.*

13. Maree, Nihongo to jendā oyobi sekushuariti and "Sei(sa) no gengotai"; Lunsing and Maree, "Shifting Speakers"; Abe, "Lesbian Bar Talk in Shinjuku, Tokyo."

14. See Maree, Nihongo to jendā oyobi sekushuariti, "Sei(sa) no gengotai," and "Ore wa ore dakara"; Lunsing and Maree, "Shifting Speakers."

15. Bahktin, *The Dialogic Imagination* and *Speech Genres and Other Late Essays.*

16. On performativity, see Austin, *How to Do Things with Words;* Derrida, *Signature Event Context;* Butler, *Gender Trouble* and *Bodies That Matter.*

17. Silverstein and Urban, *Natural Histories of Discourse.*

18. Oka's example includes *ussu,* a slang greeting with little feminine connotation, and Kenji, a popular boy/man's name.

19. Transcription conventions are as follows:

C:	speaker's initial
—	truncated word
[	simultaneous speech
=	latching
?	rising intonation
.	falling intonation
,	brief pause
(1)	pause in seconds
(umarete)	parentheses indicate unsure sections of speech
whaat	extra letters indicate extended sounds
"I'm Kenji"	quotation marks indicate quotative speech
bold	bold type indicates emphasis
<laughing>	brackets indicate quality of speech and other related features

The author's translation appears directly following the transcripts.

20. *Ojōsan-kotoba* is not a widely recognized term but one used in the roundtable to indicate differences between speech styles.

21. See Butler, *Bodies That Matter.*

22. Ōtsuka, *Queer Studies,* 50; author's translation. The original reads as follows: "Onē-kotoba ga onna no kotoba de wa nai yō ni, dorāgu wa josei no mane o suru kotode wa nai. Sore wa, gei ni totte, jendā imēji o oshi tsuke te kuru shakai ni taishite kusatta tamago wo nagetsukeru kōi de ari, otoko to neru to iu 'motto mo otoko ra-shiku nai otoko ga, 'otoko de nai mono = onna no kōzu o karite,' higoro no jatsukan o warai tobasu tame no hyōgen de mo aru."

23. Fushimi takes the character for "female" *jo* and combines it with the character for "institutionalized" *sei* to produce the term *jo-sei,* which sounds identical to the usual term for females/women, *josei.* Fushimi, *Puraibeto gei raifu* (Private gay life). Quote is from p. 21.

24. For recent references to *onē-kotoba,* see Ogawa and (Shibamoto) Smith, "The Linguistic Gendering of an Alternative Japanese Lifestyle" and "The Gendering of the Gay Male Sex Class in Japan"; McLelland, "Gay Men, Masculinity, and the Media"; Lunsing and Maree, "Shifting Speakers."

25. Nakanishi, "Kotoba kara mita Nihon no onna to otoko" (Japanese women and men from a linguistic view).

26. In the segment introduced here, co-construction of utterances by Oka and Sayuri stands out. This shows that the two speakers are in tune with each other and easily complete each other's "sentences." As partners living together, this co-construction illustrates the way in which they work together and participate in the discussion at hand. See Hayashi and Mori, "Co-construction in Japanese Revisited."

27. "Gal" refers to younger (usually between fifteen and eighteen) girls who wear what are considered heavy makeup and daring clothes.

28. Fushimi, *Puraibeto gei raifu* (Private gay life), 21.

29. For a discussion on the strategies employed by other participants see Maree, "Sei(sa) no gengotai"; Lunsing and Maree, "Shifting Strategies."

References

Abe, Hideko. The Speech of Urban Professional Japanese Women. PhD diss., Arizona State University, 1993.

———. "From Stereotypes to Context: The Study of Japanese Women's Speech." *Feminist Studies* 21, no. 3 (1995).

———. "Lesbian Bar Talk in Shinjuku, Tokyo." In Shigeko Okamoto and Janet S. Shibamoto Smith, eds., *Japanese Language, Gender, and Ideology: Cultural Models and Real People.* London: Oxford University Press, 2004.

Austin, J. L. *How to Do Things with Words,* 2nd ed., ed. J. O. Urmson and Marina Sbisa. Cambridge: Harvard University Press, 1975.

Bakhtin, Mikail. *The Dialogic Imagination.* Ed. Michael Holoquist. Austin: University of Texas Press, 1981.

———. *Speech Genres and Other Late Essays.* Trans. Caryl Emerson and Michael Holquist, ed. Vern W. McGee. Austin: University of Texas Press, 1986.

Butler, Judith. *Gender Trouble: Feminism and the Subversion of Identity.* New York: Routledge, 1990.

———. *Bodies That Matter: On the Discursive Limits of Sex.* New York: Routledge, 1993.

Derrida, Jacques. Signature Event Context. *Limited Inc.* Trans. S. Weber and J. Mahlman. Evantson, Ill.: Northwestern University Press, 1988.

Fushimi, Noriaki. *Puraibeto gei raifu* (Private gay life). Tokyo: Gakuyō Shobo, 1991.

———. *Kuia paradaizu* (Queer Paradise). Tokyo: Shōeisha, 1996.

———. *Gei to iu "keiken"* (The "experience" of being gay). Tokyo: Potto Shuppan, 2002.

Hayashi, Makoto, and Junko Mori. "Co-construction in Japanese Revisited: We Do Finish Each Other's Sentences." Ed. N. Akatsuka, H. Hoji, S. Iwasaki, and S. Sohn. *Japanese Korean Linguistics* 7 (1998).

Jugaku, Akiko. "Nyōbō kotoba: A Focus Point for Women's Language and Women's History." Trans. Claire Maree. In Haruko Wakita, Anne Bouchy, and Chizuko Ueno, eds., *Gender and Japanese History: The Self and Expression/Work and Life,* vol. 2. Osaka: Osaka University Press, 1999.

Livia, Anna, and Kira Hall, eds. *Queerly Phrased: Language, Gender, and Sexuality.* Oxford: Oxford University Press, 1997.

Long, Daniel. "Miscellany." *American Speech* 71, no. 2 (1996).

Lunsing, Wim, and Claire Maree. "Shifting Speakers: Strategies of Gender, Sexuality, and Language." In Shigeko Okamoto and Janet S. Shibamoto Smith, eds., *Japanese*

Language, Gender, and Ideology: Cultural Models and Real People. London: Oxford University Press, 2004.

Maree, Claire. Nihongo to jendā oyobi sekushuariti — negoshieshon jibun ga Jibun (atashi, boku, ore) de iru tame ni (Negotiation of Japanese language, sexuality, gender—maintaining "[my]self"). PhD diss., University of Tokyo, 2001.

———. 2002. "Sei(sa) no gengotai: Kotoba no kojinshi kara yomitoru 'jendā', 'sekushuariti', 'Fukugō-aidentiti'" (The language ecology of gender: Personal narratives of gender, sexuality, multiple identities). In Hideki Ishida and Yoichi Komori, eds., *Gengogaku to gengotai*, vol. 5: *Shakai no gengotai* (Linguistics and language ecology, vol. 5: Societys language ecology). Tokyo: Tokyo University Press, 2002.

———. "Ore wa ore dakara ['Because I'm me']: A study of gender and language in the documentary *Shinjuku Boys*." *Intersections* (2003) http://wwwsshe.murdoch.edu.au/intersections.

McLelland, Mark. *Male Homosexuality in Modern Japan: Cultural Myths and Social Realities*. Richmond, Surrey: Curzon, 2000.

———. "Gay Men, Masculinity, and the Media in Japan." In Kam Louie and Morris Low, eds., *Asian Masculinities: The Meaning and Practice of Manhood in China and Japan*. London: RoutledgeCurzon, 2003. 59–78.

Nakanishi, Kiyomi. "Kotoba kara mita Nihon no onna to otoko" (Japanese women and men from a linguistic view). *Joseigaku nenpō* 6 (1985).

Ogawa, Naoko, and Janet S. [Shibamoto] Smith. "The Linguistic Gendering of an Alternative Japanese Lifestyle: Speech Variation in the Gay Communities of Urban Japan." Paper presented at Symposium about Language and Society—Austin III (1995).

———. "The Gendering of the Gay Male Sex Class in Japan: A Case Study Based on *Rasen no sobyō*." In Anna Livia and Kira Hall, eds., *Queerly Phrased: Language, Gender, and Sexuality*. Oxford: Oxford University Press, 1997.

Okamoto, Shigeko, and Janet S. Shibamoto Smith, eds. *Japanese Language, Gender, and Ideology: Cultural Models and Real People*. London: Oxford University Press, 2004.

Queer Studies Editorial Committee, ed. *Kuia Sutadēzu '96*. Tokyo: Nanatsumori shokan, 1996.

Silverstein, Michael, and Greg Urban, eds. *Natural Histories of Discourse*. Chicago: University of Chicago Press, 1996.

Valentine, James. "Pots and Pans: Identification of Queer Japanese in Terms of Discrimination." In Anna Livia and Kira Hall, eds., *Queerly Phrased: Language, Gender, and Sexuality*. Oxford: Oxford University Press, 1997.

Yukawa, Sumiyuki, and Masami Saito. "Cultural Ideologies in Japanese Language and Gender Studies." In Shigeko Okamoto and Janet S. Shibamoto Smith, eds., *Japanese Language, Gender, and Ideology: Cultural Models and Real People*. London: Oxford University Press, 2004.

FOUR

POLITICS AND ISLAM

Factors Determining Identity
and the Status of Male-to-Female
Transsexuals in Malaysia

Yik Koon Teh

The Western definition of male-to-female transsexuals, that is, men who want to undergo sex-change operations to become women, may not be appropriate in the Malaysian context. In Malaysia, the local term *mak nyah* refers both to men who want to have the surgery as well as to those who are comfortable keeping their penises and who do not seek surgical sex change.

This phenomenon is closely linked to recent political developments in Malaysia. After achieving independence from Britain in 1957, there has been a gradual revival of Islam in Malaysia. Islam became the official religion when the nation-state of Malaysia was formed in 1963, and subsequently *Syariah* laws[1] have been implemented for all Muslims in society. In recent decades, Islam has increasingly become a political tool to gain and sustain power deployed by the ruling party.

In Islam, only *khunsa,* or hermaphrodites, are allowed to undergo sex-change operations, and so the majority of the transsexual population in Malaysia, who are not *khunsas,* are considered to be violators of the religion. Islam does not recognize the western category of transsexual. Therefore, transsexuals are regarded as nonentities. In order to force them to conform to Islamic practices, their freedom and rights are curtailed by the police and Islamic enforcement officers.[2] These officials often conduct raids to apprehend *mak nyahs* for cross-dressing, indecent behavior, and so forth under the Minor Offences Act of 1955 or under *Syariah* law. This kind of surveillance and harassment, in turn, impacts upon the kind of transsexual identity possible in Malaysia.

Although many characteristics are shared by male-to-female transsexuals all over the world, the forms that transsexualism takes are also determined by local cultural and religious factors. In most cases, transsexuals have to conform to local norms. In Malaysia, the lifestyle and self-image of transsexuals have been impacted by the country's political history and political and religious exigencies.

The Political History of Malaysia

British rule first arrived in the Malay Peninsula in 1786 when Britain established a settlement on Penang Island to protect its shipping routes between China and India. However, complete British control was not established until the late 1800s after the signing of the Pangkor Treaty in 1874.[3] Under British rule, Chinese and Indian laborers, who were non-Muslims, were imported to work in the tin mines and rubber plantations respectively. The local Malays, who were Muslims, were encouraged to farm and fish for a living. By encouraging ethnic divisions, including an ethnic division of labor, the Malays, Chinese, and Indians were kept from uniting against the British.

During the colonial period, the authority over Islamic affairs exercised by the Malay sultans or local rulers was enshrined in the treaty and the law. The rulers in each state were aided by a Council of Islamic Affairs, and since the authority over Islamic affairs was decentralized, the administration of Islam differed in every state. The Federation of Malaya gained its independence from British colonial rule in 1957 and Malaysia was formed in 1963. In 1968, under the first prime minister of Malaysia, Tunku Abdul Rahman, the National Council for Islamic Affairs was established by the federal government to coordinate Islamic affairs throughout the nation through consultation and cooperation.[4] Although Islam was established as the official religion of Malaysia, Islamic affairs were still mainly in the domain of the respective states.

At around the same time, there was an increasing resurgence of Islam among rural and urban Malays. *Dakwah* (Muslim) movements attracted many followers, including many educated Malays. Examples of these organizations include Darul Arqam and Angkatan Belia Islam Malaysia (Malaysian Islamic Youth Movement). Harold Crouch mentions that the religious attitudes of many young Malays in the universities and other educational institutions were not simply a result of bringing village beliefs and practices to the cities but, "Unlike their parents, whose practice of Islam was often ritualistic and traditional, the educated offspring came into contact with new religious ideas and interpretations through student organizations, visiting preachers and Islamic literature, much of which was translated from Arabic or Urdu. Influenced by new Islamic ideas and inspired to some extent by events such as the Iranian revolution, the *dakwah* movement reflected a desire to overhaul Malay (and indeed, Malaysian) society to bring it fully into accord with the tenets of Islam."[5]

Munro-Kua points out that this was partly an effect of rapid political and socioeconomic change, as well as the developing concept of "Malayness" which is defined, in part, by possession of a Muslim identity by the constitution.[6] A Malay who abandons Islam is no longer legally considered to be a Malay, as the federal constitution defines a Malay as "a person who professes the religion of Islam, habitually speaks the Malay language [and] conforms to Malay custom."[7] Kamarulnizam likewise points out that Islam in postindependence Malay politics, as before, was incorporated into Malay nationalism and became a defining feature of the national struggle against non-Malays, particularly the Chinese and Indians who made up almost 50 percent of the population.[8] Islam, then, was established as a central feature of Malay identity and culture.

The ruling party in Malaysia is the Barisan Nasional (National Front). It is comprised of three main ethnic units: the United Malays National Organisation (UMNO), which is the dominant component, the Malaysian Chinese Association (MCA), and the Malaysian Indian Congress (MIC). With the proliferation of the *dakwah* movements at the time, the ruling Barisan Nasional government had to promote Islam to gain support and legitimacy from the Malay/Muslim community. After the exit or expulsion of Parti Islam Se Malaysia (PAS) in 1978 from the Barisan Nasional party, UMNO had to compete with PAS on the grounds of its support for Islam.[9] PAS was the second largest Malay/Muslim political party in Malaysia whose goals were to set up an Islamic state and implement Islamic principles in all aspects of life, whereas UMNO's vision was that of a secular state.[10] In general, PAS's vision was based on Islam whereas UMNO's vision was based on Malay nationalism. PAS's popularity, with its stronghold in the Kelantan state and its appeal to the Malay peasantry, was a significant threat to UMNO. PAS challenged UMNO continually, arguing that they were the legitimate leaders of Islamic affairs in Malaysia since UMNO was based on secular ideology and, thus, was "un-Islamic." PAS, being the leading Muslim/Malay opposition party, "grew in reaction to mounting popular frustration, disillusionment and even disgust at the growing abuses of those in power."[11]

Mahathir Mohamad, from UMNO, became prime minister of Malaysia on July 17, 1981. The Mahathir administration had to deal with PAS while simultaneously trying to project the image to the world that Malaysia's interpretation of Islam was progressive rather than backward.[12] Mahathir distinguished himself from previous leaders by giving real and serious attention to the role of Islam in the administration of the country.[13] He vigorously planned and implemented programs in the government's drive towards Islamization. Eight months after Mahathir assumed the post of prime minister, Anwar Ibrahim was persuaded to join UMNO. Anwar was a former founder and leader of Angkatan Belia Islam Malaysia, a *dakwah* movement that had a membership of 40,000 mostly educated young Malay/Muslim members. Anwar's main role as deputy minister in the prime minister's department was to formulate a new Islamization policy. UMNO further enhanced its image as an administration based on Islamic values by, for example, setting up an Islamic Bank and an Islamic banking system in 1982 and founding the International Islamic University in 1983. At the state level, where policies on Islam still depended largely on local administration, there was more vigorous enforcement of Islamic laws on violators, for example, stricter enforcement of the *khalwat*[14] law and fasting rules during the month of Ramadan.

In 1983, Mahathir challenged the traditional rights of the monarchies or the Malay rulers,[15] resulting in a constitutional crisis. At this time, amendments to the Penal Code and Criminal Procedure Code conferred on the government the absolute right over *Syariah* law and its interpretation.[16] The increase in federal powers thus overrode and eroded those of the regional states and the monarchies. The different interpretation of Islamic principles by the different states was now "unified under the leadership of federal authorities headed by Dr. Mahathir."[17]

Other strategies by the Mahathir administration to more generally diffuse Islamic principles included having Islamic prayers recited at the beginning and at the end of official meetings and functions, a strict dress code for male and female civil servants, televising Friday Islamic prayers, introducing compulsory Islamic civilization courses at government universities, having more television and radio programs on Islam, and building more mosques for Malay housing areas. New regulations were also introduced at the federal level for the Muslim community, for example, the prohibition of Muslims entering casinos and the prohibition of alcohol at government functions. On the international level, there were an increasing number of cultural exchanges with other Islamic nations. For example, international conferences on Islamic issues began to be held in Malaysia, and the annual Koran reading contest in Malaysia was opened to participants from other Islamic countries. As Crouch concludes, the Islamization program enabled UMNO, at least to some extent, to undercut the criticisms of its radical Muslim opponents while at the same time appeasing the conscience of its own increasingly self-conscious Muslim members.[18] Mahathir Mohamad stepped down as prime minister of Malaysia on October 31, 2003. The new prime minister, Abdullah Ahmad Badawi, also from UMNO, won a landslide victory over PAS on March 21, 2004. This indicates that UMNO's Islamization policies have met with broad approval, in comparison with those of PAS, from a majority of Malaysian Muslims and non-Muslims.

This brief outline of the political history of Malaysia has illustrated how Islam has been used as a political tool to gain power both by the ruling and opposition political parties. It has also been used as a nationalistic tool by Malays against non-Malays, particularly the Chinese and Indians. Since Islam is not simply the official religion in Malaysia but also an important political and ideological tool wielded by politicians, its edicts are increasingly being implemented and enforced by the police and dedicated Islamic authorities on the Muslim community. The repercussions for the transsexual community, particularly its Muslim members, have included increasing marginalization and discrimination.

Changes in the Status of Male-to-Female Transsexuals in Malaysia

The local term for male-to-female transsexuals is *mak nyah*—*mak* meaning "mother" and *nyah* referring to ladylike/feminine behavior. This term was coined by members of the transsexual community themselves in 1987 when they tried to set up an official society for their community but were denied permission by the registrar of societies. The term was introduced to differentiate *mak nyah* from *pondan* or *bapok,* terms used to describe effeminate men or homosexuals. *Mak nyah* includes both individuals who have undergone sex-change operations and those who have not. In Malaysia, it has been estimated that there are about 10,000 *mak nyahs* in the country, about 70 to 80 percent of whom are Malays (who are also Muslims); the rest are Chinese, Indian, and other minority ethnic groups. Malays make up 50.7 percent of the total population whereas the Chinese, Indians, and other minority ethnic groups make up 27.5 percent, 7.8 percent, and 14 percent respectively.[19] A possible reason why there are fewer non-Malay/non-Muslim *mak nyahs* is that some of them, especially those with better employment qualifications, have migrated to other countries. Also, many non-Muslim *mak nayhs*, who face no religious objections, may well have undergone sex-change operations and become integrated into society. There are more non-Malay *mak nyahs* (with or without sex-change operations) holding better jobs than the Malay *mak nyahs* and who are consequently better integrated into mainstream society.

More than half of the *mak nyah* community is involved in sex work and about a third of them live below the poverty line of RM500 per month. Most of them (74 percent) have secondary school education, but only 4 percent have attended institutes of higher learning. The reason many *mak nyahs* turn to the sex trade is the difficulty they have in getting relatively well-paid jobs due to discrimination and nonacceptance by society.[20]

In my research, I found that the *mak nyahs* had enjoyed a better standard of living during the colonial period as the community faced less stigma and had greater employment opportunities.[21] There were fewer sex workers then as compared to the present day. Many were *mak andams*[22] (brides' attendants), *joget* dancers,[23] cooks, or artists. In my interview with a sixty-three-year-old *mak nyah*, it was related that *mak nyahs* during the colonial time were a comparatively happy lot as they were largely left alone to be who they wanted to be. The police and Islamic religious authorities did not harass them. On the contrary, the police were good to them and accepted them as they were— even sometimes giving them a treat, but never asking for sexual favors in return. Many *mak nyahs* went overseas to have sex-change operations, which they could more easily afford since they were earning good money. Those who had sex-change operations were able to have their names and gender changed on their identity cards.

At present, Malaysians generally believe that *mak nyahs* have been socialized into or actively choose to be the way they are. Common myths are that they were brought up in a household of females and therefore had only female role models; their mothers dressed them up as girls because they wanted a female child; or they were sexually abused or sodomized when they were small. These beliefs have been proven wrong in my research. Most *mak nyahs* come from big families with more than three children, generally including both male and female. Contrary to the myth, it is the female members of their families who strongly dislike them assuming the identity of *mak nyahs*. Only a small number of *mak nyahs* had the support of family members when they started cross-dressing. Moreover, the majority of *mak nyahs* were not sexually abused when they were small. In actual fact, a significant number of *mak nyahs* realized they were different from other male children when they were as young as preschool age. They liked female toys and played the female role with other female children. With such an early development, transsexualism cannot solely be a matter of preference or a product of socialization.

The changing status of transsexuals in Malaysia is closely tied to changes in the political climate, notably the ability of the community to obtain sex-change operations. Prior to 1983, sex-change operations were carried out in Malaysia, although relatively few in number due to the lack of qualified surgeons specializing in this area. The University Hospital (University Malaya Medical Centre) was one of a few hospitals that performed sex-change operations. The University Hospital had meticulous procedures to be followed before it would carry out an operation. For example, a transsexual patient opting for a sex-change operation had to undergo two years of precounseling to ensure that the operation was really what the patient wanted. They also had to go through two years of postcounseling so that they could adjust to their new roles.

In 1983, two years after Mahathir Mohamad became prime minister and the same year he challenged the Malay rulers, the Conference of Rulers in Malaysia decided that a fatwa[24] prohibiting sex-change operations should be imposed on all Muslims. Under the same fatwa, cross-dressing was prohibited. It was agreed, however, that in the case of *khunsa* (hermaphrodites, persons having both male and female sex organs), such surgery would be permitted.

In the *Hadith* of Islam,[25] gender can be divided into four groups: male, female, *khunsa,* and *mukhannis* or *mukhannas.*[26] *Mukhannis* and *mukhannas* are males whose behavior is similar to that of females. *Mukhannis* want to assume a gender identity that is associated with women—they loathe their male identity and want to be female. In contrast, a *mukhannas* is a biological male who is effeminate but does not want to change sex.[27] Islam permits *khunsa* (hermaphrodites) to undergo a sex-change operation so that a person can be rendered unambiguously either a female or a male. However, Islam forbids *mukhannis* or *mukhannas,* males who behave like females in terms of cross-dressing, wearing make-up, injecting hormones to enlarge their breasts, and so forth, from undergoing sex-change operations. For example, the *Hadith* in Sahih Bukhari, volume 7, book 72, number 774 states, "Narrated by Ibn 'Abbas: The Prophet cursed effeminate men and those women who assumed the manners of men, and he said, 'Turn them out of your houses.'"

The *Hadith* in Sunan Abu-Dawud, book 32, number 4087, states, "Narrated by Abu Hurayrah: The Apostle of Allah cursed the man who dressed like a woman and the woman who dressed like a man."

The fatwa decreed by the Conference of Rulers also prohibits Muslim surgeons from carrying out sex-change operations. Since *khunsas* are allowed to seek out sex-change surgery so that the person can be either a female or a male, they can obtain permission from the *Syariah* Department. However, they will need to produce a report from a doctor in a government hospital to prove that they are true hermaphrodites. They can then have the operation performed overseas or in Malaysia by non-Muslim surgeons.

The immediate effect of the fatwa was to increase the stigmatization of the transsexual community. Muslim *mak nyahs* were now considered violators of the tenets of Islam and consequently less moral. At present, many Muslim *mak nyahs* are afraid to undergo the sex-change operation even though they may have the means to do so. They also fear that nobody will carry out the burial rites for them when they die: in Muslim burial rites, the body of the deceased must be bathed before burial, and the body of a female can only be bathed by another female, which does not include *mak nyahs,* even though they may have undergone a sex-change operation. They are also not sure whether they will be accepted as females or considered males in heaven. Some even believe that their souls will float aimlessly when they die if they have had the operation because their bodies will not be those that God originally gave them.

As Islam is the official religion in Malaysia, the stigmatization of the community is sustained via the enforcement of religious edicts by the police and Islamic religious authorities. The fatwa allows Muslim *mak nyahs* to be charged under Islamic *Syariah* law for indecent behavior, which includes cross-dressing or behaving like a female. In addition, they can also be charged under the Minor Offences Act of 1955 according to the civil law.[28] *Mak nyahs* can be subjected to Section 377a and 377b of the Malaysian Penal Code. Section 377a states, "Any person who has sexual connection with another person by the introduction of the penis into the anus or mouth of the other person is said to commit carnal intercourse against the order of nature," and Section 377b states, "Whoever voluntarily commits carnal intercourse against the order of nature shall be punished with imprisonment for a term which may extend to twenty years, and shall also be liable to whipping." Fortunately, these laws have not so far been used against the *mak nyahs.* The last time these sections were invoked was in the infamous Anwar Ibrahim case. Anwar

Ibrahim, the deputy prime minister of Malaysia at the time, was charged with sodomy under these two sections of the Penal Code in September 1998. The charges were overturned on appeal by the Federal Court in September 2004. However, it is clear that neither the *Syariah* law nor the civil law in Malaysia accept transsexual and homosexual practices. The existence of these laws has also contributed to society's negative perception of sexual minorities.

Mak nyahs face increasing harassment from the police and religious authorities. About half of the 507 respondents in my 2001 study had been apprehended by the police, and about 28 percent had been caught by religious authorities. Many had been apprehended more than once. Although this persecution has not discouraged the Muslim *mak nyahs* from cross-dressing, many have opted not to have the sex-change operation, primarily due to the religious belief that they may not be accepted by God when they die. Indeed, some of the older and more elderly Muslim *mak nyahs* have reverted to wearing male clothing even though they had cross-dressed full time when they were younger since they want to be able to receive a proper burial as men. This clearly shows that the Muslim *mak nyahs* have a high respect for their religion, which has had a strong influence on their culture and tradition.

The religious nonacceptance and stigmatization of *mak nyahs* have increased discrimination against them. In addition to being teased and called derogatory names, they have problems getting decent-paying jobs, renting a place to live, getting bank loans to purchase homes, and legally adopting children as they are considered unfit parents.[29] Furthermore, *mak nyahs* who have had a sex-change operation cannot change their names and gender on their identity cards to that of females. Although they are permitted to add their new female names beside their original names on their identity cards, their official gender remains male. The lack of a genuine official gender status creates problems; for example, they cannot purchase health insurance because they have female organs while their identity cards state that they are males. They have problems at immigration checkpoints, as they look female but their documentation states that they are males. They cannot get bank loans. The impact of these various forms of discrimination has negatively affected the quality of life of this community.

Generally, Muslim *mak nyahs* today have accepted that they are transsexuals who are female at heart but do not opt to undergo sex-change operations. Those who do opt for surgery, which is only a small number, have it done overseas, particularly in Thailand. Since the operation is illegal for Muslims in Malaysia, this has limited the ability of *mak nyahs* to get necessary and adequate psychological support, and they do not receive counseling either before or after the operation. As a result, some have problems adjusting to their new roles, and most lack adequate social support.

In contrast, non-Muslim *mak nyahs,* mainly Buddhists, Christians, and Hindus, do not face the same level of stigmatization. They are allowed to be *mak nyahs* and are able to undergo sex-change surgery overseas if they can afford it (as there are no trained surgeons in Malaysia at present). Despite the fact that their own religions may also prohibit the operation, these prohibitions are not enforced by official religious rulings. In the absence of state-sponsored religious rulings, non-Muslims usually allow *mak nyahs* to be who they are. Reverend Wong Kim Kong, the secretary of the National Evangelical Christian Fellowship, stated, "Christians should not condemn nor judge transsexuals . . . they do not allow the transsexual activities to perpetuate. Thus, Christians will try to help transsexuals to accept themselves and lead a fulfilling life, but without going against the teachings of the bible. The transsexual, however, has a choice. The pastoral care will be carried out by Christians, but ultimately the choice is left to the person concerned."[30]

In general, Buddhists and Hindus are even more accepting of *mak nyahs* than Christians as they believe in the concept of *karma.*[31] K. Sri Dhammananda, the chief Buddhist high priest of Malaysia, explained that transsexualism was not a religious issue as long as it did not involve behavior that was immoral, harmful, or unethical.[32] In Buddhism, the term "immoral" is not related to transgressing divine edicts but to behavior that has deleterious effects on the well-being of others; and the term "harmful" refers to causing harm to oneself as well as to others.

Occasionally non-Muslim *mak nyahs* are apprehended by the police for cross-dressing and charged with indecent behavior under section 21 of the Minor Offences Act of 1955. What constitutes indecent behavior is not defined in the act, so it is up to the discretion of the police who generally define indecent behavior as that which is offensive to the general public "according to the standard of a reasonable person."[33] The police claim that their role is simply to arrest the *mak nyahs,* and it is up to the prosecutor in the court to charge them with wrongdoing. For those who have had their sex-change operation, they are subjected to the same treatment as the Muslim *mak nyahs* under Malaysian law concerning their identity cards. They will still have their original gender written on their identity card even though physically they are of the opposite gender. Although this has created problems for them in many areas, they are generally not deterred from cross-dressing or undergoing sex-change surgery. Generally, non-Muslim *mak nyahs* face less discrimination and stigmatization from the non-Muslim community. As a result, there are more non-Muslim *mak nyahs* who have professional jobs, and they are thus able to integrate better with the society.

Conclusion

The status and position of male-to-female transsexuals in Malaysia has declined since Malaysia gained its independence from the British, particularly after the fatwa condemning the behavior was decreed by the Conference of Rulers in 1983. This decline is tied directly to the revival of Islam, which has become increasingly politicized and institutionalized. The competition between rival political groups to be seen as more Islamic to gain support from the Muslim community has resulted in greater discrimination for the transsexual community.

The discrimination and lack of acceptance that the male-to-female transsexuals in Malaysia face have contributed to self-destructive behavior among the community, like drug abuse.[34] It has been estimated that about half of the *mak nyah* community and about 80 percent of transsexual sex workers are addicted to drugs. About 14 percent of the *mak nyah* community has tried committing suicide.[35] If this situation is left unchecked, it will get worse.

The transsexual phenomenon is a complex one that involves both biological and social factors as has been demonstrated in many studies. Almost all *mak nyahs* want to continue to live their lives as they do since they have a deep feeling that they are women, despite the fact they are not accepted as such by society. Instead of pushing the 10,000 or so *mak nyahs* to the fringes of society, it is time to accept them back into the fold of society by understanding and helping them. Malaysian society will only change its negative perception of the *mak nyahs* if the government first takes the lead to change its own negative perception of them, afford them equal rights, and give them the much needed support that is due all other citizens of the country.

Notes

1. *Syariah* law is Islamic law, divinely ordained, that governs both the public and private lives of Muslims (see Nair, *Islam in Malaysian Foreign Policy,* 277). The main sources of Islamic law are the Koran and the *Hadith.* The Koran is the Muslim holy book or immutable body of revelations received by the Prophet Mohammad. The *Hadith* is the "tradition" or record of action or sayings of the Prophet. *Syariah* law is implemented by the *Syariah* Court in Muslim societies ("Sharia," *Free Encyclopedia*).

2. Islamic enforcement officers are from the official Islamic Department. They are given powers similar to the police to conduct raids on Muslims who are said to have violated the tenets of Islam.

3. Ruslan, *Sejarah Malaysia*, 193.

4. Means, *Malaysian Politics*, 103.

5. Crouch, *Government and Society in Malaysia*, 171–72.

6. Munro-Kua, *Authoritarian Populism in Malaysia*, 118.

7. Crouch, *Government and Society*, 168.

8. Kamarulnizam, *The Politics of Islam in Contemporary Malaysia*, 45.

9. Means, *Malaysian Politics*, 61–69.

10. Jomo and Ahmad, "Malaysia's Islamic Movements," 93.

11. Ibid., 102.

12. Milne and Mauzy, *Malaysian Politics under Mahathir*, 86.

13. Aziz, *Mahathir's Paradigm Shift*, 67.

14. The conditions for *khalwat* are provided under the *Syariah* Criminal Provisions Act (Federal Territories), section 27: "Any man who is found together with one or more women, not being his wife or *mahram;* or any woman who is found together with one or more men, not being her husband or *mahram,* in any secluded place or in a house or room under circumstances which may give rise to suspicion that they are engaged in immoral acts shall be guilty for an offence and shall on conviction be liable to a fine not exceeding RM3,000 or to imprisonment for a term not exceeding two years or to both" (Women's Aid Organisation, "Caught in Close Proximity for 'Immoral' Acts [*khalwat*]").

15. The Malaysian monarchy is a unique system: its king or *Yang Di Pertuan Agung* is elected every five years from the nine Malay sultans from nine states. Malaysia practices constitutional monarchy. The king does not have absolute powers excepting certain powers conferred by Parliament on him under federal laws provided in the federal constitution; likewise for the sultans of the nine states.

16. Munro-Kua, *Authoritarian Populism*, 120.

17. Means, *Malaysian Politics*, 103.

18. Crouch, *Government and Society*, 172.

19. Teh, *The Mak Nyahs*.

20. Ibid.

21. Ibid.

22. *Mak andams* are employed for the day to attend to brides at weddings. They attend to the brides' makeup, their wedding clothes, the wedding ceremony, etc.

23. *Joget* is a traditional Malay dance. In the old days, there were *joget* dance halls where the *mak myahs* could work as *joget* dancers.

24. A fatwa is a religious ruling or legal opinion, usually relying on the expertise of the *ulama* (learned religious authority) and considered legally binding upon Muslims (see Nair, *Islam in Malaysian Foreign Policy*, 276–77).

25. *Hadith* is the "tradition" or record of actions or sayings of the Prophet (see Nair, *Islam in Malaysian Foreign Policy*, 276).

26. Abdul Aziz, "Islam sebagai Ad-Din" (Islam as Ad-Din), 3.

27. Wan Azmi, *Dilema Mak Nyah* (Dilemmas of a *mak nyah*), 6.

28. In Malaysia, with Islam as the official religion, there are two sets of laws governing its people: (1) the civil law inherited from the British, which applies to everyone, and (2) *Syariah* law, which is applicable only to the Muslim community. Muslims are subject to both sets of laws.

29. Teh, "Understanding the problems of *Mak Nyahs*," 176–79.

30. Teh, *The Mak Nyahs*, 114.

31. In Buddhism, our *karma* can be good or bad depending on our deeds (see Teh, *The Mak Nyahs*, 119). Both good and bad *karma* will produce rebirth—the good will provide conditions that are favorable in our subsequent birth while the bad will produce the contrary effect.

32. Teh, *The Mak Nyahs*, 120.

33. Ibid., 131.

34. Teh, "HIV/AIDS Risk among Male-to-Female Transsexuals."

35. Teh, *The Mak Nyahs*, 88.

References

Abdul Aziz Haji Hanafi. "Islam sebagai Ad-Din" [Islam as Ad-Din]. Paper presented at the seminar Mak Nyah Ke Arah Menentukan Identiti Dan Status Mak Nyah Dalam Masyarakat. Law Faculty, University of Malaya, Kuala Lumpur, October 1987.

Aziz Zarisa Ahmad. *Mahathir's Paradigm Shift*. Taiping, Malaysia: Firma Malaysia Publishing, 1997.

Crouch, Harold. *Government and Society in Malaysia*. Ithaca: Cornell University Press, 1996.

Herdt, Gilbert. *Third Sex, Third Gender: Beyond Sexual Dimorphism in Culture and History*. New York: Zone Books, 1994.

Jomo, Kwame Sundram, and Ahmad Shabery Cheek. "Malaysia's Islamic Movements." In Joel S. Kahn and Francis Kok Wah Loh, eds., *Fragmented Vision: Culture and Politics in Contemporary Malaysia*. Sydney: Allen & Unwin, 1992.

Kamarulnizam, Abdullah. *The Politics of Islam in Contemporary Malaysia*. Bangi, Malaysia: Penerbit Universiti Kebangsaan Malaysia, 2002.

Khairuddin, Yusof, Wah Yun Low, and Yut Lin Wong. "Social and Health Review of Transsexuals." Paper presented at the seminar Mak Nyah Ke Arah Menentukan Identiti Dan Status Mak Nyah Dalam Masyarakat, Law Faculty, Universiti of Malaya, Kuala Lumpur, October 1987.

Means, Gordon. *Malaysian Politics: The Second Generation*. Singapore: Oxford University Press, 1991.

Milne, Robert, and Diane Mauzy. *Malaysian Politics under Mahathir*. London: Routledge, 1999.

Munro-Kua, Anne. *Authoritarian Populism in Malaysia*. New York: St. Martin's Press, 1996.

Nair, Shanti. *Islam in Malaysian Foreign Policy.* London: Routledge, 1997.

Ruslan, Zainuddin. *Sejarah Malaysia* [History of Malaysia]. Shah Alam, Malaysia: Penerbit Fajar Bakti, 2003

Teh, Yik Koon. "HIV/AIDS Risk among Male-to-Female Transsexuals in Malaysia: The Social and Cultural Context." Proceedings of the U.S. National Institute of Drug Abuse Satellite Sessions in association with the XIV International AIDS Conference, Barcelona, 2002. 186–90.

———. *"Mak Nyahs* (Male Transsexuals) in Malaysia: The Influence of Culture and Religion on Their Identity." *International Journal of Transgenderism* 5, no. 3 (2001). Available at http://www.symposion.com/ijt/ijtv005n003_04.htm.

———. *The Mak Nyahs: Malaysian Male-to-Female Transsexuals.* Singapore: Eastern Universities Press (Times Publishing), 2002.

———. "Understanding the Problems of *Mak Nyahs* (Male Transsexuals) in Malaysia." *South-East Asia Research* 6, no. 2 (1998): 165–80.

Wan Azmi Ramli. *Dilema Mak Nyah: Suatu Illusi* [Dilemmas of a *mak nyah:* An illusion]. Kuala Lumpur: Utusan Publications, 1991.

"Sharia." *Free Encyclopedia.* Retrieved January 21, 2005, from http://en.wikipedia.org/wiki/Sharia.

Women's Aid Organisation. "'Caught in Close Proximity for 'Immoral' Acts (*khalwat*)." Retrieved January 25, 2005, from http://www.wao.org.my/news/20030104knowrghts_khalwat.htm.

FIVE

RECOGNITION THROUGH MIS-RECOGNITION

Masculine Women in Hong Kong

Kam Yip Lo Lucetta

People often called me Boy-head. My relatives used to call me that when I was playing, especially when I was yelling and playing rough in ball games. They actually sounded quite appreciative, and I didn't sense any derogatory tone. For example, I didn't cry when I was having an injection, and people would say, "Aiya, you're even better than boys!" When I was a kid, comments like this would make me very happy, because I took them as a compliment!

—Kit, twenty-eight years old

They [female colleagues] always thought that I was immature and had no clue how to behave like a lady. They naturally assumed that I wasn't dating anyone. When they spotted my new ring a few months later, their reaction was like, "Wow! How come you are wearing a ring?" They teased me about it. To them, the ring was obviously evidence of dating. I think they were overreacting, and I wonder if they were teasing me for dating or simply trying to figure out the gender of my date.

—Ted, twenty-four years old

For years I have noticed how my many masculine-styled female friends cause scenes in women's washrooms, are addressed as men by shopkeepers, and are scrutinized from head to toe by strangers on the street. More than once, my own androgynous gender presentation has resulted in similar public mis-recognition. As time passed, my curiosity about these women grew. I was eager to know about their experiences of being a differently gendered woman and how they manage to live through all the gender scrutiny and washroom dramas. Hence, I carried out research on them (and, simultaneously, research on my own masculine self).

Here I report on part of a research project I carried out between February 2002 and April 2003 in Hong Kong on the gender negotiations of eighteen Chinese women, all biological women and self-identified as women, who have been mistaken for men throughout or during certain periods of their lives (for some, the "mistake" was intended or anticipated). The gender mis-identifications happened everywhere, including in washrooms, restaurants, gas stations, on the streets, or at job interviews. I treat gender identification in this study as a continual process of negotiation. As Judith Butler puts it, gender is an assignment (or reassignment) of the tools that are available to us in any given culture.[1] We are restricted by the number of tools available to us. Yet the ways we pick up and use the tools are possible sites for cultural resignification, new forms of recognition and identification. In this chapter, I sketch a range of gender discourses in Hong Kong that are productive or repressive of the existence of women who present themselves in styles the culture recognizes as masculine.

The Gender That Has No Name

"Masculine woman" is not a commonly used term in Hong Kong. I use this term because of the lack of positive identity labels given to masculine women in local Hong Kong society (the terminological choices available in English are also limited). There is no self-identified community of "masculine women" in Hong Kong. Informants were recruited to this project through their shared experiences of being mistaken for men and their experiences of masculine identification in different periods of their lives.

The term "masculine women" and the entire research project are partly inspired by Judith Halberstam's theorization of female masculinity.[2] Halberstam's analytic framework is particularly useful for this study. She de-naturalizes masculinity from the male body and reclaims the importance of forms of masculinities displayed on female bodies for changing cultural interpretations of masculinity. In this study, I treat masculinity as a set of gender attributes that are defined by a given culture in a specific period of time. Masculinity can be actualized on all kinds of bodies, and each contributes to the overall understanding of the discourses of masculinity at work in a given culture. The current body of research on female masculinity in Hong Kong focuses on local masculine lesbian genders.[3] My research project attempted to study the gender identifications and negotiations of ethnically

Chinese masculine women in Hong Kong, both inside and outside the lesbian community and with or without same-sex desires or experiences. The study shows that masculine-styled or -identified women are not restricted to lesbians, but can also be found in women with other sexual preferences.

Using snowball sampling, I identified several possible sites where masculine women could be found. The choices were based on the popular imagination in local society and my own observations. Sampling sites included local women's nongovernmental organizations, professional women's groups, local lesbian communities, women artists' groups (including Cantonese opera societies), sportswomen's groups, women in the armed forces, Buddhist women's groups, and so on. I was open to any referral by informants that met the criteria, that is, women who have been mistaken for men or boys in Hong Kong, who have been living in Hong Kong for a significant period of time, and who grew up in an ethnically Chinese family. Face-to-face interviews were conducted individually with each informant. All interviews were conducted in Cantonese (the major Chinese dialect spoken in Hong Kong).

The eighteen informants' ages ranged from twenty-one to forty-eight. Most of them were born and grew up in Hong Kong and all of them are ethnic Chinese. All informants had completed at least secondary education, and eleven of them had tertiary education or above. When asked about sexual orientation, eight of them told me that they preferred men as their partners (one preferred celibacy due to her religion). The rest either preferred female only or female in most cases. Six informants identified themselves as lesbians or referred to themselves in lesbian identity categories (such as TB,[4] butch). One informant was in a heterosexual marriage. The rest were either single or had female or male partners. Half of the informants had undergone periods or stages of change over the years in their gender presentations or gender identifications. Among them, a few had abandoned masculine gender presentation by the time of the interview. The names of informants used in this chapter are all pseudonyms. They were either made up by the informants themselves (for example, Balance, Caterpillar, Mo) or by me. For pseudonyms that were chosen by me, I used masculine English names if the original ones were masculine (for example, Ted and Ken). I used feminine English names if the original ones were feminine (for example, Grace and May). And for those whose original names were gender neutral, I used gender-neutral pseudonyms (such as YY) or names in Cantonese (such as Kit).

Based on the interviews and my own experience as a cultural insider, I have identified a number of discourses that are relevant to the social existence of masculine women in Hong Kong. I categorized those discourses into two groups, the enabling and the disabling (see table 5.1).

Discourses can be both enabling and disabling in different contexts. They offer a social position to subjects, although that position and recognition might not be the one expected by the subjects themselves. Recognition and mis-recognition can be initiated at the same time. Therefore, the categorization of "enabling" or "disabling" discourses for masculine women is not an absolute and immutable one. The defining line is dependent on context; any discourse is simultaneously repressive and productive of subject formation. Different gender discourses in a culture can also be in conflict with each other. The social recognition and repression as well as the self-interpretation of masculine women always involve the working together of a number of discourses that are not always consistent in logic or in harmony with each other. The categorizations applied here are more an attempt to differentiate between current interpretations deeming masculine women as socially acceptable and those deeming them unacceptable. Discourses in both categories can be activated simultaneously in the process of meaning production. In the following section, I will discuss the various discourses with reference to the real-life experiences of the informants.

The Cultural Superiority of Masculinity

The cultural meaning of "masculinity" is twofold. The commonsense definition of masculinity in most male supremacist cultures tends to foreground the gender attributes of biological men; masculinity tends to be defined in relation

Table 5.1: Enabling and Disabling Discourses on Masculine Women in Hong Kong

Enabling Discourses	Disabling Discourses
1. The cultural superiority of masculinity	Masculine women as disqualified adults
2. Tomboy as a temporary phase before mature femininity	Masculine women as failed women
3. The degendering of aged women	
4. Masculine women as lesbians	
5. Defeminization as a self-defense strategy against male sexual assault	Women who dress and behave like men as pathological
6. Women who behave androgynously as capable workers	Women who dress and behave like men as wanting to be men
7. Masculine women as easygoing	

to its opposite category of femininity (foregrounding the gender attributes of biological women). Gender attributes that are more culturally acclaimed and socially productive tend to be assigned to men and naturalized as male attributes, while those opposite and less valued gender attributes tend to be categorized under the sign of femininity or female. In this way, male dominance or masculine superiority is reinforced, and the system of hierarchical genders is naturalized. Another aspect of the meaning of masculinity in a male-dominant culture is that masculine attributes are perceived as a category of ideal *human* attributes. What are culturally assigned as *masculine* qualities (always implied to belong to biological males) are presented as *universal* human ideals.

In Hong Kong, these two interpretations of masculinity coexist and are used in combination. Male dominance and male privilege are still widespread in contemporary Hong Kong society. This is evident in the predominance of males in senior professional and managerial positions in the job market, and the widespread role of women as homemakers, regardless of their employment status, as illustrated by the declining labor force participation of women after the age of thirty, given that most believe that women should get married before or when they turn thirty.[5] Male dominance is also evident in the domestic sphere. Men are expected to be the major breadwinner in a household and therefore usually receive more respect from other dependent family members. In younger generations, there is a trend toward a more egalitarian division of labor between husband and wife. However, a married woman is still expected to be the major homemaker and caretaker of the old, young, and sick members of the family. Those domestic labors culturally assigned to women are always viewed as less respectable.[6] The patriarchal culture of local society is also exemplified by the preference for sons and the higher career expectations placed on them by parents. This is less evident nowadays, for younger parents. Yet the preference for male offspring and the higher social expectations on male children were witnessed by many of my project's informants as they grew up.

It was common for many informants in this study to condemn qualities (they perceived to be) particular to women, or qualities that are culturally assigned as "feminine" and, on the other hand, to aspire to qualities that are culturally assigned to men. And yet, for most informants, this did not equate to an admiration of any men in real life or a tendency to follow men as role models. The condemned "feminine" qualities included being gossipy, physically and psychologically weak, overindulgent in external beauty, indecisive, submissive, timid, and so on. These attributes are all common stereotypes imposed on women. Under such a cultural presupposition, women showing "masculine" attributes (or nonfeminine manners) are more likely to win social acceptance or even appreciation in local society. As related by Kit in the first epigraph of this chapter, her tomboyism in childhood was appreciated by her family.

It is evident that there is a higher cultural tolerance (or even acceptance) of masculinity in teenage girls. "*Boy-head*" (*Nam chai tou*) is a popular Cantonese colloquial term widely used to describe tomboyish girls in local society. More often used as an adjective, it can also be used as a noun. Compared to the term "tomboy" in Western contexts, *boy-head* is much less frequently used as an identity. But most teenage girls who are familiar with the tomboy culture in schools refer to *boy-head* girls in school as tomboys or sometimes as abbreviated "TB." *Tomboy* is a recognized masculine gender in all-girls' schools in Hong Kong. When tomboys are contrasted with feminine teenage boys, the cultural tolerance of tomboyism becomes even more evident. Girls' engagement in activities such as rough ball games, culturally regarded as boys' activities, stirs up far less anxiety than boys' engagement in playing with dolls or wearing makeup, regarded as conventional girls' activities. Ted (twenty-four years old) recalled that she was idolized by girls in and outside her school when she was a member of the school basketball team (which Ted termed "the breeding ground for TBs" in girls' schools). In cultures that favor masculinity and operate under patriarchal logic, to be a woman (a culturally inferior gender group) with masculine attributes is a move up in the social structure, whereas to be a man (a culturally superior gender group) with feminine attributes (or even dressing style) is a move downward. As a pre-mature group, tomboys can therefore gain a positive social position in a pro-masculine culture. They can enjoy the freedom and social recognition that this culture grants to biological males. Gin (thirty-eight years old) recalled how she consciously chose to be a tomboy in order to achieve a "higher social rank" when she was a student in an all-girl secondary school:

> Although it is a mere change of wardrobe and hairstyle, the physical change itself was like a ritual. Thereafter, I was transformed into an "honorary" man, or a man ritually. Everything turned out better. There was more freedom for me. I could sit in any position I like and even talk loudly. At that time, I was quite confused and wasn't sure if I want to be a TB[7] or a guy. I thought being a guy would be better as the social status is higher. It never occurred to me that I could obtain a higher social status by simply changing the way I dressed.

Tomboy as a Temporary Phase before Mature Femininity

Tomboyism in teenage girls in Hong Kong usually does not arouse much gender anxiety. There is an understanding of tomboyism in local society as a sign of the immaturity or pre-adult status of teenage girls. As my study demonstrates, tomboy identification among teenage girl students in most all-girl schools and some coeducational schools has existed for many decades in Hong Kong. Indeed, tomboy identification remains an identifiable gender and erotic identity in many secondary schools to this day. The social acceptance of tomboy behavior, however, depends almost entirely on the belief that tomboyism is a temporary phenomenon that does not continue into adult womanhood. This belief is also prevalent in the subculture of schoolgirls themselves. To them, leaving the identity of tomboy is a rite of passage to mature femininity. The ritual leaving is characterized by the taking up of (or the "resuming" of) feminine gender styles. Externally the transition is typified by wearing longer hair and putting on more feminine attire such as dresses, and internally it entails taking up a more conventionally defined female gender role. For some, the leaving also includes a conscious change of sexual object choice; that is, it is sometimes coupled with the end of teenage lesbianism. Given the highly interactive relationship between sexual desire and gender behavior under the regulation of heteronormativity, it is not surprising to find that the successful performance of normative femininity needs to be accomplished through the "correct" choice of the gender of sexual partner. The regulatory force is strongest when teenage schoolgirls are about to graduate and enter adulthood. At that time, they prepare themselves to enter the "real" adult world, which is undoubtedly a heterosexual one. For some of them, this might indicate an urgent need to conform to the norms of the "real" outside world, and hence the farewell of the "fantasized" world of "tomboys" and "girls" in school.

Teenage tomboyism is thought of as a temporary stage prior to mature femininity. In other words, mature femininity is defined by the ritualized closure of tomboy identification, and in some cases teenage lesbian relationships. On the one hand, such a belief enables tomboy girls to exist relatively free of punishment. On the other hand, it makes the continuity of masculine identification into female adulthood, and the social recognition of teenage lesbian relationships and identifications, much more difficult to sustain.

The Degendering of Aged Women

The regulatory effects of gender conformity on aged women are relatively less severe than on younger women. Their social position is less defined by their gender than by their seniority in age and familial positions. Older women are granted more freedom to engage in less feminine acts such as speaking loudly and more assertively, being less attentive to their external appearance, walking with larger strides, and taking up leadership roles in family or other social interactions. This discourse on aged women has the effect that when masculine women get older, they may be mistaken for men less frequently and can attain greater social acceptance.

Mo (forty-eight years old) adopted a masculine style of dress for most of her life. When she was approaching middle age and was gaining weight, occurrences of being mistaken for a man in public places became less frequent. The physical changes that accompanied aging made her appear to be more feminine. Although she dressed in the same way as before, she was now more frequently addressed as a woman by others in public. Compared with the accounts of other informants who were younger but had the same body size as Mo, this situation illustrates the discursive effect of degendering on older masculine women.

Yet it is also common to categorize middle-aged or older women according to familial or kinship identities. Older women are always assumed to be married. This leads to a disabling effect on the recognition of some masculine women's gender and sexual identity. To degender and at the same time assign aged women to traditional heterosexual familial identities can lead to another kind of mis-recognition, especially for those who self-identify as lesbians or have same-sex partners. Although the degendering or desexualization of aged women allows older women in general more freedom in their gender presentations, this freedom is interpreted only within the rigid framework of heterosexuality. Mo was a living example of the dual effect of this gender discourse. She identified herself as a butch woman and a woman who loves women. In her late forties, Mo was less frequently mistaken for a male. But for the first time in her life, she was referred to by strangers as a mother. To make matters worse, she was even mistaken for her younger female partner's mother:

> Few people call me "Mister/Sir" now that I have gained weight. I was really upset when people once mistook me for Marsha's [Mo's girlfriend] mom! It was very annoying. Am I really that feminine? Again, this is a question of identity. I hate it when people see me as a *Si-Nai* [*middle-aged woman* in Cantonese, with a slightly derogatory connotation] or an old lady . . . My breasts are very obvious because I am fat. I think that's the reason why people sometimes call me *Tai-Tai* [Mrs.] on the street. When you are fat, people just naturally call you *Si-Nai* regardless of the way you dress. This upsets me a lot and makes me feel very old. This has never happened before. Even in my

thirties, people used to think I was twenty-something . . . Body shape does matter in people's perception.

By being recognized as a mother, Mo's sexual identity is denied and her masculine gender identification goes unrecognized.

It seems that the period between teen years and late middle age is the most forcefully regulated period for women's gender presentation in Hong Kong. The relatively tolerant reception of teenage tomboyism and masculinity in senior-aged women demonstrates that gender-regulatory power is most severe during women's peak reproductive years, when femininity and reproduction are tightly interlocked and regulated. During the pre-mature and postreproductive years, women are allowed to have a relatively freer choice of gender expression and identification. The tolerance for tomboys and senior-aged masculine women is actually still operating *within* the governing power of heterosexuality.

Masculine Women as Lesbians

Since the late 1980s, public sensitivity toward homosexuality in Hong Kong has grown. During the 1990s, there was a rapid development of lesbian and gay organizations and a surge of media interest in lesbian and gay topics. This sudden public and media attention can be partly attributed to the decriminalization of (male) homosexuality in Hong Kong in 1991. The increasing visibility of lesbians and gays in public space and media since the early 1990s has had a profound effect on society on the understanding of homosexuality and the formation of local lesbian and gay identities.

The emergence of *Tongzhi,* a local identity term for LGBTQs, discourses in Hong Kong during the 1980s, together with the proliferation of Tongzhi public spaces such as lesbian and gay social gatherings, political actions, and bars and cafes, has encouraged the development of Tongzhi gender and sexual identities.[8] The development of lesbian subcultural gender identifications such as *TB, TBG,* and *Pure* opens up additional gender possibilities and offers new social recognition for members of the lesbian community. *TB* is the term commonly used in the local lesbian community to refer to women who behave and dress in masculine ways and are sexually attracted to feminine women. *TBG* is the abbreviation of "TB's girl" or "TB girl." It is the opposite gender category of TB. TBGs are sexually attracted to masculine women (TB). *Pure* is a gender label for lesbian women whose gender style is ambiguous or androgynous and cannot be categorized as TB or TBG, and who might not restrict their sexual object choice to either TB or TBG. The 1990s witnessed a vibrant development of new genders and erotic identities among lesbian women in Hong Kong. However, *TB*, *TBG*, and *Pure* are the three most prominent local lesbian gender identities. The expansion of the lesbian community and its elaborated gender subculture has significantly increased its visibility in public space. Masculine lesbians or TBs are especially visible and prone to attract public attention. Unsurprisingly, masculine lesbians are usually the only image of lesbian women that appear in the media.

In my study, it became evident that local society tends to associate masculine women with lesbianism. All informants except two had been recognized as or implied by others to be lesbians. The availability of lesbian subcultural discourse was productive for some lesbian informants in interpreting their gender identities. The popular association of lesbianism with masculine gender identification made it easier for them to accept the identity label of lesbian and the gender label of TB. The interaction of sexual desire and gender identification is one of the most prominent aspects of their gender identification. Their self-identification tends to be expressed through the language of available sexuality discourses.

The repressive side of understanding masculine women in terms of recognizable sexual identities is evident in women who do not self-identify as lesbians. In such cases, the same public recognition becomes a mis-recognition. At a personal level, mis-recognition can incur bitter and prolonged discursive struggles and resistance against the imposed label. The experience of Gene (twenty-four years old) in her secondary school years was a typical case of being called into a "wrong" subject position:

> Girls from girls' schools always assume I am a *les* [a local short form for *lesbian*] or TB . . . When I was a kid, people used to call me *boy-head* all the time. To me, this only meant they thought my hairstyle was like a boy's. But TB is actually something totally different. I gradually learnt the true meaning of TB. I tried to figure out the difference between a TB and myself from their point of view. And I don't think I fit their description of a TB. I was never like that. By their definition, TB is someone who falls for girls, but I do not. I'm not even big on dating. To me, TBs always surround themselves with a crowd of girls. They enjoy attracting different kinds of girls and take pride in being womanizers. I consider myself very different from them, and I wonder why people use the term TB [to describe me].

At a broader cultural level, the appropriation by sexual discourses of gender identities can result in a reduction of possible identity categories and a premature closure of new gender identity formations. Lesbian discourse and its cultural (stereotypical) interpretations can both initiate and hinder the formation of new gender identities of masculine women.

Defeminization as a Self-Defense Strategy against Male Sexual Assault

Being defined as the physically weaker and sexually vulnerable sex in a male-dominant society, it is not uncommon for women to desexualize themselves in situations where the danger of sexual assault is present. One popular way to desexualize the female body is to dress in men's clothes. The practice of female cross-dressing as a shield to engage in activities outside the protected domestic domain can be traced as far back as imperial China. There is a rich archive of literary texts of stories of cross-dressing women participating in public events (in most cases, festive markets), joining the male-only army, and undertaking long and always dangerous journeys.

In contemporary Hong Kong society, the assumption that women are the (sexually) vulnerable sex is still prevalent. For some informants, desexualization or defeminization is used as a protective tactic against male sexual assaults. Wearing trousers and cutting their hair short are common ways that some women desexualize and so protect themselves, rendering their feminine bodily characteristics less obvious. For some, this also entails adopting masculine mannerisms such as using foul language and smoking in public so as to make themselves less (hetero)sexually attractive.

Ken (thirty-three years old) had been sexually harassed by men when she was a child. Those experiences led her to believe that women are sexually vulnerable and signs of femininity such as wearing dresses and having long hair would incite men to harass her. She confessed in her interview with me that picking up masculine manners and dressing style was a protective strategy:

> When I was a kid, I reckoned it was better to be a boy because you don't get bullied so easily. Girls always fall victim of bullies at school, as well as all other places, even at work. Most of the time boys bully girls . . . you're less likely to be bullied when you look and act like a boy. Why? Because first they have to figure out whether you're a boy or a girl. Then, if they find out you are not a "real" girl, what's the fun of bullying you at all? If they want to bully somebody, they'd rather pick on a typical girl. I reckon that was their rationale. If I put myself in their shoes, I would rather bully, or simply tease, a typical girl in a dress than someone sexually ambiguous. When you act like

a boy, that is you swear and smoke hard, you sort of protect yourself from bullies. That's all there is to it and it works! If you have boyish short hair, you can rest assured that nobody is going to attack you from behind. They will go find another easier target. It is safer to look like a boy on the street. Once, there was this girl walking on the street and a guy walked by and gave her one of those nasty looks. If it were I walking beside him, he'd definitely not give me that kind of look.

A similar interpretation was also provided by Caterpillar (thirty-four years old) who preferred to dress in dark colors and loosely fitting clothes:

Nowadays women's clothes are mostly tight fitting and the colors are too outrageous. I prefer darker colors as they're subtler. When you are wearing something that tight, people are no longer looking at *you* but at your body. There was a time when I felt that people were looking more at my breasts than my face. I felt like I was being involuntarily sucked into their sexual fantasy. This kind of invisible sexual harassment is really horrible. That's why I don't like tight-fitting clothes. You feel more comfortable both psychologically and physically in loosely fitting clothes.

Women Who Dress Themselves Androgynously as Capable Workers

Masculine women are thought to be tough, capable, efficient, and reliable at work. The positive valorization of masculine attributes in the work context interplays with the discourse of "superior masculinity" discussed earlier and also with the Chinese traditional gender discourse of femininity as belonging to the domestic domain (*nei*) and masculinity as belonging to the public domain (*wai*). The interplay between these discourses leads to the cultural logic that to be a socially recognized working subject, one has to display more masculine attributes than feminine ones.

YY (twenty-one years old) had been positively regarded by teachers for her working ability throughout her secondary school years. She interpreted herself as having the advantages of both masculinity and femininity. She was proud to tell how she was appreciated at work:

Neither boys nor girls wanted to take up the job, so I was always the one who got things done. In my seven years of secondary school education, I was made class captain for six years and class chairperson for one year. I got tons of work done. Then I ran for the students' council in Form 4 and I was appointed head prefect in Form 6. I was working all the time. My teachers appreciated me. They certainly would have liked to see more of my kind help-ing out. This is because I'm quite detail minded and willing. They reckoned it would benefit the school to have more girls with this sort of double ability, functionally speaking.

Masculine Women as Easygoing

The gender ambiguity of masculine women sometimes has the effect of dis-solving the gender boundary in mixed social groups. Their gender ambiguity enables them to mix more easily into the social groups of both sexes. Yet in the aspect of socializing, there also exist certain repressive discourses such as masculine women envy men, they are sexually threatening to (feminine) women, and they are hostile to men.

Some of the informants mixed very well socially with both sexes. Jon (thirty-five years old) was the easygoing buddy to both female and male colleagues:

> Girls usually don't smoke. My male colleagues will ask me to go to the stairwell or lift corridor for a smoke and we will chitchat. They talk to me in a coarse style and use foul language, which doesn't bother me at all. With the girls, if we go shopping, it will be "You carry the bags." If there're two bags, one bigger one smaller, I actually don't mind taking the bigger one. Sometimes people will say, "You're so stupid!" right to my face. A girl would feel bad. But my response is, "Oh yeah! And how smart are you?" I can therefore mix with my colleagues more easily.

The masculinity of the informants becomes a sign of social accessibility in day-to-day interactions. Their gender transgression has an effect of dissolving the social segregation of the two sexes. Their popularity in peer groups there-fore offers them a position accommodating of their gender ambiguity.

Masculine Women as Disqualified Adults and Failed Women

Failed womanhood is parallel to failed adulthood. These discourses inter-play with the (enabling) discourse of tomboyism. As discussed earlier, the cultural belief that tomboyism is a temporary phase before mature woman-hood is repressive to masculine-identified women in a way that makes it more difficult for them to attain a socially acceptable position when they enter adulthood. Extended tomboyism is interpreted as failed adulthood, since tomboyism is thought to be performed only by teenage girls. A mature woman demonstrating masculine attributes will be regarded as refusing to take up the adult role and responsibility that are always characterized by gender conformity and restriction.

To enter mature womanhood in a patriarchal culture always implies living with more restrictions and less freedom of mobility. The rejection of those gender restrictions will again prevent masculine women from attaining a recognized gender and social position in the adult world. They have to engage in constant struggles to obtain social recognition and new gender identities. For informants who prefer women as their sexual object choice, their survival into adulthood was even more difficult, since they did not have the help of heterosexual desire to assert and reinforce their feminine gender identification.

Balance's (twenty-three years old) masculine gender style had been violently condemned by her father for as long as she could remember. But she still boldly demonstrated her masculinity into adulthood. She was the only informant in this study who dressed unambiguously in men's fashion. She would wear a tie and men's suit to work. Her extremely masculine dressing style aroused much anxiety, discomfort, and challenge from people around her. Moreover, her young age and childish face made her even more easily categorized as a woman who had failed to attain mature femininity. "My face is a bit different from my [dress] style. My style is quite old-fashioned but my face is very childish. People take one look at me and will assume that I'm immature. They reckon that you're immature because you dress like this even though you know you're a girl."

Her overt masculinity and mannish attire also caused discomfort and negative reception within the lesbian community, of which she was an active member at the time of interview. Overt masculinity or "heterosexual" masculine identification and desire (such as preferring heterosexual women over lesbian women as partners) are usually not positively received in the local lesbian community. This is regarded as a denial of the female gender or politically immature behavior (characterized by a confusion of sexual or gender identification) and therefore regarded as a woman in denial of her "real" gender identity.

Women Who Dress and Behave Like Men as Pathological

Pathologization is a strategy used by dominant groups to marginalize culturally unrecognizable subjects. Women who challenge the "privileges" that are socially assigned to men (such as wearing "men's" attire, courting women, taking up "men's" gender roles) are often defined through pseudo-medical discourses (for instance, being labeled as "psychologically sick") and illegitimate gender categories (such as being labeled as a "non-man" or "non-woman"). Many informants mentioned being ridiculed and harassed on the street by strangers for their gender ambiguity. Their gender transgression and in some cases sexual transgression can only be understood by heterosexual logic as deviant, for they have violated the gender norms and in some cases have even broken the sexual law of heterosexuality. The only way for a heterosexist culture to appropriate non-heterosexually defined genders is to deprive them of any positive social recognition.

Women Who Dress and Behave Like Men as Wanting to Be Men

In negative discourses, masculine women are viewed by other women as sexually aggressive and threatening (this interplays with the conventional association of female masculinity and lesbianism), while by men, they are assumed to be hostile and competitive. When certain sets of behaviors and roles are culturally assigned only to males, the infringement upon male privileges by women is a socially condemned act that most often will be interpreted as a threat to the harmony of the two (heterosexual) genders, and the fault will be laid at the feet of the woman who made the infringement.

The effect of this cultural assumption was particularly felt by informants whose masculinity was more overtly displayed. The tension with males was always most obvious at the work place, as related by Ken and Balance:

> *Ken:* My male colleagues are more or less hostile to me and I can't help it. They're able to do what I can do and vice versa. If they can't stand me, I can't help it. Why can't they stand me? It's just because they feel threatened. If you couldn't do what they can do, then they wouldn't be so hostile.
>
> *Balance:* I didn't sense anything wrong when I first started to work. What men can do, I can do. I didn't think there was a problem. Later I found out that guys don't like this at all. Now if I need to carry heavy stuff or get something high up, I will ask for a male colleague's help. Men have pride. Sometimes you just have to consider their feelings.

Recognition through Mis-recognition

The gender experiences of the informants in this study demonstrate the various everyday ways that individuals use to preserve and reinforce the inner integrity of their gender identification, and also shows their individual use of the cultural resources or tools available to them to attain social recognition. The ways informants interpret and make use of these cultural resources and gender discourses open up new discursive possibilities for female genders.

The lived experiences of the informants in this study show that their very social existence is first inaugurated by the mis-recognition as the other sex. There is a discrepancy between their self-recognition and the public recognition imposed on them. Most of them struggled with public identity labels and stereotypical assumptions. And most of them did not develop into what they were recognized as by other members of society. With respect to their gender identifications, it seems that in a local context there is a lack of citational paradigms for masculine women to refer to for their gender constructions. They were repeatedly appropriated by other members of society into positions formulated through the dominant heterosexual gender discourse. Informants also interpreted their own masculinities through popular stereotypical figures such as the easygoing buddy or the capable working woman. But aside from these, other recognizable female masculine gender paradigms are absent in the local context, except the subcultural gender identifications in the local lesbian community. This explains why the "citational recognition" of masculine women in Hong Kong is always associated with female homosexuality. It also explains why this very study has been read simply by some as a research project on lesbian women. This was an oversimplification I had to combat all the time throughout my research.

The kind of gender mis-recognition discussed in this study has many implications. First, it demonstrates the limitations of existing gender discourses. The strictly polarized genders of man and woman as defined by the heterosexual framework are incapable of accommodating those genders that belong to neither of these categories. The continual appropriation of subjects into rigid male or female genders can cause those with "undefined" or "ambiguous" gender expressions or identifications to be deprived of positive social recognition.

However, the mis-recognition is also enabling in the sense that it does inaugurate subjects into *new* social positions. Through gender mis-recognition, masculine women have become a unique category of gendered subject, for they are distinguishable from the rest who have their genders "correctly" recognized by other social members. The mis-recognition is a disruption to the dominant gender framework since it demonstrates the failure of the existing system to account for all of the genders that actually exist, even though the new social recognitions of masculine women enabled by the identification mistake are not always celebrated by the women themselves, not to say the danger of being reduced to a monolithic group with no individual differences. Yet gender mis-recognition has at least made masculine women physically visible in the public eye. It is hoped that by proliferating the life experiences of people with nonnormative genders, their cultural visibility and acceptance will be enhanced. And finally a more diverse gender culture can be developed in society.

Notes

1. Butler, *Gender Trouble.*

2. Halberstam, *Female Masculinity.*

3. For examples, see Kam, "Gender: TB"; Lai, "Lesbian Masculinities"; and Tong, "Being a Tomboy."

4. *TB* stands for tomboy. TB is the queer gender identity commonly used in local lesbian community for women who behave and dress in masculine ways, and who are erotically interested in feminine women. I discuss TB in greater length with other local lesbian gender identities in later paragraphs.

5. See Mak and Chung, "Education and Labour Force Participation"; Westwood, "The Politics of Opportunity." See also the information provided by the charts of "Working Population by Sex and Occupation, 2001" and "Labour Force Participation Rates, 1991 and 2001," in *Population Census 2001: Graphic Guides.*

6. Choi and Lee, "The Hidden Abode of Domestic Labour."

7. In this quotation, *TB* is the abbreviation of tomboy. But Gin was using it more as the teenage tomboy identification that was popular in girls' schools at the time Gin was a student (the 1970s) than as the community label used today by lesbian women.

8. *Tongzhi* literally means "comrade." The term had been popularly used in the revolutionary context in early-twentieth-century China and later was adopted into the revolutionary language of Communist China. It is commonly held that Tongzhi was first used by Edward Lam, a local artist/writer and the then director of Hong Kong Gay Film Festival, to refer to sexual minorities. Since then Tongzhi has been rapidly popularized in Hong Kong, Taiwan, and later mainland China as an identity for LGBTQs.

References

Butler, Judith. *Gender Trouble: Feminism and the Subversion of Identity.* New York: Routledge, 1999.

Choi, Po-king, and Ching-kwan Lee. "The Hidden Abode of Domestic Labour: The Case of Hong Kong." In Fanny M. Cheung, ed., *Engendering Hong Kong Society: A Gender Perspective of Women's Status.* Hong Kong: Chinese University Press, 1997.

Halberstam, Judith. *Female Masculinity,* Durham: Duke University Press, 1998.

Kam, Yip Lo Lucetta. "Gender: TB" [*TB Zhe Xing Bei*]. *E-Journal on Hong Kong Cultural and Social Studies* 1, no. 1: 167–81 (in Chinese), 2002.

Lai, Yuen Ki. "Lesbian Masculinities: Identity and Body Construction among Tomboys in Hong Kong." M.Phil. thesis, Chinese University of Hong Kong, 2004.

Mak, Grace C. L., and Yue-ping Chung. "Education and Labour Force Participation of Women in Hong Kong." In Fanny M. Cheung, ed., *Engendering Hong Kong Society: A Gender Perspective of Women's Status.* Hong Kong: Chinese University Press, 1997.

Tong, Ka-man. "Being a Tomboy: An Ethnographic Research on Young Schoolgirls in Hong Kong." M.Phil. thesis, University of Hong Kong, 2001.

Westwood, Robert I., et al. "The Politics of Opportunity: Gender and Work in Hong Kong. Part I: The Gendered Segmentation of the Labour Market." In Fanny M. Cheung, ed., *Engendering Hong Kong Society: A Gender Perspective of Women's Status.* Hong Kong: Chinese University Press, 1997.

SIX

BEING A YOUNG TOMBOY IN HONG KONG

The Life and Identity Construction of Lesbian Schoolgirls

Carmen Ka Man Tong

Vicky: We don't like boys.

Betsy: We ARE boys!

Mag: Yes! We are boys already.

Vicky: We enjoy that kind of . . . that feeling of protecting others.

Betsy: And the feeling of success, when you have chased someone.

Vicky: Yes!

Betsy: When you have just chased [someone], wow! [The feeling] is fucking great!

Mag: Not only [that], but also [women's] bodies are great, with tits and butts.

Vicky: I'm more comfortable with girls, not just because of their bodies. Don't you feel it's more comfortable with girls?

Mag: Yes, right.

Betsy: You can talk about anything.

Mag: Even about M [menstruation].

Betsy: We can be ourselves.

Tong (author): Being yourself? You are a girl. Even if you like the feeling of chasing girls and protecting others, you don't have to be a boy.

Vicky: Are you asking us to chase girls as girls? The feeling is so . . . it is so . . .

[All of them laugh in a way that implies the idea is simply ridiculous.]

—Group interview, 1998

Tomboy (TB) is a term that goes back to at least the sixteenth century, when it was used to refer to a "wild romping girl" who "behaves like a spirited or boisterous boy."[1] In numerous fictional stories, tomboys are represented as girls who dislike dresses and feminine characteristics but are spirited and adventuresome, like to move freely, and are drawn to activities associated with boys. These characteristics can also be found among the tomboys in my study. However, same-sex attraction is another major criterion for one to be considered a tomboy in Hong Kong.

In this chapter, the lives, pressures, and daily resistance of young lesbian schoolgirls will be presented. On the basis of these young lesbians' daily experiences, I want to argue that their resistance to femininity and heterosexuality serves as a means to construct and consolidate their lesbian identity; but this identity is not necessarily central since multiple identities intersect, shape, and redefine their hybrid sense of female masculinity.

The Lives of Young Lesbian Schoolgirls

The tomboys in this study[2] are highly resistant to the notion of femininity; they are very different from the conventional Hong Kong image of good schoolgirls—girls who get good academic results and are hard working, obedient, quiet, gentle, caring, and feminine. The most apparent difference is their boyish appearance—when not wearing the mandatory school uniform dresses, they wore boys' sportswear, shirts, sweaters, and baggy trousers and they had trendy, short, and boyishly styled haircuts. People often mistook them for boys at first glance. Their manners and body language were also boyish: they were rude and loud and playful most of the time; they never hesitated to boldly express themselves in public places but talked loudly and played freely like they did when they were in private. They cared little about whether people around were watching them or not. In addition, their speech also made them very different from other schoolgirls: they used foul language and slang very often (as illustrated in the dialogues transcribed below), exercising restraint only in front of prefects[3] or teachers at school.

These tomboys engaged in daily activities not commonly associated with good schoolgirls. All of them loved to play basketball, not only at school but also in a neighborhood basketball court every Friday night. They enjoyed the latter more since there were fewer restrictions—for one thing, other than playing basketball, they could chat with others whenever they wanted to and could smoke whenever they liked. Smoking was regarded as an event among these tomboys; they smoked heavily in a way that they described as *bou-jin* (literally "boiling cigarettes," a Cantonese slang expression meaning chain smoking or heavy smoking). There were different reasons for them to take up smoking as a habit, but group solidarity seemed to be a central force. Smoking and hanging out with other girls were two interlocking activities for them. After school, they first went home to get changed and then met up with their friends, both tomboys and femme girls, to chat and smoke. They would *bou-jin* for the whole evening and usually go home at around 11 p.m. The friendship network of these tomboys is large and supportive; the core group of this network consisted of six girls, all of them tomboys who described themselves as "brothers" (*hing-dai*). They were all studying or have studied at Bernard College.[4] The other members of this friendship network included the tomboys' girlfriends known as tomboy girls (TBG)[5] and other tomboys who were less close.

It might seem that these tomboys were actively resisting and subverting codes associated with conventional femininity, but as young lesbians their understanding of homosexuality, especially male homosexuality, was actually highly conventional:

> *Betsy:* There are so many [homosexuals] nowadays!
> *All:* Yes!
> *Mag:* They French kiss!
> *Betsy:* I've seen man-to-man.
> *Vicky:* The men can sing so well.
> *Betsy:* Singing Faye's [a local female pop singer] songs.
> *Vicky:* You'll know if you go to a gay bar. We go to Circus.
> *Betsy:* Let's go to Circus after this [interview]! [Everyone cheered.] We
>   can bring you along. Have you been [to a gay bar] before?
> *Tong:* I've been to one at Stone Bay.
> *Betsy:* H2o?
> *Tong:* It's called "Why Not." I've seen Leslie[6] there.
> *Tobey:* Is Leslie really also [a gay man]?
> *Betsy:* I think he is.
> *Vicky:* I also think so.
> *Mag:* Andy [a local male pop singer] also!

Tobey: [He is] very sissy.

Mag: Andy and Aaron [other local male pop singers] are [gay men] too!

Tobey: Aaron as well?

Betsy: Did I tell you some of my friends saw Andy and Aaron French kissing each other?

Tobey: Wow!

Vicky: It's true? Oh!

Mag: It's so great! Aaron is [gay]!

Vicky: Help . . .

Tobey: Andy and Aaron? Fuck! Then who is what?

Mag: I think Andy is masculine and Aaron is feminine.

. . .

Tong: You don't like sissy boys?

Betsy: I dislike [them] very much.

Vicky: I saw a boy in your class one day. He touched his hair like this [placing the hair in front of the ear backward with his little finger pointing outwards]! I think he is a woman! Fuck! [It was] fucking scary and [he was] fucking ugly!

Tong: Do you think you have double standards? You behave like boys, but boys can't behave like girls.

Vicky: Don't you think it is very awful for boys to be gay?

Tobey: If you say so, but those boys may also think we are very awful.

Vicky: How could it be the same?

They expressed excitement and disgust simultaneously upon discovering that the celebrities were gay—excited because they were also seemingly homosexual, but disgusted at the thought of a feminine man. Their understanding of homosexual relationships had clearly defined gender roles, in which the heterosexual pattern was still the norm, and they had very strong ideas about how the male gender should behave. These tomboys' ideas about relationships, no matter whether heterosexual or homosexual, were still firmly attached to the masculine versus feminine/dominant versus subordinate heterosexual pattern; again, this underlines the prevalence of conventional heterosexual ideologies in Hong Kong society. On the other hand, they generally disliked boys, although they might feel less a sense of disgust and more a sense of hatred toward boys who were not feminine. Most of their comments about their male acquaintances were negative, since they regarded all boys as lustful.

In addition to resisting conventional femininity, these tomboys also resisted heterosexuality; they did not share other young girls' fantasies about heterosexual romantic relationships. In fact, they had never liked boys. Some people may believe that tomboys must have been seriously hurt by boys for them to harbor such hatred, and that becoming boys themselves is therefore a form of avoidance. This belief is neither logical nor empirically supported; for example, the tomboys in this study had never loved a male and had never been involved in any heterosexual relationships. The very first person they fell in love with was another girl, and such romantic experiences were important to their tomboy identities. All of them came to define themselves as tomboys after they fell in love, for the first time, with another girl:

> *Tong:* You might not have known that you liked girls when you were little; how did you find out?
>
> *Mag:* No! I knew when I was little.
>
> *Vicky:* Yes, I knew when I was little also but the thing is . . . you wouldn't tell others so openly before. That is, we wouldn't tell others who we are but many people know now.
>
> *Mag:* Back then, we didn't know what we were.
>
> *Betsy:* I thought it was immature.
>
> *Tong:* How about you?
>
> *Tobey:* I didn't care about relationships before. It's only after I met someone . . . That's it.
>
> *Tong:* That means you met a girl, and then you felt that you loved her, and so you realized that you like girls?
>
> *Tobey:* Yes.
>
> . . .
>
> *Tong:* You said you liked a girl when you were in primary 1. Did you feel strange about yourself?
>
> *Mag:* I didn't know what it was then. So I didn't find it strange.
>
> *Tong:* And later?
>
> *Mag:* I have never felt strange about it because all my friends accept it. I wasn't aware of any strangeness myself.
>
> *Tong:* Then when did you feel certain that you were a tomboy?
>
> *Mag:* Primary 5.
>
> *Tong:* Why was that?
>
> *Mag:* Because I started to know how to truly love a girl then.
>
> *Tong:* Have you ever thought about why you love girls?
>
> *Mag:* No, I don't know how to think about this.

Tong: It just feels natural?
Mag: Yes.

For these schoolgirls, adopting a tomboy identity was the most logical choice they could conceive of. First of all, they strongly rejected the feminine image and standards of conventional schoolgirls. For them, the biggest difficulty they face in being a girl lies in the expectations and standards concerning girls' appearance, dress, and behavior. They wanted to rebel against the normative standards: in their own narratives, they naturally could not and did not want to behave as girls were expected to, but felt a greater affinity with those qualities expected in boys. Second, they felt happier and more comfortable in girl-to-girl interactions and felt attracted to girls. In their heterosexualized understanding of relationships, becoming a tomboy—a commonly recognized identity for girls who are homosexual and who present themselves as boys—was the most obvious choice.

A surprising finding of this study is that the families of these tomboys had actually, in a way, helped them in their maintenance of a tomboy identity. The families interfered little with the way they dressed and in their personal lives. Unlike the strong adherence to the conventional good girl model of feminine ideals promoted at school, their families' acceptance or tolerance of their masculine appearance and behavior gave them a degree of freedom, if not confidence, to discover who they were or who they wanted to be. Mag and Vicky's families knew about their sexual orientation but did little to discourage their presentation of self and their relationships with other girls. This finding runs counter to the popular belief that Chinese families strictly control and regulate their children's self-expression and interaction with others. From Mag and Vicky's experience, we can see that this is not necessarily the case. Even though their families did not explicitly accept their homosexual orientation, they had done nothing to stop it. To a great extent, this allowed the girls to behave as they wished. The reason behind their families' tolerance was not clear; it could be real acceptance or an inability to interfere closely due to busy work schedules, or maybe it was simply that, as the tomboys said, their families loved them, did not think of their homosexuality as a serious problem, or expected them to change at some point in the future.

The increasing acceptance of tomboys in society may also have helped these girls assume a masculine identity. Homophobic bias and misconceptions still exist, as I will show below when I discuss teachers' attitudes towards homosexuality. However, being homosexual is not considered to be as alien or unethical as it was a decade ago.[7] More frequent media representation of homosexuals, though not always positive, might have helped open the closet. Also, people are generally more accepting of lesbians than they are of gay men.[8] The changing social climate thus helps explain the greater social tolerance toward these tomboys' behavior.

In their presentation of self, these schoolgirls said they faced little pressure as tomboys. Yet numerous feminist and lesbian writings have told us that homosexuals experience enormous pressure both socially and psychologically.[9] The lives of these tomboys, in reality, were not as easy as they themselves suggested. They faced different forms of pressure and constraints in their daily life, but they always insisted that they were happy with this identity. This may be a strategy they adopt to maintain their tomboy, masculine identity—refusing to admit any sign of weakness. On the other hand, the pressure they faced actually served as a consolidating force for the formation of their tomboy identity.

Daily Pressure and Resistance as a Young Tomboy

The public image of Hong Kong teachers and the education system is generally that of a conservative and paternalistic institution. Schools and teachers rely on control and routine to instill order and upon tradition to protect students from the perceived risks and dangers of living in the modern world. Concerning the issue of homosexuality, not only are teachers conservative but they also lack sufficient knowledge about different sexual orientations.

During an interview with Mr. Wong, the principal of Bernard College, he suggested that same-sex attraction requires the intervention of social workers. Since he regarded homosexuality as something abnormal, he considered that students displaying same-sex attraction needed help. In another interview with Miss Chu, the school counselor, she related the "problem of homosexuality" to the influence of the mass media, and she stated that she would help those who were not the "inborn type." The teachers I interviewed generally regarded homosexuality as something unnatural or pitiful. They said that students who have this orientation need to be helped and counseled. They were so caring that they wanted to help the "problem" kids. It is not hard to imagine how tiresome it must be for the tomboys to be the object of endless concern from their teachers who counseled them that they were not homosexuals and that they had the opportunity to be proper girls again. The tomboys' response was to try to ignore these concerns as nonsense, but they were not always successful. Among the tomboys in this study, Vicky had to bear much more pressure than the others because she was very protective of her girlfriend who was also a schoolmate. She tried hard to evade any concerns directed at her by the school and the social workers. Even though Vicky had gotten used to seeing the social worker regularly, she was very upset when the teachers asked her girlfriend, Sammie, to see the social worker because of their relationship. Below are excerpts from letters Vicky wrote to Sammie.

> . . . I really feel very sorry for you. If not for me, you wouldn't have become a problem girl! Maybe you think it is useless to worry but the fact is that, it is right in front of us. I am really worried about you. If anything happens to you, I will be guilty forever!
>
> I have thought about why we have to be so secretive. Should I feel guilty for liking a person? Why does it seem that I am a burden to everyone? Sometimes I think what you said is correct. We are people from two different worlds. I shouldn't have made your life so difficult. Maybe I am wrong. That's why I make you suffer so much now.
>
> . . . I wish some day we no longer have to care about other people's gaze and comments, and can develop the deepest love. Please give me a chance to love you.
>
> I have decided what I will do already. I will go to find Miss Lai [the social worker] with Mag later and ask Mag's girlfriend to pretend to be my girlfriend. This should be perfect. Don't be jealous!

After this "deceiving the social worker" incident, Vicky and Sammie went underground with their relationship. There were enormous obstacles to having a homosexual relationship in school. Vicky and Sammie had to see the social worker even when they were only suspected of being a couple. Vicky was very unhappy and blamed herself for all the troubles she had brought to her girlfriend. In another letter she wrote Sammie, "I don't know what you are thinking sometimes. Sometimes I feel that you don't want to see me and that you want me to disappear as soon as possible. Are you bothered by the gossip? If you don't want to see me, you can tell me! I don't mind. I don't want to bring you any trouble. You should not care about me. Just tell me!"

Although the school provided sex education, homosexual behavior was suppressed and treated with complete silence in the formal curriculum. So on the one hand, the school saw the tomboys' behavior as a problem that required intervention, yet on the other hand, the teachers denied that homosexuality existed by not including discussion of homosexuality in the curriculum. The tomboys expressed a sense of discomfort with the school's attitude toward sex education but also felt powerless to challenge the status quo. They chose to ignore or shy away from the school's intervention in their behavior and its failure to address homosexuality properly. This way of adapting was not easy, since they interacted with teachers almost every day. The teachers' conservative views and lack of knowledge about homosexuality were experienced as unnecessary but tangible pressure in the tomboys' everyday lives.

Other girls I met at the school generally thought tomboys were "strange," but they were in no way hostile. They all thought the ways tomboys behaved were only a matter of personality. Most schoolgirls seemed to share this tolerant and friendly attitude. When the tomboys walked around at school, many other girls greeted and chatted with them, and the atmosphere was friendly and nice. However, the tomboys seldom had such interactions with male schoolmates; on the contrary, boys were unfriendly and sometimes the source of humiliation. The excerpt below gives us some insight into why they hated boys so much:

> *Tong:* Do you mind how other people judge you?
> *Vicky:* Of course not. Everyone knows now, what is left there for me to mind about?
> *Mag:* My friends don't mind, so it's fine.
> *Tong:* Maybe some people make nasty comments?
> *Vicky:* Yes!
> *Tobey:* I haven't experienced that.
> *Vicky:* I was playing with her [Sammie]. Then a boy came and said, "Why don't you close the door and bang her? That will be more exciting!" Then I was on fire and said, "What the fuck did you say?" I swore loudly at him in school. Then [I] pushed him against the wall hard, so hard that there was a loud bang! Then I said, "Fuck your mother!" Then he said, "What is this fucking mother about? Just a joke!"
>
> . . .
>
> *Mag:* Boys think that we are wrong and that they are really something. They always say that we are "gay women" [*Gei-po;* the name does not simply refer to women who are homosexuals but there is also an explicit sense of spite and humiliation.] This happened a few days ago. It's okay now.
> *Tong:* Really? What did they say?

Mag: They said "*Gei-po* number 1," "*Gei-po* number 2," things like that.

Tong: What did you do when they said that?

Mag: I pretended that I didn't hear because if you make any response they'll say it again next time. If you ignore it, that'll be fine and they won't say it again.

Tong: Even though you ignore them, how do you feel when they say that?

Mag: Nothing, I don't regard them as human beings.

Tong: You don't regard them as human beings? Why is that?

Mag: I don't know. We are happy, that's fine. There's no need to care about what they say.

Tong: Do you feel bad being discriminated against by others?

Mag: It's okay. When [we] grow up, the discrimination may be even worse. So [we should] just treat [these] as early adaptation!

Tong: Have you thought about the reason that you have to be judged by others like this?

Mag: Because we are gay.

Such judgments and nasty name-calling often came from males. Studies on homosexuality have argued in detail that males are generally more anti-homosexual.[10] All instances of unfriendly comments the tomboys cited were from males. This helps explain their unfriendly attitude to most of their male acquaintances.

The tomboys had their own strategy of coping with unwelcome comments or humiliation. Not only did they try to evade or ignore such comments, they also built a strong friendship network for support and strength, neither of which was forthcoming from their school or families. Like the excerpted letters above, showing the pressure Vicky experienced, the tomboys also wrote to each other as a means of channeling their unhappiness. Similar to conversations, writing letters was an act they used to express and exchange feelings with their friends. Friends who were supportive and willing to listen were very important to these tomboys; they could express their views and feelings openly without too much frustration. And most of the time, friends were a group of people to have fun with, allowing them to forget about the pressures of everyday life and maintain a network of emotional support through different habits, like writing letters, chatting, playing basketball, and smoking. By actively maintaining their friendship network, they were actively creating their own space and resisting the pressure and constraints they experienced in their everyday lives.

Their collective behavior consolidated each of their individual identities as a tomboy. They all acted in boyish ways, and this made them stand out as a group with distinctive characteristics. Frequent use of foul language and slang, for example, helped to resist femininity and consolidate the masculine identity both of their group and of each of them individually. Using foul language is generally associated with local working-class male culture, and for these tomboys, it was a statement that said, "We are not good girls." They also emphasized a strong sense of brotherhood all the time, in their letters, in their casual chats, and during the interviews. No matter how much others disapproved of their behavior, they could always find approval in the group. The solidarity they felt as a group thus translated into confidence and self-acceptance. The friendship group was supportive in two ways. First, it provided a source of escape from the pressure they were facing. Studies of youth friendship and subcultural groups have suggested that friendship is an important means for establishing a positive self-identity and enhancing self-worth.[11] This was also true of the tomboys in this study: they received mutual support and confidence within their friendship group. Second, the friendship group could be considered a subcultural group since it has its own specific styles and values. Their collective styles and behavior were a form of everyday resistance, a form of the "weapons of the weak"[12] that help to deal with inequalities in everyday life. Adopting a boyish appearance and boyish manners, smoking and using foul language, staying out late and dating girls—these were all forms of everyday collective resistance to the hegemonic heterosexual feminine ideal of "good schoolgirls." Although the problems they faced because of unnecessary social pressures and constraints could not be overcome in these ways, the strong friendship network offered, at least, a way of coping with the problems they were facing.

Conclusion—The Hybrid Identity

Although the tomboy identity allowed these young lesbians to resist and subvert both heterosexuality and femininity, it was not a stable or single/central identity. Homosexual identity is often seen as a static social category that an individual identifies with,[13] but in fact, the tomboys' identity was a hybrid creation and expressed in multiple ways, one which was in the process of being (re)constructed all the time through their daily experiences. Different discourses were involved in this process of identity formation and reformation, discourses that were sometimes in conflict.

In the school context, the tomboys were expected to fulfill the "good girl" role—a role with which they refused to comply. At home, their masculinity was permitted or at least tolerated while the school tolerated their resistance to femininity but not to heterosexuality. It was in their friendship network that this tomboy identity received mutual support. When they interacted with other students, it was boys who were hostile to their tomboy identity as this was considered destabilizing of normative masculinity; but other tomboys and TBGs expected and encouraged them to act like "real" boys. Ironically, their "real" boy behaviors included lots of conventional feminine activities such as chatting and letter writing, which are not commonly associated with masculinity. Hence, their identities as tomboys were full of multiple or even conflicting ideologies—these identities were highly hybrid, being defined and redefined via different discourses. The tomboy identity cannot and will not be stabilized, and is very far from a simple or static social category.

This study of young lesbians' lives and identities gives us a sense of the strategies they deploy in resisting hegemonic femininity and heterosexuality. Because of the hybrid nature of the tomboy identity, these young lesbian girls in Hong Kong can cope with and resist the different expectations, controls, and pressures experienced in daily life by forming and reforming their individual identities in relation to the different social contexts and discourses they encounter at school, at home, and among their peer group.

Notes

All quotes from conversations are excerpted from the ethnographic research in my M.Phil. thesis, 1998–2001, at the University of Hong Kong. The name of the school, districts, teachers, and students are pseudonyms. The conversations were conducted and recorded in Cantonese, then translated and transcribed into English.

1. Thorne, *Gender Play*, 112.

2. The original focus of this research was to examine the lives of "rebellious" young girls in the Hong Kong school context. The girls selected as "rebellious" by school teachers happened to be self-proclaimed tomboys and hence the focus of my study was revised. They were enrolled in form 3 (around fourteen to fifteen years old) at the beginning of the study. During the fieldwork period, four months were spent in the school; I was not allowed to attend lessons but hung out with the girls during their breaks, lunch periods, and after school. After the fieldwork period, individual and group interviews were conducted. The girls also shared their personal letters with me, thereby providing me with different sources for understanding their friendships and romantic relationships with other girls.

3. The prefect system is common in Hong Kong schools. Prefects are usually stu-

dents with good academic standing and good conduct who serve as role models and help the school authorities to discipline fellow students.

4. Bernard College is a Christian, coeducational, government-subsidized secondary school in Hong Kong located in a lower-class district occupied by public housing and light industries. Most students in Bernard College come from the same neighborhood.

5. A tomboy girl (TBG) is a tomboy's girlfriend who is feminine in appearance and behavior.

6. Leslie Cheung was a local pop singer and actor who was openly gay. He committed suicide at the age of forty-six in 2003.

7. According to Lam Tai Hing's 1997 study, students' acceptance of homosexuality has increased significantly since 1991. Over 20 percent of boys and over 30 percent of girls accepted homosexuality in 1996.

8. Homosexuality has largely been legally and culturally defined in male terms. Accordingly, the Hong Kong legal system only deals with male homosexual acts but not with female homosexuality; as with other female identity issues, lesbianism is a cultural taboo and an invisible topic.

9. See for example Munt, *Butch/Femme,* and Smith, "Homophobia: Why Bring It Up?"

10. For example, Smith, "Homophobia"; Adam, "Structural Foundations of the Gay World"; and David Plummer, *One of the Boys,* 77–87, 149–65.

11. Griffiths, *Adolescent Girls and Their Friends,* 170.

12. Scott, *Weapons of the Weak.*

13. See, for example, Ken Plummer, *The Making of The Modern Homosexual,* and Weinberg, *Gay Men, Gay Selves.*

References

Adam, Barry. 1996. "Structural Foundations of the Gay World." In Steven Seidman, ed., *Queer Theory/Sociology.* Cambridge: Blackwell.

Griffiths, Vivienne. 1995. *Adolescent Girls and Their Friends: A Feminist Ethnography.* Aldershot: Avebury.

Lam, Tai Hing. 1997. "A Brief Report on Youth and Sexuality Survey" (in Chinese). In *Report on Youth and Sexuality Seminar.* Hong Kong: Family Planning Association of Hong Kong.

Munt, Sally, ed. 1998. *Butch/Femme: Inside Lesbian Gender.* London: Cassell,.

Plummer, David. 1999. *One of the Boys: Masculinity, Homophobia, and Modern Manhood.* New York: Harrington Park Press.

Plummer, Ken, ed. 1981. *The Making of the Modern Homosexual.* London: Hutchinson.

Scott, James. 1985. *Weapons of the Weak: Everyday Forms of Peasant Resistance.* New Haven: Yale University Press.

Smith, Barbara. 1993. "Homophobia: Why Bring It Up?" In Henry Abelove, Michèle Aina Barale, and David M. Halperin, eds., *The Lesbian and Gay Studies Reader.* New York: Routledge

Thorne, Barrie. 1993. *Gender Play: Girls and Boys in School.* Buckingham: Open University Press.

Weinberg, Thomas. 1983. *Gay Men, Gay Selves: The Social Construction of Homosexual Identities.* New York: Irvington.

SEVEN

THE ROMANCE OF THE QUEER

The Sexual and Gender Norms
of *Tom* and *Dee* in Thailand

Megan Sinnott

Lila Abu-Lughod has advocated caution in the popular tendency among anthropologists to valorize cultural practices as acts of resistance.[1] Abu-Lughod explains that in the post-1960s atmosphere of fascination with revolution and resistance, anthropologists have been tempted to see pervasive counterhegemonic meanings and acts in their search for that satisfying refusal of power in the daily activities of their research subjects. This move towards studies of resistance was accompanied by renewed interest Marxist anthropology and other approaches to the study of counterhegemonic actions.[2] Michel de Certeau's work on everyday resistance found an eager audience among anthropologists who had a predilection for teasing out moments of subversion in mundane activity.[3] De Certeau's work has been influential across disciplines, finding resonance in studies of popular culture, media studies, and ethnography. This post-1960s turn in anthropology away from static, functional models of culture to explorations of the instability of hegemonic orders and individual agency in mundane acts of resistance has made anthropologists a ready audience for the psychoanalytic/linguistically derived "queer theory," which also probes cultural expression for fissures in the reproduction of hegemonic orders.

The term "queer" or "queer theory" carries multiple meanings, but in general conveys a postmodern emphasis on destabilization and disruption of heteronormative cultural presumptions and hegemonic sex/gender orders.[4] However, linguistically derived queer theory as well post-1970s Marxist studies in anthropology do not portray unequivocal resistances to and rejections of oppressive hegemonic orders. Instead, both theoretical perspectives position these moments of resistance as rearticulations or reframings of existent norms—not absolute rejections of them. Resistance is never absolute but occurs within known frameworks of meaning that in themselves may be oppressive. Anna Livia and Kira Hall explain Judith Butler's concept of gender performance—a key element of queer theory—as existing within known meaning systems: Even activities like gender impersonation are re-iterative, because the impersonator must invoke the very essence of these "binding conventions in order for the performance to be comprehensible. Such performances should therefore be analyzed not so much as innovative discourses of resistance but as focused appropriations of existing norms."[5] Abu-Lughod comes to a similar conclusion, claiming that resistance to one set of hegemonic norms often means inclusion in another; there is no absolute point of liberation outside of hegemonic systems. Therefore, queer theory is best understood not as a study of particular kinds of sexuality or kinds of individuals (that is, homosexuality or homosexuals) and the nonnormativity of such practices and people. Queer theory is most usefully understood as an analytical approach that renders visible the cultural processes in which sexual and gender norms are constructed, reproduced, and made to appear natural.[6]

This discussion explores the production of sexual and gender norms within female same-sex sexual relationships in Thailand. Rather than positioning these relationships as nonnormative or "queer," I explore the processes in which gender and sexual norms are enacted. These gender norms are simultaneously buttressed and rearticulated in ways that implicitly destabilize or challenge the cultural presumptions upon which they are based, particularly the value accorded to women's sexual pleasure. *Toms*, masculine-identified women, and *dees*, their feminine sexual/romantic partners, engage in a sexual and gender meaning system that is consistent with Thai normative codes for female sexuality and gender. Likewise, the meanings given to male same-sex relationships in Thailand are also structured according to normative gender expectations. By shifting focus away from the dominating polarity in English-language discourse of heterosexuality/homosexuality, to gendered distinctions between male and female sociocultural practices and meanings, *tom, dee,* and *gay* identities can be understood as extensions of a gendered cultural system. Rather than focusing on resistances to heteronormativity (although these resistances occur), I suggest greater purchase on the cultural significance of these homoerotic acts is gained by understanding them as *extensions* of male or female sexuality, as they are culturally structured, rather than as oppositions to, or rejections of, heterosexuality and normative gender codes.[7] I will first explore both dominant cultural meanings assigned to *tom* and *dee* relationships, and *tom* and *dee* descriptions of self. Next, I will provide a brief description of the relationship between *gay* male sexuality and normative codes for men in the Thai context. Finally, I will show moments of reinterpretation and subtle shifts of these dominant discourses, evident in *tom* and *dee* sexual codes of *tom* sexual "untouchability."

Methods

For this chapter, I primarily rely on nine years of ethnographic research on female sexuality and gender practices in Thailand. Research includes interviews with women in same-sex relationships, long-term observational studies of female same-sex communities, review of Thai academic literature on homosexuality and gender norms, review of popular literature (magazines and newspapers) on homosexuality and gender norms, interviews with reporters and academics who wrote on the subject of homosexuality, and oral histories with elderly Thais. Research was conducted primarily in Bangkok, the capital of Thailand, but research was also conducted with individuals from a wide range of class background and regional origins/affiliations. Following convention, sources written in Thai by Thai authors list the author's given name first in both the text and the works cited page.

Gay, Kathoey, Tom, and Dee

Homosexual Thai men have been using the term "*gay*" as a self-referent since the 1960s, and soon thereafter young women began calling themselves something that sounded equally foreign, and equally English—"*tom*" and "*dee*."[8] *Tom*s I interviewed reported first hearing the term "*tom*" and using it to refer to themselves or other people they knew some time in the late 1970s, while they were teenagers or young adults, which is consistent with Peter Jackson's textual study of these terms.[9] The term "*tom*" comes from the English word "tomboy," and the term "*dee*" is derived from the last syllable of the English word "lady." For most Thais, including many *tom*s and *dee*s, the word "*dee*" is nearly synonymous with the word "woman."[10] In contrast to masculine women who often develop a strong personal identity as a *tom*, women romantically/sexually involved with *tom*s do not necessarily differentiate themselves from women in general. In contrast to the specialized subcultural discourse of *gay* men in Thailand discussed below, a remarkable consistency was expressed between descriptions of *tom*s and *dee*s by *tom*s, *dee*s, and Thais in general.[11] *Tom* and *dee* subject categories are not defined in terms of heterosexual/homosexual binary; they are not defined in opposition to heterosexuality. Greater debate exists within *tom* and *dee* communities over interpretations of these identities than between *tom-dee*s and mainstream society.[12]

*Tom*s are typically understood to be masculine beings, who express their masculinity in their personality, dress, and sexual attraction to females. Most *tom*s and *dee*s I interviewed described *dee*s as "ordinary" women (*phu-ying thammada*) who were normatively attracted to a masculine partner who could either be male or female bodied. *Dee*s are described as being capable of attraction to males or *tom*s. This description was borne out in the life stories of many of the *dee*s with whom I spoke. Many (but not all) *dee*s had had relationships with both males and *tom*s, and considered themselves to be "ordinary" women who were currently involved with *tom*s. The term *dee* includes, without distinction, women who consider themselves to be exclusively interested in *tom*s and women who perceive themselves as possible partners with either males or *tom*s. Therefore, "*dee*" is an ambivalent category, differentiating women who are sexually involved with females from women sexually involved with males, with the implicit understanding that *dee*s probably are not exclusively attracted to *tom*s, and not essentially of a different nature from women in general. In contrast, commonly among *tom*s, *dee*s, and Thais in general, a *tom* is understood as a transgendered female, with a core, inborn masculine soul (*cit-cay*).

This pattern of a gender normative person (*dee*) engaging in a sexual relationship with a transgendered person (*tom*) resonates with traditional concepts of sex and gender in Thai discourse. Peter Jackson has analyzed the Thai cultural system as one based on the primacy of gender, in contrast to a Foucaultian grid in which sexuality, sexual object choice, and sexual preference are the primary categories of the Western sex/gender order.[13] Jackson chooses to reverse Gayle Rubin's famous phrase "sex/gender system" to read "gender/sex system" to reflect the focus on gender (masculinity or femininity) in determining a person's identity in the Thai context.[14] Sexuality in Thai discourse is understood as an extension of one's gender; homosexuality is understood to be, in mainstream Thai interpretations, a result of psychological transgendering—a man in a woman's body, or vice versa. For many

Thais, including academics and psychologists, the western concept of "homosexuality" is interpreted in terms of the local concept of "*kathoey*." The term *kathoey* refers to an intersexed, transgendered, or transsexual person, usually male-to-female. As a cosmological category, the term has historical roots of at least several centuries.[15] While before the 1960s the term *kathoey* was used to refer to either male or female third genders, it now refers almost exclusively to transgendered males (although transgender females, or *tom*s, are still called *kathoey* at times). From oral histories with people over sixty years old, I have learned that masculine women were known of in the past in rural settings.[16] These women often had female partners and lived their lives as social men. While these individuals were called *kathoey* at times, people usually referred to such a masculine-identified woman as a "woman who is a man" (*phu-ying thii pen phu-chaay*). These masculine women, like *tom*s today, generally were not "passing" as men. They were known to be physically female and did not claim otherwise.

Male *kathoey* have sexual relations with gender normative men who are not linguistically marked.[17] The *kathoey* is transgressing a gender category, and therefore labeled as non-man, or a third-gender category. The male partner, however, is engaging in sexual relations with a feminine being, and his gender is consistent with being a "man." No linguistic distinction is typically made to identify the gender normative partner of either male or female *kathoey*s. *Dee*, therefore, is an innovation, in that it linguistically marks the gender normative partner of the (female) *kathoey*, although, as mentioned above, this marking is ambivalent, reflecting the persistence of concepts of gender-normality of the sexual partner of the *kathoey*.

Toms and *dee*s express their sexuality and identities in ways that are consistent with Thai expectations of women and notions of femininity. Most obviously, *tom*s and *dee*s explicitly reject the English term "lesbian" largely due to its explicit sexual associations. "Lesbian" is understood to refer to two feminine women who are engaging in sex with each other. Rather than an expression of a gendered couple, such as *tom-dee*, *tom*s and *dee*s explained to me that they understood the term "lesbian" to refer to sex acts. These sex acts could not be meaningfully contextualized within a loving female-female, gender-paired (masculine-feminine) relationship. *Tom*s and *dee*s explained that they could only see this kind of sex as a possibility when it was a performance for a lascivious male audience. For Thai women, the sameness of gender that is implied in the term "lesbian" carries an additional stigma of explicit sexuality, rather than a gendered relationship. It is these key themes of love and companionship that *tom*s and *dee*s use when describing the nature of their relationships with each other—not sexual desire. The rejection of the term "lesbian" is a meaningful linguistic act, and should be explored. One *tom* explains:

> I am a *tom*. I am not a lesbian. I feel disgusted when I hear that word. It isn't good at all: I don't like it at all. Whoever hears it probably won't like it. Who wants to be like that? Being a lesbian isn't the same at all as being a *tom*. *Tom*s are women who are capable, a little bit coarse, but not acting like a man, and not sweet and gentle like a woman. *Tom*s can protect women, can show concern for and take care of women very well. This is the most important thing. There is no way a man can understand a woman as well as a *tom* can. And women who are women (*phu-ying thii pen phu-ying*), they won't like each other. A woman who is a woman must like a *tom*.[18]

This *tom* makes a clear distinction between "women" and *tom*s. Lesbians are "women" who like "women," which implies same-gendered pairing between two feminine women. Both *tom*s and *dee*s consistently noted the difference between themselves in terms of gender. The sameness implied by the term "lesbian" does not fit the local cultural discourses in which *tom*s and *dee*s express themselves and are understood by people in general, which is premised on the assumption of a fundamental gender difference between each other. Almost all of the *tom*s and *dee*s interviewed described sexual relationships as only reasonably possible between masculine and feminine beings—men and women, *tom*s and *dee*s, *kathoey* and "men." Any suggestion of sexual relationships between two *tom*s or two *dee*s was described as bizarre and ludicrous.

In Thailand, attitudes towards homosexuality can vary according to ethnicity (Thai and Sino-Thai) and class.[19] There are social pressures for both males and females to marry and produce children, but these pressures are not absolute. However, one constant feature of the social landscape was the intense taboo against improper female heterosexuality that was held across ethnic and class boundaries. Perceived heterosexual promiscuous behavior and pregnancies outside of sanctioned relationships (not necessarily "marriage") are extremely stigmatized for Thai women. Women's improper heterosexual behavior can easily disgrace them and their families. From villagers to middle-class city dwellers, warnings to daughters about improper heterosexuality were constant in my research experiences. On the other hand, I found many cases where parents were indifferent to their daughters' relationships with *tom*s or *dee*s, or actively supported them as a good alternative to heterosexuality.[20]

Sex Versus "Caretaking" in *Tom-Dee* Relationships

*Tom*s and *dee*s often described their relationships in terms of caretaking and companionship, and when I asked about sex, most *tom*s and *dee*s downplayed its importance. For example, Um, a middle-class *dee* in her thirties, living in Bangkok, said, "We had sex when I was with the *tom,* but sex wasn't that important; it was more about emotions. Sex is only about 10 to 20 percent of being *tom* and *dee.* It is mostly about taking care of each other, paying attention to each other and helping, having good conversation, and liking the same things. When we are together we are happy." Almost all *tom*s, *dee*s, and Thais in general explained that sex between *tom*s and *dee*s was of a fundamentally different nature than heterosexual sex in terms of its moral implications. Almost all agreed that *tom-dee* sex did not constitute a loss of virginity, and could even be a way to avoid improper sexual contact with a man. Um explained further: "Having sex with women doesn't count as losing your virginity, but you do lose it if you have sex with men. If you ask men they will say sex is important, but if you ask *tom*s they will say it isn't. I don't know if this is true or not." *Tom*s and *dee*s tended to explain their relationships in terms of emotional caretaking and companionship. In particular, *dee*s described the main quality of *tom*s as their ability to caretake.

Most *tom*s and *dee*s described their relationship expectations, or *tom-dee* relationships in general, as being based on each side performing certain gendered duties. *Tom*s were thought of as responsible for taking care of the *dee,* and the *dee* as needing the emotional support of the *tom.* For example, Kralock, a middle-class *tom* living in Bangkok, described the dynamics of her relationship with *dee*s:

> I have to be more mature than she is, such as I have to protect her while crossing a street. I walk behind her to make sure that she is in my sight. I have to protect her all the time. I will do anything I can to be a leader or advisor. But in bed we are equal. I don't have to be a leader then. But about intelligence and thinking, I have to be a leader. Being a *tom* you have to take good care of her feelings. I call her several times a day. Sometimes when I am on a public phone talking to her and there is somebody waiting for the phone, I give them my phone card to use another phone so I don't have to stop our conversation. This is a small sample of how I have to be good at taking care of her feelings.

Ironically, descriptions of *tom* and *dee* relationships as based on caretaking and emotional support are not that different from the most conservative, antihomosexual voices within Thai public culture. For example, Wanlop Piyamanotham, a well-known psychologist who often writes on issues of homosexuality, describes dees.

> Dees are normal women, not noticeable from the outside. [However] they are insecure, lack love and understanding since childhood. Dees want somebody to look after them. They are well matched for toms because toms are still women inside even if not willing to act like women. It is natural for women to be sensitive to other women's feelings. Happiness for women naturally isn't about sex, but about caring, gentleness, romance, to just to be close to a lover, to hug each other is the most excellent satisfaction, not the same as men think.[21]

I doubt the toms and dees I met would agree that dees are lacking in love or are insecure. However, most toms and dees I spoke with agreed that tom and dee relationships are a form of female companionship, and that dees are not essentially different from women in general. Wanlop, and other members of Thai academia, have produced a rarified discourse of sexual pathology in which dees are awkwardly placed in the category of "homosexuality." In fact, Wanlop stood out in my review of Thai academic texts on homosexuality in that he included "dee" as a kind of homosexual identity whereas most other writers spoke only of gay men, kathoey, and toms.[22] In any case, Wanlop's assertion that the relationship that dees sought was one of caretaking and emotional closeness was quite similar to what toms and dees described. Like the normative definition of "tom" represented by Wanlop's description, toms and dees also typically described toms as female, but with a kind of masculinity that was appealing to "women." Clearly, academics such as Wanlop and others producing this pathologizing discourse have grievously misunderstood tom and dee individuals and their relationships in many ways (sex is an important part of tom and dee relationships, even if it is downplayed in discourse due to female gender norms, for example). However, toms and dees share in a hegemonic discourse of sexuality and gender.

The desexualization of tom-dee relationships places them within the realm of respectable female behavior. Of course, these statements do not reflect the actual importance of sex in these relationships, but rather are a standard way of framing these relationships as normal and morally respectable by toms and dees, which is consistent with dominant understandings of female same-sex relationships.[23] Women's choices to engage in same-sex sexual relationships must be understood within this larger cultural narrative that frames these relationships as nondisruptive of hegemonic notions of gender and sexuality.

The hegemonic imperative to desexualize their relationships is not because their relationships are homosexual. Rather, this desexualizing discourse is a reflection of the negative attitudes towards women's sexuality in general. Warunee Fongkaew's study of sexual attitudes among women and girls of northern Thailand describes this negative portrayal of female sexuality that affects all women: "Cultural norms based on gender inequality in sexual relations that expect women to be inexperienced and naïve in sexual matters, and to see themselves as passive receptacles of men's sexual passions, are widely held in this pre-urban Northern Thai society."[24]

Sexual experience *with men* is taboo for unmarried Thai women. By abstaining from improper heterosexuality, and framing one's relationship in terms of female friendship, *toms* and *dees* position themselves as moral and proper within the parameters of mainstream, hegemonic notions of sexuality and gender. Research on female sexual attitudes confirms that female homosexuality was not considered particularly deviant by young women. Amara Soonthorndhada quotes factory workers and students in Bangkok about their attitudes towards female homosexuality: "I think close relationships between women is much better than between men and women. You will never get pregnant or contract a disease. You are safe and secure."[25]

Gay Identity

In dominant, mainstream discourse, men are believed to have a natural sexual appetite, and sexual variety for men is considered necessary. What stigmatizes males and questions their male status is association with femininity or transgenderism.[26] *Kathoeys*, while generally accepted as part of the natural possibilities of gender, are not necessarily approved of by society. Herein lies the appeal of *gay* identity for Thai men.[27] Thai men who are gender normative, but have exclusive erotic attractions to other men, have adopted the English label "gay." For these men, being *gay* distinguishes them from transgendered *kathoey*'s feminine identity. The use of the English term "gay" links these men's sexuality with Western culture; it sounds cosmopolitan, modern, and respectable. While the meaning of "gay" for Thai males is not completely consistent with its meaning in other cultural contexts such as in the United States, the term's English and Western origin is an association with modernity. In contrast to Thai women's commonplace rejection of the term "lesbian," I argue that for (gender normative) Thai men, it is precisely this association with sexuality that makes the term *gay* appealing as a self-referent.[28]

The popularity of the term "gay" for some men in Thailand stems from the possibility that it presents in distinguishing homoeroticism from gender inversion. However, exclusive male homoeroticism is typically portrayed as unmanly in mainstream discourse and is presented as evidence of an inner transgenderism. Within this understanding, *gay* potentially becomes equivalent to the non-man, the *kathoey*. Therefore, the term "*gay*" uneasily slips between Western notions of sexuality as a basis for identity and Thai assumptions that such sexuality is basically a kind of gender inversion. I argue that *gayness*, as a disavowal of *kathoey* identity, is an assertion of masculine sexuality as a rearticulation of masculine gender norms in which sexual exploration and sexual pleasure are male prerogatives. The degree to which "*gay*" is a positive identity for nontransgendered Thai men is the degree to which it is explicitly associated with male sexuality instead of transgenderism. In contrast, neither *tom* nor *dee* identities are expressed as a kind of eroticism or fulfillment of sexual pleasure. The downplaying of sexual pleasure between women rearticulates dominant norms that discourage open expression of female sexual pleasure, exploration, or desire.

Queer Moments: *Tom* Untouchability and *Dee* Sexual Pleasure

One area in which *tom*s and *dee*s reverse normative discourses of sexuality is in the common practice of *tom* untouchability. Many *tom*s and *dee*s have described *tom*s as unwilling to be touched sexually by their partners or to remove their clothes during sex. Ironically, this practice is described as a natural aspect of *tom* masculinity. *Tom*s, as masculine beings, are expected to be "active" (*faay-ruk*) in sex and perform for their feminine partners. This is a normative discourse of *tom* and *dee* communities; although *tom*s and *dee*s debate whether this is true, that *tom*s must be untouched sexually by "women," it was repeated by *tom*s and *dee*s so often that it became redundant in my research notes. *Dee*s, as appropriately "passive" (*faay-rap*), expect to reach sexual climax because they are acted upon by a masculine partner. *Tom*s also generally expressed the belief that it was their duty to bring about a *dee*'s sexual satisfaction. Rules about sexual roles that *tom*s and *dee*s themselves imposed structured *tom* and *dee* identities and relationships. These rules imposed a sense of difference and complementary balance between *tom*s and *dee*s.

Both *tom*s and *dee*s consistently expressed hilarity or discomfort with the idea of a same-gendered partner. The idea that *tom*s could partner with *tom*s and *dee* with *dee*s clearly violated normative models of sexuality and identity. Khwan and Jaeng were young, urban professional women in their early thirties who talked to me about their past relationships with *tom*s and what they thought about *tom* and *dee* relationships in general. Khwan eagerly talked about her past problems and arguments with her *tom* ex-lover. I asked her if she could ever consider having a relationship with a woman who was not a *tom* (implying a *dee*). She laughed with surprise and said, "No way." Khwan explained that she could never be the "active partner," or the initiator in sex. According to Khwan, *tom*s were the ones who took the initiative in sex. Khwan said that she was a *dee* and therefore was naturally "passive." To switch roles and be the "active" partner seemed strange and even "unnatural" (*phit-pokkati*) to Khwan. Her friend Jaeng, also a *dee*, sitting nearby, said that she felt a bit differently. Jaeng said that the thought of having sex with a *dee* was bizarre, and she giggled with Khwan at the thought. However, Jaeng said she could conceivably be "active" and initiate sex, but only if her partner was a *tom*. Jaeng said she never had been "active" sexually, but she said she thought it could possibly be pleasurable. For Khwan, the sexual dynamics of *tom* and *dee* relationships made the sex act indicative of gender (active = masculine, passive = feminine). Therefore, as a *dee* she was exclusively passive sexually (meaning she was expected to reach sexual climax and not to perform sexual acts for her *tom*'s sexual pleasure). Jaeng, on the other hand, expressed greater flexibility in actual sexual practices (hypothetically, however) but insisted that *tom*s and *dee*s were natural and exclusive sexual partners. Both agreed it would only be conceivable to be with a *tom* sexually, regardless of whether they defined *tom*s as necessarily and exclusively sexual initiators or not.

*Dee*s such as Khwan and Jaeng reinforced the idea that *tom*s and *dee*s were essentially different, and this difference determined their sexual relationships: *tom*s could only reasonably be partners with *dee*s and vice versa. Khwan reinforced the norm that *tom*s, in order to be *tom*s, had to be sexually active. Even Jaeng expressed that for a *tom* to insist on being active is a natural extension of her masculinity. However, in contrast to normative expectations, the masculine partner was expected to sexually please and satisfy their feminine partner. *Tom*s consistently explained that they needed to please women in ways that men were either unable or unwilling to do to ensure that *dee*s did not abandon them for men. In contrast, research on mainstream understandings of sexuality consistently record the importance given to male sexual satisfaction. For example, John Knodel et al. summarize results from their research into Thai sexual attitudes: "In virtually all the women's focus groups and in many of the in-depth interviews, women expressed the view that it was important for wives to please their husbands sexually. Rarely did they say that sexual satisfaction was important for themselves. Discussion of marital sex among women often noted that sex was more important for men than for women. For women, providing sex for their husbands, and trying to please them in doing so, was seen as purposive in the sense that it may discourage husbands from seeking sex elsewhere."[29] Thus, in complete reversal of normative sexual code, among *tom*s and *dee*s, the masculine partner is expected to sacrifice sexual climax as a natural extension of her masculinity, and works to satisfy her feminine partner. This practice would be considered highly bizarre if it were to be found in normative heterosexual relationships; a man refusing to take off his clothes and not aiming to achieve orgasm during sex would indeed be "queer." However, I found that *tom*s and *dee*s I asked about this sexual norm reaffirmed that serving the sexual needs of *dee*s was part of *tom*s natural duties as masculine partners. *Tom*s and *dee*s allow the sexual satisfaction of the *dee* to be the definitive moment in the sex act while adhering to normative discourses of female chastity, modesty, and passivity and male sexual desire and activeness.

My reading of *tom* and *dee* sexual practices as "queer" or disruptive of normative models of sexuality is not shared by *tom*s and *dee*s themselves. *Tom*s and *dee*s rarely have expressed to me the idea that they are disruptive of the normative sex/gender order. In contrast, it appears that the pleasure that *tom* and *dee* relationships afford women may not be in their disruptive moments of resistance of a hegemonic order but in the pleasure of integrating their desire and relationships within the "normal."[30]

Conclusion

In Thailand, *tom, dee,* and *gay* are consistent with gender norms and mainstream expectations of men and women in important ways. Building on Jackson's analysis of the gender/sex system of Thailand, I suggest exploring the distinct differences between male and female same-sex identities, communities, and discourses based on hegemonic gender norms. Hegemonic concepts of male and female sexuality infuse and shape both communities in important ways.

While each category (*tom, dee, gay, kathoey*)—and the individual acts of those who are part of these subject positions—has its own spin of transgression and innovation, they must be understood as extensions of cultural practices that are strongly based on social expectations for men and women. The sexuality implied in the term "gay" accounts for its popularity among Thai men and among gender normative homosexual men in particular who shun references to transgenderism or femininity. For Thai women, it is just this allusion to sexuality in the term "lesbian" that has led to its absence in popular Thai discourse. *Tom* and *dee,* in contrast, emphasize normative gender duality (masculinity and femininity), which are embedded in normative discourses of feminine caring and emotion-based relationships. The reluctance to openly position their relationships as a form of sexuality (although these relationships *are* sexual) is an extension of Thai sex/gender norms that stigmatize female sexual expression. The deployment of these normative codes for female decorum and chastity ironically allow Thai women to engage in an open and active sexuality in which feminine sexual pleasure is prioritized and valued. If we understand "queer" to mean reiterations and reproductions of normative codes and practices that contain a strategic, though perhaps inarticulate, spin of difference, then *tom* and *dee* can arguably be considered "queer." However, rather than understanding queer as a particular kind of person or performance, a queer theory approach reveals the construction and reiterations of sexual and gender norms. Applying this theoretical approach in a cross-cultural context (or non-Euro/American context) demonstrates the need to avoid assuming the primacy of the heterosexual-homosexual binary in the construction of normativity. *Tom, dee, gay,* and *kathoey* are not united in a shared subject position (homosexual or queer) that challenges heteronormativity, but are rather extensions of an existing hegemonically constructed gender system.

Notes

A version of this chapter was presented at the Association of Asian Studies meeting in Chicago, Illinois, April 1, 2005. I would like to acknowledge and thank the editors of this volume, and Peter Jackson in particular, for their useful and insightful comments on a draft version of this paper. Funding for this research was provided by Fulbright Foundation and the Southeast Asian Studies Program at the University of Wisconsin-Madison.

1. See Abu-Lughod, "The Romance of Resistance."

2. For an overview of Marxist anthropology and the concern with political movements within contemporary anthropological work, see Vincent, *Anthropology and Politics;* and Godelier, *Perspectives in Marxist Anthropology.*

3. My thanks to an editor of this volume for this insightful connection.

4. See Butler, *Gender Trouble;* de Lauretis, "Queer Theory"; Duggan, "Making It Perfectly Queer"; and Warner, introduction to *Fear of a Queer Planet.* For a review of the multiple associations of the term "queer," see Walters, "From Here to Queer"; for an informative critique of queer theory and feminism from a linguistic perspective, see

Anna Livia and Kira Hall, "It's a Girl!" For an informative critique of anthropological studies of homosexuality, see Blackwood, "Reading Sexualities across Cultures."

5. Livia and Hall, "It's a Girl!" 11.

6. For current approaches to queer theory as an analytical approach to the construction of normativity, see the essays in the special issue of *Social Text, What's Queer about Queer Studies Now* ed. David Eng, Judith Halberstam, and Jose Esteban Munoz (Fall/Winter 2005), and Halberstam, *In a Queer Time and Place*.

7. For an excellent example of how the sexuality and identity of *gay* male Indonesians is embedded in larger sociocultural context that structures both heterosexuality and homosexuality, see Boellstorff, "The Perfect Path."

8. Jackson, "*Gay* Adaptation, *Tom-Dee* Resistance, and *Kathoey* Indifference."

9. Ibid, 213–14. For an analysis of the relationships between *tom, dee,* and other forms of female sexuality with the capitalist transition in Thailand, see Wilson, *The Intimate Economies of Bangkok.*

10. For discussion of *tom* and *dee* and their relation to gay male sexual subculture, see Sinnott, *Toms and Dees.*

11. In a similar vein, William Leap and Tom Boellstorff claim that gay language tends to be more divergent from mainstream men's language than lesbian language is from mainstream women's language. See their introduction to *Speaking in Queer Tongues.*

12. Sinnott, *Toms and Dees,* 132–61.

13. See the work of Jackson, *Dear Uncle Go;* "*Kathoey><Gay><Man*"; "From *Kamma* to Unnatural Vice"; "Tolerant but Unaccepting"; "An Explosion of Thai Identities"; and "*Gay* Adaptation, *Tom-Dee* Resistance, and *Kathoey* Indifference." See also van Wijngaarden, "Between Money, Morality and Masculinity"; and Storer, "Rehearsing Gender and Sexuality in Modern Thailand."

14. Jackson, "*Gay* Adaptation, *Tom-Dee* Resistance, and *Kathoey* Indifference," 205.

15. Jackson, "*Gay* Adaptation, *Tom-Dee* Resistance, and *Kathoey* Indifference," 210–11, and Morris, "Three Sexes and Four Sexualities."

16. Sinnott, *Toms and Dees,* 53–56.

17. Jackson, "*Kathoey><Gay><Man*" and "Tolerant but Unaccepting."

18. Chonticha does not give precise information about her informants. The six *toms* she interviewed were between twenty-eight and thirty-three years old, and five were from Bangkok and one from Chiang Mai, in northern Thailand (Chonticha, "The Development and Maintenance Process of Lesbian Identity," 66).

19. For discussion of how ethnicity and class affect male sexual norms, see Jackson, *Dear Uncle Go,* 47, 62–77. For discussion of how ethnicity and class affect female sexual norms, see Sinnott, *Toms and Dees,* 10–15.

20. Sinnott, *Toms and Dees,* 111–15.

21. Wanlop, "*Tom, Gay, Dee,* and *Tut,*" 84.

22. For example, see Jumphot, "The Legal Status of Homosexuals"; and Praphaphan, "Homosexual Identity Formation among Teenagers."

23. For a discussion of normalizing discourse of Thai gay males, see Mullaly, "Queerly Embodying the Good and the Normal," 115–229.

24. Fongkaew, "Female Sexuality and Reproductive Health in a Northern Thai Suburb," 582.

25. Soonthorndhada. *Sexual Attitudes and Behaviors and Contraceptive Use of Late Female Adolescents in Bangkok,* 28.

26. For discussion of male gender norms and the meanings of male homosexuality in Thailand, see Kittiwut Jod Taywaditep, Coleman, and Dumronggittigule, "Thailand (Muang Thai)"; Fongkaew, "Female Sexuality and Reproductive Health"; Jackson, *Dear Uncle Go,* 48–52, 179; "*Kathoey>*<*Gay>*<*Man*"; "Tolerant but Unaccepting"; and "*Gay* Adaptation, *Tom-Dee* Resistance, and *Kathoey* Indifference," 208–9.

27. The term "gay" in quotes refers to the English usage of the term and the English word itself. When the word *gay* is in italics, this refers to usage within the Thai context and its adoption in the Thai language. For a discussion of the use of English in Thai discourse, see Enteen, "Tom, Dii, and Anjaree," 99–122, and Jackson, "*Gay* Adaptation, *Tom-Dee* Resistance, and *Kathoey* Indifference," 22, for relationships between the term "gay" and modernity.

28. This appeal, however, extends to other males as well, and I have heard several well-educated *kathoey*s refer to themselves as *gay.* Particularly interesting were the comments of a student of mine at Mahidol University, Nakornpathom Province (about twelve miles west of Bangkok) during the school year of 2001. This student was a postoperative, male-to-female transsexual who effectively "passed" as a female—she consistently identified herself as *gay* to me and her classmates when discussing her life history, past relationships with men, and disapproval she has felt from society in general. However, as Peter Jackson has pointed out, there is a clear distinction within *kathoey* and *gay* subcultures over the difference between "*gay*" and "*kathoey,*" in contrast to mainstream Thai discourses that consistently conflate the two.

29. Knodel, Saengtienchai, VanLandingham, and Lucas, "Sexuality, Sexual Experience, and the Good Spouse," 99. For further discussion of normative concepts of male and female sexuality, see Cook and Jackson, *Genders and Sexualities in Modern Thailand;* and Ford and Kittisuksathit, *Youth Sexuality.*

30. Robyn Weigman presented a talk entitled "The Desire for Gender" at Yale University on February 17, 2005, in which she suggested that scholars, particularly of queer theory, need to more fully acknowledge and understand the pleasure in enacting normalcy.

References

Abu-Lughod, Lila. "The Romance of Resistance: Tracing Transformations of Power through Bedouin Women." *American Ethnologist* 17, no. 1 (1990): 41–55.

Berry, Chris, Fran Martin, and Audrey Yue, eds. *Mobile Cultures: New Media in Queer Asia*. Durham: Duke University Press, 2003.

Blackwood, Evelyn. "Reading Sexualities across Cultures. Anthropology and Theories of Sexuality." In Ellen Lewin and William Leap, eds. *Out in Theory: The Emergence of Lesbian and Gay Anthropology*. Urbana: University of Illinois Press, 2002. 69–92.

Butler, Judith. *Gender Trouble: Feminism and the Subversion of Identity*. New York: Routledge, 1990.

Boellstorff, Tom. "The Perfect Path: *Gay* Men, Marriage, Indonesia." *GLQ: Journal of Gay and Lesbian Studies* 5, no. 4 (1999): 475–510.

Chonticha Salikhubot. "The Development and Maintenance Process of Lesbian Identity" [Krabuan-kan phathanaa lae thamrong ekalak khorng ying-rak-ruam-pheet]. Master's thesis, Thammasat University, Thailand, 1989.

Cook, Nerida M., and Peter A. Jackson, eds. *Genders and Sexualities in Modern Thailand*. Chiang Mai: Silkworm Books, 1999.

De Certeau, Michel. *The Practice of Everyday Life*. Berkeley: University of California Press, 1984.

De Lauretis, Teresa. "Queer Theory: Lesbian and *Gay* Sexualities, an Introduction." *Differences* 3, no. 2 (Summer 1991): iii–xviii.

Duggan, Lisa. "Making It Perfectly Queer." *Socialist Review* 22, no. 1 (1992): 11–31.

Eng, David, Judith Halberstam, and Jose Esteban Munoz, eds. *What's Queer about Queer Studies Now?* Special issue of *Social Text* 84–85 (Fall/Winter 2005).

Enteen, Jillana. "Tom, Dii, and Anjaree: Women Who Follow Nonconformist Ways." in John Hawley, ed., *Postcolonial, Queer*. Albany: State University of New York, 2001. 99–122.

Fongkaew, Warunee. "Female Sexuality and Reproductive Health in a Northern Thai Suburb." In Virada Somswasdi and Sally Theobald, eds. *Women, Gender Relations, and Development in Thai Society*. Chiang Mai: Women's Studies Center, Faculty of Social Sciences, Chiang Mai University, 1997.

Ford, Nicholas, and Sirinan Kittisuksathit. *Youth Sexuality: The Sexual Awareness, Lifestyles, and Related-Health Service Needs of Young, Single, Factory Workers in Thailand*. Salaya, Nakornpathom, Thailand: Institute for Population and Social Research, Mahidol University, 1996.

Godelier, Maurice. *Perspectives in Marxist Anthropology*. Cambridge: Cambridge University Press, 1978.

Halberstam, Judith. *In a Queer Time and Place: Transgender Bodies, Subcultural Lives*. New York: New York University Press, 2005.

Hawley, John, ed. *Postcolonial, Queer*. Albany: State University of New York Press, 2001.

Jackson, Peter. *Dear Uncle Go: Male Homosexuality in Thailand*. Bangkok: Bua Luang Books, 1995.

————. "An Explosion of Thai Identities: Global Queering and Reimagining Queer Theory." *Culture, Health, and Sexuality* 2, no. 4 (2000): 405–24.

————. "From *Kamma* to Unnatural Vice: Male Homosexuality and Transgenderism in the Thai Buddhist Tradition." In Winston Leyland, ed., *Queer Dharma: A Buddhist Gay Anthology.* San Francisco: Gay Sunshine Press, 1997. 55–89.

————. "*Gay* Adaptation, *Tom-Dee* Resistance, and *Kathoey* Indifference: Thailand's Gender/Sex Minorities and the Episodic Allure of Queer English." In William L. Leap and Tom Boellstorff, eds., *Speaking in Queer Tongues: Globalization and Gay Language.* Urbana: University of Illinois Press, 2004. 202–30.

————. "*Kathoey*>*<Gay>*<*Man*: The Historical Emergence of *Gay* Male Identity in Thailand." In Lenore Manderson and Margaret Jolly, eds., *Sites of Desire, Economies of Pleasure: Sexualities in Asia and the Pacific.* Chicago: University of Chicago Press, 1997. 166–90.

————. "Tolerant but Unaccepting: Correcting Misperceptions of a Thai 'Gay Paradise.'" In Peter A. Jackson and Nerida M. Cook, eds., *Genders and Sexualities in Modern Thailand.* Chiang Mai: Silkworm Books, 1999. 226–42.

Jumphot Saisunthorn. "The Legal Status of Homosexuals" [Thana thang kotmaay khorng phu rak-ruam-pheet]. *Journal of Law* [Warasarn Nitisaat] 2, no. 13 (1993): 60–69.

Kittiwut Jod Taywaditep, Eli Coleman, and Pacharin Dumronggittigule. "Thailand (Muang Thai)." In Robert T. Francoeur, ed. *The International Encyclopedia of Sexuality,* vol. 3. New York: Continuum, 1997. 1192–1265.

Knodel, John, Chanpen Saengtienchai, Mark VanLandingham, and Rachel Lucas. "Sexuality, Sexual Experience, and the Good Spouse: Views of Married Thai Men and Women." In Nerida Cook and Peter Jackson, eds., *Genders and Sexualities in Modern Thailand.* Chiang Mai: Silkworm Books. 93–113.

Leap, William L., and Tom Boellstorff, eds. *Speaking in Queer Tongues: Globalization and Gay Language.* Urbana: University of Illinois Press, 2004.

Livia, Anna, and Kira Hall. "It's a Girl!: Bringing Performativity Back to Linguistics." In Anna Livia and Kira Hall, eds., *Queerly Phrased: Language, Gender, and Sexuality.* New York: Oxford University Press, 1997. 3–18.

Manderson, Lenore, and Margaret Jolly, eds. *Sites of Desire, Economies of Pleasure: Sexualities in Asia and the Pacific.* Chicago: University of Chicago Press, 1997.

Morris, Rosalind C. "Three Sexes and Four Sexualities: Redressing the Discourses on Gender and Sexuality in Thailand." *Positions* 2, no. 1 (1994): 15–43.

Mullaly, David. "Queerly Embodying the Good and the Normal." In Chris Berry, Fran Martin, and Audrey Yue, eds., *Mobile Cultures: New Media in Queer Asia.* Durham: Duke University Press, 2003. 115–229.

Praphaphan Wongsaroot. "Homosexual Identity Formation among Teenagers" [Karnphathanaa ekalak rak-ruam-pheet nai muu wai-run]. Master's thesis, Thammasat University, Thailand, 1989.

Scott, James. *Weapons of the Weak: Everyday Forms of Peasant Resistance.* New Haven: Yale University Press, 1985.

Sinnott, Megan. *Toms and Dees: Transgender Identity and Female Same-Sex Relationships in Thailand.* Honolulu: University of Hawaii Press, 2004.

Soonthorndhada, Amara. *Sexual Attitudes and Behaviors and Contraceptive Use of Late Female Adolescents in Bangkok: A Comparative Study of Students and Factory Workers.* Salaya, Nakornpathom, Thailand: Institute for Population and Social Research, Mahidol University, 1996.

Storer, Graeme. "Rehearsing Gender and Sexuality in Modern Thailand: Masculinity and Male-Male Sex Behaviors." In Peter A. Jackson and Gerard Sullivan, eds., *Lady Boys, Tom Boys, Rent Boys: Male and Female Homosexualities in Contemporary Thailand.* New York: Haworth Press, 1999. 141–59.

Van Wijngaarden, Jan Willem De Lind. "Between Money, Morality and Masculinity: The Dynamics of Bar-based Male Sex Work in Chiang Mai, Northern Thailand." In Peter A. Jackson and Gerard Sullivan, eds., *Lady Boys, Tom Boys, Rent Boys: Male and Female Homosexualities in Contemporary Thailand.* New York: Haworth Press, 1999. 193–218.

Vincent, Joan. *Anthropology and Politics: Visions, Traditions, and Trends.* Tucson: University of Arizona Press, 1990.

Walters, Suzanna Danuta. "From Here to Queer: Radical Feminism, Postmodernism, and the Lesbian Menace (Or, Why Can't a Woman Be More Like a Fag?)." *Signs* 21, no. 4 (1996): 830–69.

Wanlop Piyamanothaam. "*Tom, Gay, Dee, and Tut.*" In *Talking with a Psychologist* [Khuy kap nak citwithaya]. Bangkok: Baphitkanphim Publishing, 1992.

Warner, Michael, ed. *Fear of a Queer Planet: Queer Politics and Social Theory.* Minneapolis: University of Minnesota Press, 1993.

Wilson, Ara. *The Intimate Economies of Bangkok: Tomboys, Tycoons, and Avon Ladies in the Global City.* Berkeley: University of California Press, 2004.

EIGHT

BAD-ASSED HONEYS WITH A DIFFERENCE

South Auckland *Fa'afafine*
Talk about Identity

Heather Worth

> Modernism's crisis of legitimation, a crisis signaled in the term "postmodernism," registers the faltering recognition that this complicitous kinship of gendered binary divisions cannot be accepted complacently. . . . The hesitations that now interrupt orthodox accounts of truth and subjectivity have inevitably returned us to the perplexing questions of . . . identity.
>
> —V. Kirby, *Telling Flesh*

In the last twenty or so years, much Western theorizing has been fixated on questions of identity and its peculiar capacity for difference, ubiquity, and endurance. Identity (and difference, too) has permanence; the embodiment of sexual difference makes identity as a woman distinct from identity as a man. But the suggestion that sexual difference (that Ur-category for so many theorists over the last two decades) has a mutating existence tests our comprehension in an essential way, for it seems only natural to think of identity as fixed and discrete.

What brought home this idea that identity is paradoxically fixed and also has a curious ability to diverge and metastasize was the narratives of a group of *fa'afafine* who were interviewed as part of a research project, *Frayed at the Margins: Underclass Men Who Have Sex with Men,* a study of the relationship between poverty and unsafe sex among men who have sex with men in South Auckland (New Zealand).[1] This paper explores the narratives of this group of young *fa'afafine:*[2] Fenella, Helen, Jasmine, Lionel, Louella, Pandora,

Penny, and Rhonda, who all think of themselves in ways that are inimical to a Western view that we must be one sex or the other, or that we must choose a stable identity for ourselves. Their ability to eschew gender and sexual identity as stable hegemonic categories, their refusal to disallow multiple genders and sexual identities at the same time and in the same body is theoretically very important because they are a powerful, empirical critique of the categories that scholars have held as central to the feminist enterprise for many years now. But at the same time, their belief in both gender and sexual identities as being central to their sense of self reflects *fa'afafines'* inculcation into Western discourses of individuality, as well as in a globalized "queer" culture.

Anthropologists in the Pacific have long acknowledged the slipperiness of sex and gender. For example, Niko Besnier's work on "gender-liminality" in the Pacific has been informed by a long-ranging scholarly debate.[3] For Besnier, *fa'afafine* are not "representatives of femaleness as a coherent and unitary category, but rather they align themselves with specific instantiations of womanhood in various contexts." He argues, "the adoption by certain individuals of attributes associated with a gender other than their own is deeply embedded in the dynamics of Polynesian cultures and societies" (Besnier 1994, 285). Besnier wants to avoid terms such as "*berdache,*" "transsexual," "gay," or "homosexual" because, he argues, they "at best capture only one aspect of the category and at worst are completely miscontextualized" (308). He further asserts that the phenomena of *fa'afafine* and other modes of gender in the Pacific raise "particularly thorny categorical questions," realizing that "the distinction between gender and sex is anything but straightforward" (286). Gender is permeable, permutable, and multifarious—with exceedingly porous boundaries, varying "in form and intensity across contexts" (319). "Whatever its nature, gender liminality is the locus of a great deal of ambiguity, conflict and contestation in Polynesian societies" (328).

How do recent theoretical concerns with identity and difference fit with the experiences of a group of seven *fa'afafine* interviewees of South Auckland? In order to move these thorny questions forward, I will examine the work of a number of authors who deal with identity, but in particular I will use Derrida's essay, "The Law of Genre," which interrogates not only literary genre but also genus (from whence we get notions such as generation) and gender.[4] The law in "The Law of Genre" refers to the classification (and an enforceable principle of noncontamination and noncontradiction) of the binary opposites man/woman. But for Derrida, gender is always potentially excessive of the boundaries that bring it into being. While for Derrida binaries are not something that can be done without, the man/woman dichotomy that the law of gender tries to enforce is constitutively unable to be maintained in its absolute purity. This failing is generative (as in "genus"); it not only disrupts binary categories but is productive of the very identity (gender) that it disrupts. I am arguing here that Derrida's work helps us to think about identity and difference while realizing that the paradox of gender and sexuality can "never finally be resolved, however, because it witnesses the debt and condition of identity itself. Whether 'male' or 'female' subjectivity is a processual becoming that never arrives."[5] Thus we must view both the theorizing of gender/genre and the experiential narratives of the *fa'afafine* in this study as part of these chains of disparate signs that make up the world, both resisting and changing the binaries man/woman or straight/queer but never dissolving them.

Sex and Gender Identity in the Narratives of Pacific Island Queens

> Identity is never the same twice.
> —V. Kirby, *Telling Flesh*

Identity is central to the realization and naming of the individual's "true self" in late modernity in the West. Michel Foucault has argued that we are "dominated by the problem of the deep truth of the reality of our sex life."[6] He avers that we have come to believe that self-identity is intimately intertwined with sexuality and that sexual identity as a concept as Dowsett has argued "has assumed an existential function representing a psychic state, or a resolution of an individuated coming to the self."[7]

This idea of a resolution of identity in an individual self did not fit these women well at all. For the eight *fa'afafine* (two of whom are Maori who also called themselves *fa'afafine*, which is in itself very interesting) in this study, gender and sexual identity were extremely fluid categories. Louella heard the word "queer" before the term "*fa'afafine*."

> *Interviewer:* Had you ever heard the word "*fa'afafine*" before?
> *Louella:* Never. Never. Not *fa'afafine*. I heard . . . "queer," I heard it when I was about six. Yeah. I was walking home from school, and this chubby girl came up to me, and she goes—are you queer? I said no. She said you're queer. And I said and you're fat, and then I kept walking.
>
> I never asked anyone what *fa'afafine* was. I watched the way

people—the way they treated other people, other *fa'afafine*. And I
knew—well, they only called—these people *fa'afafine,* so they must
be *fa'afafine.* So . . . In terms of having *fa'afafine* there around me, it
was, I think it was a positive thing. . . . But even. . . . the shit that we
got as *fa'afafine,* as a whole . . . was different. . . . Because you wear a
dress, but be heterosexual, or whatever—I'm feminine, in that sense
though. And I'm quite comfortable like that.

Lionel argues that he was *fa'afafine* because his mum always wanted a
daughter and his aunties told a story that his mum used to dress him up when
he was a baby. He says, "I've never really—I've had no problems, with—my
homosexuality." Lionel realized in form 1 or 2 (aged eleven or twelve) that
he was *fa'afafine:*

> *Interviewer:* So now, you see gay men as different from *fa'afafine?*
> *Lionel:* Oh yeah. Yeah. Totally. Because . . . I'd go for a gay man, but
> I wouldn't go for a *fa'afafine.* Because *fa'afafine,* to me is . . . really,
> like, myself . . . I'd be oh no, that's incest. Do you know what I mean?
> Yeah, so, when I talk about *fa'afafine,* it's like . . . yeah. You're a girl.
> Whereas there may be a guy, a gay male, and we're, oh yum, he's deli-
> cious, it's like that. You see a guy, and it's like—yeah wow. And you'll
> see another guy and—women will go oh, but he's gorgeous, and I'll
> say well honey, that's a girl, I'm not interested in her . . . It's always—
> it's always—the guy. You know, real man.

Fenella says that she was "the only one [*fa'afafine*]. Yeah. I was the only one
in primary, only one I know, definitely, I was the only in primary, intermediate, and the only one in my high school."

Do the lived experiences of these young *fa'afafine* of South Auckland accord with the anthropological description of "a gender other than their own"?
When we examine the lived experiences, we must be attentive to the context
through which their sexual and gender identities are produced and marked.
Besnier argues that "clearly the relationship of gender liminality to social
structures and cultural processes is much more complex than traditionally
represented."[8] He also contends that the explanations of gender liminality
lie as part of "Polynesian notions of personhood which lack the consistent,
atomistic and homogeneous character of Western middle-class notions of
personhood but as capable of considerable malleability and adaptability to
changing social contexts."[9]

Besnier argues that the gender liminality in the contemporary Pacific "is further complicated by the presence, particularly the more acculturated areas of the region, of gay identities and perhaps communities that differ from 'traditional' gender liminality and resemble patterns observable in Western contexts."[10] It seems to me that for the queens in our study, identity is lived in a global context. Sex intersects with questions of class and ethnicity and with structures of poverty and colonialism. Being *faʻafafine* in Auckland at the cusp of the new millennium not only articulates with global social and cultural processes and the politics of sex, gender, and sexual orientation but also with the Pacific Island diaspora to New Zealand, the effect of HIV and the emphasis it has placed on sex and safety among marginalized groups, the effect of black American youth culture and drag personae such as Ru Paul, as well as an increasingly globalized gay culture. Thus, problematizations faced by *faʻafafine* in South Auckland at the turn of the millennium are similar to those of Harlem drag queens and straight women in general.

In our study, *faʻafafine* spoke in seemingly contradictory ways about their sex and gender during the interview—often in the same sentence or two—changing from female to male pronouns and back again at will. This was to such an extent that we, as researchers, were continually changing our minds as to whether to call them men or women. Pandora says, "I've always known, well, to me I feel that I'm—a woman. I mean, for goodness sake, I know I'm not, but my—the way I think and my habits are like a woman—I reckon. . . . We have the female side; we've got the men's,—the straight side."

However, she agrees that things can get tricky sometimes, "Yeah, I go out as a girl. And I know that sometimes I get sprung as a, as a boy, but it doesn't bother me. I think well hey, I'm who, I'm who I am." Helen speaks about being both girl and boy in this way: "I consider myself as a hundred percent female, and that's the way I live my life, every day. . . . Sometimes there was, you know, you know, you know that you are a girl, but then you know that because you're a guy, you have these needs as well." Fenella describes herself as "a bad-ass honey with a difference. That's what I'd call myself, more or less."

In the narratives above, the subjects talk about themselves as both girl and boy—as being a man but also being a woman in anything but a straightforward way. Louella has a real sense of the contradictions of sex and gender and how these categories relate to her lived experience as both male and female:

> *Louella:* I really believed that I was a woman. Female. Even male, as well. So I didn't really have a problem with being male or female. So yeah, I was a boy.

Interviewer: So you felt like both?

Louella: Yeah. . . . One day I will . . . some days I go with tits, and some days I don't. And people go—some of my queen friends go . . . why, why is it she just—be a woman or be a . . . I said it's just—don't get hung up on that—society bullshit about being either or. You know?

Her identity shifts and multiplies in time and space. She talks about hanging up her tits in her wardrobe when she didn't feel like going out as a woman. In fact, I saw Louella with tits for the very first time only a few nights ago. In all my meetings with her, she always dressed in "boy" clothes but with makeup and painted fingernails. She says, "This is the thing—I, I look at it as . . . I'm paying respect to my femininity. You know? So, I, I'll be—I'll dress up like a woman, and—you know, and have fun. And then, I'll pay respect to my masculinity, which is—dress, none of that stuff. And I feel really happy with that."

Louella is not *fa'afafine* in any "traditional" sense. Western notions of identity and difference, sex and gender inscribe her: "OK, a gay man to me, would be . . . well, yeah, I, I think I'm a gay man. Because I'm, I'm male—biologically, gender—genitalia wise, I am male, so yeah, I am, I'm a gay. But I'm also *fa'afafine*." In the very hesitancy of her statement she enunciates the difficulty in figuring out the complications of sex and gender in late modernity. But at the same time, Louella also holds the belief that identity is central to the individual's "true self," and is intimately intertwined with sexuality: "If we look at not just gender, sexual . . . like transgender or whatever, . . . everyone has their own independent individuality, and identity."

Judith Butler has argued that "performances" of gender, such as those of drag queens (and I would argue) *fa'afafine* are an imitation of femininity. She is not claiming that there is an original femininity that *fa'afafine* parody, rather, that the law of gender is experienced in the same ways as heterosexual women: "A constant and repeated effort to imitate [femininity's] own idealisations."[11] That is, there is an ideal of femininity that none of us—straight women, *fa'afafine*, or, in Butler's case, drag queens—can ever fully embody. For *fa'afafine*, identity cannot be seen as a simple imitation or a masquerade; identity as a woman is taken seriously in terms of both appearance and subjectivity. Fenella describes herself as "a real girl." And Helen says, "To me, I consider myself as a hundred percent female, and that's the way I live my life, every day." However, Helen's wish to be a girl is also undercut by her anatomical difference: "I remember when I was a lot younger, I always used to say my prayers in case I'd wake up in the morning and I've got long hair—and breasts, and one of those . . . I mean—wake up, oh it's still there! Damn it. Yeah, that was me in the mornings. I was quite young then."

This conundrum is continually pondered over by the participants. As Rhonda says, "I was born a man, you know? . . . But it . . . it doesn't just end there, you know?" Jasmine is proud of her breasts: "I have breasts. I like to grow my breasts like that—I'm the only one who has breasts." Penny felt trapped: "When I was at primary—I mean at intermediate, I felt like a real—I felt like I was a woman, trapped in a man's body. . . . Yeah." But while she and others in the study call on essentialist rhetoric about femaleness, Penny, as a queen, most importantly does not elaborate a directly feminine image; there is an articulation that grounds the very femaleness of these *fa'afafines'* morphology.

Theorizing Sex and Gender

How well do other recent attempts at theorization come to grips with these *fa'afafines'* determined multiplication of sexes and genders? In his 1996 book on gay identity in Australia, Gary Dowsett critically questions sexual identity as a concept that "has assumed an existential function representing a psychic state, or a resolution of an individuated coming to the self."[12] And while our subjects accepted Western views of individualized subjectivity in some ways, this resolution of identity did not fit the subjects of our research at all well. Dowsett's book is problematic in that it views the phenomenon of gender liminality in the metropolis though a lens of (male) homosexuality (or, as he puts it, gender-bending). In discussing one of the subjects in his book, a drag queen named Harriet, Dowsett rightly sums up the profound consequences for each person's assignment to one or other side of the man/woman binary. But Harriet is not, according to Dowsett, a transsexual even if explicitly effeminate because "I like my dick" (96). While Dowsett acknowledges the complications of feminine identity in Harriet's case, arguing that he has a clear, "purposive use for the 'essentialist' notion of identity" (97), Harriet's sexual subjectivity is in question as something constituted through practice; his sex is not: "he" is assuredly male.[13] Harriet's male body is safely quarantined outside the reach of gender. And while Dowsett makes "the historically constructed experience of living a gay life" central to Harriet's biography, this too seems inadequate to the morphology of *fa'afafine*.

Similarly, Leon Pettiway, in his book *Honey, Honey, Miss Thang,* insists that his African-American, drug-using, street-walking hustlers "are gay men [who] dress and view themselves as women."[14] However, for the majority of our respondents, identifying as gay was not an option. Fenella's response is typical: "I'm not a gay man in a dress." Being called gay was "confusing," for she considers herself *faafafine* · "Being a *faafafine*, what it means to me, or what it is to me, is that—I don't consider myself gay. . . . And . . . when—I've been called gay, when people call me gay, I look at myself and I go no, a gay man, I am [a] different thing."

> *Interviewer:* Wearing girls' clothes—is that a different thing then, or is it part of the same thing?
>
> *Fenella:* Yeah, I, I . . . I think it is. Being gay and actually—being in, in a dress, and you know, sort of—switching gender roles. I think it's . . . it's not gay at all. I don't really think it's gay.

For a number of the respondents, being gay was a "stage" that they went through, on the way to some other gender/sexual identity. Helen argues, "I consider myself as . . . really, I'm sort of halfway, just over—I'm just over the gay . . . Oh sorry, just past the gay stage—like, OK, you've got a line here, you've got your gay—your gay part, sort of like me growing up. And then—I've just sort of slightly stepped over to the transsexual side."

For Louella, being *faafafine* is a broad term: "It's very inclusive—it's not exclusive. It's [not] just that—boof, you're either gay or you're bloody heterosexuals. So like, *faafafine* is very broad. It means femininity to me. So everyone has femininity in them, so everyone's a *faafafine,* in one, some sense."

Is this identity as both woman and man ambivalent? Judith Butler's take on drag queens is that the reiteration of femaleness is pathologizing and normalizing—producing an anxiety that excludes domains of sexual possibility. Our (mine as a heterosexual woman and Louella as *faafafine*) implication in our own subordination produces loss (of identity).[15] It's an ambivalence precisely because, as Butler puts it, "There is a cost in every identification, the loss of some other set of identifications, the forcible approximation of a norm one never chooses, a norm that chooses us, but which we occupy reverse, resignify to the extent that the norm fails to determine us completely."[16]

Butler uses the term "gender" to describe the accomplishment of heterosexuality that takes place through a primary "foreclosure of homosexuality": the loss of the possibility of the same sex as an object of desire. But this loss, constitutive yet disavowed, has a continuing effect because it marks "the limit to the subject's sense of *pouvoir,* its sense of what it can accomplish and, in that sense, its power." Subjectivity thus is also "haunted by an inassimilable remainder," which emerges as gender melancholy.[17] So while on one hand Butler undermines the straight(forward) identity of the self-present subject of/as maleness, on the other the power of the law as negation, prevention, constraint, and prohibition names, assigns, and delimits identity over and over again.

Thus the only resistance possible in Butler's worldview is that which takes place outside the law. She cannot concede the possibility, indeed the inevitability, that rearticulation might occur within the law, that the law of gender might indeed be differentiating and productive. Pandora's feeling is that "I don't know who I'd class myself. . . . I like, I like to call myself a transsexual, but I know I'm not. I'm only fooling myself, but yeah, I don't know. Just as a human being, I guess. I'm just a human being." But Pandora also has a joy in this lack of closure: "Oh . . . I do really dizzy things, and—yeah. Not in, yeah, just—I just, really mental. Just a really—mental dizzy person. But in a fabulous way—in a fun way. There's that . . . being queer is fabulous, and I love it."

In summary, then, in the narratives above, the subjects talk about themselves as both being a man but also being a woman in anything but a straightforward way. If we worry about Butler's account of interpellation such that subjects are insistently "this" or "that" and continually account for themselves anew, doomed to reiterate femininity in its most subjugating form, how then do we theorize Louella's "strangeness" as both man and woman, or how do we comprehend what it means for Fenella to be a "bad-ass honey with a difference"?

Helen argues that she was born a man and that she will always be a son to her parents. But she understands that sexual and gender identities do not end at birth, that her identity "as possibly everything" signals the paradox of gender and sexuality rather than upholding the general anxiety about sexual ambiguity as a problem (and a pathology that needs fixing).

Fa'afafine: Outlaws of Genre

> Genres are not to be mixed. I will not mix genres.
> —Derrida, "The Law of Genre"

As I mentioned earlier, Jacques Derrida has written in a number of essays about the legislative character of the subject and gender. The law demands two sexes—male, female—and that we choose between them (genres are NOT to be mixed). And it also demands that we do not mix what Derrida calls "the essential purity" of gender's identity. But in the lives of these young queens and *fa'afafine* in South Auckland at the turn of the new millennium, this does not seem applicable. The law of genre does not seem to hold. They refuse such an edict, such an interdiction. Their genders are in excess of their genre, of the law of gender. In fact the very perversity of their gender, both its determination and waywardness, seems not to be a mistake that can be corrected.

But Derrida also asserts that the law of subjectivity and gender can be refused; it always potentially exceeds the boundaries that bring it into being. He posits another possibility: "Suppose for a moment that it was impossible NOT to mix genres. What if there were, lodged within the heart of the law itself, a law of impurity or a principle of contamination? And suppose the condition for the possibility of the law were the a priori of a counter-law, an axiom of impossibility that would confound its sense, order and reason."[18] As we can see from the stories of these *fa'afafine,* they disrupt the law by a spilling over of identity. It is not just that they cannot choose between genres; more importantly and problematically, they want it all. It is not as if they are free-floating or unconnected to gender. It is their very engendering that marks them. In Jasmine's story, both she and her partner are caught up in a complicated rendering of the excess of gender:

> *Interviewer:* Why did you come to New Zealand?
> *Jasmine:* I was actually engaged to a man, he didn't know I was a male, and we were together for two years, and . . . he didn't know I was a man—his mother thought I was pregnant, so . . . I came down to Auckland for a while. And I never called him since.
> *Interviewer:* And how come the mother thought you were pregnant?
> *Jasmine:* Cause he didn't know I'm a male.
> *Interviewer:* How come he didn't know that you were a male? Do you mind if I ask that; is that okay?
> *Jasmine:* It's just . . . I became . . . a prostitute when I was eleven. And I've always dealt with men. And I know how to trick men. . . . Because I am so used to having . . . a guy, because I'm not a man you know? I know how to deal with those, being open to another person.
> *Interviewer:* And how often would you have sex with him?
> *Jasmine:* Oh, I would say every day.
> *Interviewer:* And he never, ever found out?
> *Jasmine:* No.
> *Interviewer:* You screwed him?

Jasmine: I played a trick on him. Which is, to make him think how, how would he feel if I told him I was a man. And then he goes, where is your penis. And I showed it to him and he just couldn't believe it. Because we bathe together, we have a shower together, and . . . he never sees it, until the night I told him. And I showed it to him. Then he goes . . . this is not real. But it was, you know, he just thought it was not real. He just thought it was one of those put-on penises you can put on and, you know, the vibrator or what ever you call it. Then I said, let me try it out for you, because I've always wanted to do this. I want to try with him. And then we tried it, and . . . he, he's going . . . this is not real, it doesn't feel real. And then I take it out and I just— hid it again. And then when he, when he went to have a shower, I didn't bring it out again, I just hid it. And then he goes see, you're not a, you're not a man, you're a woman. And this is the Jasmine I'm in love with. The girl. You know, not a man. . . . It's just the way I look after myself and that. Because I'm so much the lady, I just don't have any manly ways.

Jasmine's story, its contradictions of gender and, even more, her boyfriend's determination that she WILL be female, is a potent empirical example of my argument. Speaking in a statement released when his film *M Butterfly* was in production, David Cronenberg stated in relation to Neil Jordan's *The Crying Game*: "*The Crying Game* made that thing of two men having a love affair— where one didn't know that the other one was a man—kind of sweet and in-nocent and pure and, in a weird way, not threatening. . . . I think it's because she (Jaye Davidson) really is a woman, even though she's got a cock."[19]

In this way the law, which is often figured as an interdiction—as the nega-tivity of a boundary that cannot be crossed, becomes a process of double af-firmation (a "yes, yes") to it all. Penny (the woman trapped in a man's body) in no way merely elaborates a directly feminine "image." And there is more than just an articulation of such a representation, more than a metaphoric and transferential articulation. As Rhonda says, "I was born a man, you know? . . . But it . . . it doesn't just end there, you know." If these *fa'afafine* identities are plastic, so also are their bodies, "materiality as a sign of writing wherein difference is its defining force."[20] Their excessive bodies are not a call for an indeterminacy of identity, part of the West's obsession with the "Other's exoticism," but a necessity born of the articulation of the femaleness of these women's morphology. If genres/genders pass into each other, this permits an engendering of *fa'afafine* that in itself engenders still further genres.

Conclusion

> [B]eyond the binary difference that governs the decorum of
> all codes, beyond the opposition feminine-masculine, beyond
> bisexuality as well, beyond homosexuality and heterosexuality,
> which come to the same thing . . . I would like to believe in the
> multiplicity of sexually marked voices. I would like to believe
> in the masses, this indeterminable number of blended voices,
> this mobile of sexually nonidentified sexual marks whose
> choreography can carry, divide, multiply the body of each
> "individual."
>
> —Derrida, "Choreographies"

Fa'afafine in South Auckland at the turn of the millennium are potent reminders that identity and difference are inextricably bound to one another. There was ample evidence throughout the interviews of the difficulty of being one or the other sex or having a stable gender or even a sexual identity, and at the same time an embracing of identity as an important part of subjectivity. This inability to be one sex or the other while at the same time making a claim to difference and identity is not a negative; it can be seen as a desire to have it all, to embrace an excessive set of genders. To conclude, however, I want to make it plain that I am not arguing that it is just the *fa'afafine* marginality that allows for an exceeding, a shattering of the law of genre. Neither is this argument some nostalgic colonial dream of exotic excess. I agree with Butler that what holds for drag queens holds for women and identity in general; that gender itself bears these characteristics as a foundational principle. Rather than being two opposing forces on either side of the binary from one another, masculinity and femininity are integral to each other's identity: "The breach in the identity and being of the sovereign subject . . . is a constitutive breaching, a recalling and differentiating within the subject, which calls it into presence. . . . This very breach opens identity to a force field of differences in which the binary divisions . . . are impossibly implicated."[21]

Notes

1. The fieldwork for the research project was carried out in the summer of 1999, and the larger study of which these interviews were a part was about the intersection between poverty and sexual and gender identities in South Auckland. An office was set up in South Auckland and contacts were made from there with interview subjects. In all, seventeen in-depth interviews were completed using snowball sampling tech-

niques. The interviews lasted up to an hour and a half and were tape recorded, then fully transcribed. This was the first time that anyone had done interviews with this group of *fa'afafine* in New Zealand. The *fa'afafine* group happened to be an interesting subsample of a larger group. I cannot tell how large the community is—especially in New Zealand as a whole. In addition, *fa'afafine* interaction with the gay community is really complicated and is a paper in its own right.

2. The term *fa'afafine* is Samoan for "the way of a woman."

3. Besnier uses the term *gender-liminal* as popularized by Victor Turner in *In the Forest of Symbols* and *The Ritual Process*. Turner elaborates three major characteristics of gender-liminality: borderline location, outsider status, and social inferiority, all of which apply to the interviewees in this study. See also the following authors: Levy, "The Community Function of Tahitian Male Transvestism: A Hypothesis"; Shore, "Sexuality and Gender in Samoa"; B. Daniellsson and M-T. Daniellsson, "Polynesia's Third Sex"; Poasa, "The Samoan Fa'afafine"; Mageo, "Male Transvestism and Cultural Change in Samoa"; Besnier, "Polynesian Gender Liminality."

4. In French, "genre" means both gender and genre.

5. Kirby, *Telling Flesh*, 67.

6. Foucault, "An Ethics of Pleasure," 379.

7. Dowsett, *Practicing Desire*, 99.

8. Besnier, "Polynesian Gender Liminality," 317.

9. Ibid., 312. Similarly, Kalissa Alexeyeff, in "Dragging Drag," argues that Cook Islands' personhood is performative of gendered roles rather than sexual desires or practices. Alexeyeff portrays *laelae* [the Cook Islands' name for gender-liminal people] and Cook Islanders as somehow not being tarnished by Western modernist ideas or influences about sexuality in the construction of gender identity and subjectivity.

10. Besnier, "Polynesian Gender Liminality," 304.

11. Butler, *Bodies That Matter*, 126.

12. Dowsett, *Practicing Desire*, 99.

13. Dowsett not only uses the male personal pronoun for Harriet, but nowhere in the chapter does he question Harriet's maleness.

14. Pettiway, *Honey, Honey, Miss Thang*, xii.

15. Butler, *Bodies That Matter*, 126.

16. Ibid., 126–7.

17. Ibid., 56.

18. Derrida, "The Law of Genre," 225, my emphasis.

19. Interestingly, most of the commentary on *The Crying Game* nominates Dil as pathological femininity-as-lack, and a renaturalization of sexual difference through recourse to an amalgam of all-too-familiar feminine stereotypes.

20. Kirby, *Telling Flesh*, 56.

21. Kirby, *Telling Flesh*, 95.

References

Alexeyeff, K. "Dragging Drag: The Performance of Gender and Sexuality in the Cook Islands." *Australian Journal of Anthropology* 11, no. 3 (2000): 297–307.

Besnier, Niko. "Polynesian Gender Liminality through Time and Space." In Gilbert Herdt, ed., *Third Sex, Third Gender: Beyond Sexual Dimorphism in Culture and History.* New York: Zone Books, 1994. 477–85.

Butler, Judith. *Bodies That Matter: On the Discursive Limits of "Sex."* London: Routledge, 1993.

Daniellsson, B., and M-T. Daniellsson. "Polynesia's Third Sex: The Gay Life Starts in the Kitchen." *Pacific Islands Monthly* (1978): 10–13.

Derrida, Jacques. "Choreographies." *Diacritics* (1982): 66–76.

———. "The Law of Genre." In Derek Attridge, ed., *Acts of Literature.* New York: Routledge, 1992. 224–25.

———. "Signature Event, Context." In *Margins of Philosophy,* trans. Alan Bass. Chicago: University of Chicago Press, 1971.

———. *Writing and Difference.* London: Routledge and Kegan Paul, 1978.

Dowsett, Gary. *Practicing Desire: Homosexual Sex in the Era of AIDS.* Stanford, Calif.: Stanford University Press, 1996.

Foucault, Michel. "An Ethics of Pleasure." In *Foucault Live (Interviews, 1966–84),* ed. Sylvere Lotringer, trans. John Johnston. New York: Semiotext(e), 1989. 371–81.

———. *Herculine Barbin: Being the Recently Discovered Memoirs of a Nineteenth-Century French Hermaphrodite.* Brighton, U.K.: Harvester Press, 1980.

Kirby, V. *Telling Flesh: The Substance of the Corporeal.* New York: Routledge, 1997.

Levy, Robert. "The Community Function of Tahitian Male Transvestism: A Hypothesis." *Anthropological Quarterly* 44 (1971): 1.

Mageo, Jeanette M. "Male Transvestism and Cultural Change in Samoa." *American Ethnologist* 19 (1992): 443–59.

Pettiway, L. *Honey, Honey, Miss Thang: Being Black, Gay, and on the Streets.* Philadelphia: Temple University Press, 1996.

Poasa, Kris. "The Samoan Fa'afafine: One Case Study and Discussion of Transsexualism." *Journal of Psychology and Human Sexuality* 5, no. 3 (1992): 39–51.

Shore, Bradd. "Sexuality and Gender in Samoa: Conceptions and Missed Conceptions." In S. Ortner and H. Whitehead, ed., *Sexual Meanings: The Cultural Construction of Gender and Sexuality.* Cambridge: Cambridge University Press, 1981.

Turner, Victor. *In the Forest of Symbols: Aspects of Ndembu Ritual.* Ithaca, N.Y.: Cornell University Press, 1967.

———. *The Ritual Process: Structure and Anti-Structure.* Chicago: Aldine, 1969.

NINE

VILLA, MONTANO, PEREZ

Postcoloniality and Gay Liberation
in the Philippines

J. Neil C. Garcia

Colonialism is all about power, but as the Foucauldian account
tells us, such power is always already ambivalent in its effects: it coerces or
subjugates at the same time that it animates the persons it hails into being.[1]

In the Philippines, American colonialism and continuing *global* neocolonialism must be seen as the ascendancy of a regulatory regime that is both
juridical and productive. While it hierarchizes and marginalizes its many
different subjects (and abjects), it also enables certain subjectivities and/or
positionalities to exist where previously they did not exist. Ironically, various dissidences and positions of resistance are made possible alongside the
inarguable fact of brute, imperialist domination.

In this chapter I argue that one such subject-position is the "homosexual"—
a pathologized identity inaugurated by the new sexual logic that was "implanted" in the Philippines during the four decades of American occupation
from 1898. From the early 1900s, the logic of *homo/hetero* became increasingly
salient in the lives of Filipinos because of the growing influence of Western
biomedicine and the modernization of local institutions of education, governance, and the mass media, all of which assumed the inevitability and "natu-
ralness" of this distinction. Soon enough, certain Filipino homosexuals began
engaging in different projects of "inversion," identifying with the very label
that pathologized and oppressed them while simultaneously refunctioning

it to serve surprisingly "liberationist" ends. In other words, while American colonialism brought the malady of "homosexuality" and all its discontents into the Philippines, it has also been the persistence and increasing virulence of this same colonialism that has provided a bit of the "cure," namely, gay liberation. The ways this liberationist discourse is articulated by Filipinos demonstrate not only instances of discursive reversal or transgressive reinscription, but also forms of hybridity and "postcolonial appropriation."

Among its neighbors in Asia, the Philippines historically has suffered from the most brutal form of direct colonization and neocolonization by American imperial power. For this reason, it would be foolish to neglect grappling with the cultural and historical fact of Americanization, and how inescapably constitutive it was and continues to be in the lives of many Filipinos. On the other hand, it is this study's major premise that Americanization, to the extent that it can be seen as a discursive rather than simply a military enforcement of hegemony, must also be read as a "representational mode." As such, Americanization was not absolute or monolithic, for once situated it was, willfully or otherwise, translated and/or resignified by the local cultures it domesticated and subsumed.

In making these arguments, I engage critically the works of Jose Garcia Villa, Severino Montano, and Tony Perez, nationally significant literary figures whose different "awarenesses" of the question of homosexuality are each curiously linked to the discourse and "experience" of America. In Villa's and Montano's cases, their permanent and transient residencies in America, respectively, occasioned the writing of texts that blatantly thematized homoeroticism. In Perez's case, on the other hand, his book may be seen to have been spurred by the Stonewall-inspired Philippines "gay liberation movement."[2] By attending to these brave and compelling texts—Villa's short stories, the trilogy called *Wings and Blue Flame* and *Song I Did Not Hear,* Montano's novel, *The Lion and the Faun,* and Perez's *Cubao 1980 at Ibang Pang Mga Katha: Ang Unang Sigaw ng Gay Liberation sa Pilipinas*—I locate and provisionally describe, in and through the operations of hybridity, the ambivalent effects of American colonial power in the domains of Filipino gender and sexuality.

My recourse to postcolonialism, and particularly to Homi Bhabha's notion of hybridity, signals an attempt to rethink—and revaluate—my earlier work on the history of homosexuality in the Philippines in order to situate it within the broader frame of transculturation and the colonial and neocolonial relations between the Philippines and the United States. My aim is to respond to the vexed and vexing question of Filipinoness. Nativist essentialism—

proposed as a heroic "remembering" of a pristine and purely indigenous past—is the dominant historiographic paradigm in the Philippines today, and an animus still exists in some Philippine academic circles against supposedly colonial-minded or foreign-derived theories.[3] Indeed, my own work has been thus critiqued. In a recent anthology edited by a group of nativist Filipino lesbian and gay critics, my four books on Philippine gay culture and criticism are not mentioned or referenced. Interestingly, this nativism is not what it seems at first glance, since the book's essays merely translate certain precepts of American lesbian and gay theories into Tagalog, without attempting to critically engage with or indeed "qualify" them.[4] Such nativism emerges from a kind of postcolonial hubris that is sadly misinformed, for it refuses to see that the national and indeed the native position themselves are made possible precisely by and inside the narrative of colonialism, of which there can be, unfortunately, no simple "essentialist" forgetting.

Among other things, what this continuity of nativist-nationalist perspectives foregoes is a productive engagement with alternative and more complicated reckonings of colonial power, and consequently, of postcolonial agency. Bhabha's theory on the ambivalent, negotiable, and fetishistic relations of mimicry and hybridity between the colonizer and the colonized offers just this reconceptualization—one that resonates with and clarifies the Foucauldian thesis on power's productivity, especially where the colonial encounter is concerned. By using the figure of sexuality—in particular, of homosexuality—in a discussion of postcolonial opposition or subversion, I am not only performing a counterintuitive move in what is, in the Philippines at least, a generally erotophobic field of knowledge that routinely ignores or glosses over the difference that homosexuality makes. I am also calling attention to what is increasingly becoming a well-known fact: that the sexual and gender questions are not merely epiphenomenal but rather, as argued by many postcolonial feminists, are central to the imperial and national projects themselves.[5]

Bhabha sees colonialism as being, in the main, a discursive or representational project imposed upon the colonized that constructs their identity as inferior and therefore needing tutelage and amelioration. And yet, precisely for this reason, this colonial identity can only exist in relation to the colonizer's, which it maintains and is maintained by it. As such, both the colonizer and the colonized are anxious positions in this relationality and are caught up in a mutually constitutive economy of fantasy and desire. Their senses of self live inside the "differentiating order of otherness."[6] That is, the Other against which they define themselves in fact resides inside them as their founding repudiation. Thus they can only simultaneously deride and desire it, revealing an ambivalence that is uneasily if only partially assuaged by fetishistic attachment. As the compulsively reiterated fetish of the colonial stereotype illustrates, even as the colonizer may outwardly revile or fear the colonized native, in the very act of reviling or fearing he silently acknowledges and actively desires him.[7]

Bhabha explains hybridity as the nonconvergence between colonial power's intentions and the affects of those who receive them. In every new encounter, colonial authority repeats itself as different from the culture it seeks to subjugate. Each repetition of its differential and discriminatory discourse undermines the very claims of this discourse to a natural and singular originality. Power repeats and imitates itself over and over, and is diluted, compromised, and hybridized at every turn. As Bhabha eloquently puts it, "In the very practice of domination the language of the master becomes hybrid—neither the one thing nor the other."[8] Thus, all colonial impositions, including those that pertain to gender and sexual identities and desires, become resignified by the other culture, split between their claims and their performances, recontextualized and syncretized from the very moment of contact with the colonized.

The Perverse Implantation, Philippine Version

To historicize homosexuality in the Philippines, we must begin by recognizing the fundamental difference between gender and sexuality.[9] We need to disarticulate the connection between the gender-transitive behaviors and identities of the local categories of *bakla, bayot, agi, bantut*,[10] and so forth, on the one hand, and the discourse and reality of homosexuality as a typically "gay" or "lesbian" question of same-sexual orientation and/or identity, on the other. From the available evidence, it seems that the history of the former stretches into the oral past not only of the Philippines but of the whole of Southeast Asia,[11] while the latter is a more recent development, a performative instance and discursive effect of the largely American-sponsored biomedicalization of local Filipino cultures. Looking at the available Spanish accounts, we know that from the earliest encounters between the *conquistadores* and the *indios,* gender-crossing and transvestism were clear cultural features of a number of early colonial—and thus, presumably, precolonial—communities across the Philippine archipelago.

A complementary—rather than a rigid and hierarchical—division of roles between men, women, gender-crossers, and others, was in place in many parts of the Philippines when the Spanish arrived. It appears that with the passing of the centuries, and as the status of native women progressively deteriorated, traditional gender-crossing became increasingly difficult to perform as the gender-crosser suffered ridicule and scorn from the Spanish brand of Mediterranean machismo. Originally likened to a species of bamboo called *bayog* in the Tagalog-speaking regions of Luzon, the native effeminate man (*bayoguin*)[12] slowly transmogrified into *bakla*, a word which also meant "confused" and "cowardly."[13] Unlike his formerly "destined" state, *kabaklaan* ("*bakla*-ness") was seen as a temporary condition away from which he might conceivably be wrested. Despite three hundred years of Spanish colonial rule and Catholic missionary activity, cross-dressing and gender-transitive behavior never left the Philippines. Rather, they were syncretized and irrevocably transformed in their encounter with the foreign into a variety of colonial and postcolonial practices.[14]

The American period—in which the postcolonial Philippines remains—saw the entrenchment of American cultural hegemony through the co-optation of the traditional mestizo creolized elite, the expansion of the newly empowered middle class, the secularization of public education, the promulgation and regulation of Western (specifically, American) notions of gender and sexuality by means of academic instruction in English, and the Americanization of all aspects of government and the mass media. This discursive regulation in and through the imposition of American culture inaugurated a sexological consciousness predicated upon a psychological style of reasoning hitherto unknown in the local context.

By virtue of American colonialism and neocolonialism, Filipinos have been increasingly socialized in Western modes of gender and sexual identity formation. This sexualization has been effected by different but nonetheless complementary discourses of public hygiene, psychosexual development, juvenile delinquency, guidance and counseling, health and physical education, family planning, civics, feminist empowerment, gay and lesbian advocacy, as well as the corporally paranoid discourse of AIDS. This has resulted in the deepening of sexuality's perverse implantation into the local soil, accompanied by the establishment and subsequent *exorbitation* of the "homo/hetero" distinction as the key organizing principle in the now-heavily-freighted *sexual* lives of Filipinos, especially those living in the large urban centers where Westernized knowledges hold most sway.

The closer to the present situation we look, the more we realize, with horror and regret, that the effeminate *bakla* has increasingly become the "homosexual": a male whose identity is primarily defined as a function of his sexual desire for *other men*.[15] This homosexualization has been premised upon a corresponding and equally foundational heterosexualization, a process that will obviously require its own painstaking historicizing in the Philippines. Taking our cue from Judith Butler's analysis of the "heterosexual matrix" in the modern West,[16] we can imagine that this process proceeded out of an initial binarization of the gendered body into anatomically mutually exclusive male and female normative "types." This is a colonial binarization, to be sure, for as I have argued, early colonial and thus presumably precolonial Philippine cultures recognized the existence of "mixed," "liminal," and/or "alternative" bodies. At the time, the male/female dualism did not exhaust all the possible somatizations of the gendered self the various Philippine *indios* could assume.[17]

While his effeminacy and transvestic ways place him as the last in a long line of "gender-anomalous" beings in the motley patchwork of the Philippines's colonial history, the *bakla* is unlike any of his predecessors in at least one key respect: he is burdened not only by his gender self-presentation, but also, and more tragically, by his "sexual orientation"—an attribute capable of defining who he is, as a matter of deep psychological being, as an innermost question of *self*.

As if coping with his swishy ways in a helplessly macho culture were not enough, the *bakla* must now also contend with private demons of self-loathing on account of his intrinsically "pathological" or "sick" desire. Nonetheless, the pathologizing of the *bakla* into and *as* a homosexual has also made available many encouraging narratives—of hybridity, appropriation, and postcolonial resistance. As the admittedly exceptional examples of Villa's, Montano's, and Perez's texts demonstrate, the very people who have been pathologized by the American sexological regime are also paradoxically "enabled" by this very stigma, which they subsequently employ in projects of reverse discourse to serve self-affirming ends.

Villa's Unheard Songs

Not many Filipinos know that the late national artist, legendary exile, and shrewish poet Jose Garcia Villa (1908–1997) published a collection of short stories in the United States[18] a few years before his first book of poems came out. Since the original collection's three most revealing stories were deleted from the local edition of this book, even fewer are aware of the fact that some of those stories, declared "autobiographical" in the preface by the book's American champion, Edward J. O'Brien, plotted the experiences of the young

Villa as a university student in Albuquerque, New Mexico. What makes these stories scandalously interesting is that they are essentially about Villa's affection and erotic desire for two American boys, a certain David from Santa Fe and the boorish and emotionally unavailable Swedish jock, Jack Wicken. In a separate story, Villa talks about a homely Jewish boy, Joe Lieberman, whose heroic and selfless love he spurns in favor of his unrequited longing for the boorish redneck, Jack.

Villa's stories provide us with the biographical and cultural context within which to read his famously beguiling, "modernist" images. They plot the "young" life of Villa as a man who loved other men, who possessed feelings of an undeniably same-sexual nature, and who, to his credit, bravely wrote out these feelings in as honest and artistic an expression as he could manage. Insofar as they can be read as autobiographical, they provide a textualized glimpse into Villa's otherwise largely irrecoverable sexual biography.

These stories are essential in *recovering* what may be the most historically relevant thing about this stubbornly quizzical figure in Philippine arts and letters. If these stories are any indication, Villa was, very early on, a socially conscious writer who confronted the social stigma attending the nature of his desire, and courageously *wrote out* and celebrated it, *in spite of everything*. We can only surmise that it is precisely because Villa was already living in the United States that he was able to articulate, in the astonishingly "early" period of the 1930s, this otherwise unspeakable "facet" of his personality—something that had obviously been hounding him even when he was a mother-loving, father-hating, brooding and sissy little boy in the Philippines.

These stories lyrically exemplify what may well be the earliest textualization by a Filipino writer of a kind of "inverted" homosexual consciousness. This consciousness was a hybrid between the *bakla* and the homosexual, as can only be the case with an expatriate like Villa, who lived his first two decades in the Philippines and thereafter permanently relocated to the United States. In Villa's revealing work, we can see that the pathologizing discourse of homosexuality that afflicted him both in the Philippines and in the United States nevertheless enabled him to speak precisely as its discursive subject, even if he could only do so mostly poetically and miserably. That he had to first migrate to the United States before he could write with some frankness on this topic suggests to us how the America that colonized his home country ironically allowed him enough personal and aesthetic distance and creative freedom to live and write as himself. If we wish to find a more affirmative articulation of this consciousness, we need to turn to the work of a contemporaneous writer, the playwright and sometime-fictionist, Severino Montano.

Montano's Woman-Hating Lion and Faun

Severino Montano (1915–1980) was posthumously declared a national artist in 2001. His work in Philippine theater in English was extensive and, in terms of his staging innovations and the sheer scale and "reach" of his productions, undeniably significant and path-breaking. He also wrote an unpublished self-consciously homosexual novel titled *The Lion and the Faun,* a photo-copied half of which I had the good fortune of acquiring ten years ago.[19] This work, written well before his death in 1980, provides another example of how American-sponsored homosexualization in the Philippines has ironically produced an abjected identity that embraces its abjection, and speaks *of* and *for* itself. As was the case with Villa, what seems to have occasioned this speech was the lived reality and experience of the United States itself.

Montano's novel is a provocative and largely autobiographical roman à clef. Comparing the known facts about Montano's life with those of his main character, Dr. Diosdado Medalla, the reader is encouraged to carry out a "biographical interpretation" of the text, which effectively parodies and sati-rizes the shallow and hypocritical lives of Manila's culturati, and makes broad hints at a possible romantic dalliance between Medalla, whose nickname is Dadong, and his famous dearest friend, the late Philippine president, Ramon "Monching" Magsaysay (1907–1957). Despite gossipy subplots and intrigues, the main story is Dadong's relationship with the younger Amihan, an Army major stationed at the Reserve Officers' Training Corps (ROTC) office of the university where Dadong teaches, and where he has founded a theater company.

Because it is likely that the American-educated Montano had been writ-ing this novel on and off for three or more decades before his death,[20] he is unlikely to have had access to feminist-inspired gay liberationist literatures that do not mandate a misogynistic attitude towards women as part of the project of articulating gayness and militating for its emancipation. Montano's appalling anti-woman attitudes are too evident everywhere in the text, from the unflattering description of the "loose" and "smelly" genitalia of Amihan's grubby tubercular wife to the characterization of women as grasping, pa-thetic, and sex-starved gold diggers.

In all probability, Montano's misogyny emanated out of the kind of mas-culinist imperative he was laboring under. To Montano's mind, it must have seemed necessary to put down women in general in order to destroy the feminized and feminizing stereotype that afflicted the Philippine *bakla,* an identity strangely missing in or perhaps deliberately "evacuated" from the novel. However, precisely because Montano has exiled all traces of effeminacy and *kabaklaan* from his text, we are forced to read the *bakla* as being in fact a central "force" in his articulation. For in repudiating this identity, he has in the end only made it all the more foundational. Indeed, despite the novel's main characters' testosterone-powered, ambisexually potent machismo, its casting aspersions on women and conceiving them as vicious "competition" for the attention and affection of men are, finally, very *bakla* things to do.

Montano's project in this text is gay-affirmative. He mentions the word "gay" only once, but it is enough to give the reader an awareness of his political agenda. That he chooses to play down effeminacy and *kabaklaan* and focus instead on the gender-intransitive aspect of male homosexuality that may be evidenced in his behaviorally bisexual yet affectively homosexual characters can only be seen as a naïve reactionism on his part. Indeed, how can a novel about male-to-male affection set in the Philippines not implicate the discourse and reality of the effeminate homosexuality embodied in the ubiquitous persona of the swishy *bakla?*

Like Villa, Montano illustrates the simultaneously coercive and "enabling" effects of Americanization—Westernization, even—which sexualized and stigmatized the local *bakla* identity but also made available a discourse and thus a discursive "position" from which the homosexualized *bakla* may now speak, from which he may come to know of and to challenge his own subjection. Montano's text represents a memorable step towards a kind of empowered self-consciousness for the homosexualized *bakla.* A more political and "fully flowered" manifestation of this self-consciousness may be found in the 1992 book *Cubao 1980* by Tony Perez (born 1951), a prolific stage, movie, and television scriptwriter, poet, and fictionist. This book is set in 1980 in metropolitan Manila's famous "armpit," the commercial and densely populated district of Cubao, in the western portion of Quezon City.

Perez's Anguished Shout

Tony Perez's book came out in 1992.[21] A personal anthology, it is composed of poems, short stories, essays, and a novella, eponymously titled *Cubao, 1980.* The book's subtitle, *Ang Unang Sigaw ng Gay Liberation Movement sa Pilipinas* (The First Shout of the Philippines Gay Liberation Movement), sounds suspiciously "inaugural" and pretentious, especially since by claiming to be the first self-consciously Filipino gay text, it effectively dismisses the fact that Villa, Montano, and even the award-winning playwrights Wilfrido Ma. Guerrero (1911–1995) and Orlando Nadres (1938–1991) had earlier attempted to articulate the homosexual question, although in tormented, "pre-gay-liberationist" ways. In availing himself of this space-clearing phraseology, Perez obviously wished to register the fact that he was acutely aware of the global gay liberation movement. Popular opinion in most gay cultures has it that this movement has an undeniably American provenance. The beginnings of contemporary gay activism and militancy are often traced to the now-mythic Stonewall riots in New York City in the summer of 1969. Looking at his book's astonishing contents, however, we are confounded by the contradictory messages they purvey.

On one hand, the novella is disturbingly anti-gay and staunchly anti-liberationist. On the other hand, the letters and essays are genuinely affirming of certain aspects of gay life. The novella's plot revolves around the initiatory and largely horrific sexual encounters of its teenage protagonist and narrator, the call boy Tom, who, by dint of financial circumstance, is forced to undergo a series of dehumanizing experiences at the hands of homosexual customers who haunt the dense commercial district of Cubao. It is from this curious boy's eyes, ears, nose, tongue, and skin that the readers get to experience the world of the novella, in all its twenty-eight, harrowingly graphic chapters.

The novella cannot claim to be "gay liberationist" short of lying through its self-righteous teeth. In many ways, even Montano's and Villa's texts, though politically guileless, do not come close to Perez's appallingly homophobic work, whose vaunted shout is the bitterly hateful one-line chapter (number twenty-five), "*Puking ina nyo mga bakla kayo*" ("Sons of bitches—you faggots"). Not only does this story reinforce the stereotype that gays are predators of the vulnerable young, it also chooses to narrate the grantedly sensitive story of lost innocence from the point of view of the boy-prostitute—a "personality" it cannot help but romanticize.

On the other hand, this book does contain lurid descriptions of male-to-male sex, a fact that distinguishes it in local literature. This creates a tension between the text's diametrically opposed performances. While ostensibly condemning the gay lifestyle for its corrupting and dehumanizing effects on the lives of vulnerable young boys, the text promotes this very lifestyle by indulging in lucidly rendered and powerfully arousing descriptions of the various sexual acts that deliciously characterize it. The novella succeeds in untying the tongue of Tagalog fiction as far as articulating the frank and visceral reality of homosexual sex is concerned. Thus, we can say that in terms of sexually explicit expressivity, Perez's book does advocate a kind of halfhearted if disingenuous "liberation."

Perez was born, raised, and established himself as a "writer of note" in a neocolonial postwar Philippines, a period characterized by the overwhelming and often blatant exercise of American cultural, economic, and military influence and power. Like many other Filipino writers and artists of his generation, Perez embraced and was vitally formed by American culture, both as he experienced it in the Philippines and, certainly, in his numerous trips to and studies in the United States (he has long served as a cultural specialist in the cultural affairs section of the American embassy in Manila).

On the question of identity, Perez takes the position that gays—who to him are synonymous with *bakla*—are biological males who should not think of themselves as "woman-hearted." He prescribes that once a gay has accepted his maleness then he will no longer suffer from the illusion that he can only have relationships with straight males. Indeed, we can see that Perez's version of gay liberationism is a unique articulation, for it is remarkably different from its American model, which takes gay identity as a revolutionary identity that no longer seeks acceptance into the dominant order, but in fact challenges the authority of that order and calls into question such "naturalized" conventions as maleness and femaleness, marriage, and even propriety itself! Appropriately enough, Foucault never more clearly illustrates his idea that "where there is power, there is resistance" than when he discusses the pathologized category of homosexuality: soon after its normalization in psychiatric and sexological discourse, there emerged homosexual subjects who identified with and embraced this selfsame label and spoke defiantly from the position it inaugurated.[22] Perez's understanding of the issue—dualistic, Catholic, and socially conservative—veers away from the distinct features of the American gay liberation movement, which he has tried his best to emulate in his own political discourse. But, as can only be expected, this emulation only partially succeeds.

In the same way that Montano's decision to exile the *bakla* from the mythic world of his woman-hating, Greek-loving, and badly written novel eventuated in the reinstating of the *bakla* as his text's founding repudiation, Perez's embracing of what he believes to be the American liberationist ideal that seeks to make the gay man a "man" and thus the object of his own homoerotic desire is itself underwritten by *kabaklaan* at heart. Like Villa's feminine-identified autobiographical persona, Perez merely repeats, in his anti-*bakla* performance, the quintessential *bakla* text. Indeed, no matter how vigorously one tries to escape *kabaklaan*, it seems it will always be an integral part of any or all "male homosexual experience" in the Philippines—and certainly, of any attempts to think and, indeed, "rethink" it.

In Conclusion: Hybridity and Bombs

And yet, Perez's prescriptive vision for *bakla* life cannot actually come to pass, for even the most determined colonialist appropriations end up becoming radically recontextualized and thus "contaminated" by the local situation, after all. Despite Perez's avowed design—strange in that unlike Villa's and Montano's own "projects," it is couched not in English but in Tagalog[23]—to bring the *bakla* closer to an identity that can be comparable to the physically liberated, erotically self-sufficient, mature, and masculinized Western gay man, his articulation remains intimately informed by local, arguably *bakla* "sentiments."

In America and other Western cultures, it is becoming increasingly possible to understand homosexuality as a question of sexual orientation independently of gender—that is to say, as a question of *whom* one sexually desires rather than of *what* masculine, feminine, or androgynous gender one fancies oneself to be. In the Philippines, on the other hand, residual indigenous valuations of gender have served to modify—that is to say, hybridize—the newly "implanted" sexual order. For instance, despite the popularly recognized fact that the *bakla* has sex with the *lalake* or "man," in Filipino cultures, it is only the former who is legitimately homosexualized by the activity. This means that the sexualization of Filipinos has so far not been very thorough. Examining this process more closely, we can see that it has, in fact, been skewed towards the further minoritization of the effeminate, "native" identity of the *bakla.* We may therefore say that in the Philippines today, the *bakla,* as a partially homosexualized identity, signifies a hybrid notion that incorporates both local and translocal conceptions of gender transitivity and homo or "same" sexuality. Thus, despite the modernizing ideologies of gender and sexuality, it continues to preserve residues of its more gender-specific, "prehomosexual" past—for instance, the idea that *kabaklaan* is simply a matter of "confusion" and "indecisiveness," which are, in the first place, the oldest genderless denotations of the word *bakla.* The popular belief that a *bakla* child can be *un*-confused and set aright by inflicting on his body acts of parental, typically fatherly, cruelty proves the persistence of earlier, "presexological" meanings even in this day and age of the homosexualized *bakla.*

This brings us to the realization that all cross-cultural encounters—including "postcolonial appropriations"—end up producing nothing purely native nor purely foreign. As these various texts suggest, the contemporary Filipino gay, like contemporary Filipino gay discourse itself, is a *syncretism* of local and Western gender and sexual constructions. Rather than adopt the nativist perspective that sees this hybridity as a symptom of weakness on the part of Filipino culture and a sign of the ultimate triumph of colonialism, we must instead argue, along with Bhabha, that, contrary to how it is usually seen in dogmatic nationalist discourse, hybridity may well be the most potent "ground" of postcolonial resistance.[24] Needless to say, we must do this because Filipinos already are, at this point in their country's multilayered history, helplessly and unquestionably hybrid anyway. Indeed, to deny or reject this fact is tantamount to denying or rejecting nothing if not their very selves.

In the fields of Philippine arts and letters and of the social sciences, the dogmatic voice of the country's many nativists and nationalists often succeeds in suppressing the publication—and celebration—of politically conscious *bakla* or gay texts. Villa's short story collection was censored of its homosexual stories before it could be published in the Philippines four decades later. Montano's novel, which made the rounds of publishing houses for a decade or more, was not published at all. And it took Tony Perez twelve years to put out his personal anthology and sadly homophobic novella.

As Bhabha explains, hybridity is premised on the idea that, from the very beginning, colonialist authority is never fully present or absolute; that as experienced by the colonized, it is always already different from its claims to a "natural" originality, truthfulness, and superiority; that there is, in the colonial setting, a radical ambivalence that lies at the heart of imperial power, which in its desire to be acknowledged as powerful has needed to be translated into the local languages and is therefore, precisely in its *translatedness,* irremediably bastardized, hybridized, transformed—needless to say, subverted *from within.* We can say that the validity of Foucault's productive theory of power[25] is all too obvious when the power in question is colonialism, for the discourse this power licenses and through which it acts is never more unstable and open to appropriation than when it isn't even self-evident to begin with—when it needs to be translated and turn "hybrid" first, just to be recognizable. Hybridity is colonial power's tenuous life and its spectacular undoing. That it animates at the same time it coerces is never clearer than in the person of the postcolonial subject herself.

When in the name of Filipinoness and puristic nationalism, nativists dismiss the hybrid spaces in Filipino life as "colonial minded," "contaminated," or "complicit," what they refuse to see is the fact that all cultures are hybrid from the very beginning. Any post- or anticolonial position that denies its own hybridity, and that refuses to recognize its history of "contamination" by colonial power, can only be at worst impracticable, and at best, delusional.

We may think of Bhabha's theory of hybridity as gesturing towards a theory of the subject that is comparable to Butler's queer-identified theory of performativity: both posit the self—be it a national or a gendered or sexual self—as the mimetic and repeatedly performed approximation of an unrealizable norm. And so, because national identity, like maleness or femaleness, is a kind of compulsory "performativity," we might say that being a Filipino is not what one is but what one does.[26] There is no simple and singular performance of Filipinoness, for it is a norm that can never be fully inhabited, only cited repetitively in a lifelong process of actualization. There is no essentially Filipino subjectivity, only its performative production as the effect of acts and discourses that do not simply characterize but actually constitute it. Agency, or the possibility of subverting the Filipino norm, therefore lies not in a presocial realm of any purely experienced "synthetically unifying" Filipino freedom, nativity, or selfhood, but in the *variation* between the ideal and its performance—in this case, between the essential fiction of Filipinoness itself, and its particular enactments by discursively *animated* Filipino subjects— as forms of negotiation with normative, "national" power. Thus, from the perspective of Butlerian theory, it is conceivable that the farther from the norm one's performance of Filipinoness goes—in Bhabha's terminology, the more "hybrid" one is—then the stronger one's exercise of negotiated agency paradoxically becomes.

Looking at the texts considered above, we realize that the exceptional "hybrid," the homosexualized *bakla* in Villa's, Montano's, and Perez's fictive worlds, owes his existence to the pathologizing discourse brought into the Philippines by American colonial rule. These *bakla*/homosexual (I would like to just say *gay*[27]) authors have been animated as sexual subjects, and, despite the stigmatizing effects of the American sexological discourse by and against which they are defined, they have embraced their own abjections, and indeed, fluently "talked back." A significant source of this fluency is the residual presence of *kabaklaan*, which has not been completed superseded by the new sexological dispensation but continues to speak to us in and through the complex and transformational discourse—and practice—that is hybridity.

As my readings of these texts by Villa, Montano, and Perez have described, this hybridity clears textual spaces for possible expressions and/or interpretations of postcolonial difference as well as the resistance and opposition this difference betokens. The Filipino homosexual as *bakla* is a trope that is irreducibly different from the homosexual in America or elsewhere in the restively globalizing world. As a cultural and political figure, he interrogates the efficaciousness and self-presence of the imperial project, for he demonstrates the persistence of the "local" and the "old" despite or precisely because of the prevalence of the "foreign" and the "new." It strikes me that this particular rhetorical "intermeshing" of anticolonial and antihomophobic strands of interests may not be as cogent or as critically generative elsewhere in current-day Asia, where an American-style queer movement seems to be unproblematically afoot. Needless to say, one of the assumptions from which this chapter proceeds is that the Philippines occupies a unique position insofar as the histories of American global imperialism and sexual and gender transculturation are concerned. The effects of this convergence are not simply repressive. The discursive enforcement that is colonialism has itself spawned the possibilities of its essential undoing, simply because it can only pluralize and disperse itself at the same time that it vanquishes the countless peoples it alternately subjects and abjects.

Admittedly, the power to *talk back* provides eloquent proof of local resilience in the face of imperialist silencing, of courageous opposition to the colonial project, of the unquestionable truth—and beauty—of postcolonial agency. The problem is, talking accomplishes very little when the smart bombs start to fall, and when embedded journalists, for the sake of the cable-TV-watching, war-mongering world, do all of the talking for the global American empire's countless, finally wordless, graves.

And so, this critical engagement notwithstanding, in the end we can only take hybridity and other similarly intransitive "discursive" models of resistance so far. Now that imperialism has turned global and has reverted to its old, brutish form[28]—upgraded in hardware and software, and televised live via satellite—theories of agency and resistance that presume a covertly hegemonic rather than an overtly "dominating" colonialism need to be rethought, precisely to register this latest, painfully familiar development.

Notes

An early version of this essay was delivered at the Sangandaan Filipino-American Studies Conference, July 9, 2003, Philippine Social Science Center, Diliman, Quezon City.

1. See Butler, *The Psychic Life of Power*.

2. For a survey of the history of gay liberationist activism in the Philippines, see chapters 2, 4, and 5 of my *Philippine Gay Culture*, 69–124 and 163–200.

3. For a critique of Filipino historians whose works evince varying affinities with nativism, see Sy Hau, "The 'Cultural' and 'Linguistic' Turns in Philippine Scholarship."

4. See Evasco, Pineda, and Rodriguez, *Tabi-tabi sa Pagsasantabi.*

5. See Eviota, "Gender Subordination. Historical and Contemporary Configurations," in *The Political Economy of Gender.*

6. Homi K. Bhabha, *The Location of Culture,* 45.

7. Ibid., 75.

8. Ibid., 33.

9. For a longer account of this history, see part 1 of my *Philippine Gay Culture.*

10. These are all culturally comparable words for "effeminate homosexual" among the Philippines's Tagalog, Cebuano, Ilongo, and Tausug ethnic communities, respectively.

11. See, for instance, studies on the Thai *kathoey* and the Indonesian *waria:* Peter Jackson, *Male Homosexuality in Thailand,* and Dédé Oetomo, "Gender and Sexual Orientation in Indonesia."

12. The diminutive term for a species of bamboo (*bayog*) meaning a "womanish man," *hombre afeminado (bayoguin),* occurs in one of the earliest vocabularies printed during the Spanish colonial period. See Pedro de San Buenaventura, *Vocabulario de Lengua Tagala,* 1613.

13. Spanish-Tagalog dictionaries in which nonsexual, ungendered definitions of the word *bakla* may be found are de Noceda and Sanlucar, *Vocabulario de la Lengua Tagala,* 49; and Serrano-Laktaw, *Diccionario Tagalo-Hispano,* 131.

14. Arguably, cross-dressing is not completely foreign to Catholicism, and folk literature suggests an equation in the popular imaginary of the fully garbed colonial priest with precolonial feminine cross-dressing. See Eugenio, *Philippine Folk Literature,* 567–68.

15. See Tan, "From *Bakla* to Gay," 85–96; and Manalansan, "Tolerance or Struggle."

16. See Butler, *Gender Trouble,* 24–25.

17. See my *Philippine Gay Culture,* specifically the chapter on precolonial gender-crossing and the *babaylan* chronicles, 125–62.

18. Villa, *Footnote to Youth.*

19. A more detailed analysis of this novel may be found in my *Philippine Gay Culture,* 237–73.

20. This was told to me in 1993 by my professor in comparative literature, the late Angelito Santos, who introduced me to Montano's unpublished novel—which had apparently been turned down for publication by several local presses in the 1970s—and allowed me to photocopy it.

21. Perez, *Cubao 1980 At Iba Pang Mga Katha.*

22. For a lucid explication of American gay liberationist discourse, see Jagose, *Queer Theory,* 30–43.

23. A hybrid Tagalog, certainly, as the book's own subtitle—which contains the English noun phrase, "Gay Liberation Movement"—vividly emblematizes.

24. Bhabha, "Signs Taken for Wonders."

25. To my mind, one of Michel Foucault's most candid discussions of this "theory" relates to the nineteenth-century production of "infantile sexuality." See the interview "Truth and Power" in Foucault, *The Foucault Reader*.

26. For more on this possibly insightful deployment of Butlerian performativity in relation to the question of national identity, see my essay "Sexuality, Knowledge, and the Nation-State," 3–15.

27. "Gay" because as Filipinos use and understand it, it is becoming more and more inclusive of both the gender-transitive and the gender-intransitive "male, homosexual" identities in the current time. Thus, "gay" is proving to be an amicably appropriated term, one that increasingly embraces both the *bakla* and his more masculine variants and/or familiars.

28. Despite protests and condemnation from almost the entire world, the U.S.-led coalition decided to attack Iraq for the purpose of regime change on March 20, 2003.

References

Bhabha, Homi K. "Signs Taken for Wonders: Questions of Ambivalence and Authority under a Tree Outside Delhi, May 1817." In Francis Barker et al., eds., *Europe and Its Others,* vol. 1, Proceedings of the Essex Conference on the Sociology of Literature, July. Colchester: University of Essex, 1985. 144–65.

———. *The Location of Culture.* London: Routledge, 1993.

Butler, Judith. *Gender Trouble: Feminism and the Subversion of Identity.* New York: Routledge, 1990.

———. *The Psychic Life of Power: Theories in Subjection.* Stanford, Calif.: Stanford University Press, 1997.

de Noceda, Juan, and Pedro Sanlucar. *Vocabulario de la Lengua Tagala.* Reimpreso en Manila: Imprente de Ramirez y Giraudier, 1860.

de San Buenaventura, Pedro. *Vocabulario de Lengua Tagala. Con licencia infresso en la noble Villa del Pila* (Manila), por Tomas Pinpin y Domingo Laog, 1613.

Eugenio, Damiana L., ed. *Philippine Folk Literature: The Riddles.* Quezon City: University of the Philippines Press, 1994.

Evasco, Eugene Y., Roselle V. Pineda, and Rommel B. Rodriguez, eds. *Tabi-tabi sa Pagsasantabi: Kritikal na mga Tala ng mga Lesbiana at Bakla sa Sining, Kultura, at Wika.* Quezon City: University of the Philippines Press, 2003.

Eviota, Elizabeth Uy. *The Political Economy of Gender: Women and the Sexual Division of Labour in the Philippines.* London: Zed Books, 1992. 167–75.

Foucault, Michel. *The Foucault Reader.* Ed. Paul Rabinow. London: Penguin Books, 1991.

Garcia, J. Neil C. *Philippine Gay Culture: The Last Thirty Years; Binabae to Bakla, Silahis to MSM.* Quezon City: University of the Philippines Press, 1996.

———. "Sexuality, Knowledge, and the Nation State." In Neil Garcia, *Performing the Self: Occasional Prose.* Quezon City: University of the Philippines Press, 2003. 3–15.

Jackson, Peter A. *Male Homosexuality in Thailand: An Interpretation of Contemporary Thai Sources,* New York: Global Academic Publishers, 1989.

Jagose, Annamarie. *Queer Theory: An Introduction.* New York: New York University Press, 1996.

Manalansan IV, Martin F. "Tolerance or Struggle: Male Homosexuality in the Philippines Today." Paper delivered at the Department of Anthropology, University of the Philippines, Diliman, Quezon City, July 17, 1990.

Oetomo, Dédé. "Gender and Sexual Orientation in Indonesia." In Laurie Sears, ed., *Fantasizing the Feminine in Indonesia.* Durham, N.C.: Duke University Press, 1996. 259–69.

Perez, Tony. *Cubao 1980 At Iba Pang Mga Katha: Ang Unang Sigaw ng Gay Liberation Movement sa Pilipinas.* Manila: Cacho Hermanos, 1992.

Serrano-Laktaw, Pedro. *Diccionario Tagalo-Hispano.* Manila: Imprenta v. Lit. de Santos y Bernal, 1914.

Sy Hau, Caroline. "The 'Cultural' and 'Linguistic' Turns in Philippine Scholarship." In Corazon D. Villareal et al., eds., *Ruptures and Departures: Language and Culture in Southeast Asia.* Quezon City: Department of English and Comparative Literature, University of the Philippines, Diliman, 2002. 36–70.

Tan, Michael L. "From *Bakla* to Gay: Shifting Gender Identities and Sexual Behaviors in the Philippines." In R. Parker and J. Gagnon, eds., *Conceiving Sexuality: Approach to Sex Research in a Postmodern World.* New York: Routledge, 1994. 85–96.

Villa, Jose Garcia. *Footnote to Youth: Tales of the Philippines and Others.* New York: Scribner, 1933.

TEN

BADING NA BADING

Evolving Identities in Philippine Cinema

Ronald Baytan

Homosexualizing the *Bakla*

The homosexual occupies a paradoxical position in Philippine cinema. On the one hand, he is everywhere—as a beautician, dancer, talent manager, guest relations officer, couturier, artist, teacher, dancer. On the other hand, his life in all its lived complexity is perpetually absent in the national cinema because of the Filipino hetero-patriarchal culture's fear of seeing two men expressing affection for each other. This study focuses on representations of *bakla,* the dominant Filipino male homosexual identity, in Philippine cinema. Simply put, *bakla* denotes a man who is effeminate and woman-hearted, who may cross-dress, and who desires a masculine man, the *lalake.* Through the years, the *bakla* has refashioned his identity by variously naming himself as *bading* (a phonologically more sonorous euphemism for *bakla*), *sward,* *atcheng,* and gay. The *bakla,* the ontological other of the privileged macho *lalake* (male), is the most visible homosexual figure in Philippine mass media. But who is the *bakla?*

Frederick Whitam notes two important things associated with the Filipino *bakla:* effeminacy and transvestism.[1] Martin Manalansan makes the same observation: "while the *bakla* conflates the categories of effeminacy, transvestism, and homosexuality and can mean one or all of these different contexts, the main focus of the term is that of effeminate mannerism, feminine physical characteristics . . . and cross-dressing."[2] Michael L. Tan adds this view: "The term *bakla*, while used loosely now to refer to homosexuals, was most probably used to refer to gender, rather than sexual orientation, with an emphasis on effeminacy."[3] Tan sheds light upon one major difference between the two entities: the *bakla* being a gender term and *homosexual* a term for sexual orientation. But the distinction is not as simple as the quote may suggest. As a former colony of the United States of America, the Philippines has experienced what Neil Garcia calls "the perverse implantation, Philippine version."[4] While *bakla* may have originally been a gender term, it has been *homosexualized* with the coming of Western (read: American) psychiatric and biomedical discourses in the twentieth century. The *bakla* has gone through resignifications in light of Western psychiatric discourse and has acquired the medical connotations of the term *homosexual*.

The *bakla*'s identity was further complicated by the entry of Western ideas of "gay" into the country from the late 1960s onwards. The *bakla*'s appropriation and *localization* of gayness is one of the most visible proofs of the implantation of Western homo/sexual discourse in the Philippines. What is interesting about the phenomenon of gayness in the country is that both *bakla* and "gay" have been irrevocably transformed because of this meeting/mating. First, local *bakla* have embraced the term "gay" as an equivalent of *bakla* to refer to themselves. Tan writes, "The terms 'homosexual' and 'gay' are now used in many Philippine languages, usually as synonyms for *bakla*."[5] It is quite common to find articles on homosexuality to contain all three words used interchangeably. Second, "gay" has also come to signify homosexual identities other than the *bakla*, particularly the Westernized masculine-acting and non-transvestic ones who previously had no place and no name in the traditional local gender mapping.

The *bakla* has become a hybrid. While formerly denoting an effeminate, transvestic homosexual identity, in the last twenty years *bakla* has become more complicated than ever: (1) there are now masculine men who call themselves *bakla* (and gay, too), and (2) there are now self-identified *bakla* who seek other *bakla* as partners when historically the *bakla*'s sex-object choice was the *lalake*, the masculine heterosexual man. Further complications arise because, as Romeo Lee shows, there are also gay men who self-identify as homosexual but are in heterosexual relationships.[6] The *bakla*/gay distinction also reflects divisions across class lines. Tan notes that "many middle-class Filipino men may identify as 'gay' but not as *bakla* because the latter are seen as low-income, effeminate males."[7]

Philippine Cinema and Gayness

In 1971, Lino Brocka—one of the Philippines' National Artists for Film— made a name for himself with *Tubog sa Ginto* (Goldplated),[8] the story of a married and closeted homosexual named Don Benito who has an affair with his driver Diego. This film looked at homosexuality seriously and explored the pathos of a non-*bakla* homosexual man, a figure who until then had remained invisible in Philippine mass media. Brocka followed this up with *Ang Tatay Kong Nanay* (My Father the Mother, 1978), a comic and poignant exploration of a lower class *bakla* and how he coped with parenthood. Another avowedly gay director, Ishmael Bernal, wrote and directed *Manila by Night* (*City after Dark*) in 1980.[9] Using the multiple-character format, the film explores the Manila of the Marcos years through a host of characters that include a gay couturier, a lesbian drug pusher, a teen-age drug addict, a reformed female prostitute, a prostitute pretending to be a nurse, a charming taxi driver, and a waitress. The film's lead, Bernardo Bernardo, was the first openly gay Filipino actor to win a Best Actor trophy for portraying a gay role (as Manay Sharon).[10]

The characters in these three landmark films transcend the Filipino stereotype of the loud and funny faggot *bakla*. But Brocka and Bernal also had to pay for their courage. Nick Deocampo writes, "But for whatever contributions Brocka and Bernal have made in terms of articulating issues of homosexual concern, they stayed in a precarious position of being censored by the state-controlled censorship board, or the risk of being shunned by commercial producers for being too serious, when what the public 'wants' are images of homosexuals audiences can laugh at."[11]

Brocka died in 1991 and Bernal in 1996, but their vision of politicized films about homosexuality has not died. The 1980s ushered in radical changes in Philippine cinema. Critics like Joel David assert that a feminist consciousness permeated Filipino films, and nonstereotypical *bakla*/gay characters started gracing the silver screen.[12] Strong and empowered *bakla*/gay characters often appeared in feminist films, positive gay films usually involved a strong heterosexual woman, and feminist films also addressed the concerns of gay men/*bakla*. There is thus a parallelism between gay and feminist politics in Philippine movies. In contemporary movies, the oppression, resistance, and affirmation of the gay subject find echoes in the struggles of women. The connections between feminist and gay politics are clear: the female, or *babae*, and the *bakla* have both been victimized by the macho, hetero-patriarchal order. The birth of feminist consciousness has helped open up spaces for strong and nontraditional gay characters and narratives. Also, given the strong currents of homophobia and religious hypocrisy in Philippine society, it is financially more viable to insert pro-gay politics into a feminist film than to produce a film with gayness as its central plot.

Now, despite the preponderance of stereotypical *bakla* representations in mass media, the last ten years have seen the arrival of more complex representations of the gay/*bakla* subject, and a boom in affirmative gay films, including *Ang Lalake sa Buhay ni Selya, Miguelle/Michelle* (1998), *Pusong Mamon* (Muffinheart, 1999), *Markova* (2001), *Duda* (2003), *Inter.m@tes* (2004), *Happy Together* (2004),[13] *Aishite Imasu 1941* (2004), and *Bathhouse* (2004). There are now more films dealing with homosexuality, and this is happening just when the average number of films produced annually in the Philippines is going down.[14] I surmise that the explosion of discourses on sexuality and the rise of gay activism in the 1990s have principally fueled this phenomenon.

It is ironic that despite the flowering of the gay culture in the Philippines and the so-called homosexualization of mass media in the 1970s and 1980s,[15] a gay political movement did not develop during that period. Though there were gay groups before the 1990s,[16] the first pride march took place in 1994. Danton Remoto says that only forty people attended the first march in 1994,[17] which was held to commemorate the twenty-fifth anniversary of the Stonewall riots in New York city in June 1969 and which mark the birth of the modern gay and lesbian political movement in the world. The first march coincided with two other important historical events, the offering of the Philippines' first gay literature class, taught by Neil Garcia at the University of the Philippines, and the publication of the first gay anthology *Ladlad: An Anthology of Philippine Gay Writing,* edited by Garcia and Danton Remoto. Around this time, many TV shows devoted episodes to the discussion of homosexuality.[18] The pride march has since become an annual event. The Pink Film Festival, the Philippines' first international gay and lesbian festival, was organized in 1999 by noted filmmaker Nick Deocampo. In 2004, Deocampo organized the second international gay and lesbian film and video festival, which featured more films than the first and generated positive media support.

The last twenty years of Philippine movies are a gold mine for gay and lesbian studies scholars, yet the sad truth is that many Filipino films are understudied. It is even sadder that many of these films are no longer extant. The most important of the limited number of studies of homosexuality in Philippines cinema are those by Roland Tolentino, Nick Deocampo, Emmanuel Reyes, and Joel David.[19] However, no one has critiqued Filipino gay films from the perspective of the *bakla*/gay dichotomy or chronicled the evolution of homosexual identities in Philippine cinema. Questions that remain unanswered include what has happened to the Filipino homosexual, particularly the *bakla,* in the movies since the 1990s and whether representations of the homosexual in Philippine cinema changed since Brocka and Bernal.

Three films produced between 1994 and 2003—*Bala at Lipstick* (Bullet and Lipstick, 1994), *Sa Paraiso ni Efren* (In Efren's Paradise, 1999), and *Duda* (Doubt, 2003)—provide good opportunities to consider issues regarding gayness or *kabaklaan* (roughly translated, "being *bakla*"). These three films, produced at crucial points in Philippine gay history, illustrate the homosexualization of *bakla* discussed earlier. They also represent the three areas of Philippine cinema discussed by Clodualdo del Mundo Jr.: the center or the mainstream, the periphery of the mainstream, and the space for independent filmmaking.[20] *Bala at Lipstick* represents the mainstream, *Sa Paraiso ni Efren* the periphery, and *Duda* independent filmmaking. These distinctions are crucial to the reading of the three films and allow us to ask: how radical is the identity politics of the three films? What are their notions of gayness or *kabaklaan*? What narrative and cinematic techniques are used to convey the films' politics? By looking at the representations in these films, it is possible to map the changing constructions of *kabaklaan* or gayness in the Philippines.

The *Bakla* under Fire: *Bala at Lipstick*

Why should a homophobic culture delight in having so many gay characters in its mass media? Film critic Emmanuel Reyes writes, "Homosexuals are tolerated in show business because they serve a function: they are entertaining. . . . Why comedy? Because that is the image of the showbiz gay that is acceptable to the Filipino public. Since much of the humor is based on how ridiculous their actions appear to the straight set, they usually end up as targets of heterosexual hostility."[21]

The *bakla*/gay character is only acceptable as long as his characterization does not question society's construction of the abject, and for as long as his so-called anomalous sexual identity is the source of jokes and verges on the ridiculous. Brocka's Coring in *Ang Tatay Kong Nanay* and Bernal's Manay Sharon in *Manila by Night* were the first exceptions in Filipino cinema.[22]

Bala at Lipstick, directed by Maryo J. de los Reyes and written by Jose Javier Reyes, is the story of twin brothers, Bambi and Bobby, who were separated at birth. Bambi is a hairdresser whose boyfriend, the dashing Greg, also has a girlfriend. His life takes unexpected turns when he crosses paths with his long-lost heterosexual twin brother Bobby, who is wanted by a criminal syndicate for laundering funds. In the end, the criminal goons are apprehended and the two brothers, who despise each other, are forced to settle their differences.

The film's take on the homosexual subject is clear from the beginning. After a prologue that explains the twins' separation, we find Bambi quarreling with a fat woman whose son has hurt his niece. The dialogue demonstrates the film's comic take on the limp-wristed *bakla* and the tomboyish fat woman. In this encounter, the real winner is the audience, who can find delight in two aberrations hurling insults at each other and pulling each other's hair. The film spectacularizes the *bakla*'s body as a source of humor.

The narrative of the film is also stereotypical in its rendition of the *bakla* as the financial benefactor of the *lalake* (man), the staunch enemy of the *babae* (woman), and a sexual predator. Bambi accepts the Filipino society's master narrative of the self-denying *bakla* who, despite his goodness and loyalty, has to give up the man he loves so that the *lalake* may marry a "real woman" (the *babae*) and sire children. Towards the end of the movie, Bambi's erstwhile boyfriend Greg appears with the woman he intends to marry and asks for Bambi's consent. The *bakla* must let go of his beloved in culturally scripted ironic lines: "I would really like you to have a family, to have a wife, to have children because I love you so much . . . I'm very, very happy . . . You are now truly free."

In the final scene, Bambi appears at the wedding, and when the sissy priest asks if anyone objects to the marriage, Bambi stands up and hollers, "Me!" Everyone is dumbstruck, and Bambi retracts, saying, "Just kidding." Bambi's complaint may be bold but, sadly, it is the only thing he can now do because he has accepted his role in the Filipino erotic triangle—the *lalake* has to leave the *bakla* for the real woman, the *babae*.

Perhaps the film's strength is the theme song *"Bading na Bading"* where Bambi intones that it is difficult to be *bading*, or *bakla*, and that no matter what happens, he will not change:

> Oh, very *badaf*[3]
> In my deeds, my heart, and my feelings.
> Do not blame me
> This is not my choice
> Very *badaf*

In the way I dress and walk
Nothing can be done about it
This is really who I am,
I am *bading,*
Very, very *bading.*

On the one hand, the song validates the *bakla's* existence by saying that it is natural, it is not something freely chosen, and it cannot be changed. This is the difference between earlier *bakla*/gay film narratives and *Bala at Lipstick.* Bambi's aunt broaches the idea of marriage to Bambi, and he instantly rejects this, saying sarcastically that he would only do it once he develops ovaries. The song also underscores the difficulty of being a *bakla* but ends with a triumphant chant, *Bading na bading ako* ("I am truly *bakla,* very *bakla*"). Yet the song also negates its own politics by saying that the *bakla,* given the choice, would have preferred to be a *lalake.* The *bakla* accepts his inferiority to the *lalake* and, thus, fails to deconstruct the *lalake/bakla* dichotomy that privileges the "real" man.

Bala at Lipstick is a "transition" film in that it contains the transgressive politics of the earlier films yet is also a counterpoint to the politicized gay movies that came after it. The absence of masculine-identified homosexuals in the film is a key point, as other art forms of the time were already showing alternative images of gay men. In a study of gay plays written in the last thirty years, Gerardo Z. Torres shows that playwrights writing between 1971 and 1989 created more masculine gay characters than femmes and that the representation in these texts was already moving away from the stereotypical effeminate *bakla.*[24] It is doubly ironic that the film was produced in 1994—when gay activism was already beginning to escalate and, as Nick Deocampo claims, a new oppositional consciousness had emerged among Filipino filmmakers during the Marcos years[25]—and that the film was written by Jose Javier Reyes, a pioneer in Philippine gay studies. Reyes taught literature and film at De La Salle University in Manila in the late 1970s and early 1980s before venturing into show business. Del Mundo states that mainstream cinema commodifies the film,[26] and it is sad that *Bala at Lipstick,* produced at the height of gay activism in the 1990s, contributed to the commodification of the *bakla.* It is caught in a time warp where the *bakla* still has to plea for the acceptance of his identity. However, it remains an important filmic text if only because, together with the other movies made by Paulate in the 1980s, it further crystallized the public's notion of "gayness" or *kabaklaan* in the 1990s, which later films would both address and challenge.

Haven of Hybridity: *In Efren's Paradise*

In Philippine gay discourse, "gay" is used to denote homosexuals across generations, class, and educational backgrounds as well as across levels of masculinity and effeminacy. Both macho and effeminate homosexuals have found a common home in the term "gay." The *bakla* as a subject position is refashioned in *Sa Paraiso ni Efren* (In Efren's Paradise, 1999). Directed by Maryo J. de los Reyes and written by Jun Lana, *Sa Paraiso ni Efren* is the story of Melvin, a soft-spoken *bakla* NGO worker who falls in love with a go-go boy (macho dancer) named Efren and decides to move into his apartment. Produced by the mainstream film matriarch Lily Monteverde (Mother Lily) for Good Harvest Films, the ambitions of the film and its homosexual theme place it more appropriately on the periphery of the industry, which, according to del Mundo, combines artistic intent and commercial viability.[27] The film was marketed as a bold flick with the sexy female and male starlets on the poster, and it showcased a lot of heterosexual sex scenes.

One of the film's strengths is Melvin's relationship with Efren, which is more social and "motherly" than overtly sexual. Efren, who grew up without a mother, is in constant search of a mother figure as an adult. Efren's endless search is foregrounded in the film's opening credits, which show a mother breastfeeding her baby. In a dream sequence, Efren dreams of a mother figure who is a man in drag, in the person of Melvin. Waking from this dream, Efren makes love to Melvin. Melvin is the nurturing "mother" Efren has been looking for, and their union can be read as a manifestation of Efren's unresolved Oedipal desires and is perhaps the "true paradise" referred to in the film's title. But their lovemaking begs the question of how it is possible that a supposed *lalake* can love a *bakla*. In one scene, Efren enters Melvin's room and tells him, "You're making me fall in love with you." In the film, desire is grounded on the capacity to nurture, not on gender. Efren wants a nurturing mother figure in his life, and Melvin is the perfect provider of this need given the construction of the *bakla* as an effeminized being.

Melvin does not have a typical *bakla* experience: he falls in love with a masculine gay man rather than a *lalake*. Melvin's friends are *bakla,* and apart from their effeminacy, the ultimate proof of their *kabaklaan* is their desire for *lalake*. Melvin, however, changes in that after his relationship with Efren, he gets a masculine gay man for a lover, whom he meets in a bathhouse, a place traditional *bakla* would not be found because a *bakla* desiring another *bakla* is unthinkable in their traditional culture.

As now used in the Philippines, "gay" denotes a host of homosexual identities, including the traditional *bakla*. It is perhaps possible to propose that the *bakla* has undergone radical changes in the last twenty years—so much so that to some, *bakla* may no longer be marked by effeminacy, but simply by a desire for the same. Likewise, the object of desire of the *bakla* has changed to now include fellow *bakla* or gay. When the *bakla* claimed gay as his name, he inevitably had to alter his vision of the beloved. He opened himself to the possibility of loving the same, which is what gay in Western discourse signifies. Melvin, therefore, represents a breakaway from the traditional *bakla,* a movement away from the search for the *lalake*. He is the embodiment of the *bakla* who not only has named himself gay but also is open to the possibility of loving another *bakla*/gay. He is a Filipino gay subject who occupies a space undefined in traditional gender constructions, a hybrid space between the traditional *bakla* and the Western gay, a "Third space," to use Homi Bhaba's term, that "resists the politics of polarity"[28] (here the dichotomy *bakla*/gay). This allows the *bakla* to recognize his otherness from gay (now being gay himself, but still *not quite*) and expands the discourse of sameness and masculinity in its construction without completely forsaking his "woman-hearted," *lalake*-desiring self.[29] This paradox attending the Filipino gay, or *bakla*, identity is the inevitable outcome of the *bakla*'s colonial past and neocolonial present and the hegemony of the globalized Western-invented gay identity. The film not only shows the fissures between *bakla* and gay but also reconstitutes the *bakla*'s identity in terms valorized by the hegemonic homophobic culture.

The New Generation Gay: *Duda*

Duda (2003) is a digital independent film written and directed by Cris Pablo.[30] It revolves around a small network TV director (Cris) and his turbulent relationship with Eric. *Duda* is the country's first digital gay film, and Pablo tapped the pink market by having this film exhibited in a major cinema chain. *Duda*'s theatrical release was an achievement for independent filmmakers, whose audience had previously been limited to cineastes and academics.

One must take note of the influences of Asian filmmaking in interpreting Pablo's filmic universe. In the 1990s, Chinese directors Ang Lee (*The Wedding Banquet,* 1993), Chen Kaige (*Farewell, My Concubine,* 1993), and Wong Kar Wai (*Happy Together,* 1997) produced three classic films that have had a profound influence on gay filmmakers everywhere. In the Philippines, this is evident in *Pusong Mamon* (Muffinheart, 1999, written by Ricardo Lee and directed by Joel Lamangan and Eric Quizon), whose plot is patterned after

The Wedding Banquet. Given the Philippines' history, one should not be surprised to find many Filipino films borrowing plots from foreign movies, especially those produced by Hollywood. In the case of Cris Pablo, critics Constantino Tejero and Gibbs Cadiz have pointed out the Wong Kar Wai influence on his work.[31]

Duda uses a multicharacter interview format to chronicle the beginning and end of Cris and Eric's relationship. The plot moves through interviews with Cris and Eric's friends, and the film's denouement involves a talk show that comes across as hilarious, witty, and cogent to the narrative and helps the film succeed in its parody of *Pinoy* (Filipino) melodrama. The film has a simple romantic plot—the protagonist's beloved is unfaithful, and this drives our hero crazy—but this is where the film's transgressive aesthetic lies. It appropriates the heteronormative narrative of romance to affirm homosexual desire. Here, the hero is an avowedly gay character whose search for true love pays off. In earlier Philippine cinema, the *bakla* or gay character always suffers for his desires—without redemption. In contrast, *Duda* is unequivocal about the message to its gay audience: *love, love, and be found.*

Duda can also be lauded for its identity politics. The film points out how the media use gays to sell. Cris objects to this vehemently and laments why and how even gay men themselves are responsible for the exploitation of gays in the mass media. The film pokes fun at a fissure in the gay community, showing how some members of the community have used the label "bisexual" not so much to denote a person's preference for both same-sex and opposite-sex partners but rather to serve as a "safer" euphemism for *bakla* or gay. This demonstrates that the self-identification as "bisexual" is symptomatic of internalized homophobia and effeminophobia. So-called bisexuals, the film subtly points out, are men who hate being labeled as *bakla,* not because the *bakla* is a sissy but because they cannot accept themselves.

In *Duda,* we can see the middle-class metropolitan gay culture and the new generation gay men who populate Manila's gay ghetto of Malate and Puerto Galera's White Beach, the summer capital of Manila's gay culture, especially during the Holy Week of Lent. We also see the spectacularization of the male body now typical of gay culture. *Duda* is unapologetic about the gayness of its characters and addresses problems of contemporary gay culture, such as obsession with the body, casual sex, fear of love, bisexuality as an excuse, marriage for convenience, and coming out. But most importantly, this film has a definite gay audience in mind. With *Duda,* we see a shift in the cinematic tradition and find gay filmmakers narrating the lives of gay characters for a gay audience.

One major difference between the *bakla* (or *bakla* gay) and the gay (the non-*bakla* gay) is the object of desire. The *bakla* desires the *lalake*, whereas the gay man desires another gay man. In traditional *kabaklaan*, the *bakla* desires the true *lalake* (real man) and this results in a love triangle: one *lalake*, one *bakla*, and one *babae*. It is, thus, typical for a macho *lalake* to have girlfriends and gay lovers simultaneously. However, in *Duda* the erotic triangle involves three gay men: Cris tries to hang on to Eric despite the latter's infidelity with another gay man, and we see Cris's friends Loyd and Mhelo in a series of casual encounters with other gay men. Loyd's philosophy is, "I'd rather enjoy sex: casual sex, quick sex, beautiful sex with the same sex, but safe sex." This notion of the "same" clearly uses the tropes of Western gay discourse, not *kabaklaan*, because the *bakla*'s desire is founded on *difference*.

Conclusion: Refashioning the *Bakla*

The last decade in Filipino filmmaking will be remembered for its production of films that continue the transgressive vision of Lino Brocka and Ishmael Bernal in the 1970s and 1980s. Between Maryo J. de los Reyes' *Bala at Lipstick* in 1994 and Cris Pablo's *Duda* in 2003, so much has happened to the homosexual in Philippine cinema. Despite *Bala at Lipstick*'s attempts at dissidence, it is engulfed by a cinema that still cashes in on the *bakla* as a source of entertainment. Its very limited notion of gayness is symptomatic of the dominant hegemonic culture's continuous attempts to fossilize the *bakla* or gay identity—to subject him to its unchanging master narrative of the suffering abject. Yet films like *Bala at Lipstick* are also a reminder of the *bakla*'s past (and present) and serve as a counterpoint to the films that came after it that are more radical in their vision of the homosexual subject. The *bakla* has transformed in Philippine movies in the last ten years.

It is understandable why *Bala at Lipstick* cannot contain a macho gay character: given the commercial aspirations of the film, it had to cater to a heterocentric audience that identifies with the *lalake* and is entertained by the stereotype of the loud and funny faggot. However, the entry of gay discourse in the country has undone the dichotomy *lalake/bakla* with its attendant categories *masculine/feminine* and *active/passive*. The *bakla* is no longer confined to the feminine mold. In *Sa Paraiso ni Efren*, we see Melvin in a relationship with a masculine gay character. Likewise, the bathhouse/bar he frequents is full of gay men ranging from the masculine to the ultra effeminate.

The *bakla* now use the word "gay" to refer to themselves. At the same time, masculine acting and upper-middle-class homosexuals who refuse to be labeled as *bakla* also use the term "gay" to name themselves. Thus, in a way "gay" has bridged the gap between the *bakla* and the non-*bakla* homosexuals in the country. We see here how the local culture has appropriated a foreign identity and how this appropriation has also affected the identity of the *bakla*. The nativizing of "gay" has produced ripples in the local culture's construction of sexual meanings and identities so much so that the traditional *lalake/ bakla* distinction is no longer the only way of interpreting Filipino genders and sexualities. We are seeing an expansion of boundaries for both the *bakla* and the gay man who may be different, or one and the same, or paradoxically both. All through the film *Bala at Lipstick* one hears the words *bakla, bading,* and *atcheng* (another word for *bakla*). But this does not signify the absence of gayness because Bambi's *bakla* friends, and enemies, are called "gay" in the film's credits. Bambi is simply *bakla* and gay, and yet not simply an unproblematic amalgam of both.

The use of "gay" to signify the *bakla* may also mark the opening of possibilities for a truly *same*-sex partnership for the *bakla*—that of two *bakla* (of whatever masculinity)—wherein the two males in the relationship take the same homosexual identity. It is also possible to assert that the *bakla* or gay subject can now shift from the *bakla-lalake* relationship to the gay-gay (*bakla-bakla*) relationship, as demonstrated in *Sa Paraiso ni Efren*. The changes in the *bakla*'s identity involve not only the creation of a masculine space within the otherwise feminized *bakla,* but also the *bakla*'s acceptance of the same-sex (or homosexual) nature of his desire (in contrast to the heteronormative version/justification of his desire above). However, a *bakla* like Bambi in *Bala at Lipstick* who adheres to the values and characteristics of the traditional *bakla* (effeminacy and choice of *lalake* partners) is not an obsolete identity. While *bakla*-identified homosexuality (for example, the *bakla* gay) is different from the masculine gay-identified homosexuality (for example, the non-*bakla* gay, or, for lack of a better term, the "gay gay"), they are not unrelated, for they share the same history of *kabaklaan* in the country, and, as the film *Duda* demonstrates, it is possible for a Filipino to be both a *bakla*- and gay-identified homosexual. What is evident here is not the annihilation of one model of homosexuality (the *bakla*) but rather its expansion in that it persists and informs the direction of the other/s. Perhaps the *bakla*'s use of gay discourse can be viewed as one of strategic appropriation, or an inevitable outcome of colonial and neocolonial discourses. This chapter demonstrates that since the onset of Western sexology, it is no longer possible to conceive of a monolithic, unified *bakla* identity. It is imperative that we conceive of a plurality of *bakla* subjectivities.

Gay—though global—cannot be completely understood outside the contexts in which it is used and negotiated. Therefore, following Neil Garcia, I believe that the Filipino gay—coming from a knowledge system and a world with specific ways of mapping sexual meanings and interpreting desires—remains irreducibly different from the Western gay.[32] Gayness in the Philippines cannot be understood without taking into account its shared history, its overlaps, and its often problematic relationship with the *bakla*.

We have seen how the *bakla* has evolved and is represented and refashioned in Filipino cinema from 1994 to 2003. The *bakla* is no longer merely effeminate. He has learned to self-identify as gay and opened the doors for more solidarity with the non-effeminate homosexuals in his culture. What used to be unthinkable has happened: though the *bakla* may wish to crossdress and act effeminately if and when he wants to, he is now open to the possibility of desiring his own kind. He no longer thinks of himself as an incomplete man or woman; he may even be masculine and nontransvestic, and he can claim that he is *lalake*, too.

The vision of Brocka and Bernal to produce a cinema that affirms the homosexual subject may still be a dream, but contemporary filmmakers have done their part to change the face of homosexuality in Philippine cinema. But much work remains to be done. Many lesbian and gay films need to be retrieved, studied, and reread, not only for their aesthetics but also for their inscriptions of the homosexual and the world to which he/she belonged. A further study of the works of Brocka, Bernal, and de los Reyes in light of gay studies/criticism and postcolonial theory should produce interesting results. The silver screen narrates the complex and often forgotten history of the Filipino male homosexual—most notably the *bakla*—and is a testament to his struggle to liberate himself from the world's limited and limiting gaze.

Notes

I would like to acknowledge the people and institutions that have made this work possible: Dr. Benedict Anderson, Dr. J. Neil C. Garcia, Eda Carreon, Maria Teresa Salazar, Cultural Center of the Philippines, De La Salle University-Manila, Sid Gomez Hildawa, Vince Groyon III, Michael Lim, Anastacio Marasigan Jr., Dr. Gerardo Z. Torres, Frances Sangil, Nonon Carandang, John Tigno, and Dr. Clodualdo del Mundo Jr.

1. Whitam, "Philippines," 980–81. For a critique of this article, see Garcia, *Philippine Gay Culture*, 330–31.

2. Manalansan, "Speaking of AIDS," 196. For a critique of Manalansan's assumptions, particularly those on masculinity and *bakla,* see Garcia, *Philippine Gay Culture,* 364. The *bakla*'s effeminacy is also discussed by Tan in "From *Bakla* to Gay," 85–96.

3. Tan, "Sickness and Sin," 209.

4. See Garcia in this volume.

5. Tan, "Silahis," 222.

6. Lee, "Psychosexual Contexts of the Homosexuality of Filipino Men in Heterosexual Unions."

7. Tan, "Silahis," 209. Also see Tan, "From *Bakla* to Gay," 87.

8. For a critical review of this film, see del Mundo, "Tubog sa Ginto (A Review)."

9. Ishmael Bernal posthumously became the country's national artist for film in 2001. For an introduction to his life and works, see Dormiendo, "The Finest Poet of Philippine Cinema."

10. Bernardo won the best actor trophy given by the *Manunuri ng Pelikulang Pilipinas,* a group of critics. The name of their award is *Urian.*

11. Deocampo, "Homosexuality as Dissent/Cinema as Subversion," 397.

12. See David, *The National Pastime* and *Fields of Vision.*

13. Not to be confused with Wong Kar Wai's *Happy Together.*

14. Del Mundo, "Philippines," 116–24.

15. See Jose Reyes, "Swardspeak in Mass Media," and Garcia, "Faggotization—Not Homosexualization—of TV."

16. See Garcia, *Philippine Gay Culture,* 77.

17. Remoto, *Seduction and Solitude,* 188.

18. Ibid.

19. Tolentino, "Transvestites and Transgressions"; Deocampo, "Homosexuality as Dissent"; Reyes, "Gay and Really Useful"; David, *Fields of Vision,* 84–97; David, *Wages of Cinema,* 180–200.

20. Del Mundo, "Philippine Movies in 2001."

21. Emmanuel Reyes, *Notes on Philippine Cinema,* 58.

22. David, *Fields of Vision,* 27.

23. "Badaf" is a synonym of "bakla." A gayspeak word, it is the contraction of two words: *ba*bae (woman) and *daf*at (should be), which means that the *badaf* or *bakla* should have been a girl instead of a biological male with a woman's heart.

24. See Torres, "Early Philippine Gay Plays."

25. Deocampo, "Homosexuality as Dissent," 398.

26. Del Mundo, "Philippine Movies in 2001," 168–69.

27. Ibid.

28. Bhabha, *The Location of Culture,* 38–39.

29. Ibid., 86. In the chapter entitled, "Of Mimicry and Man: The Ambivalence of Colonial Discourse" Bhabha uses the phrase "*almost the same, but not quite*" (italics his) in his discussion of mimicry (86).

30. I have discussed Cris Pablo's films in an earlier work. See Baytan, "Resistance and Affirmation."

31. Cadiz, "Pretty—and Proud—in Pink" and "A Calling Card for the Future of Indie Cinema." For Constantino Tejero's short review of *Duda,* please read "Pinkish."

32. See Garcia's "Philippine Gay Culture: Reflections on a Study," in *Slip/pages: Essays in Philippine Gay Criticism.*

References

Baytan, Ronald. "Resistance and Affirmation: Reflections on Cris Pablo's 'Duda' and 'Bathhouse.'" *Ideya: Journal of the Humanities* 6, no. 2 & 7, no. 1 (2006): 59–78.

Bhabha, Homi. *The Location of Culture*. London: Routledge, 2004.

Cadiz, Gibbs. "Pretty—and Proud—in Pink." *Philippine Daily Inquirer*, June 14, 2004, G2.

———. "A Calling Card for the Future of Indie Cinema." *Philippine Daily Inquirer*, January 30, 2005, A2–3.

David, Joel. *The National Pastime: Contemporary Philippine Cinema*. Anvil: Pasig, 1990.

———. *Fields of Vision: Critical Applications in Recent Philippine Cinema*. Quezon City: Ateneo de Manila University Press, 1995.

———. *Wages of Cinema: Films in Philippine Perspective*. Quezon City: University of the Philippines Press, 1998.

Del Mundo, Jr., Clodualdo. "Tubog sa Ginto (A Review)." In Nicanor Tiongson, ed., *The Urian Anthology 1970–1979*. Manila: Manunuri ng Pelikulang Pilipino and Manuel Morato, 1983. 200–203.

———. "Philippines." In Jose F. Lacaba, ed., *The Films of ASEAN*. Pasig: ASEAN Committee on Culture and Information, 2000. 89–130.

———. "Philippine Movies in 2001: The Film Industry Is Dead: Long Live Philippine Cinema." *Asian Cinema* 14, no. 1 (2003): 167–74.

Deocampo, Nick. "Homosexuality as Dissent/Cinema as Subversion: Articulating Gay Consciousness in the Philippines." In Martha Gever, ed., *Queer Looks: Perspectives on Lesbian and Gay Film and Video*. New York: Routledge, 1993. 395–402.

Dormiendo, Justino. "The Finest Poet of Philippine Cinema." In *The National Artists of the Philippines 1999–2003*, Pasig: CCP and Anvil, 2003. 29–36.

Garcia, J. Neil C. "Faggotization—Not Homosexualization—of TV." Letters to the editor, *Philippine Daily Inquirer*, May 21, 2003, C1–C2.

———. *Philippine Gay Culture: The Last Thirty Years*. Quezon City: University of the Philippines Press, 1996.

———. *Slip/pages: Essays in Philippine Gay Criticism (1991–1996)*. Manila: De La Salle University Press, 1998.

Garcia, J. Neil C., and Danton F. Remoto, eds., *Ladlad: An Anthology of Philippine Gay Writing*. Mandaluyong: Anvil, 1994.Lee, Romeo. "Psychosexual Contexts of the Homosexuality of Filipino Men in Heterosexual Unions." *Journal of Homosexuality* 42, no. 4 (2002): 35–63.

Manalansan IV, Martin M. "Speaking of AIDS: Language and the Filipino 'Gay' Experience in America." In Vicente Rafael, ed., *Discrepant Histories: Translocal Essays on Philippine Cultures*. Mandaluyong: Anvil, 1995. 193–220.

Remoto, Danton. *Seduction and Solitude*. Mandaluyong: Anvil, 1995.

Reyes, Emmanuel A. *Notes on Philippine Cinema*, Manila: De La Salle University Press, 1990.

Reyes, Jose Javier. "Swardspeak in Mass Media, Or the Myth of the Homosexualization of Manila." *Likha* 3 (1981): 23–32.

Tan, Michael L. "From *Bakla* to Gay: Shifting Gender Identities and Sexual Behaviors in the Philippines." In R. Parker and J. Gagnon, eds., *Conceiving Sexuality: Approaches to Sex Research in a Postmodern World*. New York: Routledge, 1994. 85–96.

———. "Sickness and Sin: Medical and Religious Stigmatization of Homosexuality in the Philippines." In J. Neil C. Garcia and Danton F. Remoto, eds., *Ladlad: An Anthology of Philippine Gay Writing*. Mandaluyong: Anvil, 1994. 202–19.

———. "Silahis: Looking for the Missing Filipino Bisexual Male." In Peter Aggleton, ed., *Bisexualities and AIDS*. London: Taylor and Francis, 1998. 207–25.

Tejero, Constantino. "Pinkish." *Philippine Daily Inquirer,* June 29, 2004, C1.

Tolentino, Roland B. "Transvestites and Transgressions: 'Panggagaya' in Gay Discourse." *Diliman Review* 46, no. 3–4 (1998): 91–105.

Torres, Gerardo Z. "Early Philippine Gay Plays." In Janet Tauro-Batuigas and Nonon V. Carandang II, eds., *Bin-i: New Theoretical and Critical Writings on Philippine Studies*. Manila: University of Santo Tomas Publishing House, 2004. 85–111.

Whitam, Frederick. "Philippines." In Wayne R. Dynes, ed., *Encyclopedia of Homosexuality,* vol. 2. New York: Garland Publishing, 1990. 980–81.

ELEVEN

REPRESENTATION, POLITICS, ETHICS

Rethinking Homosexuality in
Contemporary Korean Cinema
and Discourses

Jin-Hyung Park

In this chapter, I try to reconsider the significance of the historical moment of the mid-1990s for queer studies and cinematic discourses in Korea today. However, when the national label is brought to an issue like homosexuality, I meet a specific problem. In most academic writings about LGBTQ issues written in Korea, I notice that theoretical concepts such as "identity" and "sexual minority" are imported from theoretical developments based on studies done in the West, while "Korea/Korean" refers simply to the realistic context that is awkwardly added to the theoretical concepts. While, as Rey Chow observes, Western readers require writings from the non-Western world to be classified by the nation-state of their origin,[1] Korean readers, on the other hand, seem uncomfortable when the label of their nationality appears in the title of theoretical writings on homosexuality, rare though such appearances are. Sometimes, this situation implies developmentism, as in "We're not ready yet" before we can deal with homosexuality. This attitude conspires with the non-Western academic elitism that places geo-history in the realm of the "purely empirical" and requires Western concepts and theories to explain it. The division of a field into Korean "raw materials" and Western theoretical devices in Korean academia shows that the epistemological hierarchy of "the Western" and "the non-Western" is reinforced and internalized even in *non*-Western academic scenes. This situation becomes particularly apparent when academia deals with allegedly "unfamiliar" issues such as homosexuality.

Nevertheless, like other theories from the West, queer theory has arrived onto the discursive battlefield in Korea and has rapidly spread to become articulated with various other discourses, including feminism (which has been desperately seeking alliances with other theories of the oppressed) and several other political discourses on "minorities." Queer theory and criticism are the most marginalized and the most potent among the critical discourses in Korea today, at least regarding their status in academia. But queer theory faces new problems when its potential as "marginal" is acknowledged without question. Differences in race, class, or socioeconomic and geopolitical status remain unexamined under the overarching umbrella of the queer. But what really matters is that queer theory's potential as a marginal politics is in danger of being located and reabsorbed into the center of academic markets in Korea.

Starting by acknowledging my own position as a queer scholar in Northeast Asia, I wish to highlight the risk that queer theory faces in Korean academic discourses. Specifically, I raise the necessity of speculative rethinking on queer matters in Korea in the light of representations of homosexuality in contemporary Korean cinema, in their relation both to cinematic discourses and LGBTQ discourses in Korea. I think through these questions by means of a discussion of *Road Movie* (2002), a controversial Korean queer film. Analyzing the textual dynamics of *Road Movie,* I propose that the film activates a humanist desire for the interpolation of queer subjectivity and queer desire within heterosexual discourse. I also reveal the operation of discursive dynamics in Korean film criticism, which valorize and tolerate threatening homosexuality/homoeroticism in dominant cine-historical and aesthetic discourses by stressing the aesthetic category of "road movie." Based on the idea that the queer sensibility in Korean visual culture has been strongly affected and even controlled by "radical/elite" academic discourses such as sexuality studies, this analysis focuses on the specific ways that the popularization of elitism and film as "high art" in Korean cine-culture, and the politics of "identity" and universality inherent in the humanism of LGBTQ discourses, have controlled queer sensibility. How have these discourses maintained their dynamics of "othering" the queer? What can be represented and what cannot in contemporary Korean films; and what can be imagined in the gap between the representable and the unrepresentable?

Figure 11.1. Two men and a woman: trip on the unidentified road. Still from *Road Movie* (2002). Courtesy of Sidus FNH Co.

Queer, Identity and Minority

Responding to changes in social context, the 1990s, and especially the mid-1990s, are often represented as a moment of disjuncture and (dis)continuity in Korea. In sociopolitical and economic history, this moment is often described as associated with democratization, the dwindling of political struggle such as the students' anti-dictatorship movement of 1980s, and the expansion of consumerist, late-capitalist culture.

I try to relocate the moment of the mid-1990s in Korea here because this is a remarkable period in which modern Korean society absorbed new discourses and concepts, most of which came from the west, including queer theory, and when these discourses contested not only previously existing social discourses and value structures but also each other. I want to consider how the discursive dynamics of this period formed an institutional mantle controlling explanations of queer matters and their cinematic representation—a dynamic that continues to the present day. The historical context is important to consider so that we can reconsider recent social and discursive dynamics governing the way LGBTQ matters are talked about. In other words, this chapter tries to contextualize mid-1990s Korea historically in order to find a chain of cause and effect generated by discourses as discontinuous practices that are interrelated and intersect but are also ignorant and exclusive of each other. Beyond identifying this chain, I seek also to problematize its structuring logic.

Those seeking to historize LGBTQ discourses and practices in modern Korean society often collect their material from the mid-1990s, especially 1994 to 1996, as Korean society was then facing various events that played crucial roles in constructing LGBTQ cultures in the period. One of the most prominent events is the emergence of gay communities.[2] However, these communities were as yet underground. Their activities were still regarded as a "secret movement" and limited to particular spaces such as gay bars and clubs, which remained "invisible" in the broader society.[3] It was not until 1995 that this "secret" movement became visible in mainstream society. More gay communities were established on university campuses and became ready to appear in the public domain. These communities made "homosexual existence" a social issue in Korea by displaying themselves actively in the major media. Their activities were mostly cultural events like screenings of queer films, which were publicized through interviews in major newspapers and on TV. Drawing mainstream society's attention to homosexual existence and rendering it recognizable and speakable, these movements triggered social discussions on queer matters and are often cited as an "origin" for the formation of Korean LGBTQ discourse.

Alongside gay communities on university campuses, a large gay community also appeared in cyberspace. Starting with BBS-based Internet clubs for gays and lesbians, several online g/l communities were formed by the end of 1996. Unlike activist communities and campus-based g/l clubs that publicized themselves to make g/l matters visible in mainstream society, Internet g/l communities were strictly based on anonymity, security, and exclusivity so that they could gather many more gays and lesbians as members.[4] The prevalence of an anonymous, exclusive Internet g/l community (which remains the biggest form of Korean LGBTQ community) implies the difficulty that Korean LGBTQ subjects faced in revealing themselves in the public domain. But no matter how invisible and anonymous individual members of these Internet communities remained, as the communities grew bigger, they inevitably became visible and recognizable. They could raise their voices when they met discriminatory actions from ISPs. Moreover, these anonymous members gradually "came out" of cyberspace. After obtaining g/l -related information such as the locations of bars and clubs, or chatting with other members, they came out to *Nakwon-dong* or *Itaewon,* the biggest g/l street in Seoul, and gradually revealed themselves as consumers.

Again, it is important to mark the LGBTQ movements of 1995–96 in the historical context of the formation of LGBTQ discourse in Korea, since the new discourses triggered LGBTQ matters' visibility and topicality in the dominant discourses of mainstream society. Choosing the proper name for homosexuals was one of the tactical ways that was deployed for the acknowledgment of homosexual existence. Several gay activists argued that we should use the less stigmatizing term *"dong-song-e-ja"* instead of the pathologizing *"dong-song-yoen-e-ja."* Soon there emerged another word, *"i-van,"* which is sometimes compared to the English term "queer." Self-naming by gay activists and communities recognizes a social reality in which they had no (proper) name or means of representation as proper human beings and members of society, even though homosexual existence can be traced through the length of Korean history. These debates on naming and its pragmatics ostensibly show that the level of Korean society's openness and acceptance toward homosexuality had grown since before the mid-1990s. Looked at another way, the imperative that g/l communities felt to reveal themselves in mainstream society was a matter of naming, in other words, a matter of identity and identity formation. Of course, whether in Western or non-Western modern society, it is a general strategy of LGBTQ activism to assert LGBTQ identity to unite LGBTQ people and claim their rights. However, identity formation and identity politics in this period need to be reconsidered, since they are in fact problematic, especially in the way they have been deployed for the formation of LGBTQ discourse during the past decade.

It would appear that the concept of "sexual identity" that stood out in g/l activism in mid-1990s Korea was imported from Western theories. The concept and the political appropriateness of identity imported from the West were bound to have limits. First of all, while desperately searching for the essence of "homosexual identity," activism and academic research based on identity could rarely avoid an essentialist view and separatism. This essentialism could not explain the complexity of queer subject formation, and it obscured all the differences that already exist in queer subjectivities: economic, geopolitical, cultural, and even sexual.

In this regard, the adaptation of the Western concept of identity in LGBTQ activism and academic research meets its limit when it neglects the specificity of the experience of what *counts as* identity in Korean society and its historical context. While queer studies based on identity and its political use bear some similarities to minority studies and rights movements in the United States, where experiences of identity are varied by racial, national, and sexual backgrounds, matters of identity, especially identification as a minority or "the other," have contextual specificities in Korea. Not only at the level of academic concerns but also at the level of collective sentiments, in Korea matters of identity have tended to converge in a homogeneous national/ethnic identity.

More recently, much critical research has emerged in various fields on the dynamics of nationalism and ethnic identity as a dominant agent in modern Korean society. Surprisingly, however, it is difficult to find studies about the interrelation between minority groups' self-identification as "social others"—of social minorities in general, and sexual minorities like homosexuals in particular—and national identity. Therefore, it is now an urgent task to consider the matter of sexual minorities based on their relation with other social, historical, and national spectrums of identity formation, otherwise our explanations of the complexity and differences of Korean LGBTQ's social, cultural realities will run up against inevitable limits.

Acknowledging these limits warns us that we must consider the position of queer theory as well as queer matters on a broader map of the global/local. In fact, Western queer scholars have become aware of this situation and begun to question their own positions and languages as queer academics, and discussions on these issues between them and Asian queer scholars, activists, and artists continue to develop.[5] But at times, Western queer scholars coming from the perspective of positivist sociology see this situation as a new opportunity to deploy their social developmentalism, saying that queer culture and communities in non-Western regions follow a path of development when their traditional and indigenous cultures meet the more "advanced" Western queer theories.[6]

Finally, another problem with the universalization of the discourse of "sexual minority" is that it can turn the reality of minorities or social "Others" into something purely theoretical. I emphasize again that "the marginal" and "the Other" are the most provocative and controversial notions in Korea's academic discourses at present; they have opened the way for various contemporary critiques, including feminist projects that seek to reveal the oppressive structure of phallocentric patriarchy, and postcolonial projects that mount a political and theoretical critique of Western colonnial power by focusing on the third world's economic and cultural marginality. But ultimately, these radical approaches of today remain oriented toward the Western subject. The Other and the margin simply provide "the righteous position" of political correctness and theoretical legitimacy to both Western and non-Western scholars of deconstructionism and postcolonialism.

The critique of the constitutive character of otherness/othering thus leads us to consider the appropriation of the margin/other in mainstream discourses. As Tracy B. Strong describes it, "a successfully appropriated text no longer troubles the appropriator that it has become part of his or her understanding, and it is recognized by others as 'owned,' not openly available for interpretation."[7] In the light of sexuality and its power structure, the appropriation of the queer for interpolation soothes what Calvin Thomas calls "straight anxiety."[8] Queer as appropriated and interpolated margin/other plays its "productive" role in the center's normative, heterosexual subject formation.

Queer and Cinema as Art

While identity and minority and the politics based on these notions imported from the West have brought the unexpected result of LGBTQ discourse being articulated in Korean mainstream academia, it is cinematic discourse and film criticism that welcomed queer matters as a "good other" to Korea's mainstream society. In particular, the popularization of "art cinema" discourse in the mid-1990s played a critical role in raising the profile of LGBTQ's social existence in Korea.

The mid-1990s are often cited as a moment of major change in Korean cine-culture owing to various factors: the influx of big corporations and big finance into the film industry, the boom of new media, the mushrooming of film schools and departments of film studies in universities, the arrival of cinematheques and art cinema houses, the launching of popular academic film magazines, and the hosting of international film festivals of various scales. Among these factors, I would like to focus on the boom in art cinema in order to read a discursive shift in cinematic discourses in this period. I don't mean that art cinema or art cinema discourse arrived in Korea's cine-culture in the mid-1990s. Rather, I would like to emphasize the "popularization" of art cinema: art cinema enjoyed by the masses. Among the factors mentioned above, popular magazines with academic interests and their young film critics, cinematheques, and international film festivals played the most critical role in popularizing art cinema.[9] Rereading Korea's cine-culture in the mid-1990s, Hyeyoung Cho points out that in this period, art cinema discourse not only became prominent in film criticism and academia but also spread out into Korea's cine-culture more broadly.[10]

The popularization of art cinema discourse and cultural elitism helped Korean society to absorb queer matters via the movies. In the 1990s, the academic focus of film studies in universities was toward film aesthetics while not losing the political slant it inherited from earlier film studies in the 1980s. Cine-feminists' efforts to bring matters of sexuality into film studies are prominent in this period, which also brought the opportunity to introduce queer theory and films into the academic discourse on cinema. Examples of the "new queer cinema" of the early 1990s such as Todd Haynes's *Poison* and Rose Troche's *Go Fish* were repeatedly screened at campus-based cine-clubs and later in cinematheques.

It was the advent of popular film magazines with academic interests and international film festivals that pulled the starter-trigger for the cultural and visual representation of LGBTQ in Korea. A Korean art critic I spoke with a couple of years ago, who identifies himself as a former gay activist, recalls that these film magazines were the only public media open-minded toward homosexuality at that time. *Cine21*, the most popular film magazine in Korea, published a special issue on homosexuality in 1996. In a second special issue on homosexuality, the editorial argues that Korean society should start to talk about the topic:

> The advent of Korean queer theorists means that queer culture is ready to appear in Korea, too . . . the fact itself that *Cine 21* tries to talk about homosexuality (for the second time this year) under the title of "Eyes on Queer Films" reveals that our culture has been undergoing dramatic changes, even during the past year alone . . . there are reasons we would like to focus on queer movies in this week's issue. First, homosexuality exists in Korean society, but it is still distorted by our misunderstanding, prejudice, and hatred. Second, homosexuality brings important matters for our society. It can open up space for radical, subversive thought against the oppressive ideologies of our society such as capitalism, patriarchism, sexism, and familialism.[11]

This editorial clearly shows the relation between the cultural elitism of film magazines and art cinema discourse, their broader popularization, and queer matters in mid-1990s Korea. The editorial of the most popular film magazine in Korea does not hesitate to use words like "patriarchy," "ideological oppression," or "space for subversive thinking." Moreover, it suggests that readers should acknowledge the political, even ethical usefulness of queer matters. As a discursive practice, it demonstrates the privileged position of films and film magazines that allows them to discuss queer matters in Korean society, where queer matters were still otherwise unspeakable and invisible, as most of the public media from this period proves.

A few months later, one of the panelists who participated in a discussion printed in this issue was invited to a forum at the first Pusan International Film Festival (PIFF) in 1996. British film critic Tony Rayns, Chris Berry from UC-Berkeley, and Dong-jin Seo, the first gay activist known to the public in Korea and also the director of Seoul Queer Film Festival, were also invited to this forum. Since 1996, many international film festivals were established in Korea, with a variety of themes and on a variety of scales. Naturally, these film festivals provided the widest open channels for screening queer films, since general theaters had little interest in releasing films with "disturbing themes." Along with art cinema discourses, film festivals as a global circuit of the cinephile's highbrow taste made general audiences who became "art-cinema-loving" festival-goers who watched queer films far less uncomfortable. I would like to suggest that the interrelation between art cinema discourse based on cultural elitism and acceptance of queer matters via films is the most important factor that made the first Seoul Queer Film Festival possible.

Undoubtedly, the Seoul Queer Film Festival, which started in 1998, provided a stage for the encounter between queer communities' awareness of the necessity to represent themselves in society and current cultural discourses in Korea. The stage itself is politically practical, for it represents one of the social settings where queer matters were accepted by Korean society. However, under the cinephile's fascination and cultural internationalism, the film festival is also a global market of the image-economy where images are interpreted, exchanged, and translated, and it is ruled by the dominant power of the economy.

Homosexuality, for the heterosexual buyer in the film festival, can also act as a prop to cultural elitism, proving that they can afford to engage in "self-reflection on society's power structure," as stated in the editorial of *Cine21*'s special issue. Acquiring political, academic, and ethical meanings, homosexuality becomes acceptable in mainstream society. As institutions of dominant society, art discourse and cultural markets have a "disciplining" function of reconstructing deviant, "nonproductive" matters like homosexuality as "something useful" for maintaining the social structure. The discursive dynamics of art discourse and "minority" politics appropriated by mainstream social discourse as discipline govern homosexuality by the rules of the dominant norms. In popular visual cultures like film, they control the visibility of homosexual existence and desire. In this process, however, homosexuality also has to pay the high price of making invisible a key factor of its structure: *eroticism.*

Road Movie: A Korean Queer Movie?

In the case of male homosexuality, any sign of male homoeroticism or even an erotic representation of the male body (for either male or female eyes) must be erased to ease homosexuality's acquisition of social use-value. The existence of controlling heterosexual disciplinary structures can be seen in many areas of dominant society, including cinematic representation in popular film, and particularly in *Road Movie,* a controversial gay movie. Released in 2002, when queer issues were more visible in Korean society than ever before, *Road Movie* drew major public attention—enough to bring matters of male homosexuality into wider discussion.[12] It is interesting to reread *Road Movie* not only because this gay film keeps male homosexuality, especially male homoeroticism, under discipline by the genre aesthetics of the queer movie, the road movie, the art-house film, and melodrama, but also because Korean film criticism's attitudes toward the film replicate this disciplinary move.

The main characters in *Road Movie* are Suk-Won, a married heterosexual man, and Dae-Shik, a male homosexual vagabond. Suk-Won, a broker ruined in the market crash due to the economic crisis in late 1990s Korea, collapses on the streets of Seoul. Devastated by his own decay and his abandonment by his wife, he's taken care of by Dae-Shik, a leader among the guttersnipes and street-sleepers. Having lost all the joy of life, Suk-Won is bullied by other vagabonds and street youths. He starves himself and attempts suicide. Saving him with no expectation of compensation, Dae-Shik finally proposes to Suk-Won a cross-country trip together, a journey that will lead them to other people living their own desperate lives. They meet a friendly work foreman and Il-Ju, a young quasi-prostitute waitress who falls for Dae-Shik, as well as Dae-Shik's lost wife and son. But mixed feelings of despair, hatred, pity, compassion, and passion emerge between the two when Suk-Won witnesses Dae-Shik having sex with a stranger in a public toilet. Suk-Won pours out his despair and hatred for Dae-Shik's homosexuality and insults Dae-Shik's now apparent affection for him, but Dae-Shik never lets Suk-Won leave him. However, the moment of truth inevitably arrives. After a violent conflict, Suk-Won decides to leave Dae-Shik, but then discovers that Dae-Shik, who lost his will to live after Suk-Won left, has been severely injured by an explosion. Coming back and finding Dae-Shik dying, Suk-Won finally realizes and accepts Dae-Shik's true love and stays with him until his death.

Until *Road Movie*'s arrival in domestic theatres, Korean film was a barren landscape for queer cinema, lacking even a single homosexual character. Therefore, it is not surprising that film critics could praise *Road Movie* simply because "this frontier gay movie opens a new genre (of queer cinema) in Korean film culture by courageously facing up to the disturbing issue of homosexuality and through its groundbreaking depiction of graphic sex between men, even though the film itself is quite mediocre in other respects."[13]

I think this statement, which summarizes the judgments of most film critics (both Korean and foreign), reveals two dilemmas that mainstream film criticism faces in positioning *Road Movie* in Korean popular culture and film history. One is the text's identity—"Korean" queer cinema—and the other is the text's transgression—gay sex. Can we call *Road Movie* a queer movie? What criteria should we use to interpret and evaluate the film's depiction of homosexuality, from its angst to its eroticism, both of which have been uncomfortable to watch up to now? The first question (that of the film's Koreanness) implies a difficulty in positioning a particular filmic text within Korean film culture and granting a place to a gay movie on the historical map of Korean national cinema. The second question (that of the film's representation of gay sex) concerns whether the film draws general consent from society in (re)interpreting a transgression the against dominant social order. The former question is perhaps a matter of textual aesthetics; the latter, a matter of social meaning. However, these two dilemmas both arise from one central question: the signification of social margins. What kind of explanation of the marginal can be made in the interests of maintaining the dominant, homogenous society?

It is the dynamics of "interpolating the marginal into the center" that account best for these two dilemmas. The difficulty or discomfort arising from identifying the movie as "queer cinema" and positioning it as a representation of deviant sexuality was softened by bringing in the genre aesthetics of the "road movie." When it was released, in fact, the movie was publicized first and foremost as a gay movie. However, most critics focused on the film's genre aesthetics, not its queerness. Articles written from this expressionist/film-aesthetic perspective are mostly devoted to praising this "internationally acclaimed film" with abstract descriptions like "the road is life, the road is what you're living on," or by expressionist analyses emphasizing the supremacy of the movie's cinematic expression in vividly capturing the characters' inner suffering and abject reality.[14] With regard to the "queerness" of the film, most of the articles said ambiguous things like, "Graphic sex scenes between men made the movie controversial, yet these are not erotic acts but sublime ones through which the differences of class and social status between the two men were able to be transcended." Some film critics even claimed that *Road Movie* was not a queer film. They emphasize themes of liberal humanist virtues like love and mutual understanding, based on the director's own statement: "Although I am not opposed to people who watch my movie as a queer film, I am not sure that *Road Movie* can be categorized as a queer movie because it is ultimately a film about human beings, no matter their sexuality." By reading the film though an "author-as-origin" perspective, such critics willingly remove homosexuality from the movie to leave only liberal humanist virtues.

On the other hand, clearly acknowledging the identity of *Road Movie* as a queer movie, Tony Rayns praises its superiority and truthfulness by writing that it is sure to be admired as both a queer movie and a road movie. Asserting the film's identity, he mentions that it has truthfulness as a queer film by vigorously confronting the harsh reality of "being homosexual in Korean society," especially through the character of Dae-Shik, who is, according to Rayns, a "symbol of contemporary Korean gays." By suggesting the *factuality* (based on unknown research) of the idea that most Korean gays in their thirties and forties live in the closet, or else suffer in unwanted marriages, mental alienation from family, and isolation from social institutions, Rayns makes Dae-Shik a model for contemporary Korean gays' reality. In addition, criticizing Korean gay audiences' dislike of the film, he complains that they may be "laughable, silly left-wingers who think that only positive depictions of homosexuals should be made to counter the negative ones in mainstream popular culture."[15] I think Rayns' perspective is problematic not only because of his shallow positivism and vulgar realism (as in "it is by definition good to depict on screen something that exists in real life"), but also because of his remarkable innocence in appreciating the value and meanings of a filmic text based solely on its achievement in genre aesthetics. He considers the queer only as the suffering "other" in mainstream society and supports the general Western-centered evolutionist viewpoint that sees homosexuality in Korea as "still in the closet, under development, and with a long way to go." According to this perspective, *Road Movie*'s depiction of a poor, struggling and ill-fated Korean gay guy is a masterpiece of cine-realism because this is the homosexual reality in Korea today.

I want to read *Road Movie* as a symptomatic text, for it shows the discursive logic of heterosexual-centered mainstream society symptomatically, revealing that society's fear of homoeroticism as it interpolates queerness, as the other/marginal, into the circuit of dominant discourses. All this can be read in cinematic discourses and criticism of the film as well as in its own logic of representation. Rereading the film in terms of its reregistering of homosexuality and its suppression/erasure of homoeroticism, I focus below on the film's picturesque, "art-house-esque" representation of spaces as delocalized in relation to its representation of homosexual identity through a conventional abundance of melodramatic emotions, especially melancholy.

(1) High Art, Delocalized Spaces, and Identities

In the film's road-movie-style narrative structure, it is the visual representation of various spaces that most catches the eye. As Dae-Shik and Suk-Won move from place to place, different locales in Korea are captured beautifully by the camera. Picturesque spaces on their trip are contrasted with the dark side of Seoul, where they stayed before starting the trip. The complex process of transforming 16 mm film (used for shooting) to 35 mm film (for screening), has enabled the whole movie to capture unique tones. The first half of the film is shot in documentary-esque cinematography: it is characterized by grainy film and gray-toned color in dizzy handheld shots. This is obviously a visual strategy of representing Seoul as a big, cold metropolis that is cruel and harsh for vagabonds and street sleepers like Dae-Shik and Suk-Won. When the pair leaves Seoul to take their road trip, the space of the screen transforms into bright, colorful postcard-like images. The skies and sea are a more beautiful, bright blue than in any other film. The characters are carefully framed against backgrounds of picturesque scenery. As I noted above, the film's visual aestheticism is the key element praised by most film critics. The film's excessively expressionist images open up a space where the "disturbing" theme of homosexuality can be appreciated by film critics in the name of high art.

Reading Bataille's analysis of fascism, John Champagne reminds us that "the lines between 'impure' filthy heterogeneity and an 'imperative' sacred one are unstable and easily crossed," by using Bataille's example of the body of Christ: "In its bloodied and crucified form, the body of Christ represents an impure heterogeneous element that is then mobilized and transformed, via the Resurrection, into an imperative form. The ever-present danger that an 'impure' heterogeneity might be 'elevated' to an 'imperative' form, which might then serve the needs of homogeneous culture, suggests a number of caveats for a cultural criticism claiming to be 'transgressive.'"[16] Adopting

Champagne's (and Bataille's) idea for my reading of *Road Movie*'s art-house-esque visual representation, I suspect that the obsessive taste of high art plays a key role (both in the film itself and in the critics' appreciation), elevating the uncomfortable, impure life of drifters and the deviant sexuality of the queer to something imperative in the sacred form of the dominant, homogenous society, and soothing heterosexual anxiety and fear of homosexuality.

The excessively stylish, art-house-esque representation of space has another effect in *Road Movie:* delocalization of space. Beautiful, postcard-like representation of space in the country contrasts to dark, gloomy Seoul. In the late 1990s, Seoul was one of the gloomiest cities in the world due to the notorious economic collapse, which is often called "the IMF phase." In *Road Movie*, Seoul is represented through documentary aesthetics as a specific, local, historic space in a specific period. However, when Dae-Shik and Suk-Won leave Seoul, the spaces they pass through during their trip lose locality and historicity and acquire instead visual flamboyance. The deep blue sea looks like a Hawaiian beach paradise where Dae-Shik and Suk-Won can finally be happy, and the endless road is like the yellow brick road that may lead the two men to Oz. Indeed, the delocalized representation of space is found not only in *Road Movie* but in most contemporary Korean popular films. Analyzing the representation of space in Kim Ki-duk's *3–Iron* and its "exchange value" in the global economy of images, Sunah Kim writes that "understanding non-Western spaces requires not a specific historical knowledge of the spaces, but the perception to watch the spaces with a sense of unfamiliarity and fascination."[17]

To be fascinated by the representation of country spaces in *Road Movie* does not require one to remember why the men had to take their trip, but only to appreciate the spatial beauty itself. In this, homosexual Dae-Shik and post-breakdown Suk-Won can escape from their historically marked situations to unknown places where their disastrous reality is effectively erased. However, in the delocalized countryside, Dae-Shik and Suk-Won reveal quite a different mind-set about the trip. During the trip, roads are places for escape for Suk-Won, but they are places for survival for Dae-Shik. Suk-Won constantly asserts his social and sexual identities. He repeatedly claims he comes from a different class ("Do you know who I am? I was a top-notch fund manager and I am going back to my position, too"), and he emphasizes that he is a married heterosexual, even though his wife has abandoned him. ("I am not like you. I have a job and a wife. I am not a pervert like you!") However, such social markers have nothing to do with Dae-Shik. Even when his social status is revealed (it turns out he was a famous mountaineer with an ex-wife and a son), he denies all (hetero)social relations and tries to remain a vagabond who never leaves the road. The film implies that Dae-Shik's homosexuality causes him to deny all social markers and continue to wander: sexual identity is the one and only factor that determines Dae-Shik's life. Detached from the harsh reality of late 1990s Korean society, homosexuality finds its own space for survival. As Dae-Shik cannot but leave Seoul and take the trip, it is implied that homosexuality cannot survive in local, historical Seoul, only on an unending road with no destination. In other words, at the cost of losing social markers and specificity, Dae-Shik's homosexual identity can be embodied only in nameless, unknown places: the road, the countryside, the seashore, and the steep, rocky mountains.

(2) Melancholy and the De-eroticization of Gay Sexuality

On the film's relation with homosexuality, director Kim In-Shik says, "I am not offended by the public's categorization of my film as queer cinema, but strictly speaking, I think my film is a melodrama that happens to tell a story of a gay person."[18] At least the director recognizes the proper genre in which his film can be categorized. Whether recognized as a "road movie" (as its own title implies) or as a controversial "queer movie," in terms of its genre aesthetics and structure, *Road Movie* can be described best as a melodrama.

Melodramatic devices seem almost too strategic in *Road Movie*. Frustration and despair, two of the key emotions in tragic melodrama, are the dominant elements in *Road Movie*. As the provocative gay sex scene that opens the movie proves, it is Dae-Shik's gay sexuality that leads him to despair, while it is bankruptcy due to the economic collapse that frustrates Suk-Won. Frustration and despair tie the two men together, and these emotions recur over and over throughout the film. The first part of the film about the homeless people of Seoul, shot in monotoned documentary style, economically visualizes the two men's frustration and despair. Even on the road trip their remorse never ends. When Min-Seok, who also has a secret dark side and eventually commits suicide, and Il-Ju, a barmaid with a tough life, join the two men's journey, remorse and melancholy become dominant emotions in the film. However, it is the toilet scene where Dae-Shik has a sex with a stranger that illustrates the film's melodramatic economy most clearly. At the end of the scene, Suk-Won comes into the bathroom to wash his hands and sees Dae-Shik after his gay sex. The scene plays as a turning point in the narrative not only because Suk-Won finds out about Dae-Shik's homosexuality for the first time, but also because afterwards, melancholy dominates the film's melodramatic narrative: as a reward for his love for Suk-Won, Dae-Shik receives only Suk-Won's despair over his sexuality.

As a melodrama, *Road Movie* not only shows an excess of emotion, it also, even more "excessively," repeats this emotional excess over and over, especially after the toilet sex scene. The latter half of the film simply shows the two men's routine: they move, they get a one-day job at a construction site, they love and hate each other, and they fight. Nothing happens more than this "love and hate" routine, except in the scene where they visit the mountain cafe where Dae-Shik's ex-wife and son live. The scenes of this melodramatic melancholy even become boring as a result of their mechanical repetition. Generally in melodrama, emotional excess and repetition are a strategy to produce romantic fantasies, but they also play a key role in concealing various exploitations that exist in the social (based on class, economic, or sexual difference) through masochistic pleasure, as in conventional melodrama or the "women's film."[19] So, by its strategy of excessive repetition of melodramatic melancholy, what does *Road Movie* try to conceal? I propose that it is homoerotic desire that is negated and erased by the dynamics of melodrama.

Road Movie represents homosexuality but erases homoeroticism. The film asserts that we should accept two men's relationship as love, and it has succeeded in persuading audiences of Suk-Won's acceptance of Dae-Shik's love. Let's consider the final scene where the two naked men lie naked together on a salt-heap in a warehouse. This scene is the film's most melodramatic, tear-jerking moment: an act of love is accomplished and then Dae-Shik dies. Without any sign of sexual activity and with the act of "purification"—Suk-Won's washing of his body in the rain—the last scene never frames the two naked male bodies in an erotic way. Compared to the previous two gay sex scenes (one is the opening scene where Dae-Shik has sex with a guy in a dark, dirty room, and the other is the toilet sex scene), this scene merely depicts the naked male bodies in a sublime act of humanistic love. Throughout the film, Dae-Shik keeps saying "I don't want to fall in love." He refuses and denies his own desire for love. He is a classic case of the homosexual subject's "internalized negation." In the scene of purification and through Dae-shik's negative interiorization that "involves turning homosexuality inside out, exposing not the homosexual's abjected insides but the homosexual as the abject, as the contaminated and expurgated insides of the heterosexual subject,"[20] the homosexual subject becomes "a normalized otherness"; the Other that is normalized and recuperated by heterosexual mainstream discourses, and the desexualized subject that has lost its sexual pleasure of "transgression."

In the climactic moment of melodrama, in the sublime moment of melancholia, the tragic homosexual relationship is transformed into something universal in the name of love. In the disguise of a philanthropy that asserts "gays are human, too," the film reveals its dynamic of homophobic moralism that negates homoeroticism as "transgression."

Conclusion

I have been arguing that *Road Movie* and the extant criticism of it prove that mainstream heterosexual discourses never stop recuperating homosexuality as "other-margin" to resolve heterosexual anxiety. In this process, it is homoeroticism that is erased. It is interesting to take a look at the Korean word for homosexuality, *dongseongae,* compared to *seongae,* the Korean word for eroticism.[21] There is no specific word for homoeroticism. In the Korean version of this article, I have used the expression *"dong/seongae"* (homo/sexuality-eroticism) in order to foreground the representational situation in Korean contemporary cinema where homosexuality is reregistered as the "normalized other" in mainstream discourses while homoeroticism, a transgression that refuses to be recuperated by mainstream discourses, *cannot be represented.*

Given all this, what kind of blueprint can we imagine for the political and theoretical practice of queer criticism as "other-margin"? In relation to the theory of the other, John Champagne suggests an ethical criticism "that [is] ethically committed to altering the existing relations of power so that they might become more fluid, more easily reversible . . . [to] attempt to make use of the 'impure position of the culturally marginalized,' deploying the Other 'against the normalizing practices of disciplinary society.'"[22] Gay sexuality, resisting the heterosexual subject formation of disciplinary society, may be seen as a form of cultural transgression. Also, it can be theoretically transgressive because it tests the limits of dominant discourses. Queer studies should always be aware of the danger of being exposed to dominant discourse's dynamics, and should always try to intervene in the process of recuperation.

Moreover, this strategy of ethical criticism needs to consider its complex positionality. As I pointed out above, queer as "other-margin" faces the danger of being recuperated as "queer universality." The technical adoption of imported concepts from the theory of margins or minorities can overlook the complex layers of social and historical discourses where queer matters are deployed in practice. Thus, close interrogation, contextualization, and intervention are required rather than searching for some "queer essence" or the hopeless strategy of resubverting the recuperated Other. And this position requires a deconstructive tactic to read the social and cultural fluidity of subject formation where the center and the margin mutually inform one another, and actively negotiate with dominant discourses. In this way, queer criticism's politics of interpretation could become connected to ethics not only as a theoretical practice but also as a way of life.

Notes

1. Rey Chow, "Introduction: On Chineseness as a Theoretical Problem," 3.

2. See Dong-jin Seo, "Mapping the Vicissitudes of Homosexual Identities."

3. "Secretive Expansion of Underground Gay Community," *ChungAng Ilbo,* August 2, 1994.

4. The importance of Internet technology and culture for formation of LGBTQ communities in Korea cannot be overemphasized. See Chris Berry and Fran Martin, "Syncretism and Synchronicity," and Seo Dong-Jin, "Digital Bujok duel."

5. "As gay activists from non-Western contexts become more and more involved in setting political agendas, and as the rights discourse of internationalism is extended to more and more cultural contexts, Anglo-American queer theorists will have to be more alert to the globalizing—and localizing—tendencies of our theoretical languages" (Michael Warner, introduction to *Fear of a Queer Planet,* xii).

6. It may be best shown in Dennis Altman's statement: "find[ing] a balance between the view of globalization as a new stage of imperialism and the triumpalist discourse of globalization as the creation of a new world society" (Dennis Altman, "Global Gaze/Global Gays," 12).

7. Strong, "Nietzche's Political Misappropriation," 125.

8. Thomas, "Introduction," 2.

9. A couple of popular film magazines with an academic perspective came out in 1994 and 1995: *Cine 21,* a weekly magazine whose regular contributors are film scholars and serious critics, and *Kino,* a monthly magazine introducing articles and reviews based on orthodox film theories like film semiology, psychoanalysis, ideological criticism, and so on. *Cine 21* is still the top-selling magazine. *Kino* is known as the most academic film magazine.

10. Hye-young Cho, "Paranoia of the Origin."

11. Editorial, *Cine 21* 62, July 1996.

12. In 2001–02, queer sexuality in the Korean entertainment industry became a hot topic: Hong Seok-Chun, a TV actor who came out to the public, and Ha Ri-Su, a hugely popular M-to-F transsexual singer/actress, brought the homosexual topic to the surface of Korean society faster and stronger than ever before.

13. Introduction, "Special Discussion of Kim In-Shik and Seo Dong-Jin: Two Perspectives on *Road Movie,*" *Cine 21* 373, Oct. 18, 2002.

14. The later part of the film through a cinematography characterized by an excessive visual style appears close to a cliché "inherited from European art-house films" (Sang-yong Lee, "Too Road Movie-esque," *Film 2.0,* Oct.14, 2002). Indeed, the director studied filmmaking in France.

15. Rayns, "Why *Road Movie* Is Great as Both Road Movie and Queer Movie."

16. Champagne, *The Ethics of Marginality,* 31. Emphasis in original.

17. Kim, "Spaces Translatable."

18. "*Road Movie,* the Living End of the Men on the Road: An Interview with Kim In-Shik," *Kino* 90, October 2002.

19. On melodrama's dynamics of producing fantasies and reaffirming social structure based on its relation to female spectators, see Kuhn, "Women's Genres," 146–55.

20. Diana Fuss, "Inside/Out," 3–4.

21. *Ae,* meaning "love," is used in various emotions and relationships in Korean expression. For example, it is used in *jeonwooae,* comradeship between soldiers, and *hyungjeae,* brotherhood. Soyoung Kim points out that the indistinct uses of *ae* in Korean expression shows (dis)continuity of various emotions and relationships. See Soyoung Kim, "*Tell Me Something* and *JSA: Joint Security Area,*" 154–55.

22. Champagne, *The Ethics of Marginality,* xxviii.

References

Altman, Dennis. "Global Gaze/Global Gays." In John C. Hawley, ed., *Postcolonial and Queer Theory: Intersections and Essays.* Westport, Conn.: Greenwood Press, 2001.

Berry, Chris, and Fran Martin. "Syncretism and Synchronicity: Queer'n'Asian Cyberspace in 1990s Taiwan and Korea." In Chris Berry, Fran Martin, and Audrey Yue, eds., *Mobile Cultures: New Media in Queer Asia.* Durham: Duke University Press, 2003. 88–114.

Champagne, John. *The Ethics of Marginality: A New Approach of Gay Studies.* Minneapolis: University of Minnesota Press, 1995.

Cho, Hye-young. "Paranoia of the Origin: Historization of 1995's Korean Cine-culture." *Youngsang Yesul Yeonku* 1. Seoul: Youngsang Yesul Hakhoe, 2001.

Chow, Rey. "Introduction: On Chineseness as a Theoretical Problem." In Rey Chow, ed., *Modern Chinese Literary and Cultural Studies in the Age of Theory: Reimagining a Field.* Durham: Duke University Press, 2000.

Dong-Jin, Seo. "Digital Bujok duel: Jeopkyeong ui Yeonsokchei." *Munwha Kwahak* 10. Seoul: Munhwa Kwahaksa, 1997.

"Editorial." *Cine 21:* 63 (July 1996).

Fuss, Diana. "Inside/Out." In Diana Fuss, ed., *Inside/Out: Lesbian Theories Gay Theories.* New York: Routledge, 1991.

"Introduction of 'Special Discussion of Kim In-Shik and Seo Dong-Jin: Two Perspectives on *Road Movie.*'" *Cine 21* 373 (October 18, 2002).

Kim, See Soyoung. "*Tell Me Something* and *JSA: Joint Security Area:* Homosocial Fantasy in Korean Blockbusters." *Yeo/Seong e ron* 6 (July 2002): 154–55.

Kim, Sunah. "Spaces Translatable: Indexicality of Body and Film." *Film Language* 6 (2005).

Kuhn, Annett. "Women's Genres: Melodrama, Soap Opera, and Theory." In Sue Thornham, ed., *Feminist Film Theory: A Reader.* New York: New York University Press, 1999. 146–55.

Lee, Sang-yong. "Too Road Movie-esque." *Film 2.0* (October 14, 2002).

Rayns, Tony. "Why *Road Movie* Is Great as Both Road Movie and Queer Movie: A Misunderstood Masterpiece, a Future Classic." *Cine 21* 374 (October 25, 2002).

"*Road Movie,* the Living End of the Men on the Road: An Interview with Kim In-Shik." *Kino* 90 (October 2002).

"Secretive Expansion of Underground Gay Community." *ChungAng Ilbo* (August 2, 1994).

Seo, Dong-jin. "Mapping the Vicissitudes of Homosexual Identities in South Korea." *Journal of Homosexuality* (2001): 5.

Strong, Tracy B. "Nietzche's Political Misappropriation." In Bernd Magnus and Kathleen M. Higgins, eds., *The Cambridge Companion to Nietzche.* Cambridge: Cambridge University Press.

Thomas, Calvin. "Introduction: Identification, Appropriation, Proliferation." In Calvin Thomas, ed., *Straight with a Twist: Queer Theory and the Subject of Heterosexuality.* Urbana: University of Illinois Press, 2000.

Warner, Michael. Introduction to Michael Warner, ed., *Fear of a Queer Planet: Queer Politics and Social Theory.* Minneapolis: University of Minnesota Press, 1993.

TWELVE

LESBIANISM AND TAIWANESE LOCALISM IN *THE SILENT THRUSH*

Teri Silvio

In 1990, Ling Yan's novel *The Silent Thrush* (*Shisheng Huamei*) won first prize in the prestigious *Independent Evening News* (*Zili Wanbao*) One Million Fiction Contest for "Native Soil literature" (*bentu wenxue*). *Silent Thrush* was one of the first Taiwanese novels to bring together the themes of Hoklo ethnic heritage and lesbian sexuality.[1] The novel is a fictionalization of the author's own experiences as a student actress in a traveling *koa-a-hi* (Taiwanese opera) troupe in the south of Taiwan, and portrays several romantic/sexual relationships between actresses.

The first reviews of *Silent Thrush* read the lesbian relationships in the novel as a "symptom" of the "decline" of *koa-a-hi,* and traditional Hoklo culture generally, under the conditions of rapid commercialization and the KMT government's denigration of local culture in favor of a (northern) "Chinese" heritage. At the same time, several lesbian (or T/*po*) identified readers I interviewed in the early 1990s said they found the "traditional" world of the *koa-a-hi* troupe depicted in *Thrush* quite alien. While they identified with some aspects of the characters' sexuality, they did not see the novel as reflecting their own identity politics.

As Ch'iu Kuei-fen points out, the novel's content poses a serious paradox for Native Soil ideology: "On the one hand, as Mr. Yeh [Yeh Shih-t'ao, a Native Soil novelist who was one of the original judges of the novel] claims, the *koa-a-hi* troupe is a microcosm of the most traditional, Confucianist old-style feudal society. The *koa-a-hi* troupe is imbued with the symbolic aura of 'folk custom' and obviously represents tradition. Yet *Silent Thrush's* minute descriptions of the gender relations within this small society expose the fact that this most 'traditional,' most 'feudal' society is actually founded on desires between women that are the most untraditional, the farthest beyond the norms of patriarchy."[2]

Simply because *Thrush* focuses on the world of traditional opera performers, the conjunction of the themes of regional cultural identity and queer sexuality are overdetermined.[3] For centuries, Chinese opera (*xiqu*) has been both a subculture associated with nonnormative sexuality (particularly prostitution and homosexuality) and a marker of regional cultural identity.

Since the 1940s, it has been standard for women to play all of the leading roles in *koa-a-hi,* both male and female, and a complex female fan culture has developed around the women who play the *sio sing* (leading male) roles.[4] In my interviews with *koa-a-hi* actresses and fans in the 1990s, I found that romantic and sexual relationships between actresses, or between actresses and women fans, were universally acknowledged to be common, regardless of individual informants' views on homosexuality.[5]

If Chinese opera as a subculture has been associated with queer sexuality, as an art form it has been associated primarily with subnational regional culture. The names of most Chinese opera genres are simply the name of a place followed by some term for drama—for example *jing xi* refers to Peking opera, and *yue ju* refers to the drama of the Yue, or Zhejiang, region. Local operas, like local cuisines, are integral to the Chinese concept of regional culture. In contexts in which regional identity is foregrounded, such as tourism, local opera genres are often cited as representative local traditions. In Taiwan, where the relationship between regional and national culture (that is, between "Taiwan" and the "Republic of China") has been highly contested, Native Soil activists' definition of *koa-a-hi* as "Taiwanese opera" was a political act.

Silent Thrush came out within six years of the end of martial law in Taiwan, at the beginning of a period of great diversification in Taiwanese politics and the arts. Between 1992 and 2000, when Chen Shuibian was elected president, Hoklo cultural identity went from being oppositional (to the Chinese cultural identity promoted by the Chinese Nationalist Party [KMT]) to being legitimated through academic discourse and government cultural policy. During these same years, a gay and lesbian political movement, largely based in universities, developed and became a visible part of Taiwanese public life. A wide variety of sexual identity categories emerged, such as those suggested by Song Hwee Lim in this volume, that had been unthinkable in the martial law period between 1947–1987. Yet these two identity discourses were, and remain, largely separate; in Taiwan, homosexuality is rarely discussed in relation to Hoklo ethnicity, or vice versa.

The revolutionary implications of the paradox that *Thrush* reveals—that lesbian desire is not only not un-Taiwanese but foundational to local identity—have been largely lost in the subsequent development of both ethnic and queer identity politics in Taiwan. I believe this loss is due to the rejection of mass culture by both Hoklo ethno-nationalism and queer activism in Taiwan. By mass culture, I mean all that is purged from both folk culture and the avant-garde as "inauthentic"—the kitschy, the generic, the commercial, and the feminine.

A film version of *Silent Thrush* came out in 1992, directed by Chen Sheng-fu. I analyze the film because it reveals the paradox of *koa-a-hi* as both traditional folk art and queer subculture more clearly than the novel precisely because of the film's deeper participation in the abjected realm of mass culture. The film heightens the paradox of queer folk culture not by historicizing it but by structuring audience identification through contradictory genre conventions. I should note that my reading is a perverse one; the film is in many respects very homophobic, and many Taiwanese lesbians found the film quite offensive. Yet if the film obviously participates in a discourse of exclusionary ethno-nationalism, it also offers a glimpse of the potential for both queering Hoklo identity and localizing queer identity.

Silent Thrush was a box-office flop. It closed in Taiwan after only one week, and lost so much money that the producer had to sell his home.[6] But its failures make it interesting. The film is a work of commercial culture that, at the same time that it tries to maintain the novel's status as Native Soil art, crassly attempts to appeal to the Taiwanese mass audience's desires. The transparency of this pandering—the film's sensationalism and uneven style—reveals how contradictory, and how queer, those desires are assumed to be. In the way it sensationalizes lesbian sexuality, the film reveals a nostalgic yearning for abjection itself at the heart of Hoklo identity.

The Plot

Mu Yun has been enchanted by *koa-a-hi* since she was a little girl, and has always dreamed of becoming an actress. When she graduates from technical high school, Mu Yun runs away from home to join a traveling *koa-a-hi* troupe. The troupe is a "tape-recorded troupe" (*luyin tuan*). The actresses do not sing and improvise dialogue themselves, as actresses in "flesh-and-sound troupes" (*rou sheng tuan*) do, but lip-synch to cassette tapes.

As the troupe moves from town to town, Mu Yun grows increasingly disillusioned with life in the troupe, and increasingly pessimistic about the future of the theater she loves. The film is set in the mid-1980s, the period of "lottery fever," so the troupe has plenty of work at temple festivals where worshippers pray for gambling tips or give thanks for lottery winnings.[7] But the audiences in the small towns are bored by *koa-a-hi*, and the troupe often switches to "varieties"—comedy routines and sexy dancing—after the ritual "representation of the gods" (*pan sian*) is done. The sponsors are continually pressuring the troupe to do strip shows.

Only one couple in the troupe is in a normative heterosexual marriage. All of the other women are in various unorthodox relationships. Ah Kim is the "little wife" of the troupe's owner, and Ba Gam Yi (Fleshy-Sexy Auntie) is the "little wife" of a gambling taxi driver. Hung Hung (Phoenix) is divorced and engages in prostitution on the side. Tau Iu Ko (Brother Soy Oil), the troupe's butch lesbian manager and teacher, is in a relationship with another actress. The star *sio sing* (male role) and *sio toa* (female role) actresses, Ka Hung and Ai Cheng, are in a long-term relationship and have bought a house together. The dramatic climax of the film comes when Ka Hung attempts to violently seduce Mu Yun, and Ai Cheng makes an unsuccessful suicide attempt. After this Mu Yun learns that her grandfather has died and decides to leave the troupe.

Genre and Style

The film presents a jarring mixture of different styles. In fact, there seem to be three films colliding here: a didactic, social realist melodrama; a soft-porn film; and a nostalgic art film. The ambivalent relationship between ethnic identity and queer female sexuality is manifest in the way these three styles both contradict and infect each other. I will briefly describe these three styles and then discuss the relationships among them.

Social Realist Melodrama

Most of the film seems to present the story in the same way it was read by Native Soil writers. That is, the film shows the "degradation" of the actors' lives through the gaze of the "normal" (middle-class) Mu Yun. Several scenes emphasize the financial conditions of the troupe and make causal connections between the materialist environment of rural Taiwan in the 1980s and the "vulgar" morality and affect of the actresses. The film's didacticism is manifest primarily in heavy-handed montages. For example, in the first scene in which the actresses are forced by their sponsors to dance in skimpy costumes, the camera pans from the dancers to Mu Yun sitting by the side of the stage, facing away. The next shot is presumably from her point of view—she is watching some butchers slaughtering and carving up chickens and pigs. In Taiwan, the term "beef market" (*niu rou chang*) refers to strip show venues. The montage's "meat market" pun reads very similarly in Taiwan to the way it would in the United States. The film ends with another montage alternating between shots of skyscrapers (including Taipei's International Trade Center) and of abandoned traditional-style homes and temples (for example, a shot of a courtyard overgrown with weeds with a broken high chair lying in the foreground), implying cause and effect between the growth of the cold, gleaming international capital and the death of the warm, family-centered environment of the village. This montage visualizes what Ch'iu Kuei-fen calls a "recurring trope in Native Soil novels . . . : folk custom = childhood memories of agricultural society = ideal; contemporary culture = industrial society = decadence."[8]

The actors in the film rely heavily on stereotyped and exaggerated gestures to mark working-class identity. This style may be seen as simply unprofessional; as one Taiwanese filmmaker with whom I watched the video described it, "It's like in the 1970s, when they first started to try and do social realism, but they hadn't quite got it right." Yet gestural stylization is also a prominent feature of *koa-a-hi* itself (as well as other Chinese operas) and of the Holo dialect television soap operas in which many *koa-a-hi* actresses moonlight. The film's melodramatic style is distinctly "popular" in contrast with the almost expressionless acting style favored by Taiwanese art film directors such as Hou Hsiao-hsien and Tsai Ming-liang.

One significant exception is Mu Yun, whose expressions and gestures are far more reserved than any of the other characters.' The actress who played Mu Yun, Li Yushan, was hired late, to replace another actress. Perhaps the director was therefore forced to unintentionally replicate Hou Hsiao-hsien's directing techniques (Hou generally refuses to give the actors a script for a scene until the day of filming). At any rate, the differences between Li's low-key performance and those of the other actors serves to highlight Mu Yun's framing position as an intellectual "artist" observing the "masses" from an emotional distance.

Soft Porn

If Mu Yun's narratorial gaze disapproves of the sexualization and commodification of the actresses, the film also revels in it. The abundant scenes of the actresses' exotic dancing are filmed in a way reminiscent of the strip show VCDs on sale in every night market in Taiwan. These scenes make the female body the object of scopophilia in the ways outlined by Laura Mulvey;[9] they break the narrative and fragment and fetishize the female body with overhead shots to show cleavage, shots which follow the lines of isolated legs and arms, close-ups in which the actress looks directly, and seductively, into the camera.

The film production process replicated precisely the de-skilling and sexualization of *koa-a-hi* that the novel critiqued. Only one actress in the cast had any experience performing *koa-a-hi*. Although there were plans to invite *koa-a-hi* actresses to teach the film actresses the stylized movements of *koa-a-hi*, they apparently received minimal training. Li Yushan was a fashion model with only two minor film roles to her credit. Another of the actresses in the film, Gu Jie, was previously known only for having appeared as a *Playboy* centerfold. She showed up in a revealing outfit at a press conference for the film and distributed nude photographs of herself to the reporters.[10]

If the strip dance scenes are reminiscent of the simplest genre of soft porn available in Taiwan, the lesbian sex scenes are filmed in a manner more reminiscent of Hong Kong "Category III" (adult only) feature films, particularly the genre of ancient-costume erotic feature film. The style of the soft porn parts of *Thrush* is coded as "traditional" through oblique references to classical Chinese erotic literature and painting. For instance, Kim Lian, the stripper hired to spice up the troupe's shows, has the same name as the heroine of the Ming dynasty erotic classic *Jin Ping Mei*. In the sex scene between Ka Hung and Ai Cheng, Ka Hung forces herself on a reluctant Ai Cheng, and stuffs a plum into her mouth to keep her from making noise. Ai Cheng's orgasm is represented by her biting into the plum and letting its juice and pulp run down her face. The plum is a well-known symbol of sexuality in classical Chinese literature. In terms of both the erotic use of this specific fruit and the bullying nature of the sex, this scene resonates obliquely with a famous scene in *Jin Ping Mei* in which Ximen Qing punishes Pan Jinlian by throwing plums into her vagina. In terms of how these scenes function in the film, the relationship between the moralistic framing of the overall story and the scopophilic displays of the female body replicate the overall structure of *Jin Ping Mei* and other classical erotic novels in which the sensational eroticism is framed within a didactic Buddhist/Confucian lesson on the wages of excessive attachment to the pleasures of the flesh.[11] Davis and Yeh note the same combination of scopophilia and moralistic framing in Hong Kong ancient-costume Category III films.[12] The stylistic conventions through which the female body and sexuality are represented in *Thrush* associate female sexuality, and particularly lesbianism, with the imperial Chinese past. Thus, although there is nothing in these scenes other than the Holo dialogue to mark them as specifically Taiwanese, the film's particular style of soft pornography undercuts any reading of lesbianism as a symptom of "modernization" or "Westernization."

Nostalgic Art Film

This aspect of the film appears in scenes that represent Mu Yun's memories or thoughts. These sequences contain no dialogue, only the folky theme music, which is played on traditional instruments, and include images of clichéd symbols of Hoklo folk culture such as temple architecture, rural trains, and sunsets over rice paddies. The general tone of these sequences is melancholy.

The visual style of these sequences is very different from that of more internationally known Taiwanese art films that also thematize nostalgia for rural life, such as Hou Hsiao-hsien's films. They contain theatrical or surreal elements alien to the Taiwanese art cinema aesthetic. Nevertheless, they are clearly marked as "arty" and separate from the melodramatic realism of the diegesis.

Intersections

The connection between lesbian sexuality and Hoklo identity lies primarily in the echoing of certain symbols and themes between the lesbian soft porn sections of the film and the memory sequences. Many of these symbols and themes are established in the opening sequence, which warrants a detailed description.

The film opens with a shot of a child's eye peeking out from under a cloth as a lullaby-like folk melody plays. We realize that the child is peeking under the cloth siding of a temporary stage as the next shot shows us a *koa-a-hi* actress in costume, nursing a baby. A subtitle tells us that it is 1974, and this is the Iok Siu Koa-a-hi Troupe (identified as a "flesh-and-sound" troupe where actresses do their own singing and dialogue). As the credits appear in the corner, the camera continues to pan around the backstage space, showing us older male actors eating noodles and napping on their trunks, a group gambling, the *sio sing* and *sio toa* putting on their makeup. The camera closes in on the face of the *sio sing* as she begins to put on her costume. In the next shot, the child lifts the cloth over her head, and we see the whole face of a girl of about seven, gazing with longing. We then return to the *sio sing* and *sio toa* dressing. The *sio sing* takes a pack of cigarettes from her sock and lights one. She throws the empty packet on the ground and goes up a ladder to the stage. As she passes the string and wind section of the orchestra, she places the cigarette in the mouth of an old man playing the banjo-like *goekhim* and walks off camera. The camera zooms in on the old man's face. He places the cigarette down next to a packet of betel nuts (*binlang*). The music changes to the traditional gongs and strings signaling the opening of a *koa-a-hi* performance, and we see shots of the various traditional instruments being played. We then return to a shot of the cigarette burning, and then see a shot of the old male *goekhim* player, completely isolated on the left side of the screen, in front of a plain cloth backdrop. The girl lowers the cloth back over her face, and we see a (more delicate) cloth drop gently down in front of the old man like a curtain, forming a billowing backdrop for the title of the film. The entire sequence is shot with a blue filter.

Four motifs are established in this scene and repeated through the movie, which later link lesbianism to nationalist nostalgia. These are cigarettes and betel nut, the *goekhim,* the falling curtain of silk, and the blue filter. Cigarettes and betel nut are multivalent symbols in Taiwan. Both are associated with masculinity, particularly working-class masculinity. Betel nut is a mild stimulant, native to the island, and was introduced to the Chinese settlers by the aboriginal peoples. Betel nut chewing is a habit particular to Hoklo, Hakka, and aboriginal men in Taiwan, as opposed to the Chinese immigrants who came with Chiang Kai-shek after 1949 and their children. It is also generally associated with the working class and the criminal underclass. The shots of the betel nuts and the burning cigarette thus condense the themes of addictive sensual pleasure, working-class or underclass masculinity, "native" identity, and the fleetingness of time.

The cigarette, which passes from the mouth of the *sio sing* actress to that of the old musician, creates a direct and eroticized link between Mu Yun's fascination with the women who play the male roles (on and offstage) and a more mainstream, clichéd image of "authentic" Hoklo folk culture. It also serves to emphasize the performative nature of gender. The detachability of this symbol from biological sex parallels the general way in which *koa-a-hi* performance constructs the gendered role through symbolic costuming and stylized gesture.

Cigarettes, betelnut, and the *goekhim* are all associated metonymically with Tau Iu Ko, who once played the *sio sing* roles. Tau-Iu Ko's masculine gender identity is established at once through her betel nut chewing and smoking. She also plays the *goekhim,* and gives her *goekhim* to Mu Yun as a gift. Through her position as teacher, Tau Iu Ko is clearly established as a "father figure" to Mu Yun. She is the holder of tradition, the person who both excites and prohibits Mu Yun's desires.

The combination of the blue filter and the falling silk are particularly significant because they appear both in scenes that represent Mu Yun's idealized memories of, or hopes for, Taiwanese opera and in the lesbian sex scenes. After Ka Hung and Ai Cheng make love, we see a blue silk cloth fall over the body and melancholy face of Ai Cheng, and Ka Hung seduces/rapes Mu Yun in front of a blue curtain. The use of these tropes in both scenes simultaneously eroticizes traditional Hoklo culture and imbues lesbian sexuality with an aura of ethnic nostalgia.

In the climactic scene, Mu Yun sits in her curtained-off sleeping space backstage, looking through a photo album given to her by Tau Iu Ko. The album lies open, showing black and white photographs of Taiwanese opera actresses in the Kung Lok Sia, once the largest and most popular troupe in Taiwan. Tau Iu Ko's *goekhim* lies on the mat beside it. Ka Hung enters Mu Yun's sleeping space, startling her. She tells Mu Yun that twenty years ago, when *koa-a-hi* was in its heyday, she could have been a star, and she offers to teach Mu Yun the proper movements for the heroine role. Ka Hung stands behind Mu Yun and molds her body into the proper position. When she forms Mu Yun's fingers into the "lotus fingers" gesture, she intertwines her fingers with Mu Yun's and draws her down to a sitting position. As Ka Hung enfolds and strokes Mu Yun's body, Mu Yun's face is isolated in a close-up, with a billowing blue screen behind her. Her facial expression alternates between distress and contentment. The seduction/rape ends abruptly when Mu Yun sees blood running across the straw floor mat—Ai Cheng has slashed her wrists.

This scene is not in the novel, where Mu Yun only observes, but does not participate in, the sexual/romantic relations among the troupe members. This original scene in the film places the narratorial position within, rather than outside, the web of lesbian relationships. The novel's controlled separation of traditional earthiness from modern dirtiness is rendered impossible in the film once Mu Yun's love for traditional Hoklo culture is explicitly linked to an erotic attachment to the *koa-a-hi* actresses who play the male roles. It is because Mu Yun has already developed an erotic attachment to Tau Iu Ko—not the Tau Iu Ko who manages the contemporary troupe, but the former actress posing in the photographs—and to the *sio sing* actress from the memory sequences—that she ambivalently accepts Ka Hung's seduction.

This is suggested by the sequence—Mu Yun looks at the photos, Ka Hung suggests she could have been a star in the female roles, the intimate physicality of movement training—and by the motif of the actors isolated against the billowing silk background. Despite Ka Hung's violence, the desire driving the scene, indeed the entire movie, is Mu Yun's.

"Environmental" Lesbianism

The idea of "environmental" homosexuality ran throughout contemporary reviews of both the novel and film. For example, Li Kangnian, the screenwriter for the film, told an arts reporter, "The actors in *koa-a-hi* troupes are with each other day and night, and they are all girls. Not only are the girls who play the *sio sing* roles handsome in appearance, they are more sensitive and caring than most males, and they have a better understanding of women's needs. Naturally they become the partners that the other troupe members admire and depend on. If romance follows from this, that's really quite natural."[13]

Although gay and lesbian activists have criticized the environmental "explanation" of homosexuality for many valid reasons, it opens up some interesting possibilities within the context of an ethno-nationalist discourse that is obsessed with defining a unique Taiwanese culture. If the lesbianism in *Thrush* is environmental in the sense that it is *caused by* the milieu of the *koa-a-hi* troupe, it must also be read as environmental in the sense that it is *constitutive of* the milieu of the troupe, that it is a "local custom" of this microcosmic world. In other words, the idea of environmental lesbianism opens up the possibility that not only does *koa-a-hi*, a local tradition, make women queer, but that queer women make *koa-a-hi*, and by extension, make Hoklo culture.

The theme of environment is explicitly established in the trope of the silent thrush, which is transposed directly from the novel to the film. Mu Yun passes a bird seller and notices that one of the caged thrushes will not sing. When she asks the shopkeeper why, he tells her that it is because it was only recently taken from the forest. The wild bird's environment has changed too rapidly—perhaps it will be able to sing again if it is allowed to slowly adjust. *Koa-a-hi*, Mu Yun decides, is just like that thrush—its musical voice is no longer heard because its environment has likewise changed too rapidly. But the metaphor applies equally well to Mu Yun herself, who literally cannot sing because she cannot adjust to the environment of the troupe.

Here it is interesting to compare the way that *koa-a-hi* training is represented in *Thrush* with how opera training is represented in Chen Kaige's *Farewell, My Concubine* (*Ba Wang Bie Ji*, 1993). In *Farewell*, the student actors "become the role" (*cheng jiao*) through painful work on the body. The film shows numerous scenes of the boys enduring torturous stretching exercises and physical punishments for every mistake. I have argued elsewhere that the process by which the boy Douzi literally incorporates the female role works as a trope for the ideal of the Maoist subject transforming his or her consciousness through physical praxis; in its portrayal of opera training and the visual and narrative linking of that training process to the struggles of the Cultural Revolution, *Farewell* reveals a nostalgic attitude towards the lost ideals of Maoism.[14] In *Silent Thrush*, in the two scenes in which Mu Yun actually receives coaching, the training works more like a laying on of hands. In each case, a *sio sing* actress (Tau Iu Ko and Ka Hung, respectively) stands behind her, molding her body into the proper position. She is literally enveloped. In the climactic scene described above, this enveloping molding leads into the lesbian seduction. We could read Mu Yun's failure to become an actress as a result of her resistance to, or the interruption of, her seduction/envelopment. In comparison with *Farewell*, we might read *Thrush*'s representation of failed opera training as an equally nostalgic longing for a complete envelopment within a "traditional" milieu, which is no longer possible in modern, industrialized Taiwan.

Lesbianism as a "Local Custom" of Jianghu

The trope of environmental lesbianism takes on a particularly ambivalent relationship to ethno-nationalist nostalgia if we read *Thrush* in view of Taiwanese conceptions of opera as part of a specific cultural milieu—*jianghu*. *Jianghu* literally means "rivers and lakes." It is best known as the chronotope of *wuxia* (knights-errant) fiction. It is where swordsmen fight for fame and honor, although it cannot be located in any particular geographical space. The precise nature of *jianghu* is different in different historical periods and genres, but it is almost always outside of the realm of the Confucian officialdom.[15] *Jianghu* is usually also outside of the Confucian family system; the most important relations in *jianghu* are generally the fictive kin relations of sworn brothers or teachers/pupils.

In modern Chinese fiction and cinema, *jianghu* is often a trope through which the power structures of contemporary political and economic systems are critiqued. Many interpretations of Hong Kong *wuxia* and gangster films focus on the allegorical relationship between *jianghu* and the politically ambiguous situation of Hong Kong before and after 1997.[16] Like novels and films that depict Chinese homosexuality, works that focus on *jianghu* can be seen as challenging state discourses that posit a hermetic, homogenous "Chinese" or "Asian" Confucian society.

In contemporary Chinese dialects, *jianghu* refers metaphorically to real social spaces as well, those that are marginal to or outside of all legitimate institutions, particularly the underground world of triads. Thus, in Hong Kong cinema, the word *jianghu* appears in the titles of many gangster films, and in the dialogue of virtually all of them. In contemporary Taipei, run-down neighborhoods, singers with smoky voices, and cheap hostess bars (*te-tiam-a*) are all referred to as having "*jianghu* flavor."

In Chinese societies, actors, like beggars and itinerant peddlers, are often described as "*jianghu* people." "*Jianghu* tunes" are sung not only in *koa-a-hi* but also, until recently, in markets, by beggars or peddlers selling patent medicines to attract a crowd. *Jianghu* people are those who are always in transit, unbound to and unprotected by hometown authorities or biological family, and who rely, like the swordsmen of *wuxia* fiction, on networks of fictive kinship and the ethics of personal honor. What I am most interested in here is the way that the term *jianghu*, in its particular use in the Taiwanese term *jianghu ren* (or *kangho lang* in Holo) both blends associations with traditional (outdated, feudal) ethics and criminality, and is set in opposition to both the legitimate state and corrupt modernity. Thus, if the *koa-a-hi* troupe is seen as a microcosm corrupted by both the KMT state and the commercialization resulting from its economic policies, it can also be read as a cultural space outside both the national community and the global marketplace, as a manifestation of *jianghu*.

Nostalgia for *jianghu* can be seen as a constant strain within Taiwanese Native Soil discourse, one that counters the rural-communitarian nostalgia of the more mainstream ethno-nationalist discourse. Hou Hsiao-hsien's films *A Time to Live, A Time to Die* (*Tong Nian Wangshi,* 1985) and *Goodbye, South, Goodbye* (*Nanguo, Zaijian, Nanguo,* 1996), with their petty gangster protagonists, are prominent examples. Yet Hou's *jianghu* nostalgia is usually distinctly masculine. What sets *Thrush* apart is that it makes female sexuality, particularly lesbian sexuality, constitutive of *jianghu*. It is significant that in the film, neither the words "lesbian" nor "homosexuality" are ever uttered. "It" is simply referred to as something that is "common in [*koa-a-hi*] troupes." In *Thrush*, lesbianism, along with stripping, prostitution, bigamy, betel nut chewing, and gambling, becomes one of the defining "local customs" (*fengsu*) of a specifically Taiwanese *jianghu*.

Mu Yun's erotic attachment to both Taiwanese opera and the actresses who play the male roles queers a prescient nostalgia for the freedom that came with being outside of the arena of political power, freedom from interpellation by the state. In the years following the film's release, Native Soil consciousness became the dominant discourse of the state, and "local custom" was transformed from the surrounding environment of everyday life to a museum piece, framed and placed at an untouchable, and therefore tantalizing, remove. The sensationalization and exoticization of the actresses' lesbianism in this film acknowledges precisely what may be lost in this process, the self-alienation entailed in the drawing of boundaries around Hoklo culture.

Conclusion

Since the early 1990s, a great deal has changed, both in terms of trends in Taiwanese identity discourse and in terms of the social positioning of both homosexuality and *koa-a-hi*. As the Native Soil movement gained political ground, the government increasingly took on the task of preserving local culture, including *koa-a-hi,* which is now performed at the National Theater and taught in public schools. At the same time, the mainstream of Taiwanese identity discourse has also become more inclusive. Hoklo identity is now constructed, both in DPP rhetoric and in local cinema, television, and literary productions, as part of a Taiwanese identity and history that includes aboriginal peoples, Hakka, and mainland immigrants and their children. The birth of a lesbian political movement in Taiwan is often dated to the founding of the group Between Us (*Women Zhi Jian*) in 1990, the same year the novel *The Silent Thrush* was published, and this movement has become increasingly visible and effective since then.[17] Along with other identity-based movements, such as feminism and the aboriginal rights movement, the claims of the gay and lesbian movement are acknowledged, in rhetoric if not in practice, by the government.

What has been lost in this civilization of both Hoklo "folk culture" and gay and lesbian identity is their connection. The gay and lesbian movement is largely university based, and deeply influenced by American gay and lesbian politics. Within the discourse of the movement, although there is much discussion of the differences between the situations of gay men and lesbians in Taiwanese, or pan-Chinese, societies and in "the West," very few connections are made between this construction of sociocultural difference and the continuing movement to construct a distinctive Hoklo ethnic identity. In fact, Hoklo working-class identity is often "othered" or simply ignored within Taiwanese "*ku'er*" ("queer") discourse, just as homosexuality is often "othered" or simply ignored within Hoklo ethno-nationalist discourse.

Some of the connections made between homosexuality and Hoklo ethnic identity in *Silent Thrush* may, however, be seen in more recent Taiwanese literature and television. One example is the 1996 novel *Ni Nü (Rebel Daughter)*, and the Taiwan Television miniseries adaptation of 2001. Like *Silent Thrush*, *Rebel Daughter* was seen as a "sympathetic" treatment of lesbianism by an (at least publicly) straight female writer, Du Xiulan; like *Silent Thrush*, it won a prestigious literary prize. In *Rebel Daughter*, the narrator, Angel, grows up in poverty with an abusive Hoklo mother and an impotent old mainlander father. She falls in love with sweet, demure girls (whom she sees as the opposite of her mother) in junior high school and high school, and later older women in college and after. At the end of the novel, Angel dies of cancer while still in her twenties, rejecting her natal family for her lover and her more supportive network of friends. As Ding Naifei and Liu Jenpeng have pointed out,

> Angel's short life is filled with . . . her silent shame of, resistance to, and attempts to get away from her Hoklo mother's torrential vocal abuses and performances of victimized motherhood in front of an audience of avidly interested neighbors. . . . Despite the author's disclaimer in her preface, where she warns that she does not mean the novel to be read as a statement to the effect that dysfunctional families in general and abusive mothers in particular will produce a rebel, an unfilial, a lesbian (quasi-T, or butch) daughter; nonetheless, the novel could very well be read as an allegory of precisely such a trajectory.[18]

In other words, the trope of "environmental lesbianism" drives the novel, although here the daughter's lesbianism is a reaction against, rather than a conforming to, her vulgar, working-class Holo-speaking environment.

Significantly, in the miniseries of *Rebel Daughter*, *koa-a-hi* serves as a trope condensing the mother's "vulgarity"—her shamelessness and performativity. In the first episode, when Angel's voice-over first describes her mother, she says, "As for my mother, she had nothing to do with the positive adjectives people usually think of—benevolent, warm, concerned, protective. What my father said was right, my mother should have been a *koa-a-hi* actress." Immediately after this voice-over we see the mother beating the daughter.

Ding and Liu analyze *Rebel Daughter* as part of a critique of the fatally homophobic aesthetics and politics of "reticence" (*hanxu*). They argue that the novel *Rebel Daughter* is itself a reticent text but despite this manages to reveal the oppressive force of reticence in Taiwanese lesbians' lives. They take issue with the ethnonationalist argument that coming out (that is, being nonreticent) is an inappropriate strategy for Chinese gay and lesbian movements simply because it is "Western." Based on my perverse reading of *Silent Thrush,* I would suggest that rejecting "Chinese" reticence could be framed as part of a localizing project rather than as part of a globalizing one. Embracing the most abject aspects of Hoklo ethnicity—shamelessness, nonnormative female sexualities, performativity—might be a resource for Taiwanese antihomophobic activism.

The trope of "environmental homosexuality" has been a thread connecting homosexual desire to Hoklo ethnicity. If, as in *Silent Thrush,* "environment" is defined in terms of (sub)cultural milieu—a Taiwanese *jianghu*—rather than the psychic environment of the individual family, this trope also holds the possibility of queering Hoklo identity. The disjunctures and aesthetic failures of the film of *Thrush* reveal internal contradictions within Taiwanese ethnonationalism that might be exploited. Taiwanese ethno-nationalism, in setting itself in opposition to the Chinese nationalism promoted by the KMT, has had to use the categories of Chinese nationalism while changing the content. In order to construct a "Taiwanese culture" equivalent to, but not the same as, the "Chinese culture" of classical philosophy, literature, and art, Taiwanese nationalist discourse has often relied on that culture produced outside of state support. This necessarily includes not only the petty criminal *jianghu* world celebrated by many male Native Soil artists, but also the popular, commercial culture that has thrived precisely by pandering to the "vulgar" tastes of the masses—including the queer desires of Hoklo women.

Notes

Research for this chapter was partially funded by grants from the Jacob K. Javits Foundation, the American Council of Learned Societies, the Chiang Ching-Kuo Foundation, and the Asian Cultural Council. I am grateful for the comments of Fran Martin, Sara Friedman, Liu Jen-peng, Ding Naifei, and Zheng Yadan, as well as this volume's anonymous reviewers. All translations from the Chinese are my own, unless otherwise noted.

1. *Hoklo* generally refers to the descendants of Chinese farmers from Fujian and Guangdong provinces who settled on Taiwan between the seventeenth and nineteenth centuries, whose mother tongue is the Taiwanese Hokkien (Minnan), or Holo, dialect. Hoklo are usually said to make up approximately 70 percent of the Taiwanese population (Government Information Office, *Taiwan Yearbook*), although intermarriage, generational changes in linguistic practice, and changing definitions of ethnicity makes such statistics problematic.

2. Ch'iu, *Zhongjie Taiwan Nüren*, 92.

3. In fact, *Silent Thrush* is but one instance of what we might call a mini-genre of Chinese language productions that bring together these themes through a focus on *xiqu* actors. These include Li Pikhua's (Hong Kong) novel *Farewell My Concubine* and the film version by Chen Kaige (1993) and Ellen Pau's video *Song of the Goddess* (1993). These films, as well as *Silent Thrush*, were cited by Chris Berry when he noted that the opera is emerging as a privileged Chinese site or trope in the "discursive construction of homosexuality" ("Sexual DisOrientations," 171). *Koa-a-hi* also features briefly in the HK-Taiwan coproduction *Twin Bracelets* (*Shuang Zhuo*) (Yushan Huang, 1992), which was seen as a "lesbian film" in the United States and by some people in Taiwan (Friedman, "Sexuality and Culture in the Global Media Market"). An ambiguous relationship between a *koa-a-hi* actress of the male roles and a wealthy widow features in the Taiwanese novel *Osmanthus Alley* (*Gui Hua Xiang*) (Xiao Lihong, 1977) and the 1997 film directed by Chen Kunho based on it.

4. For standard histories of *koa-a-hi*, see Lin and Liu, *Bianqian Zhong de Tai Min Xiqu yu Wenhua*. For a history of the rise of all-girl *koa-a-hi* troupes, see Wang, "Guanyu Rizhi Shiqi Taiwan de Gezaixi."

5. Silvio, "Reflexivity, Bodily Praxis, and Identity in Taiwanese Opera."

6. Lan, "Tong Xing zhi Ai, Di Di Ling Ren Xie Lei."

7. The KMT government periodically ran "patriotic lotteries" from the 1950s through the 1970s. In the 1980s, a period of economic boom in Taiwan, both legal government-run lotteries and underground lotteries were extremely popular.

8. Ch'iu, *Zhongjie Taiwan Nü ren*, 91.

9. Mulvey, "Visual Pleasure and Narrative Cinema."

10. Anonymous, "Shisheng Huamei Wei Kai Jing Qun Ci Jiaojing Shifei Duo" [Before the Cameras Start Rolling, *Silent Thrush*'s Crowd of Females Competing and Calling Each Other Names]. Gu Jie was originally cast in the role of Mu Yun. She quit the lead role, but she is still in the credits. Because the credits list only the names of the actors and not their roles, I am not sure which role she did play in the film.

11. McMahon, *Causality and Containment in Seventeenth-Century Chinese Fiction*.

12. Davis and Yeh, "Warning! Category III: The Other Hong Kong Cinema," 14.

13. Lan, "Tong Xing zhi Ai, Di Di Ling Ren Xie Lei."

14. Silvio, "Chinese Opera, Global Cinema, and the Ontology of the Person."

15. Chen, *Qiangu Wenren Xiake Meng*, 187–201.

16. For example, see Chan, "Figures of Hope and the Filmic Imaginary of Jianghu in Contemporary Hong Kong Cinema"; Pang, "Chivalric Stories in Hong Kong Media"; and Teo, "Tsui Hark: National Style and Polemic."

17. Zhuang, ed., *Yang Qi Caihong Qi*.

18. Ding and Liu, "Wen Jing: Hanxu Meixue yu Ku'er Zhenglue" [Asking Shadow: Reticent Aesthetics and Queer Politics]; translation by Ding and Liu.

References

Anonymous. "Shisheng Huamei Wei Kai Jing Qun Ci Jiaojing Shifei Duo" [Before the Cameras Start Rolling, *Silent Thrush*'s Crowd of Females Competing and Calling Each Other Names]. *Lianhe Bao* July 16, 1991, p. 28.

Berry, Chris. "Sexual DisOrientations: Homosexual Rights, East Asian Films, and Postmodern Postnationalism." In Xiaobing Tang and Stephen Snyder, eds., *In Pursuit of Contemporary East Asian Culture*. Boulder, Colo.: Westview Press, 1996. 157–82.

Chan, Stephen Ching-kiu. "Figures of Hope and the Filmic Imaginary of Jianghu in Contemporary Hong Kong Cinema." *Cultural Studies* 15, no. 3/4 (2001): 486–514.

Chen Pingyuan. *Qiangu Wenren Xiake Meng* [The Literatis Age-Old Dream of the Swordsmen]. Taipei: Maitian, 1995.

Ch'iu Kuei-fen. *Zhongjie Taiwan Nü ren* [Mediating Taiwanese Women]. Taipei: Yuan Zun Wenhua, 1997.

Davis, Darrell W., and Yeh Yueh-yu. "Warning! Category III: The Other Hong Kong Cinema." *Film Quarterly* 54, no. 4 (2001): 12–26.

Ding, Naifei, and Liu, Jenpeng. "Wen Jing: Hanxu Meixue yu Ku'er Zhenglue" [Asking Shadow: Reticent Aesthetics and Queer Politics]. *Xing/Bie Yanjiu* 34 (1998): 487–554.

Friedman, Sara L. "Sexuality and Culture in the Global Media Market: The Film *Shuang Zhuo* and Debates Over Representing the Hui'an Woman." Paper presented at the International Conference of Asia Scholars, Singapore, August 19–22, 2003.

Government Information Office. *Taiwan Yearbook* 2005. Http://www.gio.gov.tw/taiwan-website/5-gp/yearbook/02PeopleandLanguage.htm#EthnicComposition (accessed April 2006).

Hsiau, A-chin. *Contemporary Taiwanese Cultural Nationalism*. New York: Routledge, 2000.

Lan, Zuwei. "Shisheng Huamei Piaofang Can Pei" [*Silent Thrush* Loses at the Box Office]. *Lianhe Bao*, April 24, 1992, p. 22.

———. Tong Xing zhi Ai, "Di Di Ling Ren Xie Lei" [Same-Sex Love, an Actors Blood and Tears]. *Lianhe Bao*, April 27, 1992, p. 22.

Lin Bozhong and Liu Huanyue. *Bianqian Zhong de Tai Min Xiqu yu Wenhua* [Taiwan-Minnan Opera and Culture in the Midst of Change]. Taipei: Tai Yuan, 1990.

Ling Yan. *Shisheng Huamei* [*The Silent Thrush*]. Taipei: Zili Wanbao She Wenhua Chuban Bu, 1990.

Lü Su-shang. *Taiwan Dianying Xiju Shi* [*A History of Cinema and Drama in Taiwan*]. Taipei: Yinhua, 1961.

McMahon, Keith. *Causality and Containment in Seventeenth-Century Chinese Fiction*. Leiden: E. J. Brill, 1988.

Mulvey, Laura. "Visual Pleasure and Narrative Cinema." In Philip Rosen, ed., *Narrative, Apparatus, Ideology.* New York: Columbia University Press, 1986. 198–209.

Pang, Kenneth Ka-fat. "Chivalric Stories in Hong Kong Media." In Georgette Wang and Wimal Dissanayake, eds., *Continuity and Change in Communications Systems: An Asian Perspective.* Norwood, N.J.: Ablex Publishing, 1984. 215–230.

Qiu Kunliang. *Xiandai Shehui de Minsu Quyi* [Folk Theater in Modern Society]. Taipei: Yuan Liu, 1983.

Silvio, Teri. "Reflexivity, Bodily Praxis, and Identity in Taiwanese Opera." *GLQ* 5, no. 4 (1999): 585–604.

Silvio, Teri. "Chinese Opera, Global Cinema, and the Ontology of the Person: Chen Kaige's Farewell My Concubine." In Jeongwon Joe and Rose Theresa, eds., *Between Opera and Cinema.* Routledge, 2002. 177–97.

Teo, Stephen. "Tsui Hark: National Style and Polemic." In Esther C. M. Yau, ed., *At Full Speed: Hong Kong Cinema in a Borderless World.* Minneapolis: University of Minnesota Press, 2001. 143–58.

Wang Jianchuan. "Guanyu Rizhi Shiqi Taiwan de Gezaixi" [On Taiwanese Koa-a-hi during the Period of Japanese Rule]. *Yilan Wenxian Zazhi* 38 (1999): 77–100.

Zeng Yongyi. *Taiwan Gezaixi de Fazhan yu Bianqian* [The Development and Transformation of Taiwanese Koa-a-hi]. Taipei: Lian Jing, 1988.

Zhuang Huiqiu, ed. *Yang Qi Caihong Qi: Wo de Tongzhi Yundong Jingyan 1990–2001* [Raise the Rainbow Flag: My Experience in the Gay and Lesbian Movement 1990–2001]. Taipei: Xinling Gongfang, 2002.

THIRTEEN

HOW TO BE QUEER IN TAIWAN

Translation, Appropriation,
and the Construction of a Queer
Identity in Taiwan

Song Hwee Lim

In their 1995 essay, "What Does Queer Theory Teach Us about X?" Lauren Berlant and Michael Warner note that queer theory is "less than five years old" and ask, "Why do people feel the need to introduce, anatomize, and theorize something that can barely be said yet to exist?" Two lines down, they quip, "Queer is hot."[1] What they might not have realized is, a year before on the other side of the Pacific, the term *queer* had been translated as *ku'er* in Taiwan by a radical intellectual journal *Isle Margin* (*Daoyu bianyuan*). The compound term *ku'er* consists of the Chinese characters *ku* (meaning "cruel" and "cold" as well as "very" and "extremely"; it is also the transliteration of the English slang "cool" meaning fashionable or having street credibility) and *er* (meaning "child," "youngster," and "son").[2] This chapter traces the appearance of the term *ku'er* and aims to answer the following questions: What impact does the translation of *queer* as *ku'er* have on existing discourses of same-sex sexuality in Taiwan? To what extent does this translation and appropriation construct a new queer identity in Taiwan? How does it problematize issues of local/global identities and cross-cultural politics in the name of hybridity? Or, to put it another way, what does queer theory teach us about Taiwan?

This chapter is divided into four parts. Section one provides a historical account of the various discursive terms in Chinese for same-sex sexuality until the 1990s; section two locates the instance of the translation of queer as *kuer* and argues that this translation is foregrounded by an imperative of difference and differentiation from earlier discursive terms; section three examines how the *kuer* discourse attempts to imagine a queer community in Taiwan and the identity politics embedded in the process of translation and appropriation; section four concludes the discussion by interrogating the notion of hybridity in the construction of a queer identity in Taiwan.

One: Speaking of Same-sex Sexuality in Chinese

As Kevin Kopelson notes, "It is by now a commonplace of Foucauldian criticism that homosexual identities, as opposed to homosexual acts, arose only after a number of relatively recent, and primarily sexological, discourses breathed life into them."[3] The distinction between same-sex behavior and identity is noteworthy here because it echoes premodern Chinese understanding of sexuality. There has been a long tradition of same-sex relationships in China from antiquity to the late imperial periods, documented in Bret Hinsch's *Passions of the Cut Sleeve: The Male Homosexual Tradition*. Hinsch highlights in particular the care to be taken when discussing same-sex sexuality in the Chinese context "because classical Chinese [language] lacked a medical or scientific term comparable to 'homosexuality' or 'homosexual,'" and "instead of saying what someone 'is,' Chinese authors would usually say whom he 'resembles' or what he 'does' or 'enjoys.'"[4] However, since the early twentieth century, with "a Westernization of Chinese sexual categories and a Westernization of the overall terms of discourse about homosexuality," Hinsch believes that the "fluid conceptions of sexuality of old, which assumed that an individual was capable of enjoying a range of sexual acts, have been replaced with the ironclad Western dichotomy of heterosexual/homosexual." As a result, the "Chinese now speak of 'homosexuality' (*tongxinglian* or *tongxingai*), a direct translation of the Western medical term that defines a small group of pathological individuals according to a concrete sexual essence."[5]

In her study on the Chinese translation of Western sexological terms in Republican China (1912–1949), Tze-lan Deborah Sang notes that the characters *tongxingai* (literally same-sex love; the same characters are read as *doseiai* in Japanese) "was coined in Japan at the end of the Meiji [1868–1912] and the early Taisho [1912–25] period as Japanese intellectuals translated European sexology." There is "reason to believe that *tongxingai* was a direct adoption of the Japanese *doseiai*, based on which the Chinese then invented the variants *tongxing lianai* and *tongxing lian* [both meaning same-sex love]."[6]

While Sang concurs that the "range of Chinese discourses on homosexuality narrowed after the 1920s," she nevertheless argues that "the idea of there being an extraordinary homosexual nature confined to a small percentage of the population did not become the overruling paradigm for understanding homoerotic desire," because "*tongxing'ai* is primarily signified as a modality of love or an intersubjective rapport rather than as a category of personhood, that is, an identity."[7]

It is probably fair to say that, through the course of the twentieth century, *tongxing'ai* and *tongxinglian* have not only become the most common Chinese discursive terms for homosexuality but also have gradually solidified into an identity category. The latter is perhaps exacerbated in the past few decades with the arrival of post-Stonewall gay identities and discourses and the concomitant tropes of the closet and coming out. Moreover, there are differences in the development of these discursive terms among China, Taiwan, and Hong Kong. For example, while it is not unknown for those familiar with Western gay parlance to directly use the English word *gay*, it has been translated as *gei* (meaning "foundation") in Cantonese, the common language in Hong Kong, and is usually rendered as *gei-lo* (*lo* meaning "male"), which Wah-shan Chou reads as derogatory "since *lo* carries the connotation of a male who comes from the lower classes" and as sexist "because it totally ignores and rejects lesbians and bisexual women."[8] In Taiwan, there is a translation of *gay* as *gaizu* (*gai* functions as a transliteration of gay and means, among other things, "lid" or "cover," while *zu* denotes "clan" or "tribe"), though as far as I am aware, it has never circulated widely.[9]

Up until the 1990s, *tongxinglian* and *tongxing'ai* remain the most commonly used Chinese discursive terms especially in writing, with *gei-lo, gay,* or *gaizu* functioning as regional and subcultural terms. This began to change with the appropriation of the term *tongzhi* (literally "same will"), the Chinese translation of the Soviet Communist term *comrade,* as a discursive term for same-sex sexuality.[10] The popular use of its original meaning can be traced to a quote by Sun Yat-sen (1866–1925), the founding father of Republican China, whose dying wish was "The revolution has yet to triumph; comrades still must work hard" (*Geming shang wei chenggong; tongzhi reng xu nuli*), and it became the most common form of political address in China following the establishment of the People's Republic of China in 1949. The term *tongzhi* was first publicly appropriated for same-sex sexuality by the organizers of Hong Kong's inaugural lesbian and gay film festival in 1989, and it was introduced to Taiwan in 1992 when the Taipei Golden Horse international film festival featured a section on lesbian and gay films. It has since gained popular currency in Taiwan, Hong Kong, and overseas Chinese communities. Even in China, where there is potential ambiguity and confusion in its use resulting from the conflation of its appropriated meaning with its political reference, the term has increasingly been used to refer to same-sex sexuality. The term *tongzhi* has replaced *tongxinglian* or *tongxing'ai* in most post-1990 publications in the Chinese language, except in China for the reasons of ambiguity and confusion delineated above.[11] The term's popularity can be attributed to "its positive cultural references, gender neutrality, desexualization of the stigma of homosexuality, politics beyond the homo-hetero duality, and use as an indigenous cultural identity for integrating the sexual into the social."[12]

Two: Translating Queer in Taiwan

The translation of queer as *ku'er* made its first appearance in Taiwan in the January 1994 issue of the journal *Isle Margin*, with a cover bearing the title "*KU'ER* QUEER." Guest edited by up-and-coming novelists and translators Hung Ling (also known as Lucifer Hung), Chi Ta-wei, and Tan T'ang-mo, the timing of this issue coincided with the publication of the Chinese translations of Jean Genet's *A Thief's Journal* by Hung and of Manuel Puig's *Kiss of the Spiderwoman* by Chi. The special feature, which runs to nearly seventy pages, includes, among others, the translators' prefaces to and excerpts from the two foreign novels and an article entitled "Little *Ku'er* Encyclopaedia" with forty-nine entries (a different version with thirty-eight entries appeared in a 1997 book edited by Chi),[13] interspersed with images seemingly culled from Western pornographic sources.

It must be noted, however, that queer has also been translated into other Chinese terms. As mentioned above, queer was translated as *tongzhi* at the 1992 Taipei international film festival in the section on lesbian and gay films featuring "New Queer Cinema" (translated as *xin tongzhi dianying*), a short-lived cinematic movement in the West at the turn of the 1990s. The term "queer" also appears in the June 1994 issue of the lesbian journal *Ai Bao* (literally "love paper"), where it is translated as *tongzhi* in the special section entitled "Queer Nation" (*tongzhi guo*; English words set alongside Chinese translation), while its preface uses the term "queer tribe" (*guaitai yizu*; literally "strange fetus one tribe").[14] *Guaitai* already existed in Taiwan as a colloquial term referring to people who are strange or eccentric, thus making it particularly apt for denoting the double entendre in the English word *queer*. As Fran Martin points out, *guaitai* "is one of several terms which attempt more precisely to translate the meaning of queer, in this instance, as a literal translation of 'queer' as a refunctioned term of homophobic abuse: *Guaitai* might be translated as 'weirdo' or 'freak.'"[15] Feminist scholars (such as Chang Hsiao-hung) in particular seem to prefer the term *guaitai* as a translation of queer.[16]

Despite their chronological appearance, the terms *tongxinglian, tongzhi, ku'er,* and *guaitai* do not supersede each other in terms of currency and circulation. For example, postdating the January 1994 issue of *Isle Margin* and the June 1994 issue of *Ai Bao,* the October 1994 special issue of *eslitebookreview* (a highbrow artistic magazine on reading published by the upmarket book chain the Eslite Book Store) was entitled *"Tongxinglian,"* appealing perhaps to its more bourgeois readers while differentiating itself from the two radical journals. On the other hand, the glossy lifestyle magazine *G&L* (simultaneously standing for Glory & Liberty, Gentlemen & Ladies, and Gay & Lesbian, as declared on its cover; founded in June 1996), calls itself a "Chinese *tongzhi* magazine," thus avoiding both the pathological connotation of *tongxinglian* and the radicality of *ku'er* and *guaitai.* As translations for the term "queer," both *ku'er* and *guaitai* are confined to limited circulation within the realms of academia and radical politics until today, while *tongzhi* is perceived as the most all-encompassing term, which may partly be due to the fact that it is understood chiefly as the appropriation of the communist term *comrade* rather than as a translation of the English term *queer.*

While the choice of different Chinese translations for the term "queer" may have been dependent upon the preference of the translators, the material context in which these terms came into circulation in Taiwan should not be overlooked. As the term *ku'er* was introduced in an intellectual journal, its translation can be seen as a form of competition between publications for readers' attention and thus in terms of market segmentation. Bearing in mind Pierre Bourdieu's concept of "the field of cultural production,"[17] the translators of *ku'er* can be perceived as operating within the structural relations between themselves and the possible positions and position takings that determine the production, dissemination, and reception of cultural products in any given context. As the translation of queer as *ku'er* was partly occasioned by the publication of two translated novels, the introduction of a queer discourse in Taiwan may have as much to do with marketing strategies as with identity politics. In post-martial-law (1987) Taiwan—which witnessed a booming industry of homosexual-themed literature and publication, and with the term *tongzhi* occupying a central discursive position for same-sex sexuality—what better way to highlight one's publication and translation by introducing something new, something hot, and indeed something as cool as *ku'er*?

I would therefore argue that this instance of translation can be appreciated in the context of competing discursive terms for same-sex sexuality in contemporary Taiwan. That is to say, with *tongzhi* largely replacing *tongxinglian* as the dominant discourse for same-sex sexuality in the 1990s, the translation of queer as *ku'er* is foregrounded by an imperative of difference and differentiation. Moreover, while *ku'er* must compete for discursive space with other terms such as *tongxinglian* and *tongzhi,* its introduction has also had the effect of complementing, complicating, and even confounding them, requiring the terms to perform positional shifts in the realm of meanings to accommodate *ku'er,* literally creating a subcategory in the imagined community of homosexuals. In my analysis of the translation of queer as *ku'er,* my concern is not what the term *ku'er* means but rather its legitimizing discourses, how and why they are deployed, in what contexts, in whose names, by whom, for whom, and to what ends. In other words, I am interested in what Lydia Liu calls "the rhetorical strategies, translations, discursive formations, naming practices, legitimizing processes, tropes, and narrative modes" that bear upon the historical conditions of, in this instance, the translation of queer as *ku'er* in Taiwan.[18] I draw my materials primarily from the above-mentioned article, "Little *Ku'er* Encyclopaedia," both its 1994 version in *Isle Margin* and the 1997 version in Chi Ta-wei's edited book *Queer Archipelago* (*Ku'er qishilu*). My analysis focuses on entries related to the *ku'er* identity, and by cross-examining *ku'er* along the matrices of age, attitude, location, and gender, I ask what kinds of processes of othering does *ku'er* invariably, if inadvertently, perform, and what kinds of imagined communities does it at once inaugurate and exclude?

Three: Imagining a Queer Community

The most discernable form of same-sex expression in contemporary Taiwan has always been literary production. Pai Hsien-yung's 1983 novel, *Crystal Boys* (*Niezi*), is commonly regarded as the first homosexual novel and thus "an iconic text for the representation of homosexuality in Taiwan."[19] By the 1990s, homosexuality had become the most fashionable topic in literary writing, with three major awards inaugurated in that decade (each with a top prize of one million New Taiwan dollars) won by novels with a lesbian or gay theme in their respective years of inception.[20] This led to the following observation in an entry on "Class" in "Little *Ku'er* Encyclopaedia": "In Taiwan, whenever homosexual(ity) [*tongxinglian*] is mentioned, normal people will associate it with such attributes as romantic, artistic circle, high educational achievement, middle-class, yuppie, and so on. Homosexuals without these attributes are in an awkward position: their existence is even unthinkable by society. Where can homosexuals living in rural areas, with no educational achievement, bourgeois banknotes, or young, tempting bodies go?"[21] This entry underpins the identity politics of the translation of queer as *ku'er* in Taiwan, where the appropriation and construction of a queer identity is premised on a reaction against the perceived bourgeois form of homosexuality dominating the popular imagination. This antagonism is reinforced in the 1994 entry on *ku'er* ("Queer"; the English term appears in original): "Those with homosexual orientation but who react against a *gaizu* (gay)[22] ideology: they do not meddle with mainstream society but rather reflect honestly on their position and behavior without any regard for social convention, rationality or legality; they especially have no intention of sucking up to normal people. . . . Queer is otherwise translated as '*guaitai.*' However, as the fetus has grown and matured, and has a cool and sly appearance of a kid, hence it is translated here as '*ku'er.*'"[23] The translators' rhetorical strategies and naming practices are first and foremost an opposition of *ku'er* against a gay ideology. As I noted earlier, the term *gaizu* has never gained popular currency, and whether there was an identifiable gay ideology in Taiwan in the early 1990s against which *ku'er* could react is open to debate. In the years immediately after martial law was lifted in Taiwan, while awareness of same-sex sexuality had certainly increased and a nascent *tongzhi* community had begun to emerge, discourses on same-sex sexuality still resided primarily in the literary and intellectual fields. A gay community, and in particular a gay ideology, can be said to exist mainly in the imaginary. One could only speculate that the object of opposition (that is, the embodiment of a gay ideology) refers to an earlier generation of literary writers whose works teeter on homoerotic and homosexual themes but who are not "out and proud" gays.[24] Recalling my earlier mobilization of Bourdieu's concept of "the field of cultural production," and bearing in mind the translators' other personas as budding novelists and that the translation of queer as *ku'er* appears in an intellectual journal, I am inclined to read this constructed opposition not only as imagined rather than real in terms of identity politics but, more importantly, as a struggle for cultural capital in the literary and intellectual fields, with the young upstarts attempting to stamp their mark on the map of discourses on same-sex sexuality in Taiwan. This tension, I will add, also reflects an intergenerational struggle as the translators were in their early twenties at the time, while their (imagined) objects of opposition were a generation older.

The 1997 entry on *ku'er* further elaborates on the relationship between the Chinese terms: "Since the import of 'queer' in Taiwan, there have appeared translations as different as '*tongzhi*,' '*guaitai*' and '*ku'er*,' but each differs slightly from the 'original meaning' of 'queer.' '*Tongzhi*' emphasizes 'similarity' whereas 'queer' emphasizes 'difference,' so they should naturally not be equated; '*guaitai*' possesses the playfulness and agility of 'queer' theory but is not as confrontational as 'queer.' . . . Because the word '*ku*' already has the connotation of 'young people being obstinate and unruly' in Taiwan culture, thus the term '*ku'er*' naturally also gives such associations as playful, rebellious, youthful, and polyvalent in sexual culture."[25] It is confusing that while the term "queer" has been variously translated as *tongzhi, guaitai* and *ku'er,* the term *tongzhi* is taken to stand for "lesbian and gay"[26] as well as "queer,"[27] and *tongzhi*'s association with lesbian and gay is probably stronger than with queer. However, while the translators emphasize that "the tension between 'queer' and 'lesbian and gay' in English-speaking societies does not equate to the relationship between Taiwan's version of '*ku'er*' and '*tongzhi*,'"[28] the reaction against *gaizu* in the 1994 entry and the distinction between *ku'er* and *tongzhi* in the 1997 entry have, to a certain extent, replicated that tension. The emphasis on age and attitude in the two entries on *ku'er,* coupled with the intergenerational antagonism towards a "gay ideology," clearly privilege young, rebellious queers in the translation of queer as *ku'er.* The biases in age and attitude raise the following questions: Can generations of homosexuals predating the emergence of the *ku'er* discourse make claims to it, or is the term *lao ku'er* (old queer) destined to be an oxymoron in the Chinese language?[29] Can someone who is queer but uncool be a *ku'er*?

In fact, one could argue that the translators have also failed to address the issue of those homosexuals highlighted in the entry on "Class" who live in rural areas, with minimal education, young tempting bodies, or economic or cultural capital, who are the real homosexual subalterns who, in line with Gayatri Spivak's thesis, cannot speak. As Chong Kee Tan asks, "What would happen when young urban gay and lesbian discourse encounters older rural working-class lesbians; or Fukkienese, Hakka [two regional languages spoken in Taiwan as opposed to Mandarin, the "standard" language], and aboriginal, identity discourse?"[30] Martin also argues that "Taipei is the definitive centre of the *tongzhi* movement, whereas the Minnan-dominated [Minnan is synonymous with Fukien in this context] cities and regions of the island's centre and south appear to be experienced and represented as somewhat peripheral to the emergent *tongzhi* culture that continues to mirror the northern bias of the waning KMT [Kuomintang, or the Nationalist Party] colonizer culture."[31] Moreover, given the male gender bias of the word *er* (which can also mean "son"), would female queers prefer to stick to more feminine-inflected terms like *leisibian* (transliteration of lesbian; literally "lace whip" or "lace border")[32] rather than be subsumed by *kuer* (the way that lesbian can be subsumed by gay but not vice versa), or as I have shown earlier, to adopt the term *guaitai* instead?[33] Add to this the aforementioned Taipei-centrism of the discourse and the biases in terms of age and attitude and the imagining of a queer community through the *kuer* discourse has also performed an exclusionary function as much as it purports to promote difference. In this instance of translingual practice,[34] the introduction of a new discursive term has reified an identity category that empowers and celebrates at the same time as it marginalizes and divides.

Four: Hybridity Is Not Enough

By way of a conclusion, I would like to interrogate the notion of hybridity as mobilized by the translation of queer as *kuer*, and to further point out the contradiction embedded in this discourse. As a much-celebrated concept in postcolonial studies, the notion of hybridity poses a challenge to essentialism on the one hand and points to a more diversified future on the other. In an introduction to his edited book *Queer Archipelago,* Chi Ta-wei argues that *kuer* does not equate to queer by highlighting the linguistic and contextual aspects of the two terms. For Chi, the pejorative connotation of the term queer has not been reproduced in the term *kuer,* and the association of *kuer* with "coolness" also cannot be translated back to queer.[35] Calling *kuer* a "hybridised/bastardised" (*zazhong*) product of cultural exchange and miscegenation, Chi suggests that *kuer* has to continue a dialogue with queer on the one hand and to inscribe local history on the other.[36]

The rhetorical device deployed by Chi is an increasingly familiar one: the interaction between global discourse and local experience produces a "glocalized" hybrid manifestation that somehow deserves celebration. For example, in his study on Taiwan's gay and lesbian discourse in the 1990s, Chong Kee Tan argues that "the resulting cultural hybridity is not a bad copy of any 'original' but a demonstration of the fluid possibilities of sexual politics and an indirect challenge to ideological stand off between queer radicalism and gay conservatism such as what we see in the U.S. today," though Tan does qualify that this "cultural hybridity is so far still unstable," and it may, in the future, "also function as a warning not to fall too easily back onto stock positions of ideological polemics."[37] However, as I have shown above, the translation of queer as *ku'er* in Taiwan does replicate the standoff between a self-constructed queer radicalism and a self-perceived gay conservatism. Moreover, as Martin acutely argues, "Given that 'cultural hybridity' appears to constitute for the current generation of scholars the object of collective desire that 'cultural tradition' was for a previous one, it would be all too easy merely to celebrate Taiwan's palpably syncretic cultures as though their hybridity were itself proof against the continuing effects of unevenly held power."[38] My delineation of the biases along the matrices of age, attitude, (urban) location, and gender clearly illustrates the continuing effects—and some newly reified forms—of unevenly held power embedded in the discourse of hybridity in this instance.

In an article entitled "Beyond Happy Hybridity," Jacqueline Lo identifies two uses of the term hybridity and links them to Mikhail Bakhtin's distinction between organic and intentional hybridity. The first is what Lo calls "happy hybridity," which resembles Bakhtin's organic hybridity and "celebrates the proliferation of cultural difference to the extent where it can produce a sense of political in-difference to underlying issues of political and economic in-equalities."[39] The second, more akin to Bakhtin's intentional hybridity, "holds the potential to unsettle and dismantle hegemonic relations because it fo-cuses on the process of negotiation and contestation between cultures" and serves as "a form of political intervention."[40] It seems to me that the staging of identity politics in the translation of queer as *ku'er* and the discourse of hybridity mobilized begin as an intentional hybridity aimed at negotiating between cultures but too quickly solidify into an organic or happy hybridity that "serves a stabilising function to settle cultural differences and contesta-tions."[41] Moreover, if we accept that "translation is an essentially hybridizing instance,"[42] and if pre-*ku'er* terms such as *tongxing'ai, tongxinglian,* and *tongzhi* are also hybridized translations in their own right (via Europe, Japan, and the Soviet Union), why is the hybridity in the *ku'er* discourse privileged over earlier instances of hybridity, which are not even acknowledged as such? Do the poststructuralist and postcolonial contexts of this hybridity make it more hybridized than others?

I would suggest that the exclusionary tendency of the hybridity of the *ku'er* discourse is inextricably bound to the source of its translation: as queer theory originates from elite U.S. universities as an academic discourse, its transmutation into *ku'er* cannot completely be extricated from its inherent elitism. Indeed, in order to readily recognize *ku'er* as a transliteration of *queer,* to appreciate its "coolness" and to comprehend its epistemological ground-ing in poststructuralism, one cannot do without postsecondary education, a good command of English, familiarity with the development of the latest and hippest academic theories and social movements in Anglo-American universities and societies, and a certain degree of metropolitan if not cos-mopolitan background. Ironically, while constructing an opposition to pre-*ku'er* ideologies (whether *tongxinglian, gaizu,* or *tongzhi*), the translators of *ku'er* themselves possess similar attributes (the aforementioned romantic, artistic, educational achievement, middle-class, and yuppie) as students of the Department of Foreign Languages at the National Taiwan University (the most prestigious humanities department in Taiwan's most elite university) and as budding novelists. That is to say, the very attributes under fire from *ku'er* must somehow be reincarnated upon those who "get" the translation of queer as *ku'er* and even those who self-identify as *ku'er* and the translators themselves. In coining a neologism to differentiate themselves from exist-ing discursive terms for same-sex sexuality, the translators have, willy-nilly, resurrected the very ideological attributes that they have been attempting to dissociate from. If the *ku'er* discourse does unveil itself as producing a hierarchy of identity politics organized along the matrices of age, attitude, location, gender, education, and class, one needs to question if this hybrid-ized discourse and identity is only available and affordable to some but not to others. Yes, it may be cool to be a *ku'er* in Taiwan, but apparently not everybody is entitled to be a "cool kid."

So, what price hybridity? As Martin argues along with Lo, "any uncritical endorsement of 'hybridity' that produces it as a general, abstract, positive value to be celebrated and fails to engage with the messy materiality of this state as lived by social subjects" should be open to criticism.[43] By examining the messy materiality of this instance of translated hybridity that is *ku'er,* I hope I have demonstrated that, if it is impossible to comprehend the mean-ing of *ku'er* without recourse to queer (theory), and if hybridity invariably incorporates and demands some knowledge of an Other, one needs to ask who benefits from such a cross-cultural exchange and cross-fertilization. To maintain its unsettling power as a form of intentional rather than organic hybridity, instead of becoming the terminator of this process of negotiation, it should be the starting point for another type of interrogation, raising ques-tions such as: Is hybridity enough? Who needs hybridity? In whose terms is hybridity perceived as both desirable and legitimate? Is hybridity a voluntary choice or a euphemism for a process that is either unavoidable or forced upon the party on the receiving end? By delineating the translation, appropriation, and construction of a queer identity in Taiwan, and the process by which one instance of translation attempts to show how one could be queer in Taiwan, I hope I have not concretized the *ku'er* discourse but rather have prized it open for continual negotiation, contestation, and intervention.

Notes

1. Berlant and Warner, "What Does Queer Theory Teach Us about X?" 343.

2. All translations from the Chinese sources are mine. All Taiwanese and Hong Kong names are romanized in the Wade-Giles system whereas names of mainland Chinese are rendered in pinyin. All Chinese names appear with surname first, followed by given names, unless otherwise in original English publication. Earlier versions of this paper were presented at the Edinburgh China Institute; Third International Convention for Asia Scholars, Singapore; Center for Emergent Cultural Studies, National Chiao-Tung University, Taiwan; Institute of Chinese Literature and Philosophy, Academia Sinica, Taiwan; European Association for Taiwan Studies conference, London; Queer Matters conference, London; and National Boundaries and Cultural Configurations conference, Singapore. I thank the British Academy for a research grant that enabled the development of the bulk of the research and the writing of an earlier draft of this paper at the Academia Sinica from October to December 2003. I also thank Michel Hockx (discussant at the EATS conference) and the anonymous readers of an earlier draft of the chapter for their insightful comments.

3. Kopelson, *Love's Litany,* 8.

4. Hinsch, *Passions of the Cut Sleeve,* 7.

5. Ibid., 169.

6. Sang, *The Emerging Lesbian,* 278.

7. Ibid., 297, 292–93.

8. Chou, *Tongzhi: Politics of Same-Sex Eroticism,* 79.

9. The term *gaizu* probably makes its first appearance in the science fiction of Taiwanese writer Chang Hsi-kuo, though it does not signify same-sex sexuality. I thank Professor Shu-chen Chiang for bringing this to my attention. The use of *zu* to denote a subcultural group probably comes from the Japanese *zoku* (same Chinese/ *kanji* character) which since as early as 1971 has been used in a same-sex context in Japan with the publication of the gay magazine "Rose Tribe" (*Barazoku*). See Aoki, "The Rose Tribes," 14.

10. Chou, *Tongzhi: Politics of Same-Sex Eroticism,* 1. I suspect the Chinese translation of *comrade* as *tongzhi* (or *doshi* in Japanese) may have also been borrowed from the Japanese, which has been used in homosexual argot in Japan since at least the end of WWII, though I am not aware of its influence on Taiwan's discourse on same-sex sexuality. On *doshi,* see McClelland, *Queer Japan,* 98 n25.

11. This is reflected in the titles of books published on homosexuality in China.

See, for example, Fang, *Homosexuality in China;* Li, *Subculture of Homosexuality;* Li and Wang, *Their World: A Clear Look into China's Male Homosexual Community;* and Zhang, *Homosexuality.* Even a Taiwanese publication on homosexuality in China uses the term *tongxinglian.* See An, *Black Souls under the Red Sun: Live Report on Homosexuality in Mainland China.* In Hong Kong, Chou Wah-shan has consistently used *tongzhi* in the titles of his books, including one on China. See his *Beijing Tongzhi Stories.* This arguably does not reflect the term's usage among its subjects of inquiry at the time who, according to An K'e-Ch'iang, use a host of other terms but *tongzhi* (An, *Black Souls,* 80–82). This, however, is not suggesting that those in China are not aware of the appropriated meaning of *tongzhi,* which is circulated on the World Wide Web and increasingly used in the media.

12. Chou, *Tongzhi: Politics of Same-Sex Eroticism,* 2.

13. As authors of this article, the translators appear under pseudonyms Hung Shui-hsien, Chi Hsiao-wei, and Tan T'ang-mo, with the 1997 version indicating the author (again appearing in different names or pseudonyms) at the end of each entry.

14. I thank Teri Silvio for lending me her copy of the journal.

15. Martin, *Situating Sexualities,* 4.

16. For example, when guest editing a special issue on "Queer Sexuality" (English in original; May 1998) for the journal *Chung Wai Literary Monthly* (published by the foreign languages department at the National Taiwan University), Chang uses the term *guaitai* for queer, as she does in her book *A Queer Family Romance.*

17. Bourdieu, *The Field of Cultural Production.*

18. Liu, *Translingual Practice,* xviii.

19. Martin, *Situating Sexualities,* 54.

20. The novels are Ling Yan's *The Silent Thrush* (*Shisheng huamei*), winner of the Independence Daily Award, 1991; Chu T'ien-wen's *Notes of a Desolate Man* (*Huangren shouji*), China Times Award, 1994; and Tu Hsiu-lan's *Adverse Woman* (*Ni Nü*) (or *Rebel Daughter,* see Silvio, this volume), Crown Award, 1996.

21. Hung, Chi, and Tan, "Little *Ku'er* Encyclopaedia" (Xiaoxiao ku'er baike), 62–63.

22. The English term is used in the original.

23. Hung, Chi, and Tan, "Little *Ku'er* Encyclopaedia" (Xiaoxiao ku'er baike), 64.

24. For a list of literary works with a homoerotic or homosexual theme, see the appendix in Chi, ed., *Queer Carnival,* 247–67.

25. Hung, Chi, and Tan, "Little *Ku'er* Encyclopaedia" (Xiaoxiao ku'er baike), 56–57.

26. Ibid., 38; Martin, *Situating Sexualities* 3.

27. Chang, "Queer Politics of Desire," 9.

28. Hung, Chi, and Tan, "Little *Ku'er* Encyclopaedia" (Xiaoxiao ku'er baike), 57.

29. I thank Frances Weightman for highlighting this to me in an e-mail exchange.

30. Tan, "Transcending Sexual Nationalism," 132.

31. Martin, *Situating Sexualities,* 14.

32. There are two different translations for *bian:* (1) "border" as used in the June 1994 issue of *Ai Bao* and Sang, *The Emerging Lesbian,* 341 (2) "whip" as used in Hung, "Intercourse Between the Lace and the Whip" (1996) and Hung, Chi, and Tan, "Little *Ku'er* Encyclopaedia" (Xiaoxiao ku'er baike), 70, or 59 in the 1997 edition.

33. On the gender bias of the English term queer, see Annamarie Jagose, *Queer Theory,* 116.

34. Liu, *Translingual Practice.*

35. Chi, "On *Ku'er,*" 10.

36. Ibid., 11.

37. Tan, "Transcending Sexual Nationalism,"132.

38. Martin, *Situating Sexualities,* 35–36.

39. Lo, "Beyond Happy Hybridity," 152–53.

40. Ibid., 153.

41. Ibid., 152.

42. Sakai, *Translation and Subjectivity,* 3.

43. Martin, *Situating Sexualities,* 36.

References

An, K'e-Ch'iang. *Black Souls under the Red Sun: Live Report on Homosexuality in Mainland China (Hong taiyang xia de hei linghun: Dalu tongxinglian xianchang baodao).* Taipei: Shibao wenhua, 1995.

Aoki, Darren. "The Rose Tribes: Sexual Solidarity and the Ethico-Aesthetics of Manliness in Japan in the Early 1970s." PhD diss., University of Cambridge, 2004.

Berlant, Lauren, and Michael Warner. "What Does Queer Theory Teach Us about X?" *PMLA* 110, no. 3 (1995): 343–49.

Bourdieu, Pierre. *The Field of Cultural Production: Essays on Art and Literature,* ed. Randal Johnson. Cambridge: Polity Press, 1993.

Chang, Hsiao-hung. *A Queer Family Romance (Guaitai jiating luomanshi).* Taipei: Shibao, 2000.

———. "Queer Politics of Desire" (Tongzhi qingren, feichang yuwang: Taiwan tongzhi yundong de liuxing wenhua chuji). *Chung Wai Literary Monthly (Zhongwai wenxue)* 25, no. 1 (June 1996): 6–25.

Chi, Ta-wei. "On *Ku'er*: Reflections on Contemporary Taiwan *Ku'er* and *Ku'er* Literature" (Ku'er lun: sikao dangdai Taiwan ku'er yu ku'er wenxue). In Chi Ta-wei, ed., *Queer Archipelago: A Reader of the Queer Discourses in Taiwan* [English in original] (*Ku'er qishilu: dangdai Taiwan Queer lunshu duben*). Taipei: Yuanzun wenhua, 1997. 9–16.

Chi, Ta-wei, ed. *Queer Carnival: A Reader of Queer Literature in Taiwan* (Ku'er kuanghuan jie: Taiwan dangdai QUEER wenxue duben); Taipei: Yuanzun wenhua, 1997. 247–67.

Chou, Wah-shan. *Tongzhi: Politics of Same-Sex Eroticism in Chinese Societies*. New York: Haworth Press, 2000.

———. *Beijing Tongzhi Stories* (*Beijing tongzhi gushi*). Hong Kong: Xianggang tongzhi yanjiushe, 1996.

Fang, Gang. *Homosexuality in China* (*Tongxinglian zai Zhongguo*). Changchun: Jilin renmin chubanshe, 1995.

Hinsch, Bret. *Passions of the Cut Sleeve: The Male Homosexual Tradition in China*. Berkeley: University of California Press, 1990.

Hung, Ling. "Intercourse Between the Lace and the Whip: The Flow of Lesbian Desire in Contemporary Taiwanese Fiction" (Leisi yu bianzi de jiaohuan: cong dangdai Taiwan xiaoshuo zhushi nü tongxinglian de yuwang liudong). *Chung Wai Literary Monthly* (*Zhongwai wenxue*) 25, no. 1 (June 1996): 60–80.

Hung, Shui-hsien [Hung Ling], Chi Hsiao-wei [Chi Ta-wei], and Tan T'ang-mo. "Little *Ku'er* Encyclopaedia" (Xiaoxiao ku'er baike). *Isle Margin* (*Daoyu bianyuan*) 10 (January 1994): 47–71. A different version appears in Chi Ta-wei, ed., *Queer Archipelago: A Reader of the Queer Discourses in Taiwan*. Taipei: Yuanzun wenhua, 1997. 27–61.

Jagose, Annamarie. *Queer Theory*. Melbourne: Melbourne University Press, 1996.

Kopelson, Kevin. *Love's Litany: The Writing of Modern Homoerotics*. Stanford, Calif.: Stanford University Press, 1994.

Li, Yinhe. *Subculture of Homosexuality* [English in original] (*Tongxinglian yawenhua*). Beijing: Jinri Zhongguo chubanshe, 1998.

Li, Yinhe, and Wang, Xiaobo. *Their World: A Clear Look into China's Male Homosexual Community* (*Tamen de shijie: Zhongguo nantongxinglian qunluo toushi*). Shangxi: Shangxi renmin chubanshe, 1992.

Liu, Lydia H. *Translingual Practice: Literature, National Culture, and Translated Modernity—China 1900–1937*. Stanford, Calif.: Stanford University Press, 1995.

Lo, Jacqueline. "Beyond Happy Hybridity: Performing Asian-Australian Identities." In Ien Ang, Sharon Chalmers, Lisa Law, and Mandy Thomas, eds., *Alter/Asians: Asian-Australian Identities in Art, Media, and Popular Culture*. Annandale, New South Wales: Pluto Press Australia, 2000. 152–68.

Martin, Fran. *Situating Sexualities: Queer Representation in Taiwanese Fiction, Film, and Public Culture*. Hong Kong: Hong Kong University Press, 2003.

McClelland, Mark. *Queer Japan from the Pacific War to the Internet Age*. Lanham, Md.: Rowman and Littlefield, 2005.

Sakai, Naoki. *Translation and Subjectivity: On "Japan" and Cultural Nationalism*. Minneapolis: University of Minnesota Press, 1997.

Sang, Deborah Tze-lan. *The Emerging Lesbian: Female Same-Sex Desire in Modern China*. Chicago: University of Chicago Press, 2003.

———. "Translating Homosexuality: The Discourse of *Tongxing'ai* in Republican China (1912–1949)." In Lydia H. Liu, ed., *Tokens of Exchange: The Problem of Translation in Global Circulations*. Durham: Duke University Press, 1999. 276–304.

Tan, Chong Kee. "Transcending Sexual Nationalism and Colonialism: Cultural Hybridization as Process of Sexual Politics in 90s Taiwan." In John C. Hawley, ed., *Postcolonial, Queer: Theoretical Intersections* Albany: State University of New York Press, 2001. 123–37.

Zhang, Beichuan. *Homosexuality* (*Tongxing'ai*). Shandong: Shandong kexue jishu chubanshe, 1994.

FOURTEEN

KING VICTORIA

Asian Drag Kings,
Postcolonial Female Masculinity,
and Hybrid Sexuality in Australia

Audrey Yue

Going South—The Ex-centric Queer Asian Diaspora in Australia

Asian drag kings in Australia are mobile parasites who dwell at the threshold of many borders: as migrants between Asia and Australia, as racialized lesbians in a predominantly white queer scene, as performers between genders and sexualities, and as subjects of knowledge between disciplines and theoretical frameworks. This chapter will critically examine how Asian drag kings in Australia have produced a new hybrid sexuality that reflects this parasitic politics of the border. Central to this is its ex-centric diasporic position in Australia.

Australia has been described as the south of the West.[1] This distinction emphasizes its geography and cultural heritage. It is similar to the West because of its Anglo-Celtic settler history, but also different from the West because of its Aboriginal indigeneity. Australia has also been described as between Asia and the West.[2] Privileging the Asian diaspora in Australia as an alternative site of knowledge disrupts the fixity of Australia as a south in between the West and Asia. This alternative episteme involves "going south": "Inscribed in a migratory movement of literal displacement and reoriented in the racialized landscape of a postcolonial settler Australia, (going south) aligns itself with south of Asia, south of China and south of the East and the West."[3]

As a geographical movement of physical migration, "going south" attends to the history of Asian migration to Australia. This orientation differentiates the Asian diaspora in Australia from those in the West. As a critical trajectory centered on the trope of movement, "going south" foregrounds the ex-centricism of the Asian diaspora. "To be ex-centric, on the border or margin, inside yet outside is to have a different perspective."[4] Unlike the south in between the West and Asia, "going south" does not rely on the margin or the periphery in relation to a fixed center. Its ex-centricity circumvents the fixity of place by interrogating its ontology and reconfiguring its locality. "Going south" questions how Australia's hybrid identity has emerged through its relational location to the Orient (south of Asia), the East (south of the East), and the West (south of the West).

This chapter demonstrates how "going south" is evident in the performances of Asian drag kings in Australia. Section one explores "going south" as a geographical movement of physical migration through global and gender border-crossing by showing how the globalization of drag king cultures has localized the Australian "scene" and produced performances that showcase postcolonial female masculinity. Postcolonial female masculinity is a hybrid sexual identity that questions the normative settler conventions of race, gender, and sexuality. Section two extends "going south" as a critical trajectory by examining how the performances of Asian Australian drag kings produce diasporic female sexuality as an example of postcolonial female sexuality. These performances are characterized by the diasporic Asian Australian tomboy as a desirable form of hybrid sexual identity. This sexuality inscribes the gendered migration of the Asian Australian diaspora.

Framing this chapter is also the critical framework of "going south" as a productive methodology that can resituate a queer and Asian diaspora studies in Australia. The ex-centricism of "going south" enables a reorientation of the academic hegemony of North American-centric diaspora studies by historicizing and differentiating the Asian diaspora in Australia from other global Asian diasporas elsewhere.[5] This ex-centricism also enables transdisciplinarity through a mode of trafficking that interrogates the ontology of disciplines as the "place" that makes its epistemic claims to specialized bodies of knowledge. Using a range of analytical techniques such as ficto-criticism, ethnography, cultural geography, diasporic media and gender studies, Hong Kong action film theory, and the queer performativity of cross-dressing, this chapter hopes to produce a critical framework for queer and Asian diasporic studies in Australia that not only communicates between disciplines but problematizes the mobility of sexuality currently evident in its many border-crossing valencies, from the globalization of gay and lesbian studies, the emergence of queer modernities, and the proliferation of middle-class material sexualities.[6]

King Victoria: Australian Lesbian Subculture and Postcolonial Female Masculinities

Situated in the city of Melbourne, King Victoria is Australia's first and only drag king institution that emerged against the backdrop of a 1990s coalition queer culture that witnessed the proliferation and the endorsement of multiple sexualities and genders. Unlike the controversial transsexual debates in the major cities' lesbian communities a few years earlier that questioned the gender politics of sexuality through its politically correct and radical-feminist-inspired "are transsexuals allowed in lesbian-only spaces" query, there was no controversy surrounding King Victoria's emergence. It was celebrated and quickly endorsed in a "scene" hungry for the diversity of a female cross-dressing nightclub subculture. Operating since 2000, it enjoys a seminal place in Australia's gay and lesbian culture, and it is the only institution to have achieved national media interest and international acclaim. Outside of Club Casanova in New York and Klubstitute (now defunct) in San Francisco, King Victoria is one of the world's longest-running drag king nightclubs.

King Victoria began with a drag king competition featuring the Butoh-dancing Drastic Boy (Tomoko Yamasaki) and the gangsta-rapping Muthafucka MC (Mandy Siegel). With the success of the competition, King Victoria quickly became a Friday night institution at the Star Hotel with weekly cabaret shows and translesbian readings. Since 2000, King Victoria has produced a lesbian porn video (*King Porn 1*), organized numerous boi band and arm wrestling competitions, traveled interstate and overseas to compete in more drag king competitions, performed nationally at Pride festivals, been featured in a center spread in the mainstream Melbourne newspaper *The Age,* and now topped more than 200 shows featuring a troupe of twenty to thirty regular performers—women passing as sexist rednecks, gay men as heteros, transsexuals as male feminists, women as men as femmes pretenders, and so forth—such as Neil Dominant (Di Marshall), LeeBruceLee (Ray Jalil), Dr La Fist (Bumpy/E. Eldridge), Moira Finucane, Tom Urge (Katie Hamilton), Maurice Valentino (Mandy Siegel), and Hung Low (Raquel Bacatan).[7]

Central to the King Victoria institution is the emergence of a lesbian subculture consisting of a community of drag king performers, queer writers, and regulars who simply like to dress up like a man for a Friday night out at the Star Hotel. Although drag king acts existed in Australia before King Victoria, they appeared only sporadically across the major cities of Perth, Sydney, Adelaide, and Brisbane. King Victoria sets the stage for an emerging lesbian-identified nightclub culture. Its competition drew hundreds of lesbians and allowed a range of masculinities to be articulated. Some of these are now incorporated into its regular shows.

As an inner-city venue, the Star Hotel in Collingwood's Hoddle Street occupies a culturally marginal location south of the Yarra River compared to mainstream queer nightclubs in the northern suburbs. On the outside, it is a nondescript corner pub and hotel in a mixed zone of gentrified warehouse conversions and industries. Part owner Andy Stevens describes the Star Hotel as a place that was once "the rough domain of 'junkies and cops.'" [8] This seediness is also mythologized in *The Age*, as "surreal . . . like a scene out of a David Lynch film; deep burgundy colors, CDs and mirror balls glittering from the ceiling."[9] The Star Hotel shows how inclusion is enabled through exclusion: as legal and illegal, popular and deviant, this otherness foregrounds its politics of class, life/style, and sexuality.

It is institutionally iconic as a gay hotel renowned as a venue for queer subcultures: Lotus Club gatherings of rice queens, Asian drag queen shows, bootscooting, and bear nights. Not mainstream like the buffed bodies of muscle fairies at the Peel dance club or hardcore as the leather men at the Trade Bar or cosmopolitan like its hip, north-of-the-river Market Hotel types, the Star Hotel supports a marginal masculinity expressed through the deviance of race, desire, size, and taste. Masculinity as a political, social, and cultural expression of maleness, patriarchy, and power is a discourse constructed not only in relation to an orthodox femininity but also to alternative masculinities. With diasporic Asian drag queens theatricalizing the worlds of Suzie Wong or even Sakura, older Anglo men actively seeking out younger Asian men, suburban gay nesters in cowboy boots line dancing to country and western steps, and big hairy men attracting equally chunky chubby cubs, the Star Hotel destabilizes normative gay masculinity by exposing how it is discursively constituted through the subordination of other masculinities of color, erotic preference, lifestyle, and body shape. Reflecting either excessive (rice, bear, or cowboy fetish) or insufficient masculinities (Asian), these minority or postcolonial masculinities call to task and make legible how normative Anglo Australian gay masculinity is constructed as white, middle-class, young, blond, toned, and hip.

King Victoria extends these postcolonial masculinities with its drag king performances of female masculinity. Different from the cross-dresser, the butch dyke, or the male impersonator, the drag king is "a female (usually) who dresses up in a recognizably male costume and performs theatrically in that costume."[10] Unlike the cross-dresser who wears men's clothes as an everyday practice, or the butch dyke who does not perform but embodies masculinity, or the male impersonator who attempts to reproduce maleness as part of the act, or lesbian camp that follows gay male monopolies of femininity and uses theatricality to expose excessive femininity rather than excessive masculinity, the drag king exposes the theatricality of maleness in the performance.[11] "Passing" as a man is an art form consisting of pompadours, stuffed pants, clipped hair applied to the face with gum, and creating a persona that heightens the performance of masculinity.[12]

Female masculinity is often perceived as sexist, misogynist, patriarchal, and pathological by feminists and heterosexuals and in homosexual and lesbian discourses.[13] It is sometimes considered a variation of the heterosexual paradigm, a form of social rebellion or an identity of sexual otherness. It is a site of productive anxiety because it questions the normative histories of femininities by exposing the limits of binary gender relations. Halberstam coined the term "gender deviant" or "gender-ambiguous" to describe a hybrid identity that is "not-woman and not-man" but "an unholy union of femaleness and masculinity."[14] King Victoria's cofounder, Bumpy (E. Eldridge) describes this identity as "transient boy stuff" and drag is "whatever the boygrrl or grrlboy wanted to make of it."[15] By subverting the spelling of "grrl" but keeping the normative spelling of "boy," King Victoria makes clear that the practice of drag kinging has "the power to reorganize masculinity" by challenging "how masculinity is constructed as masculinity."[16] Its parodic name foregrounds a politics that decenters hegemonic Australia's colonial British heritage that promotes a settler masculinity through the exemplars of convicts, bushmen, diggers, and blokes.[17]

The border-crossing performances of drag describe a range of dissonances surrounding gender, sex, appearance, and reality.[18] Drag kings parody male stereotypes, exaggerate heterosexual gender, destabilize the intelligibility of heteronormative masculinity, and reveal how the gendered body itself is performative. The following section will critically show how Asian drag kings in Australia problematize the dominant racialized masculinities that produce the social histories of gender relations, questioning the reciprocities surrounding patriarchy, privilege, and female empowerment.

Asian Drag Kings in Australia

LeeBruceLee is a disco-dancing, kung fu prancing Melbourne-based Malay-Chinese drag king. Just like the real thing, he begins his act by ripping off his Bonds singlet, revealing a bound chest, but unlike the real thing or even the movies, nothing much else is hard-boiled or hard-bodied. The kok is synthetic, homemade. Made in China. LeeBruceLee performs best to a Barry White croon. He gyrates a Travolta swagger with the balletic grace of the real thing. He chopsticks a fly in slo-mo tai chi precision. He even tops it off with the trademark squeal. The chicks at the Star Hotel love their chinky boi. None of these hormone-puffed transmen, just a subtle modern touch,

Figure 14.1. LeeBruceLee (Ray Jalil) with Dr La Fist (Bumpy/ E. Eldridge). Photograph from *Slit Magazine*. Photo taken by Andrea Van Steen.

like the unassuming little Nokia that LeeBruceLee carries in the palm of her handsome clutch.

Malay-Chinese LeeBruceLee (Ray Jalil) (LBL) appears regularly at King Victoria. As the name suggests, LBL performs a recognizable male persona, martial arts icon Bruce Lee. He carries a mobile phone, wears a 1970s styled polyester striped shirt, high-waisted bell-bottomed pants, a white flat cap, moustache, and very little makeup. His main act consists of lip-synching and dancing. Sometimes he slows down in mid-act with a stylized display of kung fu fist fights in the air. At other times, he continues by taking off his clothes to reveal a singleted flat chest, a stuffed crotch, or a strap-on. Occasionally he pairs with Dr La Fist (Bumpy/E. Eldridge), an Anglo femme pretender, for a Viagra fix. LBL also personifies as Dirk ReDiggler, an innocent postadolescent boy with a huge gift, in an Afro wig, a tight yellow T-shirt, and with an oversized foam penis over his white jocks. Dirk always adventures with the entrepreneurial but equally innocent BumpaBar (Bumpy/E. Eldridge), a pimp-wanna-be, but their dreams always remain just that, dreams. Dirk is more fantastical than LBL. LBL also performs as Annabel Lee and Tiger Lee: the former a blond-wigged Hong Kong socialite traveling the festivals of the world, the latter a sex slave/nymph with long black hair.

At its basic, LBL's fist fighting appropriates the style of Bruce Lee as a style of performance. Here, the act can be read as an earnest copy of kung fu masculinity and a homage to the kung fu king. Such a worship reflects the preeminent place Bruce Lee holds in the kung fu and popular imagination. Stephen Teo writes that after Lee's premature death in 1973, the cult legend became "an object, even a fetish."[19] As a signifier for the practice of kung fu, Lee's masculinity conveys a trained body connoted through muscles or, following Yvonne Tasker, "hardness."[20] He is an icon for a postcolonial Chinese masculinity. Always an underdog defeating opponents from the West or Japan, his postcolonial Chinese masculinity is a fetish for an imagined Chinese national pride and solidarity during colonial conditions because it shows empowerment through self-defense.[21] As the trailer to Lee's final film *Enter the Dragon* (Robert Clouse, 1973) eulogizes, Lee the legend is "part man, part myth, part magic." This myth is exposed as a social construction when the term, *gongfu,* is rendered in the Chinese language. The Chinese term, *gongfu,* translates as "a learned skill from hard work." This translation exposes the myth behind the muscles that support the body, resonating with Meaghan Morris's suggestion that it is Bruce Lee's status as "an iconic film teacher" rather than a "generic action hero" that makes him an ideal teacher to learn from.[22]

Against this, although LBL's imitation of kung fu can be read as a form of appropriated flattery (LBL admits to being a fan of martial arts in his star biography), LBL's tactic of copying-as-kinging reveals that there is no essence to kung fu masculinity except as a physiological form of body training that can be acquired. Writing on the differences between white and black king performances in the United States, Halberstam suggests many drag-king-of-color performances are not as successful as white performances because they imitate rather than parody.[23] Here, LBL's female masculinity—her copying-as-kinging—is subversive because it reveals that the masculinity that is connoted by hardness, strength, and power is an artificial skill that can be learned. LBL's copy displaces Bruce Lee's postcolonial Chinese masculinity and inscribes diasporic Asian female masculinity as a new form of sexual identity.

Perhaps it is the myth of Bruce Lee that he is part man and part magic that allows a diasporic lesbian like LBL growing up in Asia in the 1970s to see him as a role model who she can secretly emulate and take pride in. In one translesbian reading, LBL performed a short story entitled "The Tailor of Sea Park." Read as an autobiographical excerpt from his childhood, LBL recounts the life of a twelve-year-old tomboy growing up in Kuantan and Kuala Lumpur in Malaysia playing in monsoon-filled drains catching fish, and how he acquired his first three-piece suit for his birthday that year:

> I picked my material for the suit. It was off white with fine blue stripes. Very Travolta. My father had pants made from the same material. And my shirt was exactly the same as one of Pa's, but miniature. Men's style, dark blue cotton, with a pattern of white fern. I got measured up. I proudly showed off my fabric stapled receipt to all my friends at school.
>
> At my birthday party all my friends were excited to view my new 3 piece suit. My Dad was there, my grandmother, my sister, aunties, cousins and my girlfriend, Tina Shereen who was very impressed. I felt proud. I felt very suave, groovy, handsome, in vogue, dancing in my white 3 piece suit to The Pointer Sisters and The 3 Degrees, from my father's record collection.[24]

LBL's suit reflects a resistance to gender conformity evident in tomboyism. Another example of female masculinity, tomboyism is usually experienced prepubescently.[25] It is sometimes pathologized as a form of gender dysphoria when it extends beyond adolescence. Punished because it refuses a subscription to normative femaleness, it represents a desire for the freedom and mobility enjoyed by boys, or a subversion of adulthood and adult femininity.[26] LBL's reclamation of tomboyism as adult female masculinity is reflected in the spelling of "boi" in his star biography.[27] Initially mobilized as a lingo in Western lesbian subculture to describe a young butch dyke, "boi" has now

Figure 14.2. Drastic Boy (Tomoko Yamasaki) in shadow mask.

taken on a specific sexuality of its own: "(A) boi . . . is someone whose biological sex is female, or close to female, who socially identifies as male, but who is not currently on hormones."[28]

This reclamation of tomboyism is also evident in the performances of Japanese drag king Drastic Boy (Tomoko Yamasaki) (DB), who uses the persona of Ultraman in his cyber-Butoh dance performances. *Ultraman* was a Japanese science fiction television series popular between 1966 and 1998. Ultraman is the hero of the series, an extraterrestrial who arrives with a mission to save the Earth from destruction. DB's star biography shows how he has turned the television hero Ultraman into the postcolonial mimic man:

> The Ultra-man is a character of animation in Japan.
> When I was a child, I watched the Ultra-man's
> TV program after I returned from kindergarten.
> At kindergarten, only boys did the Ultra-man play.
> I was looking at it from outside. I also wanted to play role
> of the Ultra-man. When I looked at real Ultra-man in TV,
> the Ultra-man was not a man or a woman.
> The Ultra-man is just an Ultra-man for me.
>
> Now, there is the Ultra-man in me.
> The Drastic Boy is just a Drastic Boy for you.[29]

In the above, mimicry exposes the tactics of the postcolonial who has the capacity to successfully copy the culture of the colonizer through the technique of gender repetition. By imitating the cyborgic Ultraman, DB not only reclaims the cultural heteronormativity of his childhood, he also exposes the constructedness of masculinity connoted by the superhuman male hero. This performance repeats the original and destroys the myth of a postwar Japanese masculinity symbolized by the death of the father (the loss of the war) and its substitution through a problematic techno-masculinity evidenced in Japan's accelerated technological expansion.[30] Such a destabilization is further evidenced in his other performance of the Japanese salary man.

As a Japanese salary man, bespectacled DB wears a pin-stripped office suit, and carries a briefcase with a bento lunchbox. This act mixes Butoh dance steps with techno music in a rhythm that accelerates as he eats noodles and strips bare to reveal the sexy butch masculinity of a tomboy. The salary man's status as an ideal of Japanese postwar masculinity[31] is displaced by DB's tactic of "layering" that oscillates between being and acting, showing how queerness is performed through the play with multiple identities.[32] This performance exposes the hegemonic heterosexual middle-class masculinity of the Japanese salary man as the white-collar product of Japan's successful postwar economic expansion by reinscribing it with diasporic Asian female masculinity.

Diasporic Asian female masculinity in Australia is characterized by the emergence of the Asian tomboy as a desirable sexual identity. This identity narrates migration by returning to cultural memory through the media. The performances of LBL and DB share a mediated childhood through the local, inter-Asian, and global popular culture of *Ultraman,* Bruce Lee, and disco. These cultural memories are not simply nostalgic, as indicated by Martin Manalansan in his study of Filipino drag queens in America.[33] They return to reinvest the heteronormative "home" with new queer imaginings. Their tactics of mimicry and differential repetition decenter the roots of the child-hood home with the routes of popular media, where the everyday practices of watching television, going to the movies, and listening to music are affective events that function as alternative sites for a queer desire.

This critical trajectory of "going south" shows how cultural reimaginings are differently inflected when the diaspora is considered through as an alternative episteme. Unlike the other chapters in this collection such as the lesbian tomboy and the masculine woman in Hong Kong that show female masculinity through the effects of local socialization and mis-recognition, the diasporic Asian tomboy in Australia does not rely on these genealogies as sites for new constitution. This is not to suggest that nativist claims about home cultures do not exist; rather, it is to foreground the fact that masculinity's current hybridity is constituted by its articulation in an English-language address where "the Asian tomboy in Australia" is interpellated through self-recognition and group mis-recognition: the former mediated through the reimagined childhood of an Asian "home" culture, the latter the politics of the Asian race and gender in the Australian "host" culture.

Consider, for example, the three-piece white-suited LBL preening as he prepares to lip-synch to the deep soul bass of Barry White and gyrate the Travolta groove. This authenticates the 1970s set by staging a realism that intertextualizes not the scene in Tony Manero's (John Travolta) room in *Saturday Night Fever* (John Badman, 1977), but a similar scene in the Singapore-Miramax blockbuster *Forever Fever* (Glen Goei, 1998) where, repeating a similar narrative, the male protagonist is framed preening himself as he prepares for a disco dance competition. *Forever Fever's* bedroom, similar to the mise-en-scène in *Saturday Night Fever,* is walled by a row of posters that includes Tony Manero, Rocky (Sylvester Stallone), and Bruce Lee. LBL's quotation shows the kinging tactic of understatement where realism strips the stage of props to convey masculinity through the body rather than the spectacle of the costume. His impersonation stages the theatricality of a hybrid masculinity personified by Lee, Travolta, and Stallone in a genre characterized by the physicality of the body. This performativity highlights how the coincidence to the physicality of the body complicates the roots of popular media to show the potential of cultural memory as an intermediary that connects "home" and "host." It allows a new queer imagining that is not simply a retrieval of the past; rather, it stages the past through a present where Travolta returns as a king role model that is reimagined in the Asian Australian diasporic circuits of *Forever Fever* and Bruce Lee.[34] This tactic also foregrounds how the diasporic Asian tomboy queers heteronormative desire by visually embodying the physicality of the sexed body.

Cultural memories are also reworked through migration to Australia as a physical event constituted in the daily experiences of discrimination caused by the stereotyping of Asian men and women in Australian history, popular media, and culture. Two genealogies engender this memory. First, Asian women have been orientalized through a hypersexuality sensationalized by media representations of pornography, sex workers, and mail order brides. As Annabel and Tiger Lee, LBL's repertoire parodies a wide range of these stereotypes such as Singapore porn star Annabel Chong, Hong Kong superstar Maggie Cheung, and Filipino-Australian icon Rose Porteous.[35] Similar interventions include LBL's reinvention of the 1970s porn king Dirk Diggler. These performances use racialized sex and gender to reflect and disrupt the excessive sexuality of the Asian woman in Australia. Newer stereotypes such as the model minority high-achieving swot or the computer geek show how the prudent Asian woman is lacking in sexuality. Both excess and lack contribute to the effacement of the Asian tomboy in the circuit of normative lesbian butch desirability. This desirability casts the butch/femme "as a form of self-representation for lesbians" and produces the butch as a "distilled and visible embodiment of lesbian desire."[36] The Asian tomboy in an Anglo-dominated lesbian scene is simply not butch or masculine enough when compared to other Anglo or European counterparts. As the gaze of butch-baiting, the diasporic Asian tomboy exposes how normative butchness idealizes an impossible category complicit in the shame of the failure of a projected masculinity.

The second genealogy of the white Australia legacy that has constructed the impotent Asian man supports this emasculated logic and measures the "masculinity" of the Asian butch against this stereotype. Where normative butchness maintains the boundaries of masculinity through the reciprocity of looking and being looked at, the Asian butch is unable to refigure her selfhood because the sex that constitutes the body's virility is dematerialized by a prescribed social body that projects Asian masculinity as diminished and debased. DB's appropriation of Ultraman and the Japanese salary man further shows how techno-orientalism, as the Western construction of a futuristic and dystopic Japan, is used to maintain this stereotype of the Japanese as detached, asexual, and emotionally remote. The diasporic Asian butch occupies this site of impossibility where sexual and racial difference has erased the specificity of queer identity through the overdetermined representations of Asian women as hypersexualized and Asian men as desexualized. LBL and DB reclaim this identity by constituting the sexy Asian tomboy as a hybrid of both genealogies. For LBL, it is the expropriation of sex through hyperbole; for DB, the inscription of sex through layering.

This parallel tactic of the expropriation and inscription of sex is evident in another Asian drag king, Hung Low (Raquel Bacatan) (HL). Of Filipino background, Hung Low is King Victoria's backstage "groupie" made famous through name appropriation and commodity consumption. Hung Low's groupie homage is spectacularized by the sight of a gym-fit, six-packed Asian dyke with a crew cut and ripped jeans slithering topless on the pool table at the front of the bar during the intervals between the staged performances. These interjections have become a supplementary event that jettisons the orthodoxy of the Aussie beer-drinking and pool-playing lesbian scene. HL reinvents the erotica of tabletop dancing by inverting the hypersexuality of the Asian woman and introducing a hybrid tomboy sexuality that reposi-

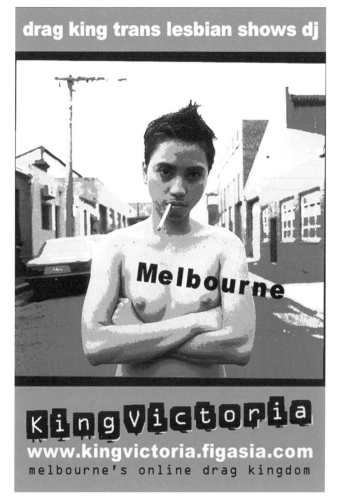

Figure 14.3. Hung Low (Raquel Bacatan) advertising the King
Victoria fridge magnet.

tions the players as voyeuristic spectators to-be-looked-at. This hybridity
counterappropriates hypermasculinity through the visual embodiment and
the practice that surrounds the name "Hung Low."

The name is also an appropriation of a popular Vietnamese-Australian co-
median, Hung Le. As a comic talent in mainstream Australian media, Hung
Le's status and performances expose indirect racism by showing how minor-

ity groups are represented in the media: in center-stage roles, and through discursive humor, as subjects and objects to be laughed at. HL challenges this indirect racism in her pose in an image on King Victoria's famous fridge magnet. Launched at the King Victoria's drag king extravaganza as part of Melbourne's annual Midsumma Gay and Lesbian Festival in 2004, the HL fridge magnet has become the iconic mark of the success of the King Victoria institution in Australia. This week-long extravaganza featured drag king workshops, seminars, photographic exhibitions, fashion shows, a sold-out cabaret program, and a range of best-selling accessories including combs, monogrammed pocket handkerchiefs, T-shirts, and refrigerator magnets. Together, these events and accessories shape the subculture consisting of a subterranean community with shared rituals and a mainstream commodity with hierarchies of taste. The fridge magnet exemplifies this liminality through its status as both a marketing and customizing device. Usually in the form of an advertising business card that is used to personalize the ubiquitous white fridge, the queer fridge magnet in particular (for example, the iconic rainbow fridge magnet) has come to function as a device for public disclosure and domestic reinscription. It reveals and hides through its subcultural capital of "being in the know." The HL fridge magnet reflects this double function of public and private, mainstream and deviant, proclamation and concealment, and collective and singular. This fridge magnet shows a pixellated black and white image that recalls the gym-fit topless Asian tomboy with folded arms smoking and returning the gaze of the camera. She is standing in the middle of a road abutting suburban terrace houses and warehouse conversions. Her to-be-looked-at-ness historicizes the omnipresent gaze of the camera as the symbolic apparatus of othering. Her defiant nakedness foregrounds a body politic sedimented by the direct and indirect racisms of both the Australian mainstream and the antipodean queer. As a mainstream commodity, she embodies the universality of a feminized and ethnicized erotica; as a queer accessory, she particularizes the social taste of the fetishished multicultural toygirl; and as a diasporic Asian butch, she is the butt of butch-baiters. The HL fridge magnet, in its public display and its domestic reinsciption, reflects and disrupts these sedimentations through the sexiness of the diasporic Asian tomboy as a border agent that expropriates and inscribes the gendered migration of the Asian Australian diaspora.

Conclusion

As sections one and two have argued, central to the performativity of drag kings in Australia is the practice of border-crossing, both as a form of physical displacement and a critical mode interrogation. Not only do Asian kings cross gender boundaries when they perform, these performances are also imbued with the literal experiences of physical migration. When LBL and DB cross-race in their double act as a boy band collective, the Golden Bois, they mime the ubiquity of MTV boy bands. They expose the discursive sameness that categorizes the genre, choreography, and style. This is also the same indirect racist discourse that stereotypes the Asian lesbian in the public lesbian culture. The public display of Asian kings, whether or not they engage in cross-racial performances, is always already a hypervisualized performance encoded in the racial politics of the Asian in Australia.

As public display, Asian kings represent the collective face of a minority group of Asian lesbians in Australia. The last decade that celebrated multicultural sexuality as a politics of identity in the country has witnessed the coming out of many gays and lesbians from non-English-speaking backgrounds. Aleph Melbourne, Greek and Gay, Gay Asian Proud, and Yellow Kitties comprise some of these support and activist groups in the Melbourne queer community. Despite the profile given to these community groups, and despite the fact that the Asian GLBTQ community is the largest non-Western group of queers in Australia, Asian lesbians, unlike gay Asian men, have never encountered a sustained visible platform until King Victoria emerged. Multicultural sexuality recognizes the complexities of sexuality through its intersection with the discourses of ethnicity, immigration, science, and English-language proficiency.[37] While this framework has enabled the articulation of a multicultural queer identity, it constructs a minority sexuality in relation to an Anglo Australian hegemony. This can be understood through the 1989 implementation of multiculturalism as a social management policy that uses the governance of "ethnic"/migrant cultures to construct a national identity. This identity disavows race and maintains a social structure that contains cultural difference into an acceptable form for the dominant culture by celebrating a benign type of cultural diversity.[38] It leaves intact a dominant white Australia as the unmarked center that incorporates "ethnic" subjects into a monocultural nationalism.

King Victoria problematizes official multiculturalism by showing how postcolonial female masculinity can expose the racialized and sexualized hierarchies of identities and desires. These performances work over an aggregate array of stereotypes so that they distanciate and disidentify by refusing to affirm the conventions of the dominant culture. More significantly, by engaging the queer migration of the Asian diaspora in Australia, the performances of Asian drag kings show how the diaspora is an ex-centric episteme to displace normative monocultural nationalism. These performances also mobilize the transnationality of cultural memories and show how a new hybrid sexuality has emerged without negotiating a dominant center. As diasporic Asian female masculinity, these hybrid sexualities find pleasure and eroticism in the spectacle of kings—as butches, femmes, and lover bois all at once.

Drag king performances are public performances. Their success depends on how audience members have been hailed into the act. Are performers subversive, are they cute, or do they silence? These are the usual questions asked of their potential transgression. The success of drag kings in Australia reflects both subcultural and mainstream consumption. Within the lesbian subculture, consumption is evident through the nightclub culture as part of "scene," as well as through the shared kinging rituals of the performers and the audience. Kung fu and manga have emerged as taste cultures within this community; new role models are also evident. Commodity consumption is also reflected in the otherness of the multicultural drag king. The Asian tomboy has become an "ethnic" flavor that adds to the diverse and popular range of performances in King Victoria.

Asian drag king performances have clearly challenged normative masculinities. Their performances of diasporic female masculinities show queer hybridities and new sexual identities. For the Asian drag kings, the tomboy is reclaimed through the gendered and queer routes of media and physical migration. Through the ex-centric diaspora, kinging in postcolonial Australia has become a site of critical hybridity where diasporic female masculinities have emerged through the contestations of "home" and "host" cultures. This contingency is its performability.

Notes

Earlier versions of this paper were presented at the "Performing Gender Forum," Drag King Festival, Victoria College of the Arts, Melbourne, Australia, January 29, 2004, and Third International Convention for Asian Scholars, National University of Singapore, Singapore, August 19–22, 2003.

1. Gibson, *South of the West.*
2. Ang, *On Not Speaking Chinese.*
3. Yue and Hawkins, "Going South," 51.
4. Hutcheon, *The Poetics of Postmodernism,* 60–67.
5. This decentering is evident in two drag king studies of the American heartland and Australian kings developed as a response to Halberstam's monocultural and urban-centric study. See Piontek, "Kinging in the Heartland," 125–34, and Crowley, "Drag Kings 'Down Under,'" 298–308, in *The Drag King Anthology,* ed. Donna Troka, Kathleen LeBesco, and Jean Bobby Noble.

6. The research for this chapter began informally six years ago when the drag king subculture first emerged in Melbourne in Australia. I was first involved as a support crew to my friends who started the drag king competition. Through the years, this insider-out status has enabled many new friendships and also allowed my "belatedly acquired" outsider-in researcher status the subcultural capital required for my informal participant observation, both as a member of the backstage outer support group as well as a viewing spectator of the audience. This paper would not have been possible without the trust of the cast and crew of King Victoria who have generously provided ad hoc interviews, anecdotes, photographs, and reflections through the years, especially Bumpy/E. Eldridge, Ray Jalil, Raquel Bacatan, Mandy Siegel, and Di Marshall. My sincere thanks to all of them. I alone, however, am responsible for any aberrant interpretations that may not accord with the views of the performers. Reflecting the transdisciplinary framework formulated in this chapter, my research methods deliberately did not deploy the "authenticity" of voice through the in-text citations of interviews promoted by disciplines such as sociology, anthropology, and media reception studies. This "lack" does not reflect the subsumption of the voices of the researched at the expense of the researcher's authorial voice; rather, this chapter hopes to show, through its deployment and interrogation of disciplines, how communication and dialogue can be produced at the intersection of the different registers of voice and authority.

7. The spelling of "boi" in this chapter follows the conventional spelling used by King Victoria to describe the sexuality of one who is biologically female but socially male (personal interview, Ray Jalil, July 12, 2003).

8. Merz, "Drag Kings Create a Hairy New Scene," 14.

9. Ibid, 4.

10. Halberstam. *Female Masculinity,* 232.

11. See, for example, Wheelwright, *Amazons and Military Maids;* Munt, ed. *Butch/ Femme;* Ferris, ed. *Crossing the Stage;* Morreale, "Xena: Warrior Princess as Feminist Camp."

12. On academic writings of drag kings in the West, see Halberstam, *Female Masculinity;* Halberstam and Volcano, *The Drag King Book;* and Troka, LeBesco, and Noble, eds., *The Drag King Anthology.*

13. See, for example, Rottnek, *Sissies and Tomboys.*

14. Halberstam, *Female Masculinity,* 21, 29.

15. Bumpy/E. Eldridge, "History," *King Victoria Online Drag Kingdom,* http://www.kingvictoria.figasia.com/history.htm (June 2, 2003). The spelling *grrl* follows the postfeminist spelling convention that describes a grrl as a self-aware woman who subverts patriarchal norms. *Grrl* was first associated in the West in the mid-1990s with subcultures such as cyberfeminists, riot girl bands, and girl punk subcultures.

16. Halberstam, *Female Masculinity,* 29, 1. See also Knights, *Writing Masculinities.*

17. See Connell. *Masculinities,* and Tomsen and Donaldson, eds., *Male Trouble.* A "digger" is an iconic Australian term to describe a working-class battler; it is derived

from the heroic status given to Australian soldiers during the first world war. The term "bloke" is a colloquial Australian term to describe an ordinary Australian man.

18. Newton, *Mother Camp*. See also Butler, *Gender Trouble* and *Bodies That Matter*.

19. Teo, *Hong Kong Cinema*, 120.

20. Tasker, "Fists of Fury," in Stecopoulos and Uebel, eds., *Race and the Subject of Masculinities*, 317.

21. Li, "Kung Fu."

22. Morris, "Learning from Bruce Lee," in Tinkcom and Villarejo, eds., *Keyframes*, 178.

23. Halberstam, *Female Masculinity*, 257.

24. Ray Jalil, "The Tailor of Sea Park," *King Victoria Online Drag Kingdom*, http://www.kingvictoria.figasia.com/readings/taylorofsea.htm (June 3, 2003).

25. See, for example, Rottneck, *Sissies and Tomboys*.

26. Halberstam, *Female Masculinity*, 5–9.

27. LeeBruceLee, "Stars," *King Victoria Online Drag Kingdom*, http://www.kingvictoria.figasia.com/stars/leebrucelee.htm (June 3, 2003).

28. *A Boi's Life Website*, http://biodyke78.tripod.com/aboislife/id4.html (June 3, 2003).

29. Drastic Boy, "Stars," *King Victoria Online Drag Kingdom*, http://www.kingvictoria.figasia.com/stars/drasticboy.htm (June 3, 2003).

30. Napier, *Anime from Akira to Princess Mononoke*, 170–72.

31. Kinmonth, *The Self-made Man in Meiji Japanese Thought*; Roberson and Suzuki, eds., *Men and Masculinities in Contemporary Japan*.

32. Halberstam, *Female Masculinity*, 258–60.

33. Manalansan, *Global Divas*.

34. Personal interview with Ray Jalil, October 15, 2003.

35. Rose Porteous was a Filipino maid who married her now-deceased Australian mining tycoon employer, Lang Hancock. Constructed as a stereotype by the Australian media, she was flamboyant in her display of her new wealth and was later accused by the media and his family of plotting his death in the early 1990s. Her hyperbolic status was renewed in 2003 when she hosted her own reality television show on mainstream television. She has become an icon of Asian femininity in Australia: orientalized, eroticized, debased, and stereotyped.

36. Munt, ed., *Butch/Femme*, 4, 6.

37. Jackson and Sullivan, *Multicultural Queer*.

38. See Ang, *On Not Speaking Chinese*; and Hage, *Against Paranoid Nationalism*.

References

Ang, Ien. *On Not Speaking Chinese: Living between Asia and the West*. London: Routledge, 2001.

A Boi's Life Website. http://biodyke78.tripod.com/aboislife/id4.html (June 3, 2003).

Butler, Judith. *Bodies That Matter: On the Discursive Limits of "Sex."* New York: Routledge, 1993.

———. *Gender Trouble: Feminism and the Subversion of Identity.* New York: Routledge, 1990.

Connell, Robert W. *Masculinities.* Sydney: Allen and Unwin, 1995.

Ferris, Lesley, ed. *Crossing the Stage: Controversies on Cross-dressing.* New York: Routledge, 1993.

Gibson, Ross. *South of the West: Postcolonialism and the Narrative Construction of Australia.* Bloomington: Indiana University Press, 1992.

Hage, Ghassan. *Against Paranoid Nationalism: Searching for Hope in a Shrinking Society.* Annadale, Victoria: Pluto Press, 2003.

Halberstam, Judith. *Female Masculinity.* Durham: Duke University Press, 1998.

Halberstam, Judith "Jack," and De LaGrace Volcano. *The Drag King Book.* London: Serpent's Tail, 1999.

Hutcheon, Linda. *The Poetics of Postmodernism: History, Theory, Fiction.* London: Routledge, 1988.

Jackson, Peter A., and Gerard Sullivan, eds. *Multicultural Queer: Australian Narratives.* New York: Haworth Press, 1999.

Jalil, Ray. "Personal Interview." July 12, 2003.

King Victoria Online Drag Kingdom. http://www.fig.net.au/kingvictoria/ (August 13, 2003).

Kinmonth, Earl H. *The Self-made Man in Meiji Japanese Thought: From Samurai to Salary Man.* Berkeley: University of California Press, 1981.

Knights, Ben. *Writing Masculinities: Male Narratives in Twentieth-Century Fiction.* New York: St. Martin's Press, 1999.

Li, Siu Leung. "Kung Fu: Negotiating Nationalism and Modernity." *Cultural Studies* 15, no. 3/4 (2001): 515–42.

Manalansan, Martin. *Global Divas: Filipino Gay Men in the Diaspora.* Durham: Duke University Press, 2003.

Merz, Mischa. "Drag Kings Create a Hairy New Scene." *The Age,* August 11, 2001, 4, 14.

Morreale, Joanne. "Xena: Warrior Princess as Feminist Camp." *Journal of Popular Culture* 32, no. 2 (1998): 79–86.

Munt, Sally, ed. *Butch/Femme: Inside Lesbian Gender.* Washington: Cassell, 1998.

Napier, Susan. *Anime from Akira to Princess Mononoke: Experiencing Contemporary Japanese Animation.* New York: Palgrave, 2001.

Newton, Esther. *Mother Camp: Female Impersonators in America.* Chicago: Chicago University Press, 1979.

Roberson, James, and Nobue Suzuki, eds. *Men and Masculinities in Contemporary Japan: Dislocating the Salaryman Doxa.* New York: Routledge, 2003.

Rottnek, Matthew. *Sissies and Tomboys: Gender Nonconformity and Homosexual Childhood.* New York: New York University Press, 1999.

Stecopoulos, Harry, and Michael Uebel, eds. *Race and the Subject of Masculinities.* Durham: Duke University Press, 1997. 315–36.

Teo, Stephen. *Hong Kong Cinema. The Extra Dimension.* London: British Film Institute, 1997.

Tinkcom, Matthew. *Working Like a Homosexual: Camp, Capital, and Cinema.* Durham: Duke University Press, 2002.

Tinkcom, Matthew, and Amy Villarejo, eds. *Keyframes: Popular Cinema and Cultural Studies.* New York: Routledge, 2001.

Tomsen, Stephen, and Mike Donaldson, eds. *Male Trouble: Looking at Australian Masculinities.* North Melbourne, Victoria: Pluto Press Australia, 2003.

Troka, Donna, Kathleen LeBesco, and Jean Bobby Noble, eds. *The Drag King Anthology.* Haworth Press: New York, 2002.

Wheelwright, Julie. *Amazons and Military Maids: Women Who Dressed as Men in the Pursuit of Life, Liberty, and Happiness.* Boston: Pandora, 1989.

Yue, Audrey, and Gay Hawkins. "Going South." *New Formations* 40 (Spring 2000): 49–63.

CONTRIBUTORS

RONALD BAYTAN is an associate professor of literature at De La Salle University-Manila, where he teaches creative writing, Philippine literature, and queer/gender studies. He is the author of *The Queen Sings the Blues: Poems, 1992–2002*. He coedited *Bongga Ka Day: Pinoy Gay Quotes to Live By* with J. Neil C. Garcia and Ralph Semino Galan. His forthcoming book is *The Queen Lives Alone: Personal Essays*.

J. NEIL C. GARCIA teaches creative writing and comparative literature at the University of the Philippines-Diliman, where he also serves as an associate for poetry in the Institute of Creative Writing. He is the author of numerous poetry collections and works in literary and cultural criticism, including *Our Lady of the Carnival, The Sorrows of Water, Kaluluwa, Philippine Gay Culture: The Last Thirty Years, Slip/pages: Essays in Philippine Gay Criticism, Performing the Self: Occasional Prose, The Garden of Wordlessness,* and *Misterios and Other Poems*. His latest critical work is *Postcolonialism and Filipino Poetics: Essays and Critiques*. He is currently working on a full-length book, a postcolonial survey and analysis of Philippine poetry in English.

PETER A. JACKSON is a senior fellow in Thai history in the Research School of Pacific and Asian Studies at the Australian National University in Canberra. He specializes in the cultural history of modern Thailand, and his main research interests are the histories of Buddhism, gender, sexuality, and globalization in Thailand. His books include *Dear Uncle Go: Male Homosexuality in Thailand, Buddhadasa: Theravada Buddhism and Modernist Reform in Thailand,* and *Genders and Sexualities in Modern Thailand* (coedited with Nerida Cook). He is currently writing a history of Thailand's same-sex and transgender cultures, conducting research on the impact of globalization and capitalism on Thai religion in the 1990s, and exploring the history of Thai perceptions of the West since the reign of King Mongkut in the mid-nineteenth century.

KAM YIP LO LUCETTA is a doctoral student and part-time lecturer in gender studies at the Chinese University of Hong Kong. Her current research is about *lalas* (women with same-sex desires) in Shanghai, China. Her publications include "Gender: TB" (in Chinese), "Noras on the Road: Family and Marriage of Lesbian Women in Shanghai," and "Queer Guise for the Straight Guy: The Construction of Metrosexuals in Hong Kong." She is the editor and illustrator of *Lunar Desires: Her First Same-Sex Love, in Her Own Voice* (in Chinese) and is currently working on the Oral History Project on Women-Loving-Women in Hong Kong.

SONG HWEE LIM is a senior lecturer in film studies at the University of Exeter, UK. He is the author of *Celluloid Comrades: Representations of Male Homosexuality in Contemporary Chinese Cinemas,* coeditor of *Remapping World Cinema: Identity, Culture and Politics in Film,* and founding editor of the *Journal of Chinese Cinemas.*

J. DARREN MACKINTOSH is a lecturer in Japanese cultural studies at Birkbeck College, University of London. His interests include gender and sexuality in contemporary Japan and East Asia with a focus on masculinities, the relationship between the body and narratives of the Japanese nation, and East Asian identity in diaspora. He is currently completing a book on the representations of men and male sexualities in postwar Japan and coediting a volume on cultural studies and cultural industries in East Asia.

CLAIRE MAREE is an associate professor in multicultural studies and Japanese language studies at Tsuda College, Japan. She is author of *Hatsuwasha no Gengo Sutoratejii toshite no Negoshiēshon Kōi no Kenkyū* (Research into negotiation as speakers linguistic strategies). Her English-language publications include "The Un/State of Lesbian Studies in Japan" and "Shifting Speakers" (with W. Lunsing). Her research interests include the intersections of gender, sexuality, and language in contemporary society; discourse studies; and cultural studies.

FRAN MARTIN is a lecturer in cultural studies at the University of Melbourne, Australia. She is author of *Situating Sexualities: Queer Representation in Taiwanese Fiction, Film, and Public Culture,* translator of *Angelwings: Contemporary Queer Fiction from Taiwan,* coeditor with Chris Berry and Audrey Yue of *Mobile Cultures: New Media and Queer Asia,* and coeditor with Larissa Heinrich of *Embodied Modernities: Corporeality, Representation, and Chinese Cultures.* Her new book titled *Backward Glances: Contemporary Chinese Cultures and the Female Homoerotic Imaginary* is forthcoming from Duke University Press.

MARK MCLELLAND is a lecturer in sociology at the University of Wollongong, Australia. He is the author and coeditor of several books about the history of Japanese queer cultures and histories, including *Queer Japan from the Pacific War to the Internet Age, Queer Voices from Japan,* and *Genders, Transgenders, and Sexualities in Japan.* He also writes on new media in Japan and its region, and is the coeditor of *Japanese Cybercultures* and the forthcoming collection *Internationalizing Internet Studies.*

JIN-HYUNG PARK is a lecturer in film criticism and visual culture at Chung-Ang University in Seoul. He is editor-in-chief of *eBuddy,* the online edition of *Buddy,* the first Korean LGBT magazine. He is also active in the Korean Sexual-Minority Culture and Rights Center (http://www.kscrc.org), the first center for sexual minorities, people living with HIV/AIDS, and those who support the rights of sexual minorities in Korea.

TERI SILVIO is an assistant research fellow at the Institute of Ethnology, Academia Sinica, Taipei. She is an anthropologist whose research interests include media technologies and social change, gender and sexuality, and the historical relationship between popular and intellectual culture in Taiwan. Her recent ethnographic projects have focused on transforming local performance genres, including opera and puppetry.

MEGAN SINNOTT worked in Thailand and studied Thai sexual and gender formations for nine years. Her book, *Toms and Dees: Transgender Identity and Female Same-Sex Relationships in Thailand,* won the 2004 Ruth Benedict Prize. She has taught anthropology and women's studies at University of Colorado-Boulder and Yale University and is currently an assistant professor of women's studies at Georgia State University.

YIK KOON TEH is an associate professor in criminology and sociology at Universiti Utara Malaysia. Her research interests include gender and transsexual issues, fraud and corruption, prisoner rehabilitation, and criminological theory. She is the author of *The Mak Nyahs: Malaysian Male to Female Transsexuals.*

CARMEN KA MAN TONG teaches sociology at HKUSPACE Community College in Hong Kong. With a strong interest in studying her local Hong Kong society, she has also been involved in social research at the Centre for

Criminology at the University of Hong Kong, covering topics including club drugs and teenagers, the Hong Kong illicit drug market, violence and drugs, and social support for battered women.

JAMES WELKER is a PhD student in the Department of East Asian Languages and Cultures at the University of Illinois at Urbana-Champaign. He is coeditor of and translator for *Queer Voices from Japan: First Person Narratives from Japan's Sexual Minorities* (with Mark McLelland and Katsuhiko Suganuma) and coeditor of "Of Queer Import(s): Sexualities, Genders, and Rights in Asia," a special issue of *Intersections: Gender, History, and Culture in the Asian Context* (with Lucetta Kam). His article "Beautiful, Borrowed, and Bent: Boys' Love as Girls' Love" in *Shōjo* Manga was awarded the 2006 Crompton-Noll Award for best essay in lesbian, gay, and queer studies.

HEATHER WORTH is the deputy director and an associate professor of the National Centre in HIV Social Research at the University of New South Wales, Australia, where she heads the international HIV research program. She is the author of several books, including *Gay Men, Sex, and HIV in New Zealand*, and many articles. Her work combines her interests in gender, sexuality, and globalization in the era of AIDS with a passion for continental theory.

AUDREY YUE is a lecturer in cultural studies at the University of Melbourne. She is coeditor of *Mobile Cultures: New Media in Queer Asia.* Her most recent essays on diaspora queer cultures, Hong Kong cinema, and cultural policy appear in *International Journal of Cultural Policy, Asian Migrations: Sojourning, Displacement, Homecoming, and Other Travels,* and *Between Home and World: A Reader in Hong Kong Cinema.* She is currently completing two book projects: *Queer Asian Migrations in Australia* and *Sexuality and the Creative City in Singapore.*

INDEX

Abu-Lughod, Lila, 131, 132
activists: queer studies by, 24n20
Adon, 29
Adonis Boy, The, 29
aesthetics (*tanbi*), 50
aged women: degendering of, 105–7
Allan, 47, 49; personal ads in, 50–51, 53; readership, 60n6; self-referents in, 55; terms used in, 51, 53–54, 56
Ang Tatay Kong Nanay, 183, 185
Aniisu, 58
Anwar Ibrahim, 88, 92–93
Aoyama Tomoko, 50
Asian, the: as object, 4, 23n3
AsiaPacifiQueer (APQ), 2, 4, 7; hybridity in, 7
AsiaPacifiQueer (APQ) Network, 2, 23n2
Australia: Asian lesbians in, 265; Asian queer diaspora, 22; cultural location of, 5; role in queer studies in Asia, 4, 6. *See also* going south

badaf, 194n23
Bakhtin, Mikhail, 244
bakla, 14, 20, 21, 167, 171; in cinema, 181–93; homosexualization of, 168, 174, 182, 185, 189; hybridity of, 169, 175–76, 182; relationship with "gay," 192–93; stereotypes of, 172, 186
Bala at Lipstick, 20, 185–87, 191, 192
bapok, 19, 89
Barazoku, 29, 30, 41, 52, 54; female voices in, 62n37; publishing figures, 41n2

Barisan Nasional, 87
beautiful boys. *See* boy's love
Berlant, Lauren, 235
Bernal, Ishmael, 183
Besnier, Niko, 150, 152
Bhabha, Homi, 164, 165–66, 175, 176, 189
bodily idioms, 42n13
boi, 258
boy-head (*nam chai tou*), 19, 104
boy's love (*boizu rabu*); homosexuality in, 48–49; influence of, 47, 49, 56, 58; manga, 46
Brocka, Lino, 183
Butler, Judith: on drag queens, 156–57; on gender, 57, 100; heterosexual matrix, 168; on performance, 132, 154; on self-referents, 55

Center for the Study of Sexualities (Taiwan), 12
Chakrabarty, Dipesh, 15–16
Champagne, John, 209, 213
Chen Kaige, 227
Chi Ta-wei, 238, 240, 243
Ch'iu Kuei-fen, 217, 221
cinema: in Korea, 198, 203–5, 207; in the Philippines, 183–84, 190, 191; queer Asian, 20–21
Cine21, 204, 205
colonialism, 3, 8, 16, 165–66
Cronenberg, David, 159
Crouch, Harold, 86–87, 89
Crying Game, The, 159

The University of Illinois Press
is a founding member of the
Association of American University Presses.

Composed in 10.5/13 Adobe Minion Pro
with Helvetica Neue LT Std display
at the University of Illinois Press
Designed by Kelly Gray
Manufactured by Cushing-Malloy, Inc.

University of Illinois Press
1325 South Oak Street
Champaign, IL 61820-6903
www.press.uillinois.edu